PAUL CHADWICK'S

Concrete®

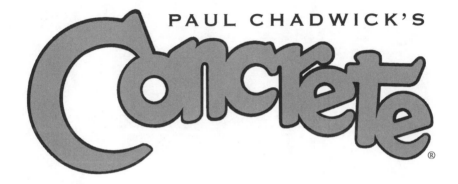

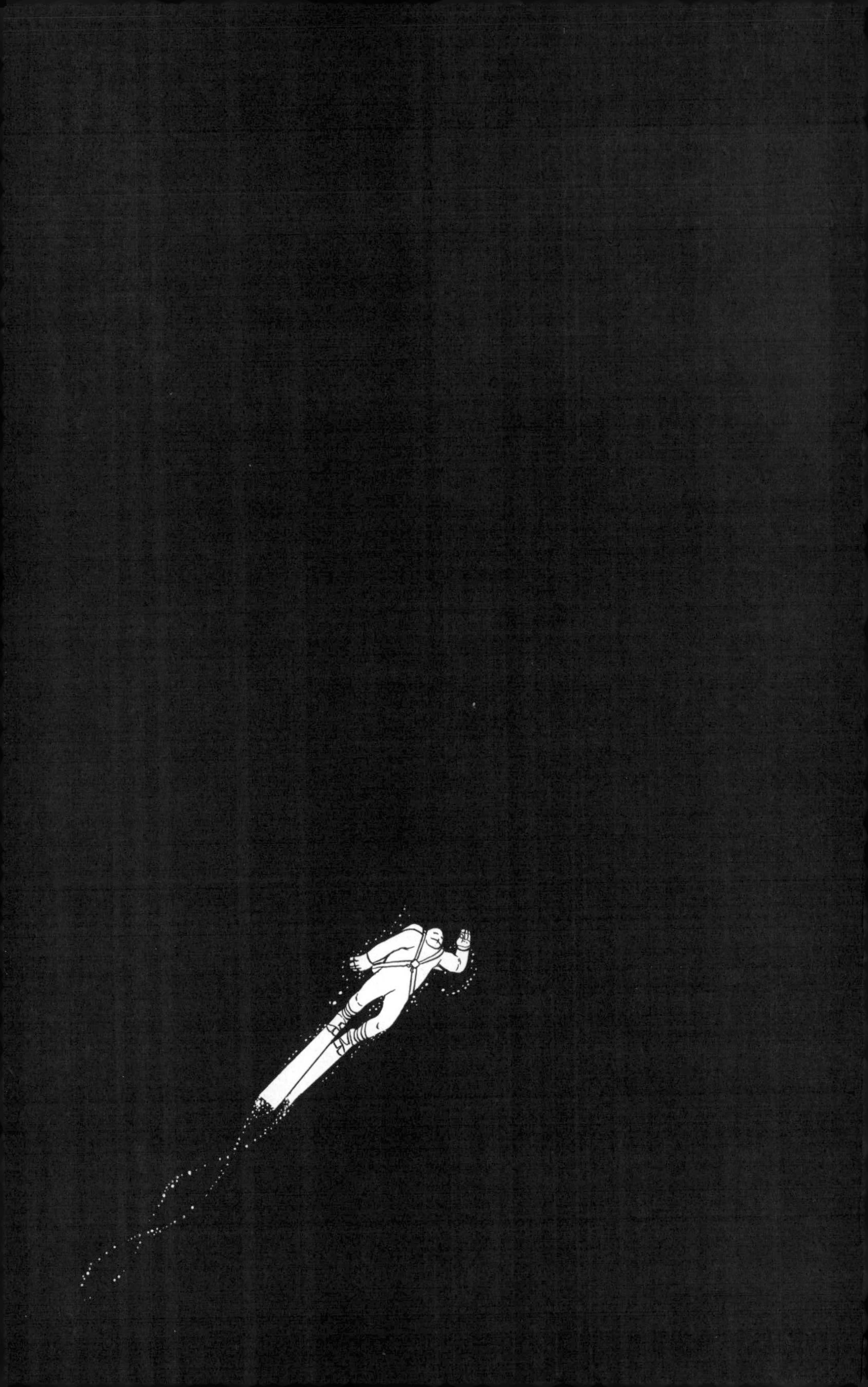

PAUL CHADWICK'S

1
DEPTHS

STORY AND ART
PAUL CHADWICK

LETTERING
BILL SPICER

DARK HORSE BOOKS™

INTRODUCTION

Here's the ground floor. These are the early stories showing Concrete's very secret origin, and very public impact upon emerging into the world. They represent the best I could do in playing out, rationally (if not entirely soberly), what might really happen to someone whose life was so changed.

At the time, this approach was quirky—even radical—in comics. I was asked whom he would fight, what super-foes? How else could there be conflict? And the aliens— they just *leave*? No *revenge*, no final *obliteration* of the enemy?

Nope. Just one hapless rock-coated fellow, enduring the consequences of my asking the question: what would I do in his shoes?

That many of these stories involve going underground and undersea often enough to justify the title for this collection speaks to a continuing bane to Concrete's existence: gravity.

Anthony Greenbank's brilliant how-to, *The Book of Survival*, is organized around extremes. Chapter titles were "Too Lonely, Too Crowded, Too Hot," etc. Concrete would do well to reread the chapter "Too Low."

Life's that way when you weigh 1200 lbs. You sink. You fall. Things break and bury you.

I'm drawn to survival stories, which I guess is why I write and draw so many of them. The question, "What would I do?" intrigues me. That I am a personality more given to ambivalence than action is probably part of it. Touching this danger safely, mentally, is a way to quicken the blood without actually experiencing the horror and despair of mortal fear.

Safety, and the desire for it, is at the root of making a rock-coated man the vehicle for my fantasies. How lovely to be so hard to hurt. But someone who never experiences danger and trouble can't generate much of a story. So I find ways, and Concrete suffers.

Not all his challenges are mortal. Concrete craves acceptance, barred as he is from normal human warmth by his freakish body. So the criticism he receives in "A Stone Among Stones" and the awkward social interactions in "The TransAtlantic Swim," "Water God," and "Sympathy from a Devil" are especially stinging.

So is his ineptitude at caving, showcased in "Orange Glow." In fact, I see Concrete's existence as one of sustained low-level embarrassment, punctuated by episodes of acute humiliation. How this relates to my life I prefer to leave unexplored.

The very first Concrete story, "Lifestyles of the Rich and Famous," takes place at a party. Everyone knows parties are agony, socially. How better to introduce a character for whom abashment is life's main dish?

Concrete's origin is a story I keep returning to. The silent, full-page panels in this printing are from a fix-up for a one-shot republication, *A New Life*. I tried again in two (unproduced) screenplays and in a longer comics treatment, *Strange Armor*. I'm working through a novelized version now. I hope someday to get it right.

This version, whatever its deficiencies, has the virtue of springing fresh from my brow, like the sweat of a fever dream. What I find interesting now is how many "throwaways" these stories have—visual ideas, gags, "bits"—that are inessential to the plot. They're simply things I wanted to do. I tend to be more disciplined, now, in this regard. But I wonder if that's entirely a virtue. Those throwaways are really pretty fun, rather like searching for the hidden animals in a children's magazine puzzle picture. Every page promises a new "bird" or "squirrel". . . or a moon that echoes Concrete's bullet-cratered head, or a sculpture of a backstabber in the mansion of a betraying rock star.

In the early days I made lists, independent of plots, of shots I wanted to do, potential gags, and "moments." I fit them in when I could.

I have always been enamored of film directors with a gift for shot design for its own sake: Nicholas Roeg, Terrence Malick, Carroll Ballard (as well as Stephen Spielberg, though his skill at shot design is always welded to a sprightly sense of storytelling). Some of their shots are echoed here. Comics master Jim Steranko gave me a taste for lots of little panels. Such were the seeds of my aesthetic.

Although chronologically clustered, as far as Concrete's life goes, these stories range from 1986 to 2000. My artwork has evolved, though perhaps less than I'd like. "Vagabond" is an autobiographical vignette from the anthology *Streetwise*. This "road" strip is perhaps not in keeping with the title theme, but accommodating it with the title "Depths and Widths" would be inflicting a tongue-twister on the bookselling world (try it).

—Paul Chadwick
Friday Harbor, WA 2005

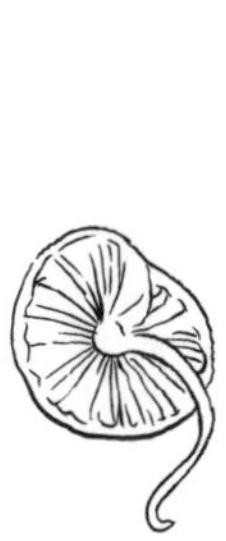

PUBLISHER
MIKE RICHARDSON

COLLECTION EDITOR
CHRIS WARNER

COLLECTION DESIGN
HEIDI FAINZA & DEBRA BAILEY

ART DIRECTOR
LIA RIBACCHI

CONCRETE VOL. 1: DEPTHS

© 1986, 1987, 1999, 2000, 2005 by Paul Chadwick. All rights reserved. No portion of this publication may be reproduced, in any form or by any means, without the express written permission of the copyright holders. Names, characters, places, and incidents featured in this publication are either the product of the author's imagination or are used fictitiously. Any resemblance to actual persons (living or dead), events, institutions, or locales, without satiric intent, is coincidental. Dark Horse Books™ is a trademark of Dark Horse Comics, Inc. Dark Horse Comics® is a trademark of Dark Horse Comics, Inc., registered in various categories and countries. All rights reserved.

This volume collects issues one through five of the Dark Horse comic-book series *Concrete* and stories from issues one, eight, ten, and one-hundred-fifty of the Dark Horse comic-book series *Dark Horse Presents*; the Dark Horse comic book *Dark Horse Presents Annual '99: DHP Junior*; the Dark Horse comic book *Dark Horse Maverick Annual 2000*; and the TwoMorrows comic book *Streetwise*.

Dark Horse Books
A division of Dark Horse Comics, Inc.
10956 SE Main Street
Milwaukie, OR 97222

darkhorse.com

To find a comics shop in your area,
call the Comic Shop Locator Service toll-free at
1-888-266-4226

First edition: July 2005
ISBN: 1-59307-343-7

10 9 8 7 6 5 4 3 2 1

PRINTED IN CANADA

TABLE OF CONTENTS

A Stone Among Stones. 10

Lifestyles of the Rich and Famous 35

The TransAtlantic Swim 43

Water God 77

A New Life. 85

Straight in the Eye. 147

An Armchair Stuffed with Dynamite 155

Sympathy from a Devil. 183

Orange Glow 191

Vagabond. 199

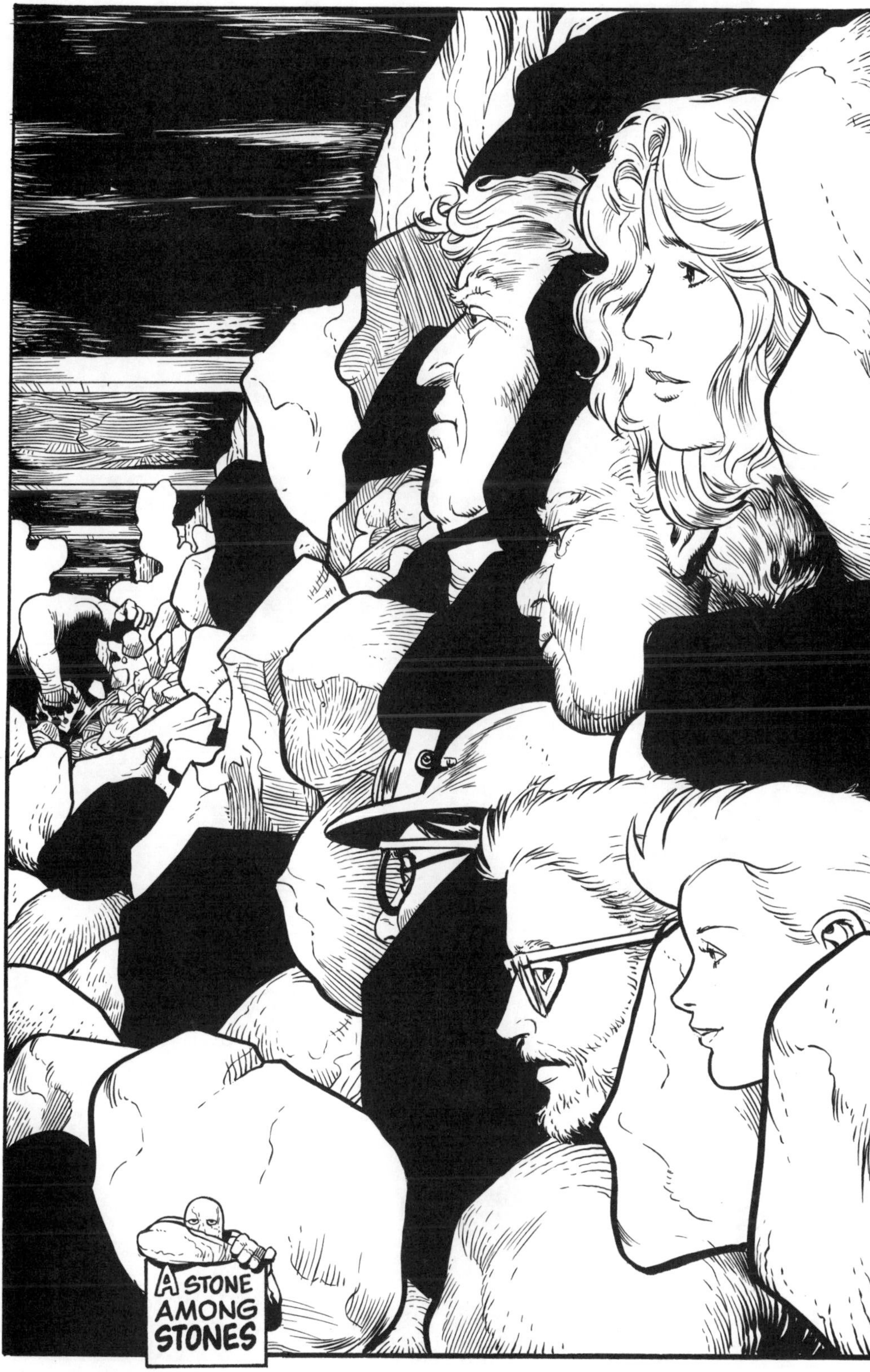
A STONE AMONG STONES

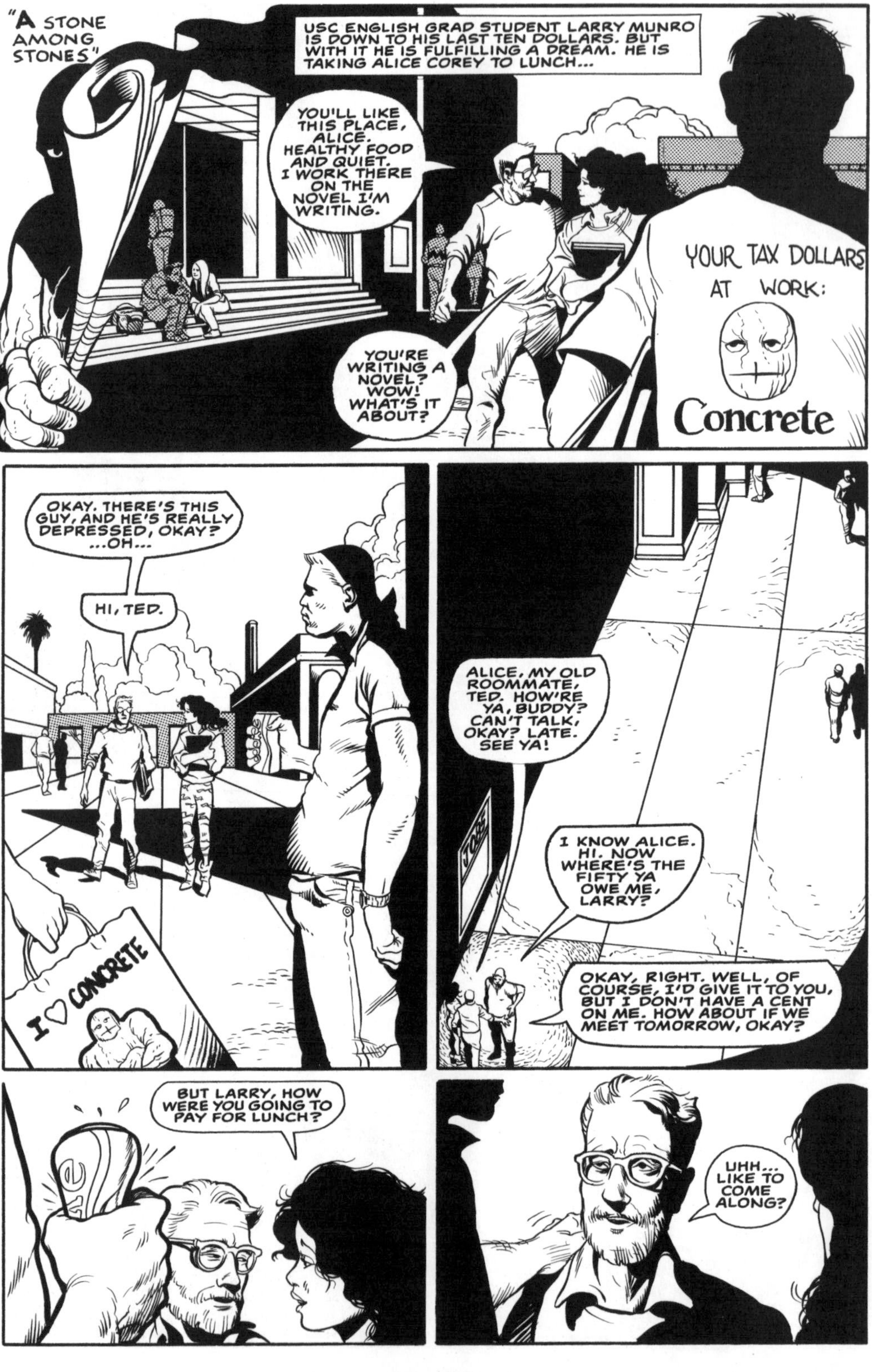
"A STONE AMONG STONES"
USC ENGLISH GRAD STUDENT LARRY MUNRO IS DOWN TO HIS LAST TEN DOLLARS. BUT WITH IT HE IS FULFILLING A DREAM. HE IS TAKING ALICE COREY TO LUNCH...
YOU'LL LIKE THIS PLACE, ALICE. HEALTHY FOOD AND QUIET. I WORK THERE ON THE NOVEL I'M WRITING.
YOUR TAX DOLLARS AT WORK:
Concrete
YOU'RE WRITING A NOVEL? WOW! WHAT'S IT ABOUT?
OKAY. THERE'S THIS GUY, AND HE'S REALLY DEPRESSED, OKAY? ...OH...
HI, TED.
I ♡ CONCRETE
ALICE, MY OLD ROOMMATE, TED. HOW'RE YA, BUDDY? CAN'T TALK, OKAY? LATE. SEE YA!
I KNOW ALICE. HI. NOW WHERE'S THE FIFTY YA OWE ME, LARRY?
OKAY, RIGHT. WELL, OF COURSE, I'D GIVE IT TO YOU, BUT I DON'T HAVE A CENT ON ME. HOW ABOUT IF WE MEET TOMORROW, OKAY?
BUT LARRY, HOW WERE YOU GOING TO PAY FOR LUNCH?
UHH... LIKE TO COME ALONG?

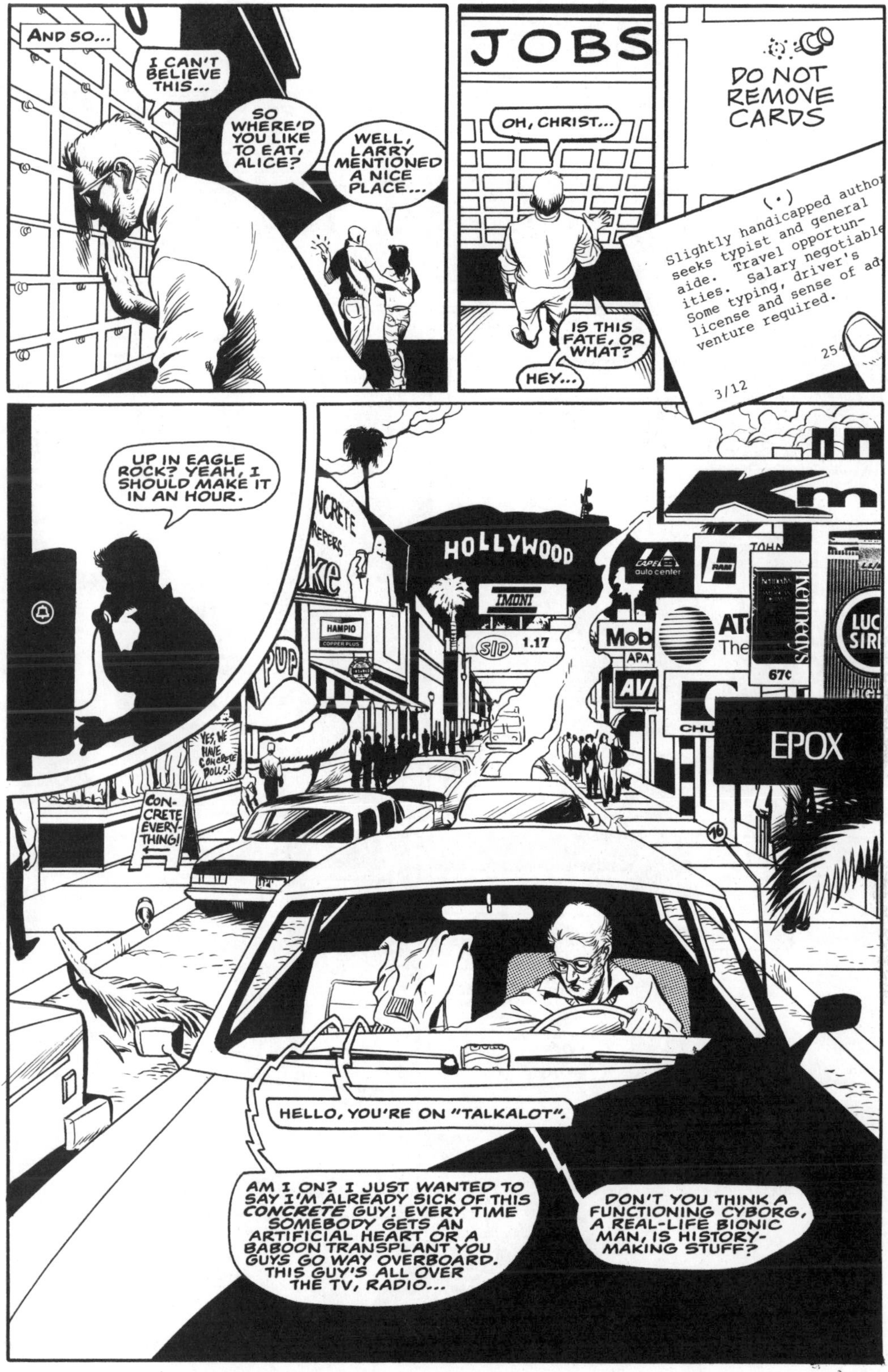
AND SO...
I CAN'T BELIEVE THIS...
SO WHERE'D YOU LIKE TO EAT, ALICE?
WELL, LARRY MENTIONED A NICE PLACE...
JOBS
OH, CHRIST...
IS THIS FATE, OR WHAT?
HEY...
DO NOT REMOVE CARDS
Slightly handicapped author seeks typist and general aide. Travel opportunities. Salary negotiable. Some typing, driver's license and sense of adventure required.
254
3/12
UP IN EAGLE ROCK? YEAH, I SHOULD MAKE IT IN AN HOUR.
HOLLYWOOD
YES, WE HAVE CONCRETE DOLLS!
CONCRETE EVERYTHING!
EPOX
HELLO, YOU'RE ON "TALKALOT".
AM I ON? I JUST WANTED TO SAY I'M ALREADY SICK OF THIS CONCRETE GUY! EVERY TIME SOMEBODY GETS AN ARTIFICIAL HEART OR A BABOON TRANSPLANT YOU GUYS GO WAY OVERBOARD. THIS GUY'S ALL OVER THE TV, RADIO...
DON'T YOU THINK A FUNCTIONING CYBORG, A REAL-LIFE BIONIC MAN, IS HISTORY-MAKING STUFF?

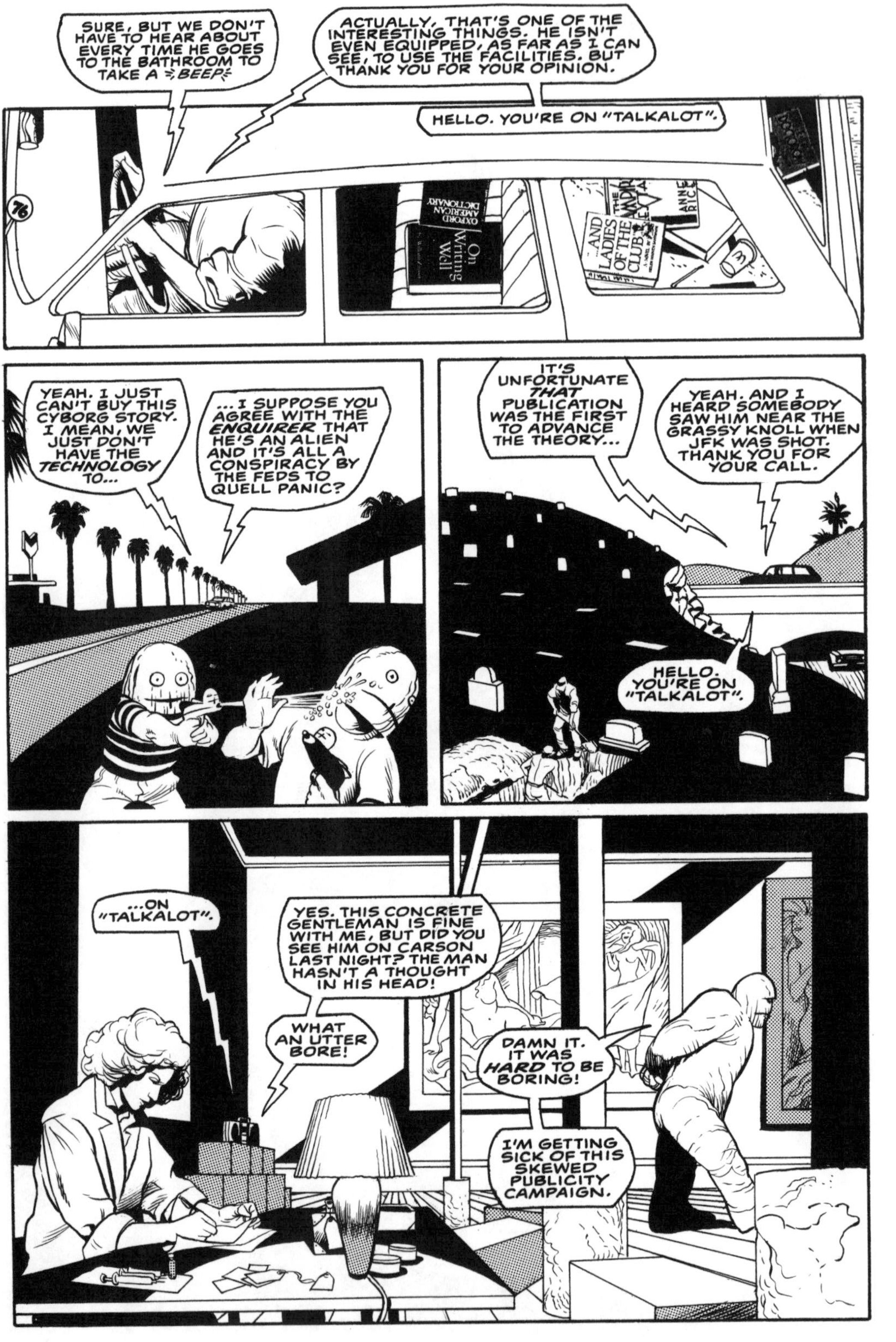
SURE, BUT WE DON'T HAVE TO HEAR ABOUT EVERY TIME HE GOES TO THE BATHROOM TO TAKE A BEEP
ACTUALLY, THAT'S ONE OF THE INTERESTING THINGS. HE ISN'T EVEN EQUIPPED, AS FAR AS I CAN SEE, TO USE THE FACILITIES. BUT THANK YOU FOR YOUR OPINION.
HELLO. YOU'RE ON "TALKALOT".
OXFORD AMERICAN DICTIONARY
On Writing Well
...AND LADIES OF THE CLUB
YEAH. I JUST CAN'T BUY THIS CYBORG STORY. I MEAN, WE JUST DON'T HAVE THE TECHNOLOGY TO...
...I SUPPOSE YOU AGREE WITH THE ENQUIRER THAT HE'S AN ALIEN AND IT'S ALL A CONSPIRACY BY THE FEDS TO QUELL PANIC?
IT'S UNFORTUNATE THAT PUBLICATION WAS THE FIRST TO ADVANCE THE THEORY...
YEAH. AND I HEARD SOMEBODY SAW HIM NEAR THE GRASSY KNOLL WHEN JFK WAS SHOT. THANK YOU FOR YOUR CALL.
HELLO. YOU'RE ON "TALKALOT".
...ON "TALKALOT".
YES. THIS CONCRETE GENTLEMAN IS FINE WITH ME, BUT DID YOU SEE HIM ON CARSON LAST NIGHT? THE MAN HASN'T A THOUGHT IN HIS HEAD!
WHAT AN UTTER BORE!
DAMN IT. IT WAS HARD TO BE BORING!
I'M GETTING SICK OF THIS SKEWED PUBLICITY CAMPAIGN.

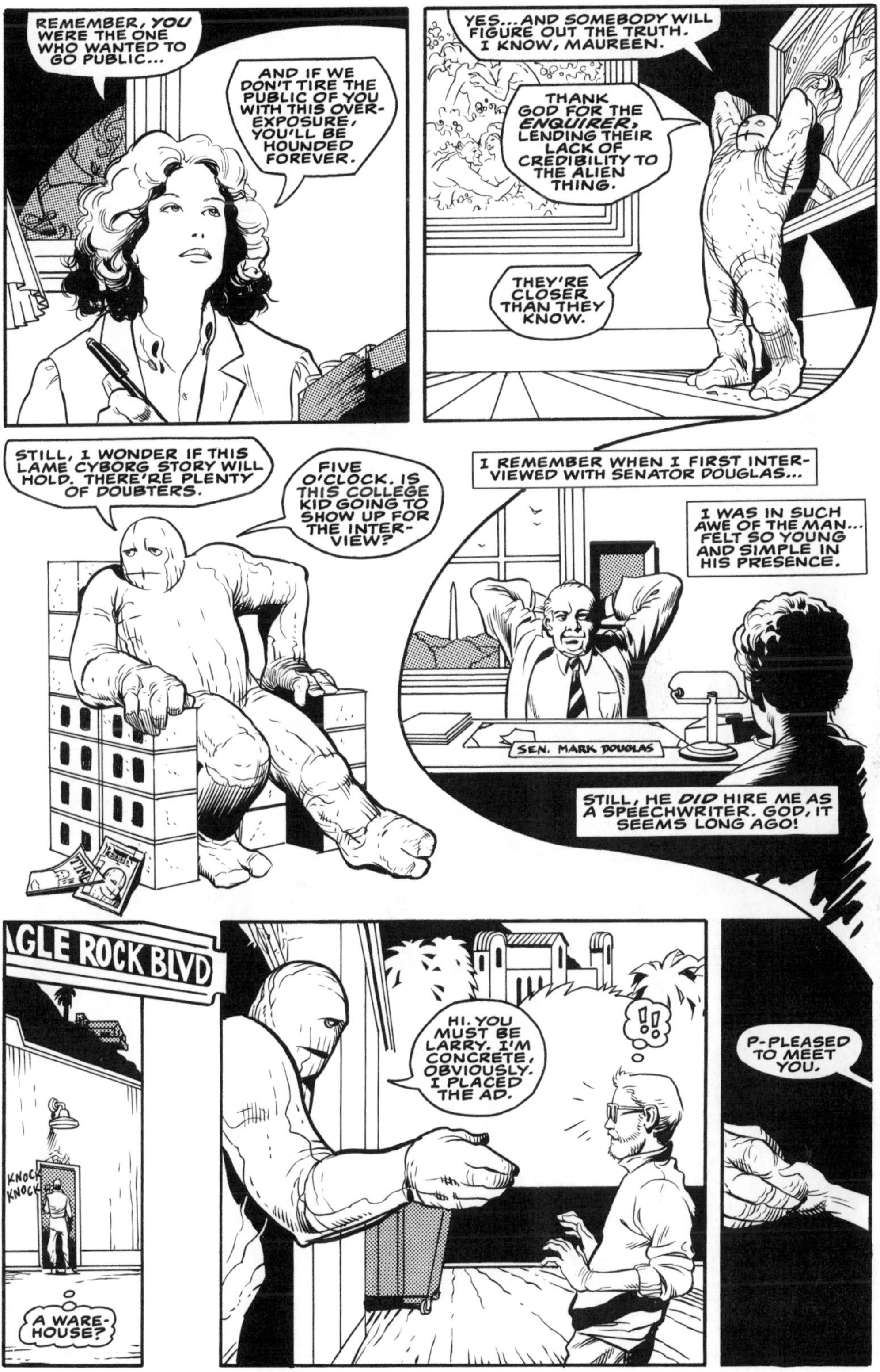

REMEMBER, *YOU* WERE THE ONE WHO WANTED TO GO PUBLIC...
AND IF WE DON'T TIRE THE PUBLIC OF YOU WITH THIS OVER-EXPOSURE, YOU'LL BE HOUNDED FOREVER.
YES... AND SOMEBODY WILL FIGURE OUT THE TRUTH. I KNOW, MAUREEN.
THANK GOD FOR THE *ENQUIRER*, LENDING THEIR LACK OF CREDIBILITY TO THE ALIEN THING.
THEY'RE CLOSER THAN THEY KNOW.
STILL, I WONDER IF THIS LAME CYBORG STORY WILL HOLD. THERE'RE PLENTY OF DOUBTERS.
FIVE O'CLOCK. IS THIS COLLEGE KID GOING TO SHOW UP FOR THE INTER-VIEW?
I REMEMBER WHEN I FIRST INTER-VIEWED WITH SENATOR DOUGLAS...
I WAS IN SUCH AWE OF THE MAN... FELT SO YOUNG AND SIMPLE IN HIS PRESENCE.
SEN. MARK DOUGLAS
STILL, HE *DID* HIRE ME AS A SPEECHWRITER. GOD, IT SEEMS LONG AGO!
GLE ROCK BLVD
KNOCK KNOCK
A WARE-HOUSE?
HI. YOU MUST BE LARRY. I'M CONCRETE, OBVIOUSLY. I PLACED THE AD.
!!
P-PLEASED TO MEET YOU.

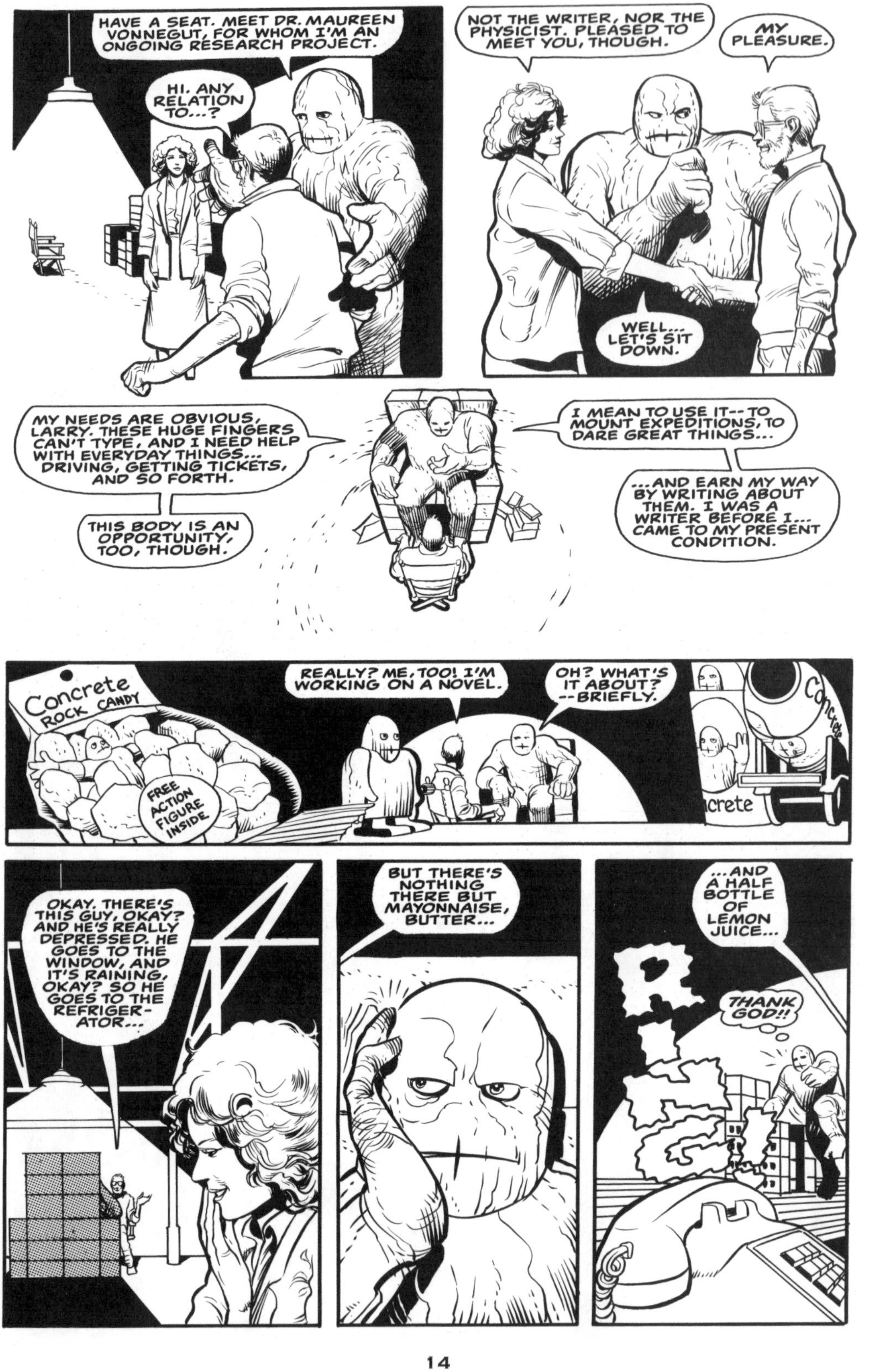
HAVE A SEAT. MEET DR. MAUREEN VONNEGUT, FOR WHOM I'M AN ONGOING RESEARCH PROJECT.
HI. ANY RELATION TO...?
NOT THE WRITER, NOR THE PHYSICIST. PLEASED TO MEET YOU, THOUGH.
MY PLEASURE.
WELL... LET'S SIT DOWN.
MY NEEDS ARE OBVIOUS, LARRY. THESE HUGE FINGERS CAN'T TYPE, AND I NEED HELP WITH EVERYDAY THINGS... DRIVING, GETTING TICKETS, AND SO FORTH.
THIS BODY IS AN OPPORTUNITY, TOO, THOUGH.
I MEAN TO USE IT-- TO MOUNT EXPEDITIONS, TO DARE GREAT THINGS...
...AND EARN MY WAY BY WRITING ABOUT THEM. I WAS A WRITER BEFORE I... CAME TO MY PRESENT CONDITION.
Concrete ROCK CANDY
FREE ACTION FIGURE INSIDE
REALLY? ME, TOO! I'M WORKING ON A NOVEL.
OH? WHAT'S IT ABOUT? --BRIEFLY.
Concrete
ncrete
OKAY. THERE'S THIS GUY, OKAY? AND HE'S REALLY DEPRESSED. HE GOES TO THE WINDOW, AND IT'S RAINING, OKAY? SO HE GOES TO THE REFRIGER-ATOR...
BUT THERE'S NOTHING THERE BUT MAYONNAISE, BUTTER...
...AND A HALF BOTTLE OF LEMON JUICE...
RING
THANK GOD!!

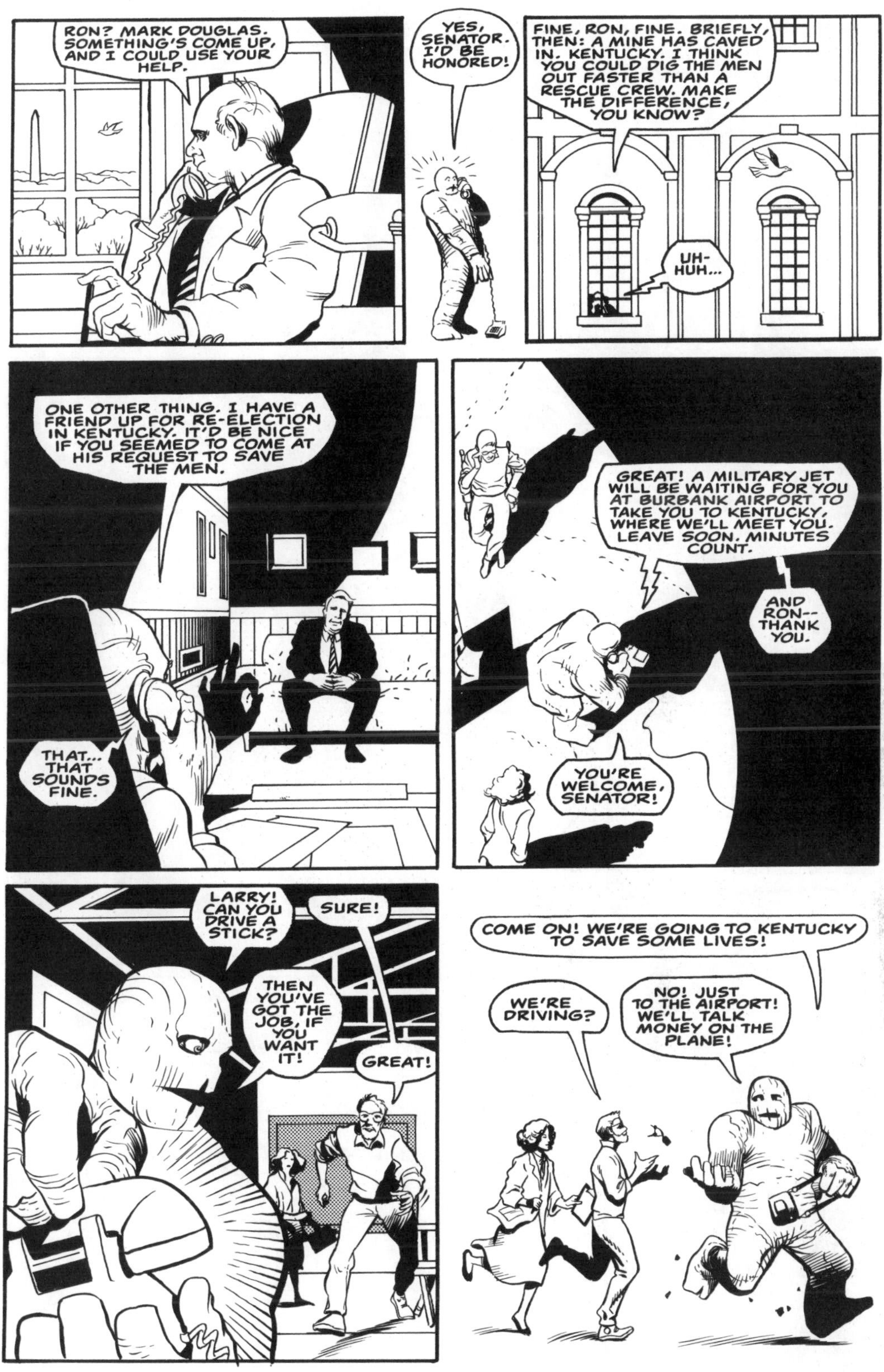
RON? MARK DOUGLAS. SOMETHING'S COME UP, AND I COULD USE YOUR HELP.
YES, SENATOR. I'D BE HONORED!
FINE, RON, FINE. BRIEFLY, THEN: A MINE HAS CAVED IN. KENTUCKY. I THINK YOU COULD DIG THE MEN OUT FASTER THAN A RESCUE CREW. MAKE THE DIFFERENCE, YOU KNOW?
UH-HUH...
ONE OTHER THING. I HAVE A FRIEND UP FOR RE-ELECTION IN KENTUCKY. IT'D BE NICE IF YOU SEEMED TO COME AT HIS REQUEST TO SAVE THE MEN.
THAT... THAT SOUNDS FINE.
GREAT! A MILITARY JET WILL BE WAITING FOR YOU AT BURBANK AIRPORT TO TAKE YOU TO KENTUCKY, WHERE WE'LL MEET YOU. LEAVE SOON. MINUTES COUNT.
AND RON-- THANK YOU.
YOU'RE WELCOME, SENATOR!
LARRY! CAN YOU DRIVE A STICK?
SURE!
THEN YOU'VE GOT THE JOB, IF YOU WANT IT!
GREAT!
COME ON! WE'RE GOING TO KENTUCKY TO SAVE SOME LIVES!
WE'RE DRIVING?
NO! JUST TO THE AIRPORT! WE'LL TALK MONEY ON THE PLANE!

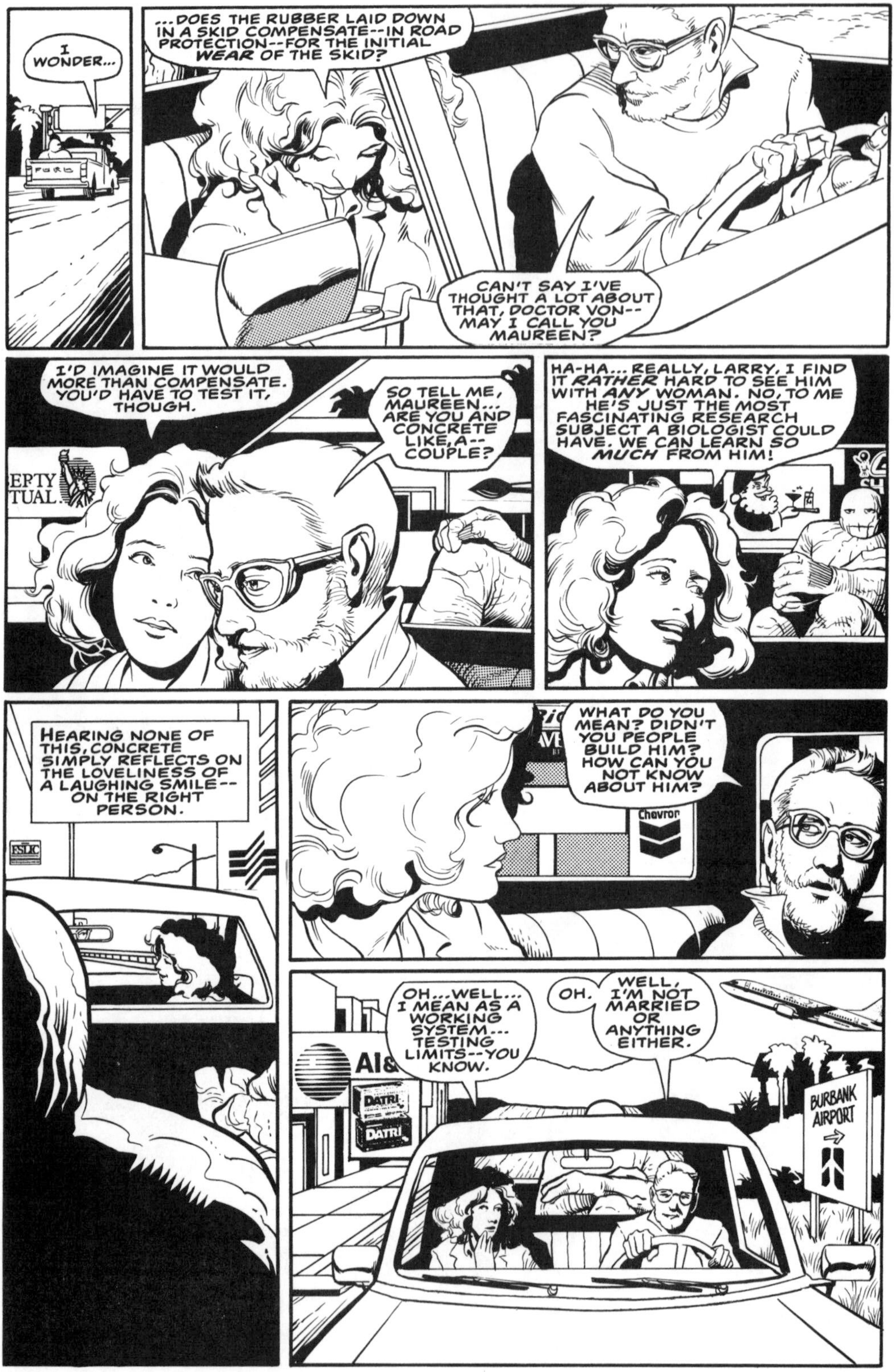
I WONDER...
...DOES THE RUBBER LAID DOWN IN A SKID COMPENSATE--IN ROAD PROTECTION--FOR THE INITIAL *WEAR* OF THE SKID?
CAN'T SAY I'VE THOUGHT A LOT ABOUT THAT, DOCTOR VON-- MAY I CALL YOU MAUREEN?
I'D IMAGINE IT WOULD MORE THAN COMPENSATE. YOU'D HAVE TO TEST IT, THOUGH.
SO TELL ME, MAUREEN... ARE YOU AND CONCRETE LIKE, A-- COUPLE?
HA-HA... REALLY, LARRY, I FIND IT *RATHER* HARD TO SEE HIM WITH *ANY* WOMAN. NO, TO ME HE'S JUST THE MOST FASCINATING RESEARCH SUBJECT A BIOLOGIST COULD HAVE. WE CAN LEARN SO *MUCH* FROM HIM!
HEARING NONE OF THIS, CONCRETE SIMPLY REFLECTS ON THE LOVELINESS OF A LAUGHING SMILE-- ON THE RIGHT PERSON.
WHAT DO YOU MEAN? DIDN'T YOU PEOPLE BUILD HIM? HOW CAN YOU NOT KNOW ABOUT HIM?
Chevron
OH... WELL... I MEAN AS A WORKING SYSTEM... TESTING LIMITS--YOU KNOW.
OH.
WELL, I'M NOT MARRIED OR ANYTHING EITHER.
DATRI
BURBANK AIRPORT

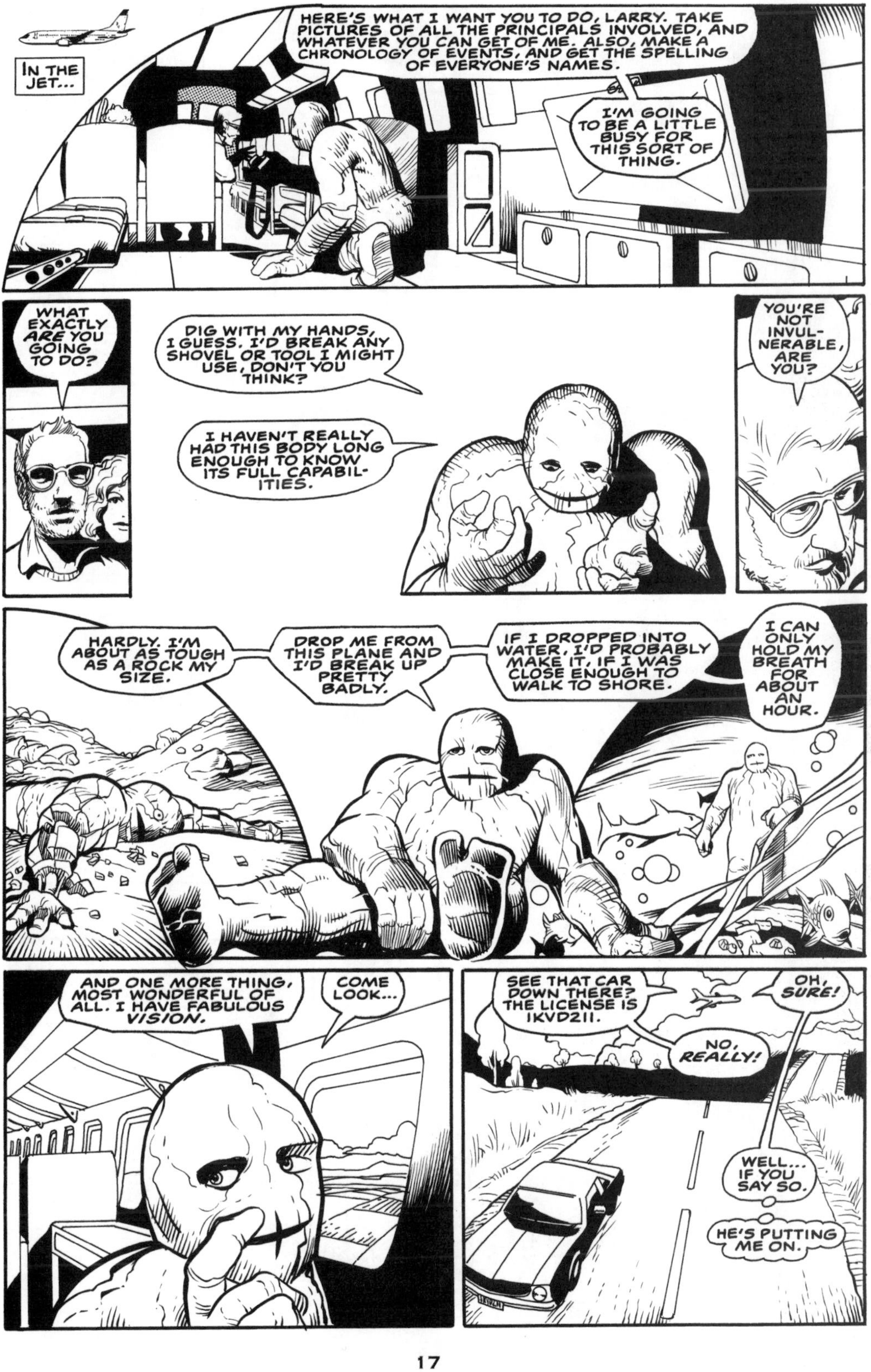

IN THE JET...
HERE'S WHAT I WANT YOU TO DO, LARRY. TAKE PICTURES OF ALL THE PRINCIPALS INVOLVED, AND WHATEVER YOU CAN GET OF ME. ALSO, MAKE A CHRONOLOGY OF EVENTS, AND GET THE SPELLING OF EVERYONE'S NAMES.
I'M GOING TO BE A LITTLE BUSY FOR THIS SORT OF THING.
WHAT EXACTLY *ARE* YOU GOING TO DO?
DIG WITH MY HANDS, I GUESS. I'D BREAK ANY SHOVEL OR TOOL I MIGHT USE, DON'T YOU THINK?
I HAVEN'T REALLY HAD THIS BODY LONG ENOUGH TO KNOW ITS FULL CAPABIL-ITIES.
YOU'RE NOT INVUL-NERABLE, ARE YOU?
HARDLY. I'M ABOUT AS TOUGH AS A ROCK MY SIZE.
DROP ME FROM THIS PLANE AND I'D BREAK UP PRETTY BADLY.
IF I DROPPED INTO WATER, I'D PROBABLY MAKE IT, IF I WAS CLOSE ENOUGH TO WALK TO SHORE.
I CAN ONLY HOLD MY BREATH FOR ABOUT AN HOUR.
AND ONE MORE THING, MOST WONDERFUL OF ALL. I HAVE FABULOUS *VISION*.
COME LOOK...
SEE THAT CAR DOWN THERE? THE LICENSE IS IKVD211.
OH, *SURE!*
NO, *REALLY!*
WELL... IF YOU SAY SO.
HE'S PUTTING ME ON.

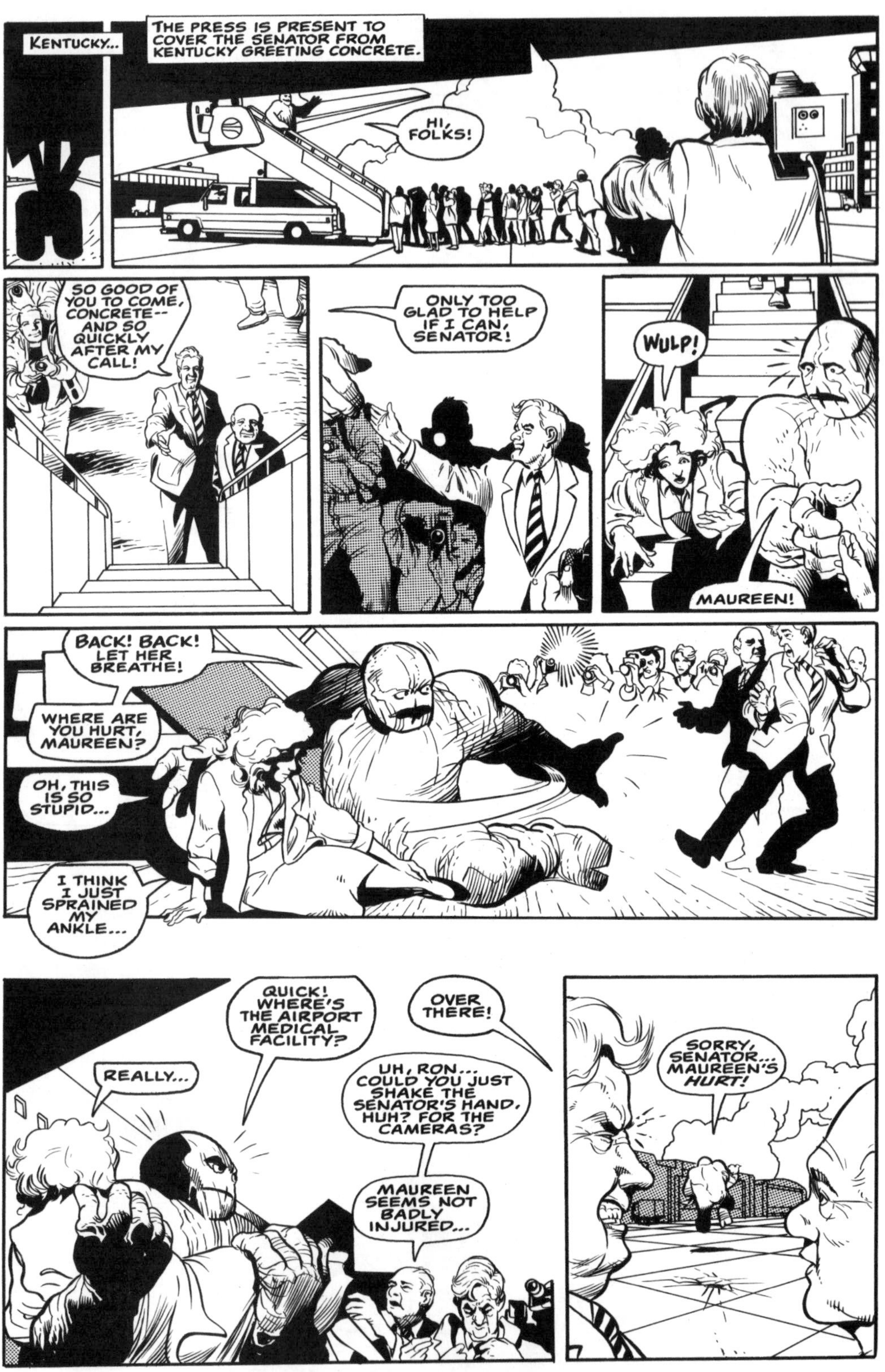
Kentucky...
The press is present to cover the senator from Kentucky greeting Concrete.
Hi, folks!
So good of you to come, Concrete-- and so quickly after my call!
Only too glad to help if I can, senator!
Wulp!
Maureen!
Back! Back! Let her breathe!
Where are you hurt, Maureen?
Oh, this is so stupid...
I think I just sprained my ankle...
Really...
Quick! Where's the airport medical facility?
Over there!
Uh, Ron... could you just shake the senator's hand, huh? For the cameras?
Maureen seems not badly injured...
Sorry, senator... Maureen's *hurt*!

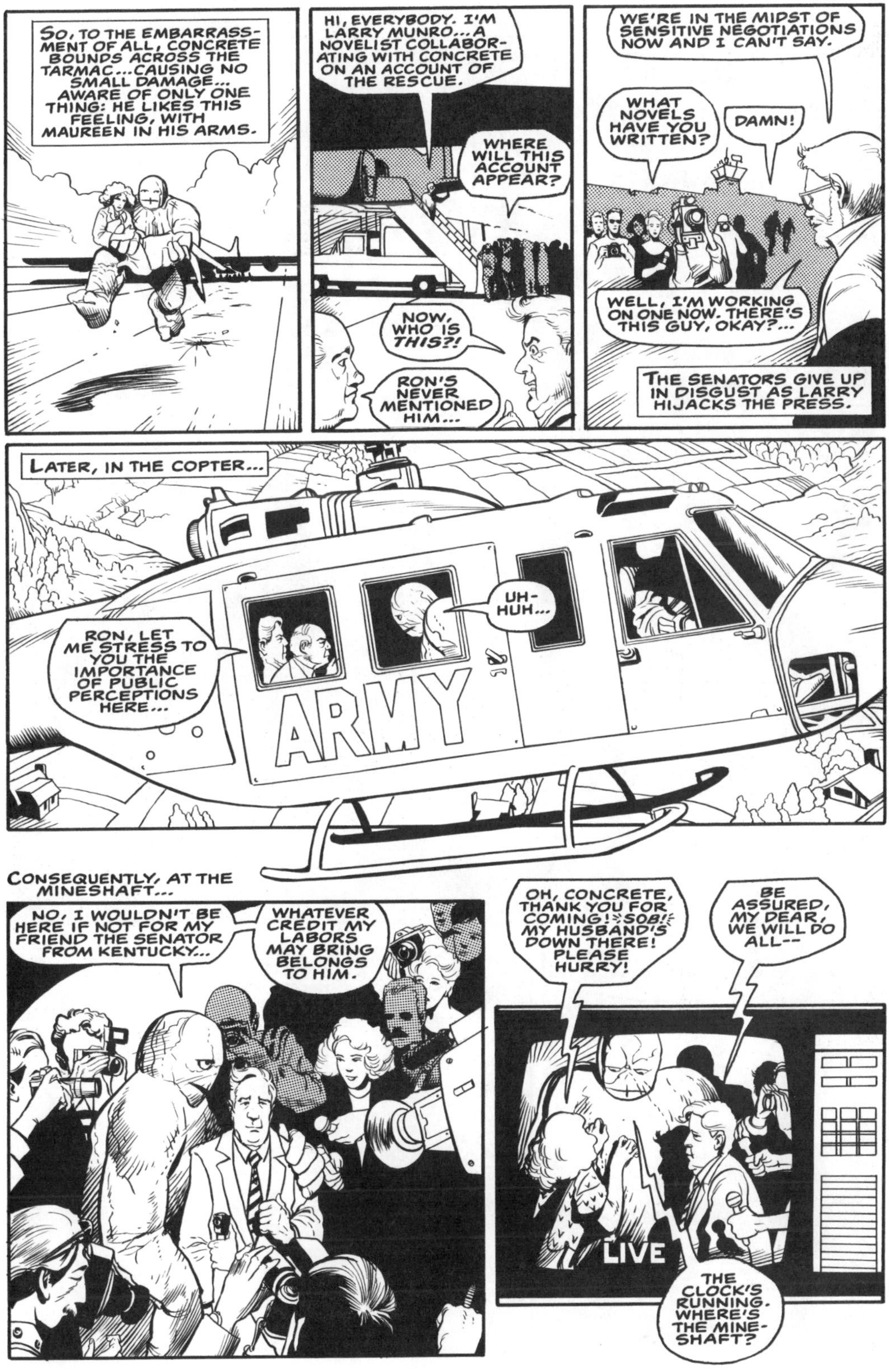
So, to the embarrassment of all, Concrete bounds across the tarmac...causing no small damage... aware of only one thing: he likes this feeling, with Maureen in his arms.
Hi, everybody. I'm Larry Munro... a novelist collaborating with Concrete on an account of the rescue.
Where will this account appear?
Now, who is *this?!*
Ron's never mentioned him...
We're in the midst of sensitive negotiations now and I can't say.
What novels have you written?
Damn!
Well, I'm working on one now. There's this guy, okay?...
The senators give up in disgust as Larry hijacks the press.
Later, in the copter...
Ron, let me stress to you the importance of public perceptions here...
Uh-huh...
ARMY
Consequently, at the mineshaft...
No, I wouldn't be here if not for my friend the senator from Kentucky...
Whatever credit my labors may bring belongs to him.
Oh, Concrete, thank you for coming! *sob!* My husband's down there! Please hurry!
Be assured, my dear, we will do all--
LIVE
The clock's running. Where's the mineshaft?

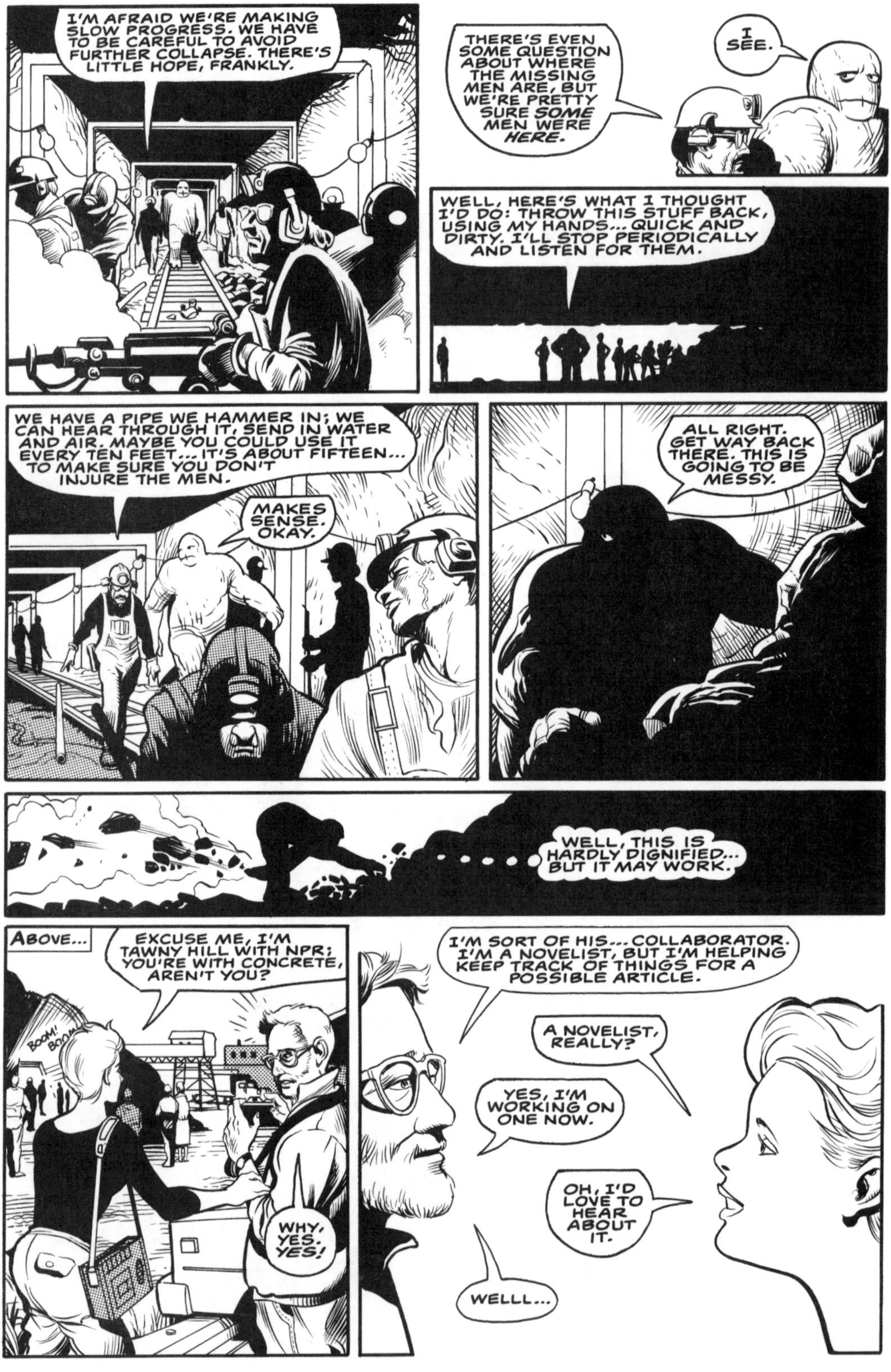

I'M AFRAID WE'RE MAKING SLOW PROGRESS. WE HAVE TO BE CAREFUL TO AVOID FURTHER COLLAPSE. THERE'S LITTLE HOPE, FRANKLY.
THERE'S EVEN SOME QUESTION ABOUT WHERE THE MISSING MEN ARE, BUT WE'RE PRETTY SURE *SOME* MEN WERE *HERE*.
I SEE.
WELL, HERE'S WHAT I THOUGHT I'D DO: THROW THIS STUFF BACK, USING MY HANDS... QUICK AND DIRTY. I'LL STOP PERIODICALLY AND LISTEN FOR THEM.
WE HAVE A PIPE WE HAMMER IN; WE CAN HEAR THROUGH IT, SEND IN WATER AND AIR. MAYBE YOU COULD USE IT EVERY TEN FEET... IT'S ABOUT FIFTEEN... TO MAKE SURE YOU DON'T INJURE THE MEN.
MAKES SENSE. OKAY.
ALL RIGHT. GET WAY BACK THERE. THIS IS GOING TO BE MESSY.
WELL, THIS IS HARDLY DIGNIFIED... BUT IT MAY WORK.
ABOVE...
EXCUSE ME, I'M TAWNY HILL WITH NPR; YOU'RE WITH CONCRETE, AREN'T YOU?
BOOM! BOOM!
WHY, YES. YES!
I'M SORT OF HIS... COLLABORATOR. I'M A NOVELIST, BUT I'M HELPING KEEP TRACK OF THINGS FOR A POSSIBLE ARTICLE.
A NOVELIST, REALLY?
YES, I'M WORKING ON ONE NOW.
OH, I'D LOVE TO HEAR ABOUT IT.
WELLL...

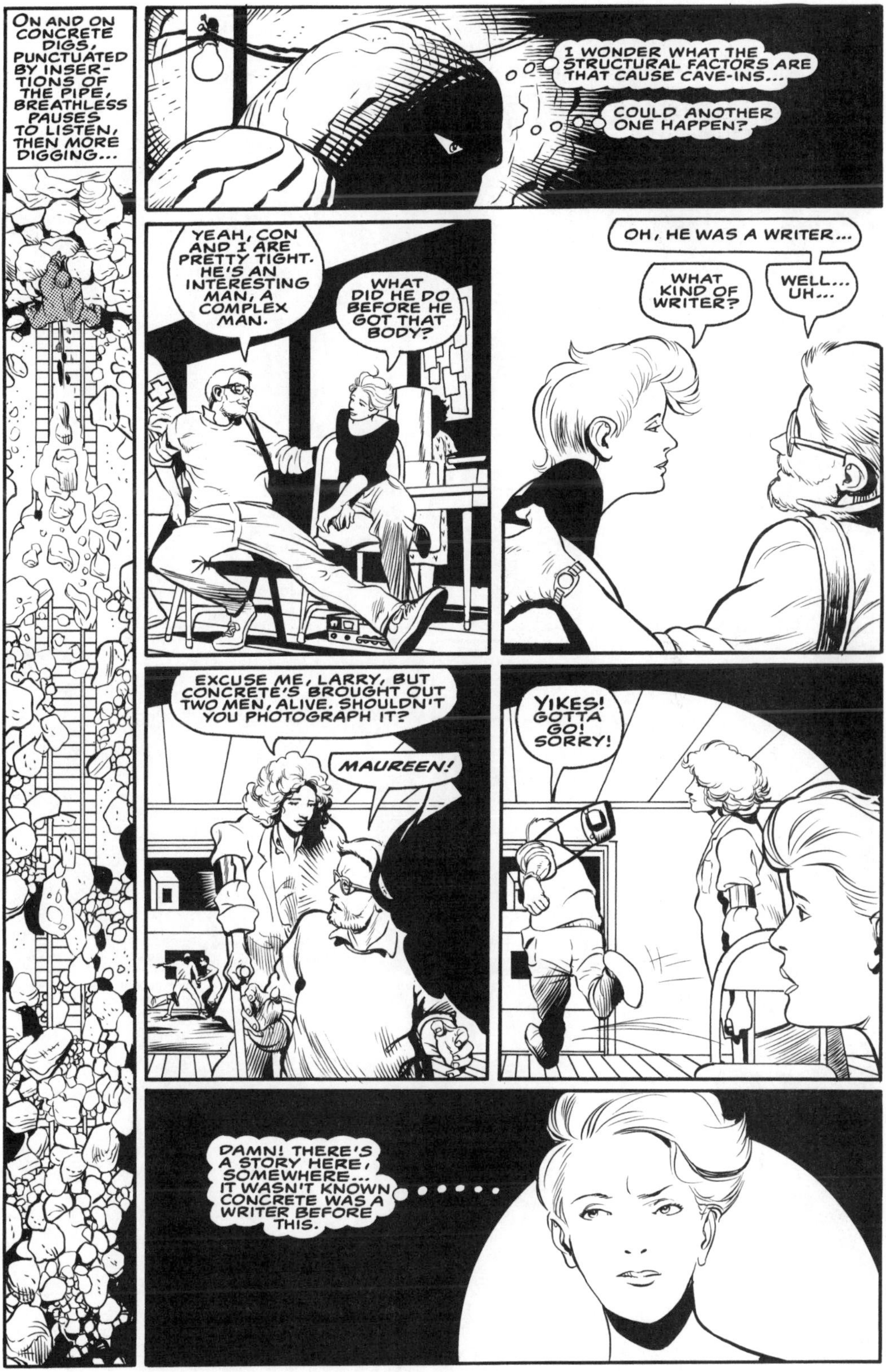
ON AND ON CONCRETE DIGS, PUNCTUATED BY INSERTIONS OF THE PIPE, BREATHLESS PAUSES TO LISTEN, THEN MORE DIGGING...
I WONDER WHAT THE STRUCTURAL FACTORS ARE THAT CAUSE CAVE-INS...
COULD ANOTHER ONE HAPPEN?
YEAH, CON AND I ARE PRETTY TIGHT. HE'S AN INTERESTING MAN, A COMPLEX MAN.
WHAT DID HE DO BEFORE HE GOT THAT BODY?
OH, HE WAS A WRITER...
WHAT KIND OF WRITER?
WELL... UH...
EXCUSE ME, LARRY, BUT CONCRETE'S BROUGHT OUT TWO MEN, ALIVE. SHOULDN'T YOU PHOTOGRAPH IT?
MAUREEN!
YIKES! GOTTA GO! SORRY!
DAMN! THERE'S A STORY HERE, SOMEWHERE... IT WASN'T KNOWN CONCRETE WAS A WRITER BEFORE THIS.

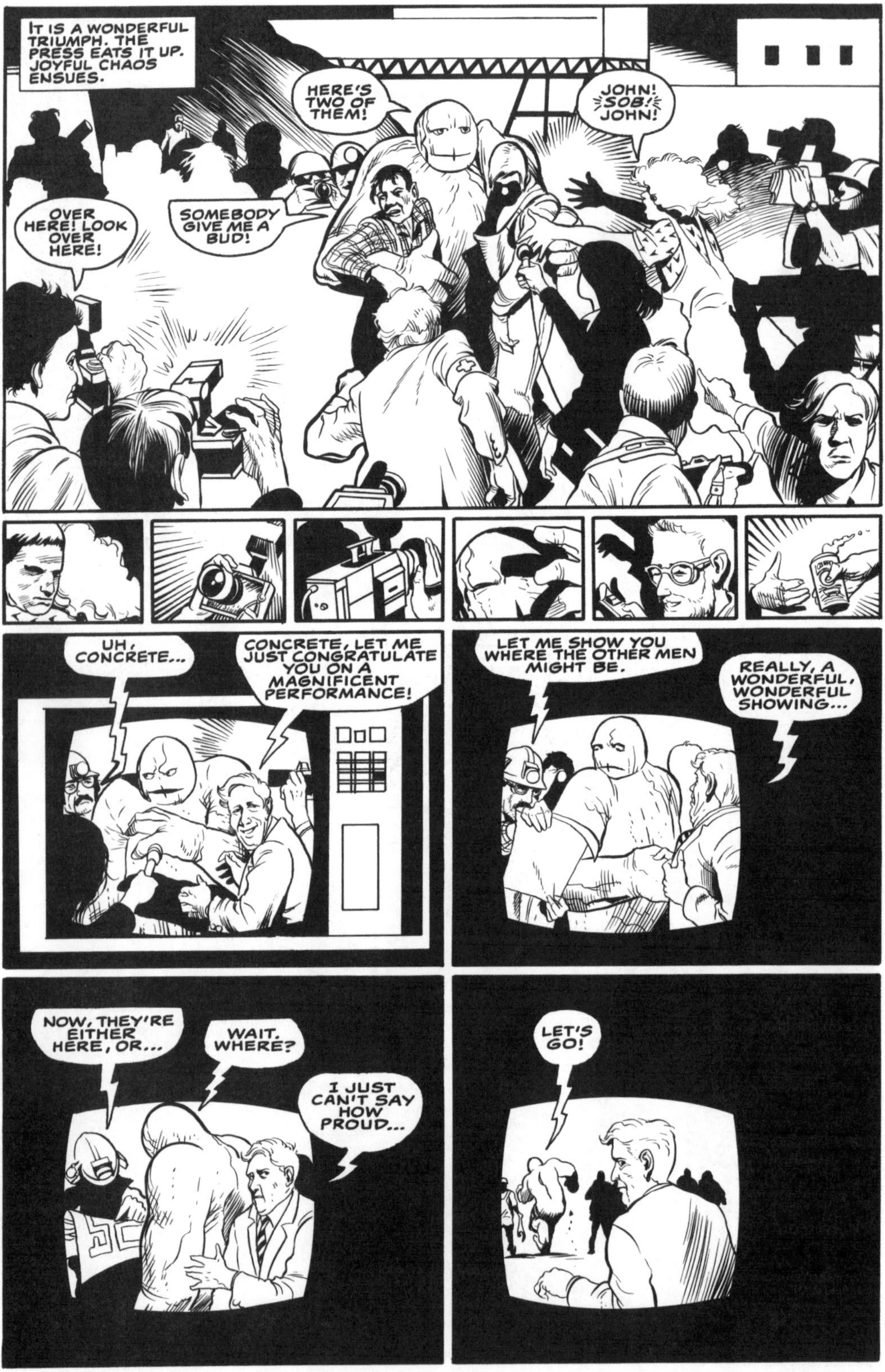
IT IS A WONDERFUL TRIUMPH. THE PRESS EATS IT UP. JOYFUL CHAOS ENSUES.
HERE'S TWO OF THEM!
JOHN! SOB! JOHN!
OVER HERE! LOOK OVER HERE!
SOMEBODY GIVE ME A BUD!
UH, CONCRETE...
CONCRETE, LET ME JUST CONGRATULATE YOU ON A MAGNIFICENT PERFORMANCE!
LET ME SHOW YOU WHERE THE OTHER MEN MIGHT BE.
REALLY, A WONDERFUL, WONDERFUL SHOWING...
NOW, THEY'RE EITHER HERE, OR...
WAIT. WHERE?
I JUST CAN'T SAY HOW PROUD...
LET'S GO!

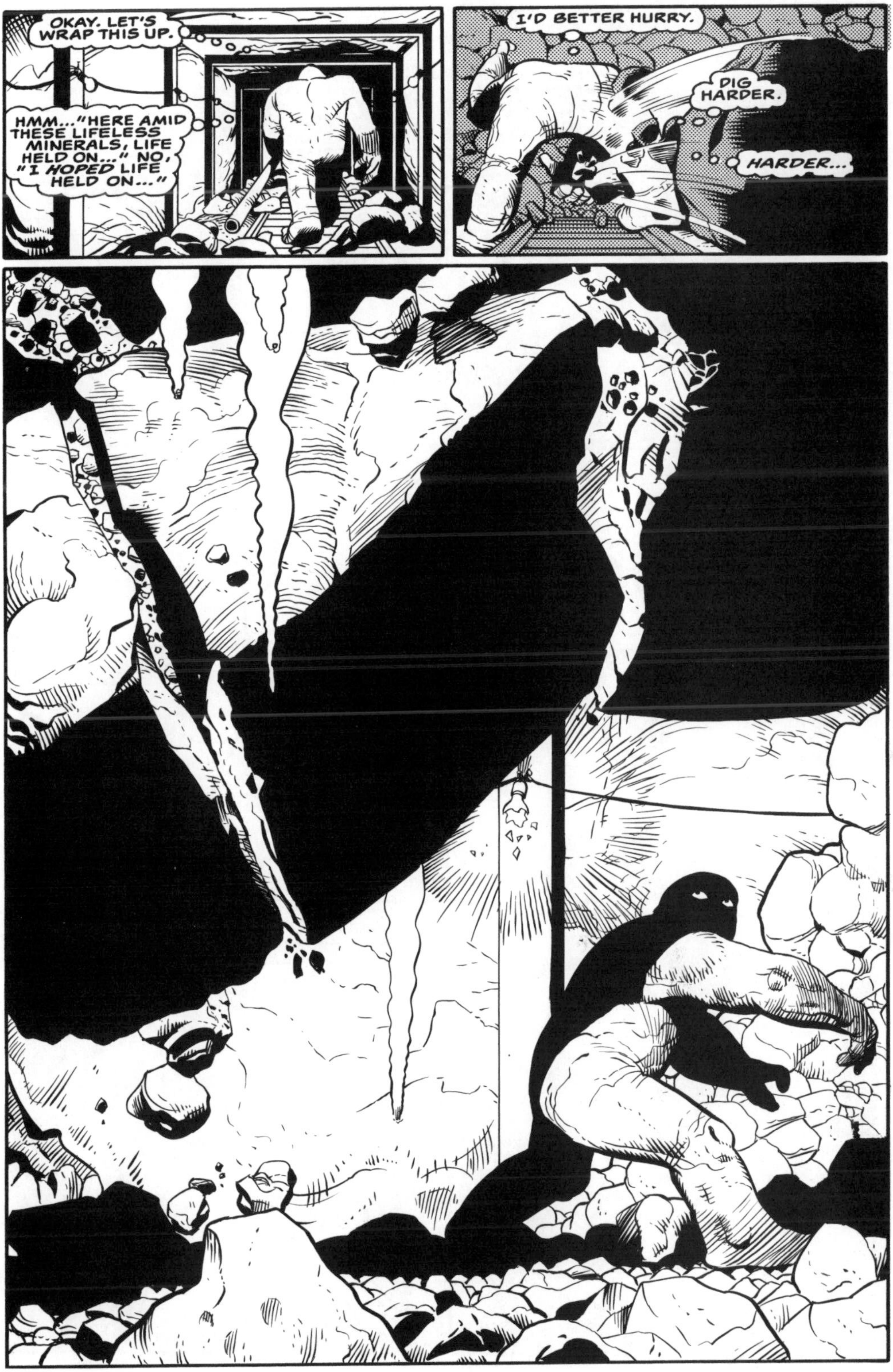
OKAY. LET'S WRAP THIS UP.
HMM... "HERE AMID THESE LIFELESS MINERALS, LIFE HELD ON..." NO, "I HOPED LIFE HELD ON..."
I'D BETTER HURRY.
DIG HARDER.
HARDER...

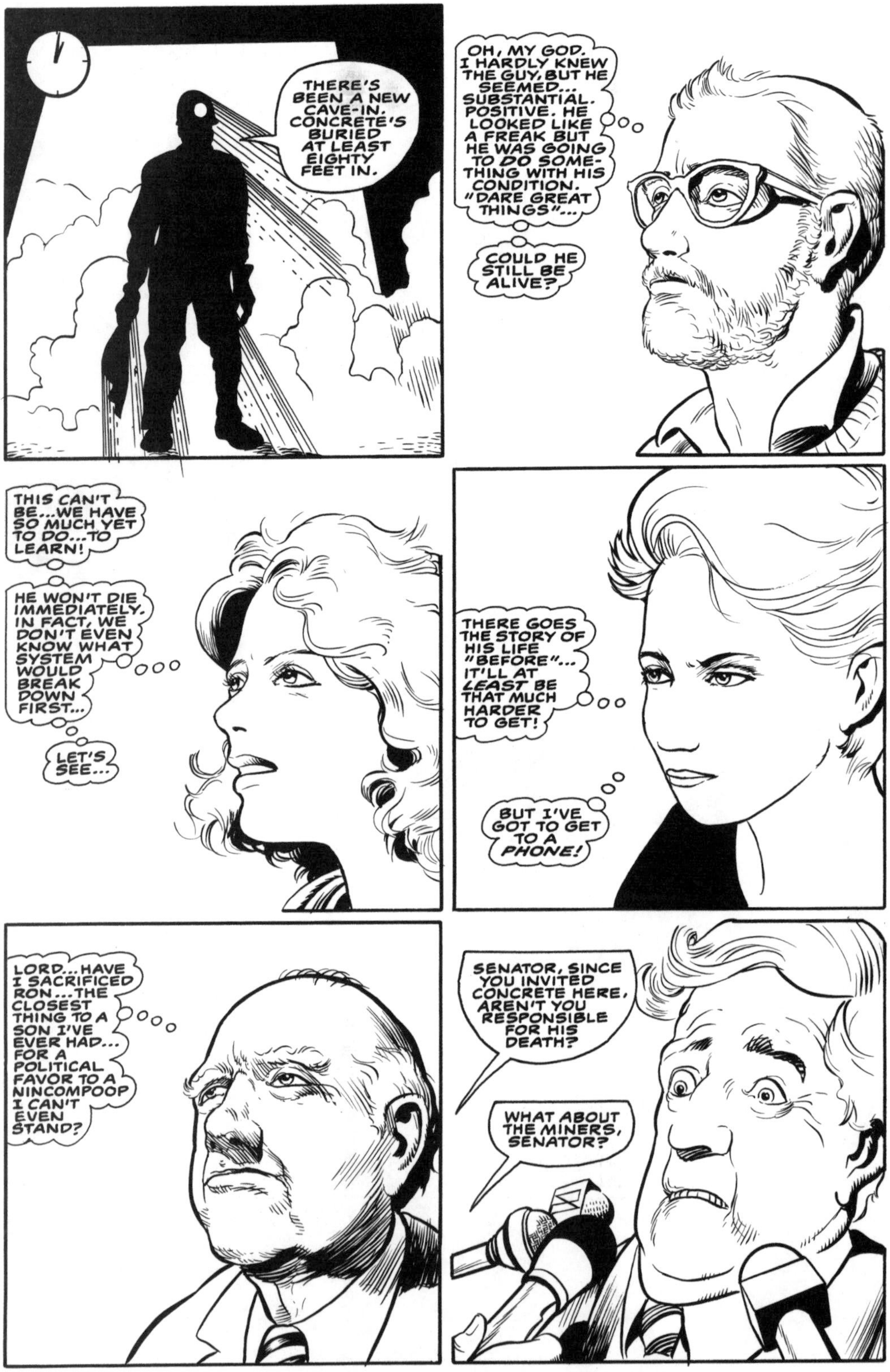
THERE'S BEEN A NEW CAVE-IN. CONCRETE'S BURIED AT LEAST EIGHTY FEET IN.
OH, MY GOD. I HARDLY KNEW THE GUY, BUT HE SEEMED... SUBSTANTIAL. POSITIVE. HE LOOKED LIKE A FREAK BUT HE WAS GOING TO *DO* SOMETHING WITH HIS CONDITION. "DARE GREAT THINGS"...
COULD HE STILL BE ALIVE?
THIS CAN'T BE...WE HAVE SO MUCH YET TO DO...TO LEARN!
HE WON'T DIE IMMEDIATELY. IN FACT, WE DON'T EVEN KNOW WHAT SYSTEM WOULD BREAK DOWN FIRST...
LET'S SEE...
THERE GOES THE STORY OF HIS LIFE "BEFORE"... IT'LL AT *LEAST* BE THAT MUCH HARDER TO GET!
BUT I'VE GOT TO GET TO A *PHONE!*
LORD...HAVE I SACRIFICED RON...THE CLOSEST THING TO A SON I'VE EVER HAD... FOR A POLITICAL FAVOR TO A NINCOMPOOP I CAN'T EVEN STAND?
SENATOR, SINCE YOU INVITED CONCRETE HERE, AREN'T YOU RESPONSIBLE FOR HIS DEATH?
WHAT ABOUT THE MINERS, SENATOR?

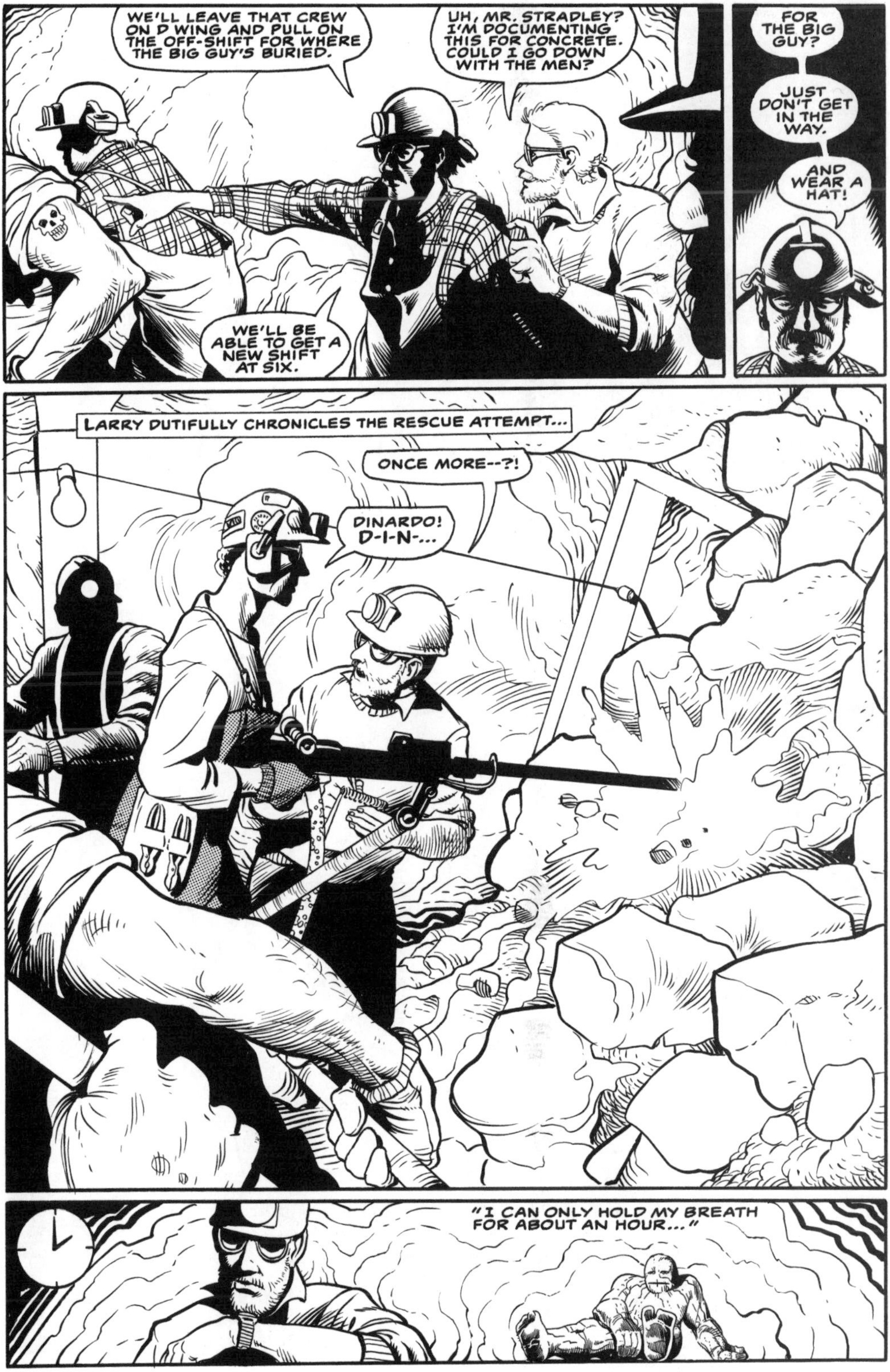
WE'LL LEAVE THAT CREW ON D WING AND PULL ON THE OFF-SHIFT FOR WHERE THE BIG GUY'S BURIED.
WE'LL BE ABLE TO GET A NEW SHIFT AT SIX.
UH, MR. STRADLEY? I'M DOCUMENTING THIS FOR CONCRETE. COULD I GO DOWN WITH THE MEN?
FOR THE BIG GUY?
JUST DON'T GET IN THE WAY.
AND WEAR A HAT!
LARRY DUTIFULLY CHRONICLES THE RESCUE ATTEMPT...
DINARDO! D-I-N-...
ONCE MORE--?!
"I CAN ONLY HOLD MY BREATH FOR ABOUT AN HOUR..."

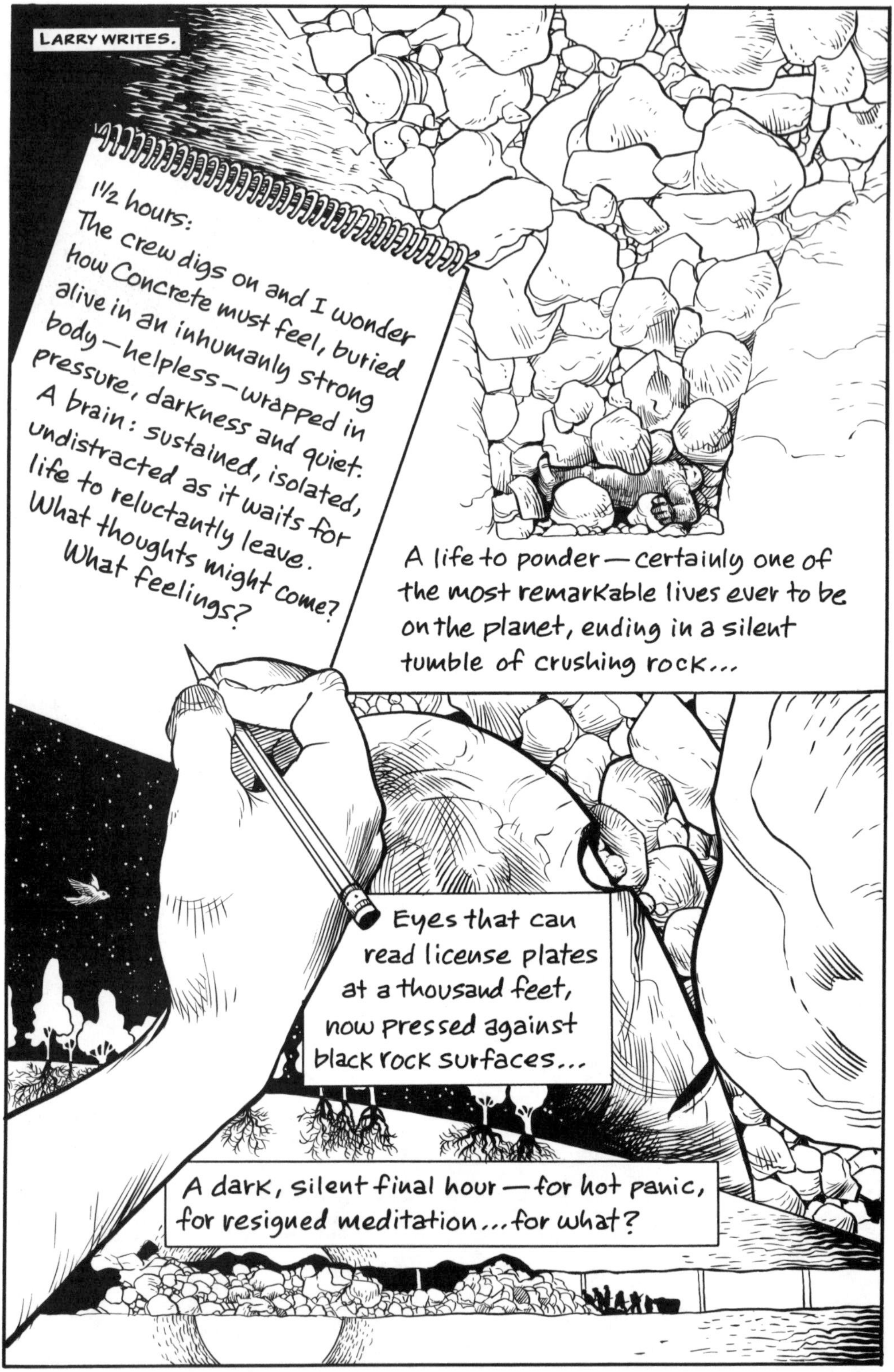
LARRY WRITES.
1½ hours:
The crew digs on and I wonder how Concrete must feel, buried alive in an inhumanly strong body—helpless—wrapped in pressure, darkness and quiet.
A brain: sustained, isolated, undistracted as it waits for life to reluctantly leave.
What thoughts might come?
What feelings?
A life to ponder—certainly one of the most remarkable lives ever to be on the planet, ending in a silent tumble of crushing rock...
Eyes that can read license plates at a thousand feet, now pressed against black rock surfaces...
A dark, silent final hour—for hot panic, for resigned meditation...for what?

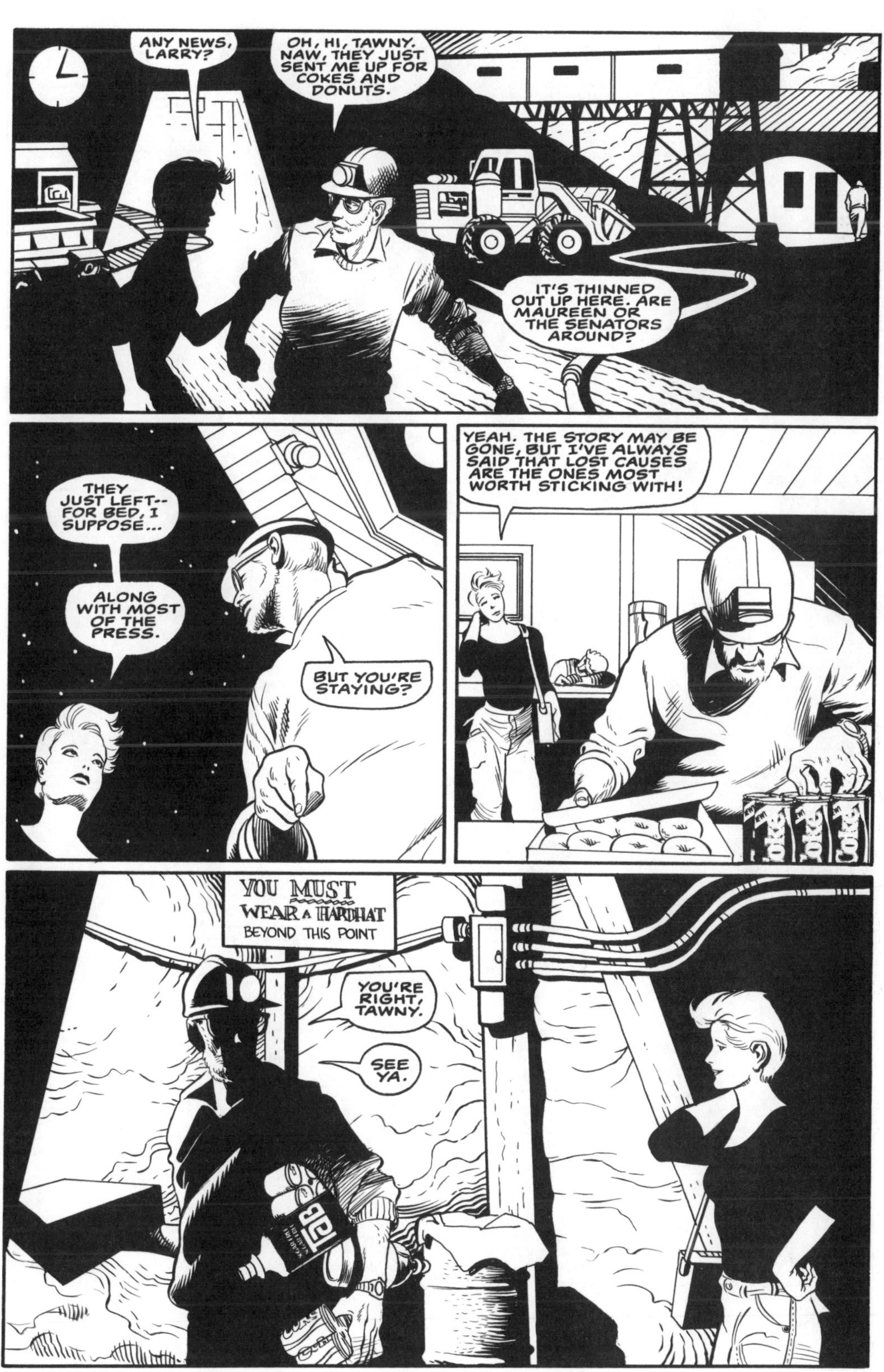
ANY NEWS, LARRY?
OH, HI, TAWNY. NAW, THEY JUST SENT ME UP FOR COKES AND DONUTS.
IT'S THINNED OUT UP HERE. ARE MAUREEN OR THE SENATORS AROUND?
THEY JUST LEFT-- FOR BED, I SUPPOSE...
ALONG WITH MOST OF THE PRESS.
BUT YOU'RE STAYING?
YEAH. THE STORY MAY BE GONE, BUT I'VE ALWAYS SAID THAT LOST CAUSES ARE THE ONES MOST WORTH STICKING WITH!
YOU MUST WEAR A HARDHAT BEYOND THIS POINT
YOU'RE RIGHT, TAWNY.
SEE YA.

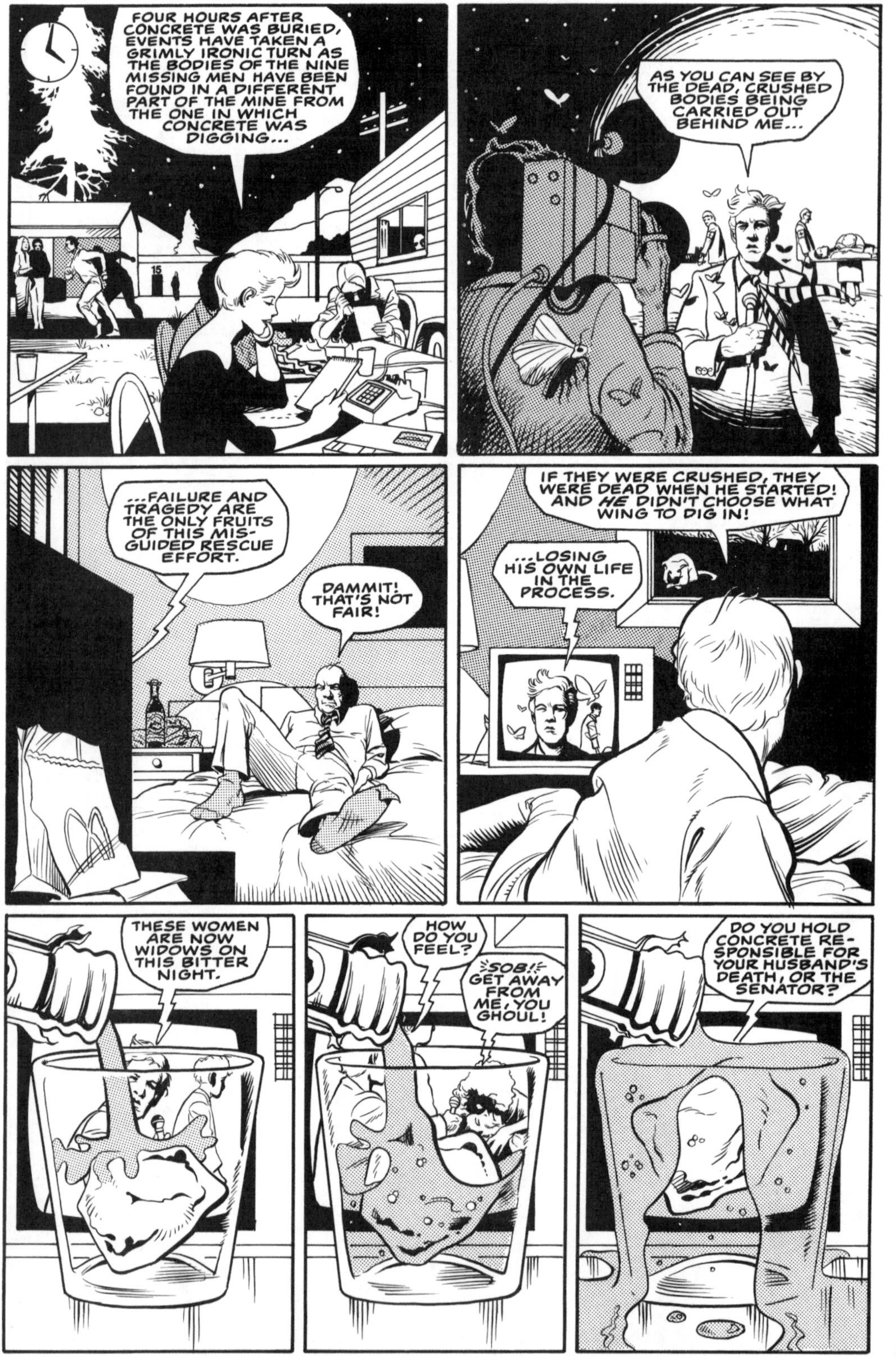
FOUR HOURS AFTER CONCRETE WAS BURIED, EVENTS HAVE TAKEN A GRIMLY IRONIC TURN AS THE BODIES OF THE NINE MISSING MEN HAVE BEEN FOUND IN A DIFFERENT PART OF THE MINE FROM THE ONE IN WHICH CONCRETE WAS DIGGING...
15
AS YOU CAN SEE BY THE DEAD, CRUSHED BODIES BEING CARRIED OUT BEHIND ME...
...FAILURE AND TRAGEDY ARE THE ONLY FRUITS OF THIS MISGUIDED RESCUE EFFORT.
DAMMIT! THAT'S NOT FAIR!
IF THEY WERE CRUSHED, THEY WERE DEAD WHEN HE STARTED! AND HE DIDN'T CHOOSE WHAT WING TO DIG IN!
...LOSING HIS OWN LIFE IN THE PROCESS.
THESE WOMEN ARE NOW WIDOWS ON THIS BITTER NIGHT.
HOW DO YOU FEEL?
SOB! GET AWAY FROM ME, YOU GHOUL!
DO YOU HOLD CONCRETE RESPONSIBLE FOR YOUR HUSBAND'S DEATH, OR THE SENATOR?

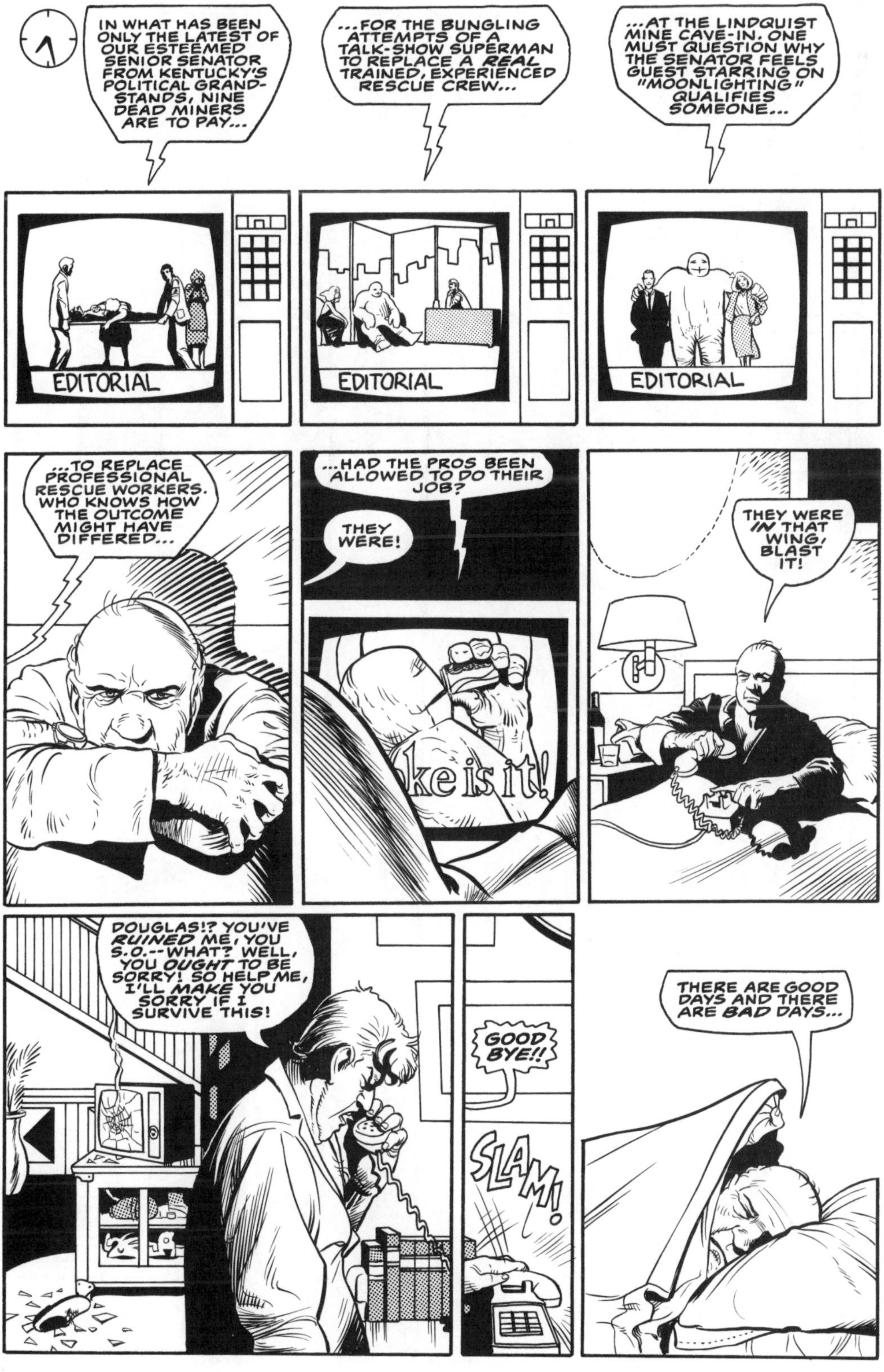
IN WHAT HAS BEEN ONLY THE LATEST OF OUR ESTEEMED SENIOR SENATOR FROM KENTUCKY'S POLITICAL GRAND-STANDS, NINE DEAD MINERS ARE TO PAY...
EDITORIAL
...FOR THE BUNGLING ATTEMPTS OF A TALK-SHOW SUPERMAN TO REPLACE A REAL TRAINED, EXPERIENCED RESCUE CREW...
EDITORIAL
...AT THE LINDQUIST MINE CAVE-IN. ONE MUST QUESTION WHY THE SENATOR FEELS GUEST STARRING ON "MOONLIGHTING" QUALIFIES SOMEONE...
EDITORIAL
...TO REPLACE PROFESSIONAL RESCUE WORKERS. WHO KNOWS HOW THE OUTCOME MIGHT HAVE DIFFERED...
...HAD THE PROS BEEN ALLOWED TO DO THEIR JOB?
THEY WERE!
ke is it!
THEY WERE IN THAT WING, BLAST IT!
DOUGLAS!? YOU'VE RUINED ME, YOU S.O.--WHAT? WELL, YOU OUGHT TO BE SORRY! SO HELP ME, I'LL MAKE YOU SORRY IF I SURVIVE THIS!
GOOD BYE!!
SLAM!
THERE ARE GOOD DAYS AND THERE ARE BAD DAYS...

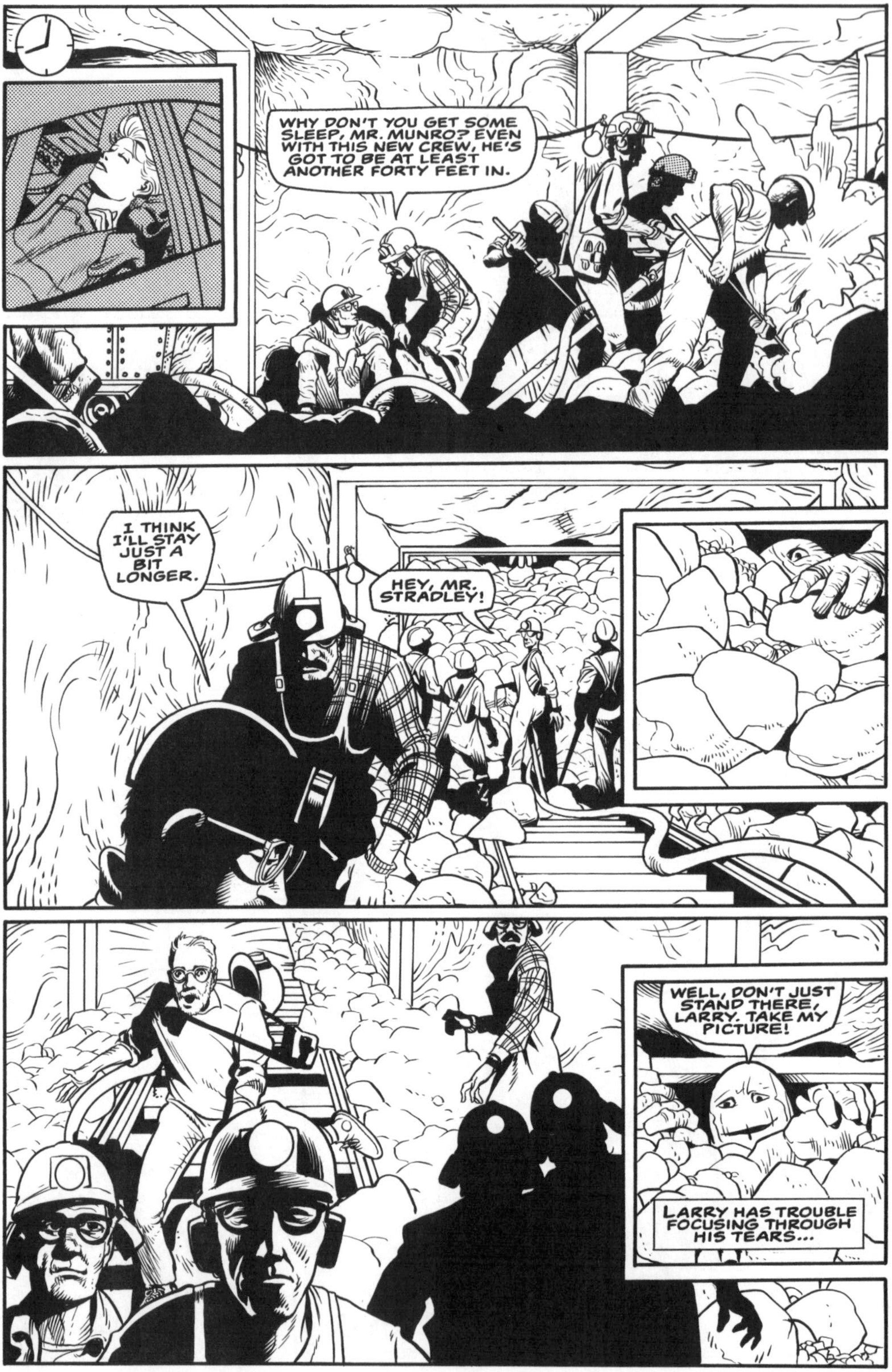
WHY DON'T YOU GET SOME SLEEP, MR. MUNRO? EVEN WITH THIS NEW CREW, HE'S GOT TO BE AT LEAST ANOTHER FORTY FEET IN.
I THINK I'LL STAY JUST A BIT LONGER.
HEY, MR. STRADLEY!
WELL, DON'T JUST STAND THERE, LARRY. TAKE MY PICTURE!
LARRY HAS TROUBLE FOCUSING THROUGH HIS TEARS...

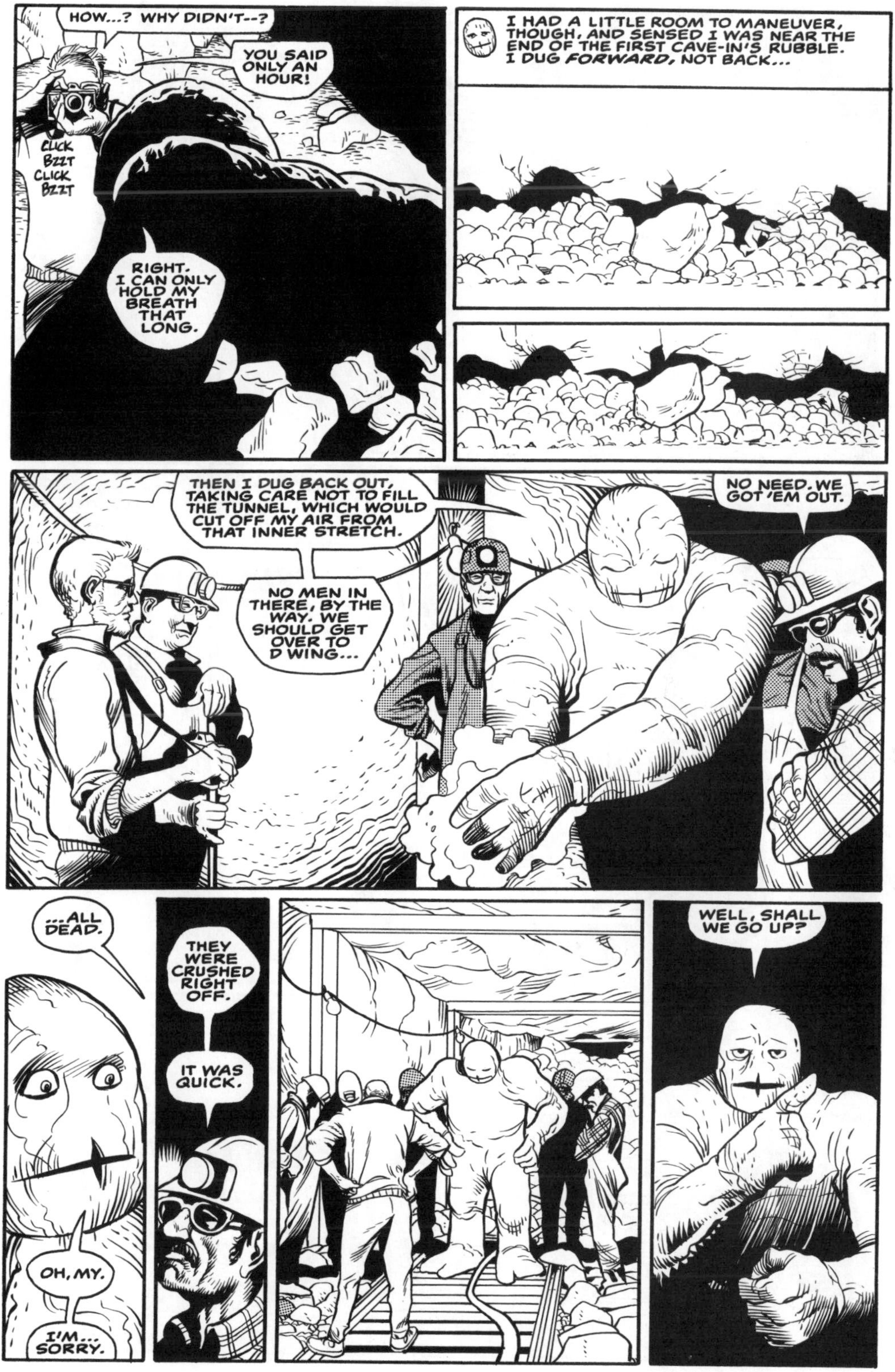
HOW...? WHY DIDN'T--?
YOU SAID ONLY AN HOUR!
CLICK BZZT CLICK BZZT
RIGHT. I CAN ONLY HOLD MY BREATH THAT LONG.
I HAD A LITTLE ROOM TO MANEUVER, THOUGH, AND SENSED I WAS NEAR THE END OF THE FIRST CAVE-IN'S RUBBLE. I DUG FORWARD, NOT BACK...
THEN I DUG BACK OUT, TAKING CARE NOT TO FILL THE TUNNEL, WHICH WOULD CUT OFF MY AIR FROM THAT INNER STRETCH.
NO MEN IN THERE, BY THE WAY. WE SHOULD GET OVER TO D WING...
NO NEED. WE GOT 'EM OUT.
...ALL DEAD.
THEY WERE CRUSHED RIGHT OFF.
IT WAS QUICK.
OH, MY.
I'M... SORRY.
WELL, SHALL WE GO UP?

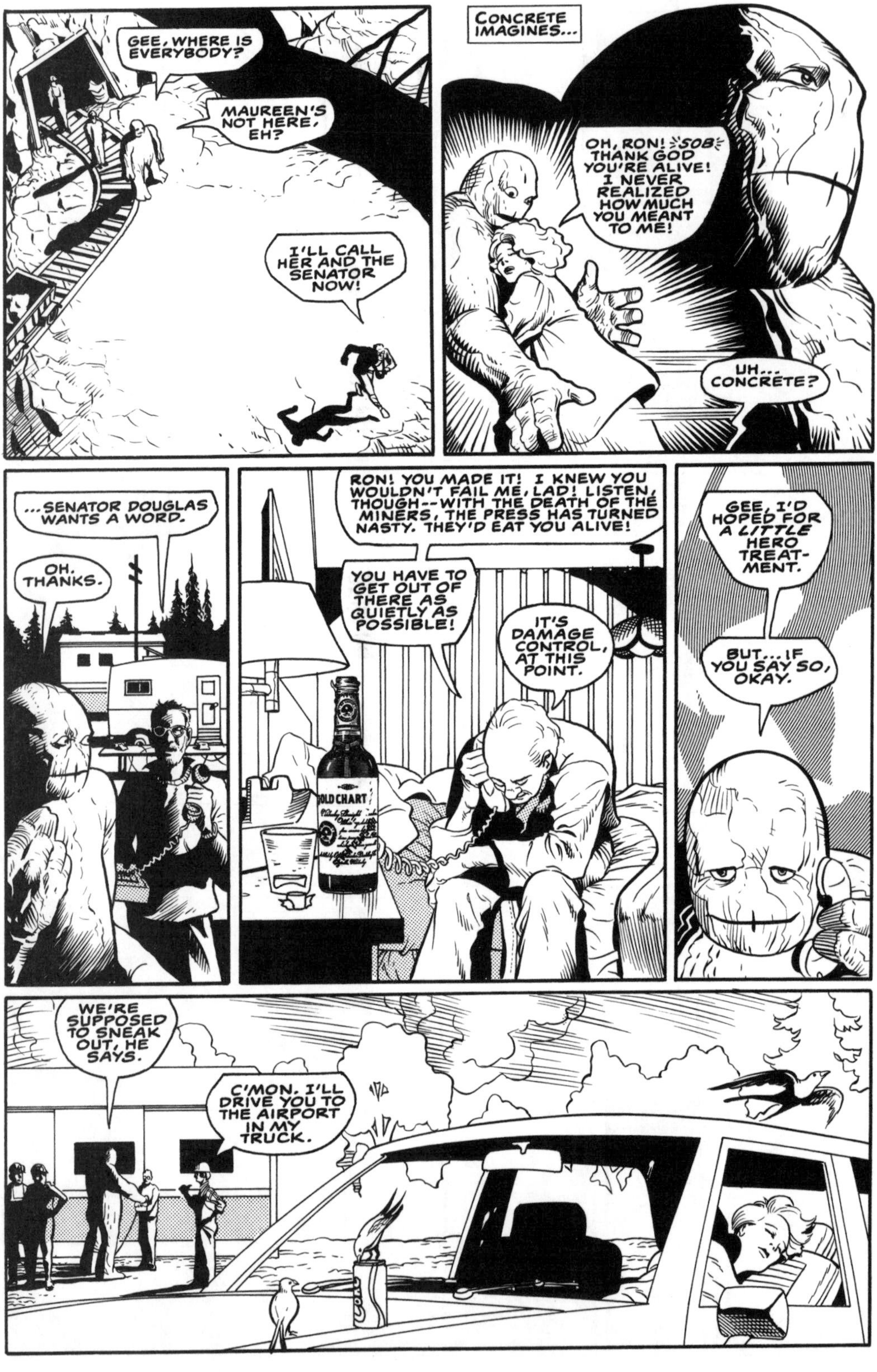
GEE, WHERE IS EVERYBODY?
MAUREEN'S NOT HERE, EH?
I'LL CALL HER AND THE SENATOR NOW!
CONCRETE IMAGINES...
OH, RON! SOB THANK GOD YOU'RE ALIVE! I NEVER REALIZED HOW MUCH YOU MEANT TO ME!
UH... CONCRETE?
...SENATOR DOUGLAS WANTS A WORD.
OH. THANKS.
RON! YOU MADE IT! I KNEW YOU WOULDN'T FAIL ME, LAD! LISTEN, THOUGH--WITH THE DEATH OF THE MINERS, THE PRESS HAS TURNED NASTY. THEY'D EAT YOU ALIVE!
YOU HAVE TO GET OUT OF THERE AS QUIETLY AS POSSIBLE!
IT'S DAMAGE CONTROL, AT THIS POINT.
OLD CHART
GEE, I'D HOPED FOR A *LITTLE* HERO TREAT-MENT.
BUT... IF YOU SAY SO, OKAY.
WE'RE SUPPOSED TO SNEAK OUT, HE SAYS.
C'MON. I'LL DRIVE YOU TO THE AIRPORT IN MY TRUCK.

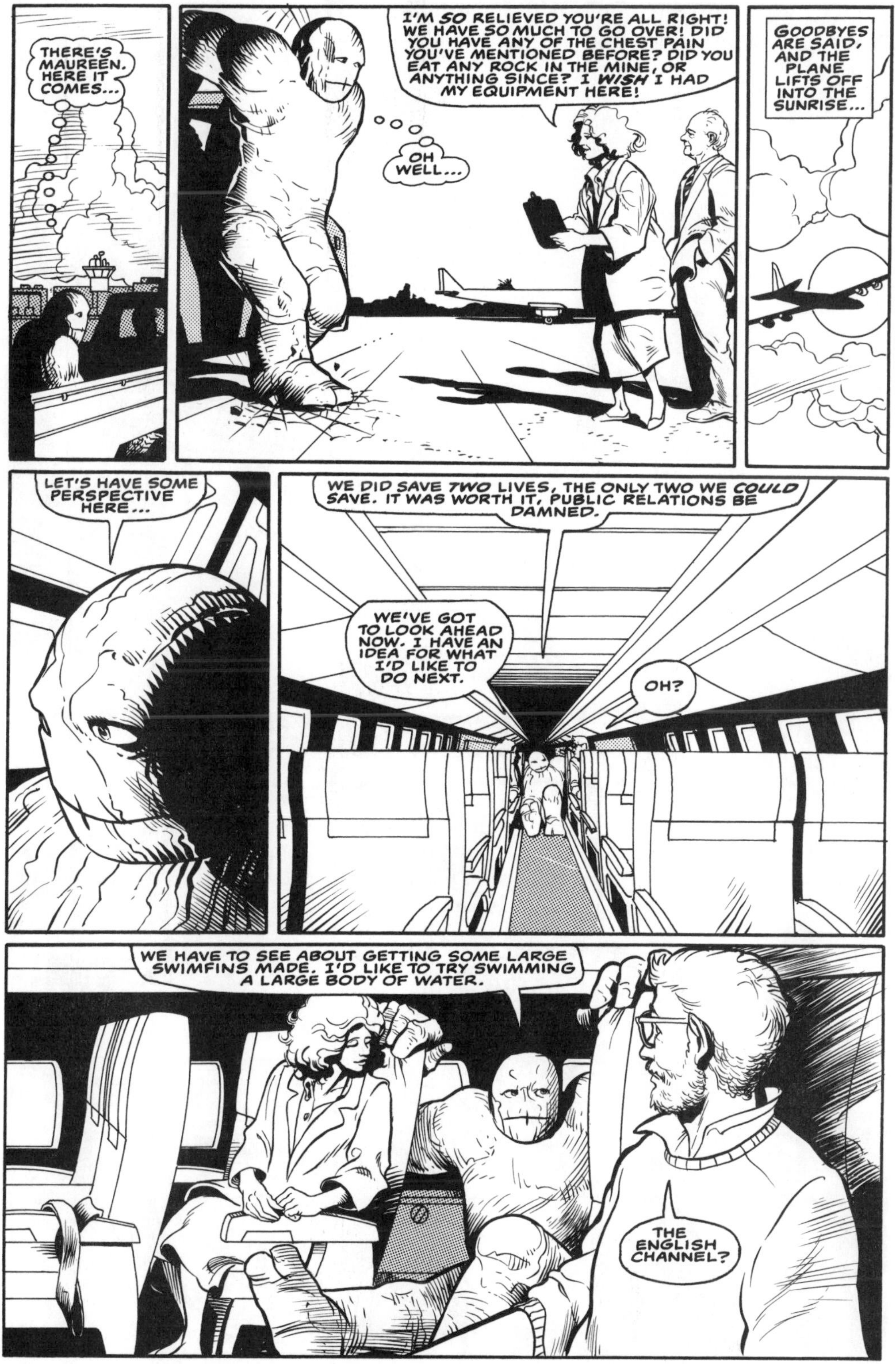
THERE'S MAUREEN. HERE IT COMES...
I'M SO RELIEVED YOU'RE ALL RIGHT! WE HAVE SO MUCH TO GO OVER! DID YOU HAVE ANY OF THE CHEST PAIN YOU'VE MENTIONED BEFORE? DID YOU EAT ANY ROCK IN THE MINE, OR ANYTHING SINCE? I WISH I HAD MY EQUIPMENT HERE!
OH WELL...
GOODBYES ARE SAID, AND THE PLANE LIFTS OFF INTO THE SUNRISE...
LET'S HAVE SOME PERSPECTIVE HERE...
WE DID SAVE TWO LIVES, THE ONLY TWO WE COULD SAVE. IT WAS WORTH IT, PUBLIC RELATIONS BE DAMNED.
WE'VE GOT TO LOOK AHEAD NOW. I HAVE AN IDEA FOR WHAT I'D LIKE TO DO NEXT.
OH?
WE HAVE TO SEE ABOUT GETTING SOME LARGE SWIMFINS MADE. I'D LIKE TO TRY SWIMMING A LARGE BODY OF WATER.
THE ENGLISH CHANNEL?

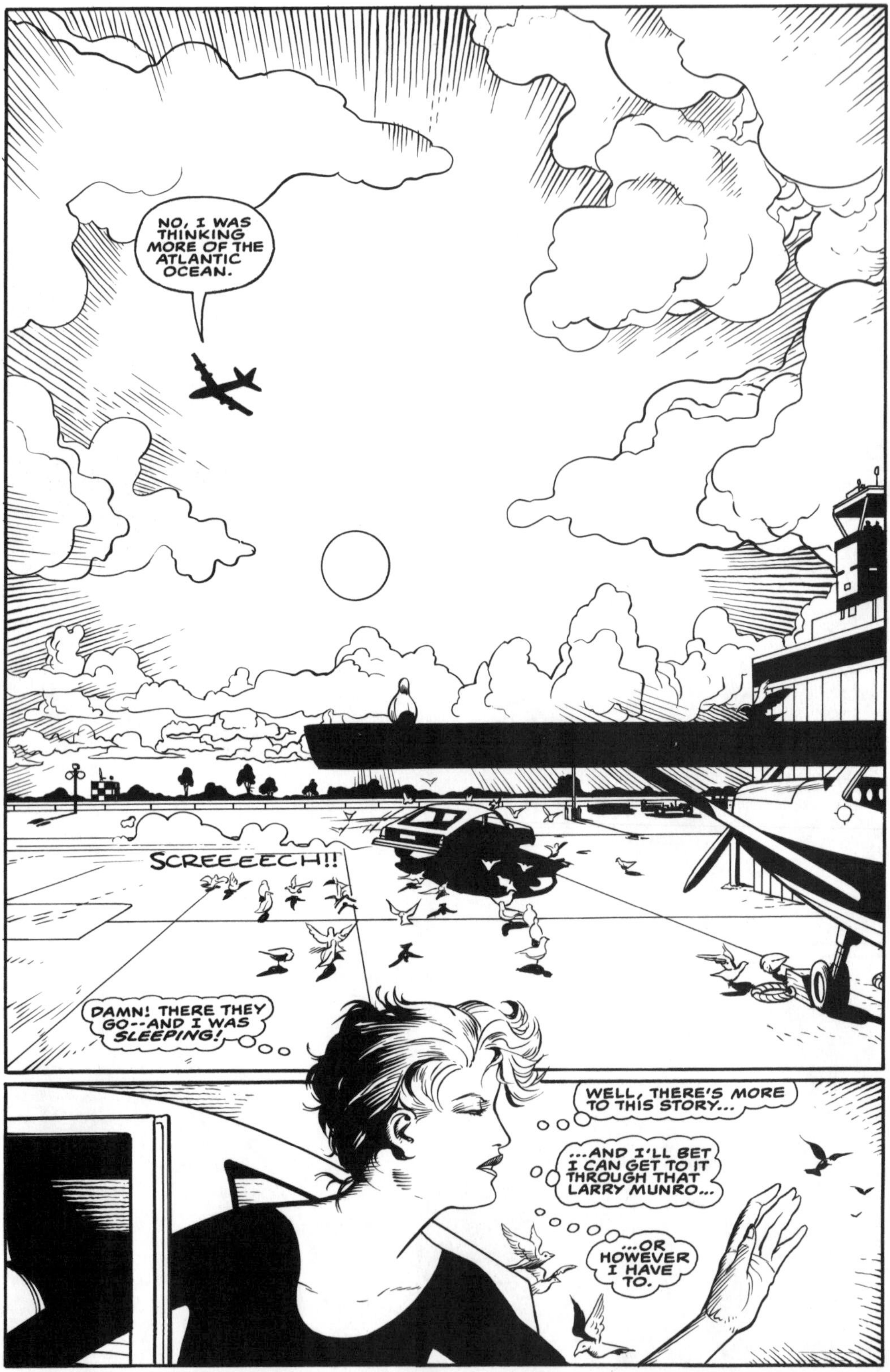
NO, I WAS THINKING MORE OF THE ATLANTIC OCEAN.
SCREEEECH!!
DAMN! THERE THEY GO--AND I WAS SLEEPING!
WELL, THERE'S MORE TO THIS STORY...
...AND I'LL BET I CAN GET TO IT THROUGH THAT LARRY MUNRO...
...OR HOWEVER I HAVE TO.

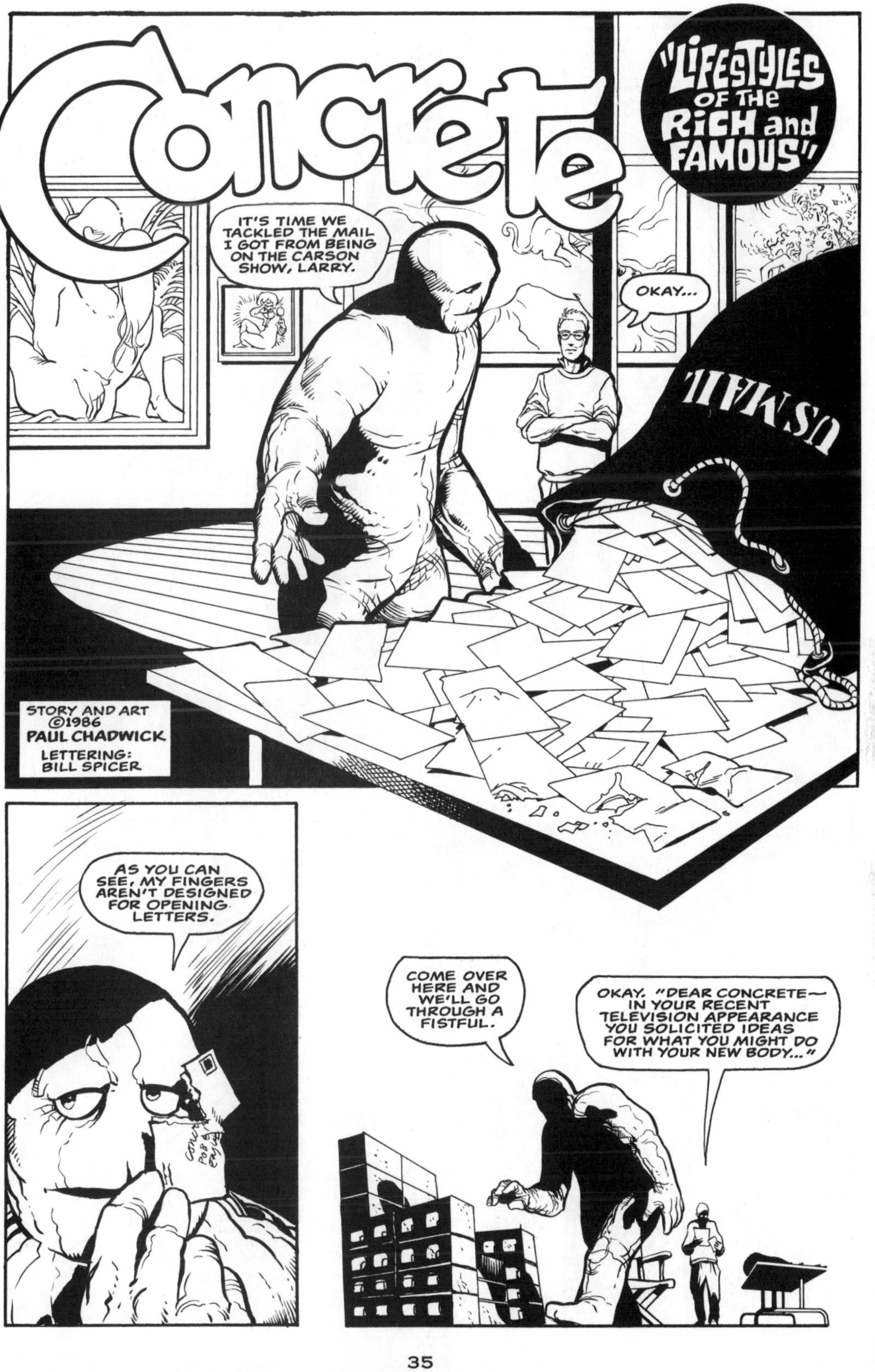
Concrete
"Lifestyles of the Rich and Famous"
IT'S TIME WE TACKLED THE MAIL I GOT FROM BEING ON THE CARSON SHOW, LARRY.
OKAY...
STORY AND ART ©1986 PAUL CHADWICK
LETTERING: BILL SPICER
AS YOU CAN SEE, MY FINGERS AREN'T DESIGNED FOR OPENING LETTERS.
COME OVER HERE AND WE'LL GO THROUGH A FISTFUL.
OKAY. "DEAR CONCRETE— IN YOUR RECENT TELEVISION APPEARANCE YOU SOLICITED IDEAS FOR WHAT YOU MIGHT DO WITH YOUR NEW BODY..."

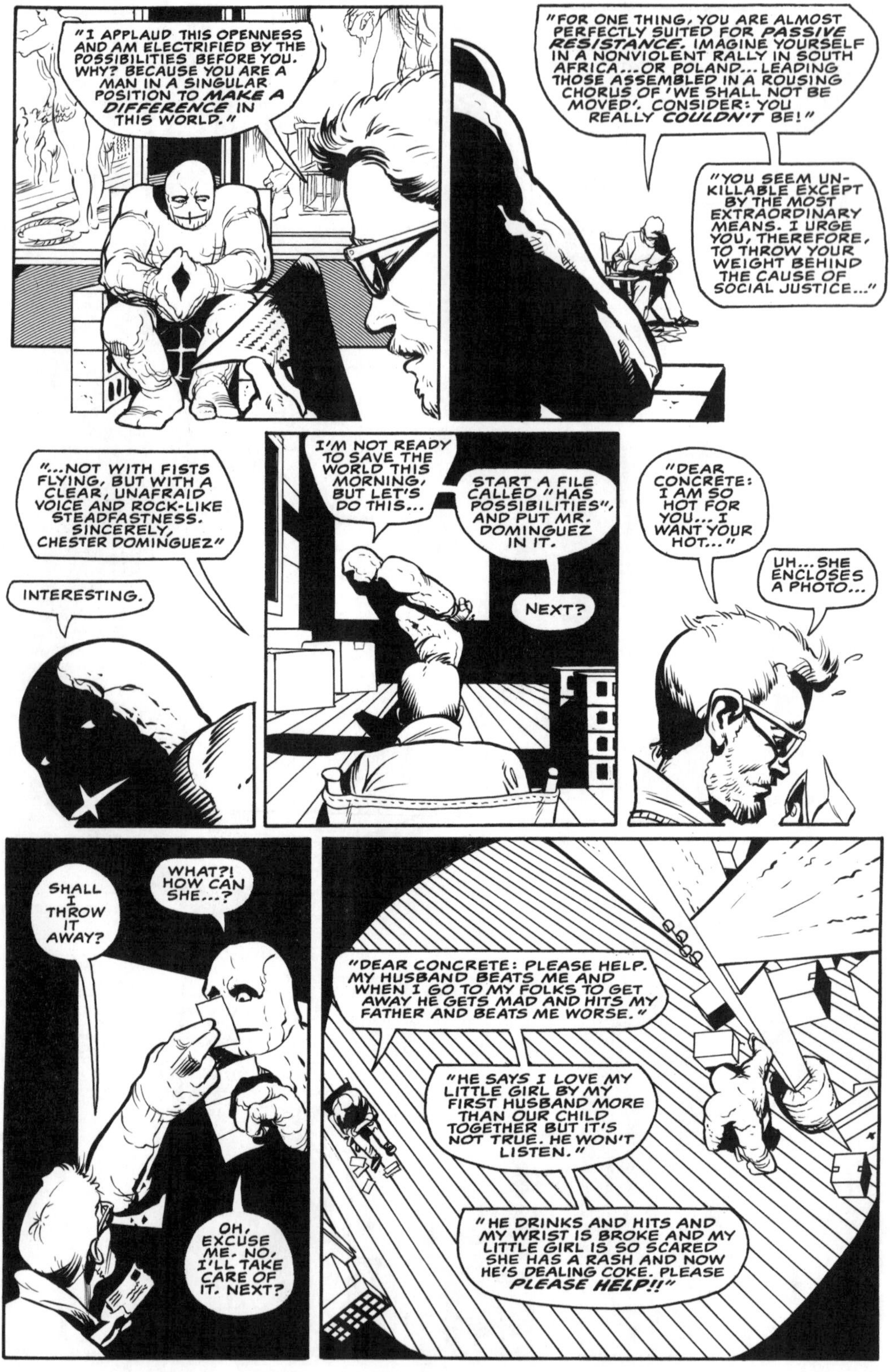
"I APPLAUD THIS OPENNESS AND AM ELECTRIFIED BY THE POSSIBILITIES BEFORE YOU. WHY? BECAUSE YOU ARE A MAN IN A SINGULAR POSITION TO MAKE A DIFFERENCE IN THIS WORLD."
"FOR ONE THING, YOU ARE ALMOST PERFECTLY SUITED FOR PASSIVE RESISTANCE. IMAGINE YOURSELF IN A NONVIOLENT RALLY IN SOUTH AFRICA...OR POLAND...LEADING THOSE ASSEMBLED IN A ROUSING CHORUS OF 'WE SHALL NOT BE MOVED'. CONSIDER: YOU REALLY COULDN'T BE!"
"YOU SEEM UN-KILLABLE EXCEPT BY THE MOST EXTRAORDINARY MEANS. I URGE YOU, THEREFORE, TO THROW YOUR WEIGHT BEHIND THE CAUSE OF SOCIAL JUSTICE..."
"...NOT WITH FISTS FLYING, BUT WITH A CLEAR, UNAFRAID VOICE AND ROCK-LIKE STEADFASTNESS. SINCERELY, CHESTER DOMINGUEZ"
INTERESTING.
I'M NOT READY TO SAVE THE WORLD THIS MORNING, BUT LET'S DO THIS...
START A FILE CALLED "HAS POSSIBILITIES", AND PUT MR. DOMINGUEZ IN IT.
NEXT?
"DEAR CONCRETE: I AM SO HOT FOR YOU... I WANT YOUR HOT..."
UH...SHE ENCLOSES A PHOTO...
WHAT?! HOW CAN SHE...?
SHALL I THROW IT AWAY?
OH, EXCUSE ME. NO, I'LL TAKE CARE OF IT. NEXT?
"DEAR CONCRETE: PLEASE HELP. MY HUSBAND BEATS ME AND WHEN I GO TO MY FOLKS TO GET AWAY HE GETS MAD AND HITS MY FATHER AND BEATS ME WORSE."
"HE SAYS I LOVE MY LITTLE GIRL BY MY FIRST HUSBAND MORE THAN OUR CHILD TOGETHER BUT IT'S NOT TRUE. HE WON'T LISTEN."
"HE DRINKS AND HITS AND MY WRIST IS BROKE AND MY LITTLE GIRL IS SO SCARED SHE HAS A RASH AND NOW HE'S DEALING COKE. PLEASE PLEASE HELP!!"

I WONDER WHAT SHE WANTS ME TO DO... KNOCK SOME SENSE INTO HIM?

FROM ALL I'VE HEARD IT'S TOUGH TO REFORM A WIFE-BEATER. ALL YOU CAN DO IS ESCAPE HIM.

IS SHE IN L.A.?

YEAH.

CAN YOU FIND OUT WHAT KIND OF WOMEN'S SHELTERS ARE IN HER AREA? THERE'S A HOTLINE NUMBER.

SURE.

I THINK THAT'S THE BEST WE CAN DO, SHORT OF SENDING GETAWAY MONEY-- AND I'M NOT READY FOR THAT. NEXT?

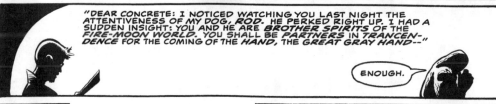

"DEAR CONCRETE: I NOTICED WATCHING YOU LAST NIGHT THE ATTENTIVENESS OF MY DOG, ROD. HE PERKED RIGHT UP. I HAD A SUDDEN INSIGHT: YOU AND HE ARE BROTHER SPIRITS OF THE FIRE-MOON WORLD. YOU SHALL BE PARTNERS IN TRANCEN-DENCE FOR THE COMING OF THE HAND, THE GREAT GRAY HAND--"

ENOUGH.

TWO FILES: BENIGN NUTS AND HOSTILE NUTS. PUT MR. FIREMOON IN NUMBER ONE.

THE PROCESS WEARS ON, CUTTING THROUGH STRATA OF HUMANITY...

...YIELDING A BOUNTY STRANGE, WRY, TRAGIC...

...AND INTRIGUING.

Dear Concrete:

...I THINK WE'RE READING THIS RIGHT. SHE'LL PAY ME A COOL FIFTEEN HUNDRED TO MINGLE WITH A BUNCH OF RICH PARTY GUESTS FOR A COUPLE OF HOURS! SOUNDS TOO GOOD TO BE TRUE!

BUT IT'S NICE STATIONERY AND A WEST L.A. ADDRESS, RIGHT BY BEVERLY HILLS.

THIS SATURDAY.

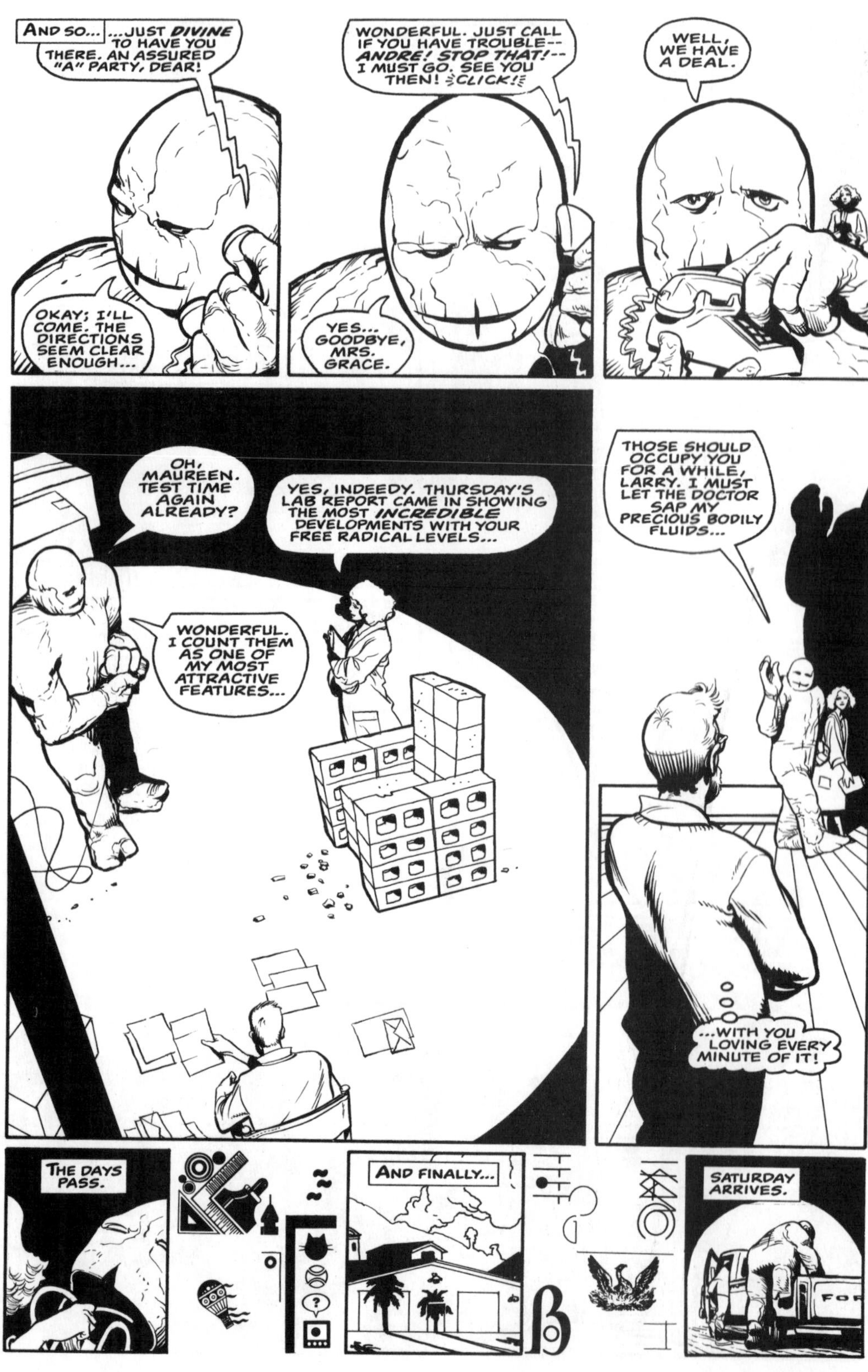

AND SO...
...JUST DIVINE TO HAVE YOU THERE. AN ASSURED "A" PARTY, DEAR!
OKAY; I'LL COME. THE DIRECTIONS SEEM CLEAR ENOUGH...
WONDERFUL. JUST CALL IF YOU HAVE TROUBLE-- ANDRE! STOP THAT!-- I MUST GO. SEE YOU THEN! CLICK!
YES... GOODBYE, MRS. GRACE.
WELL, WE HAVE A DEAL.
OH, MAUREEN. TEST TIME AGAIN ALREADY?
YES, INDEEDY. THURSDAY'S LAB REPORT CAME IN SHOWING THE MOST INCREDIBLE DEVELOPMENTS WITH YOUR FREE RADICAL LEVELS...
WONDERFUL. I COUNT THEM AS ONE OF MY MOST ATTRACTIVE FEATURES...
THOSE SHOULD OCCUPY YOU FOR A WHILE, LARRY. I MUST LET THE DOCTOR SAP MY PRECIOUS BODILY FLUIDS...
...WITH YOU LOVING EVERY MINUTE OF IT!
THE DAYS PASS.
AND FINALLY...
SATURDAY ARRIVES.
FOR

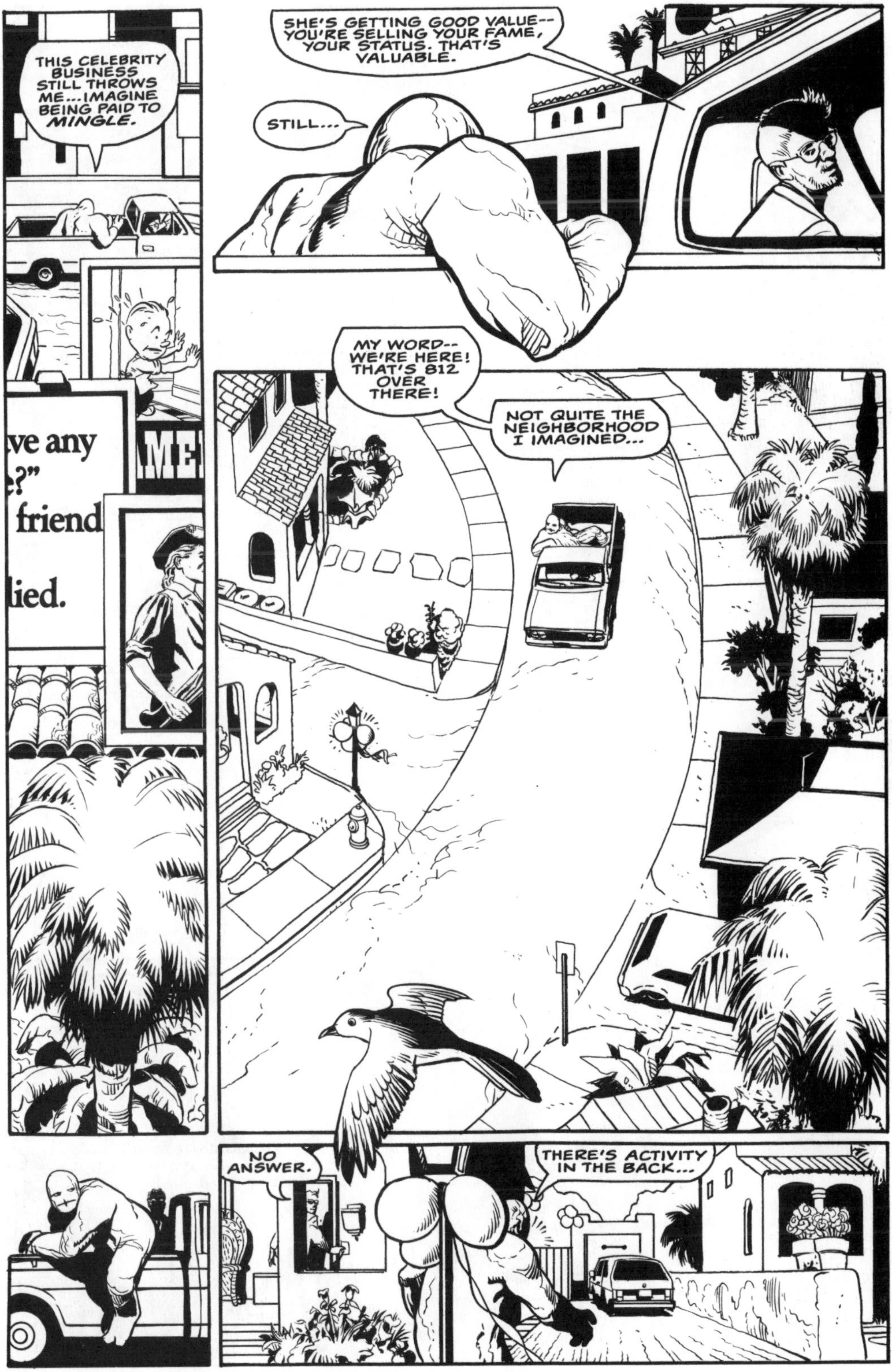
THIS CELEBRITY BUSINESS STILL THROWS ME...IMAGINE BEING PAID TO *MINGLE*.
SHE'S GETTING GOOD VALUE-- YOU'RE SELLING YOUR FAME, YOUR STATUS. THAT'S VALUABLE.
STILL...
friend
MY WORD-- WE'RE HERE! THAT'S 812 OVER THERE!
NOT QUITE THE NEIGHBORHOOD I IMAGINED...
NO ANSWER.
THERE'S ACTIVITY IN THE BACK...

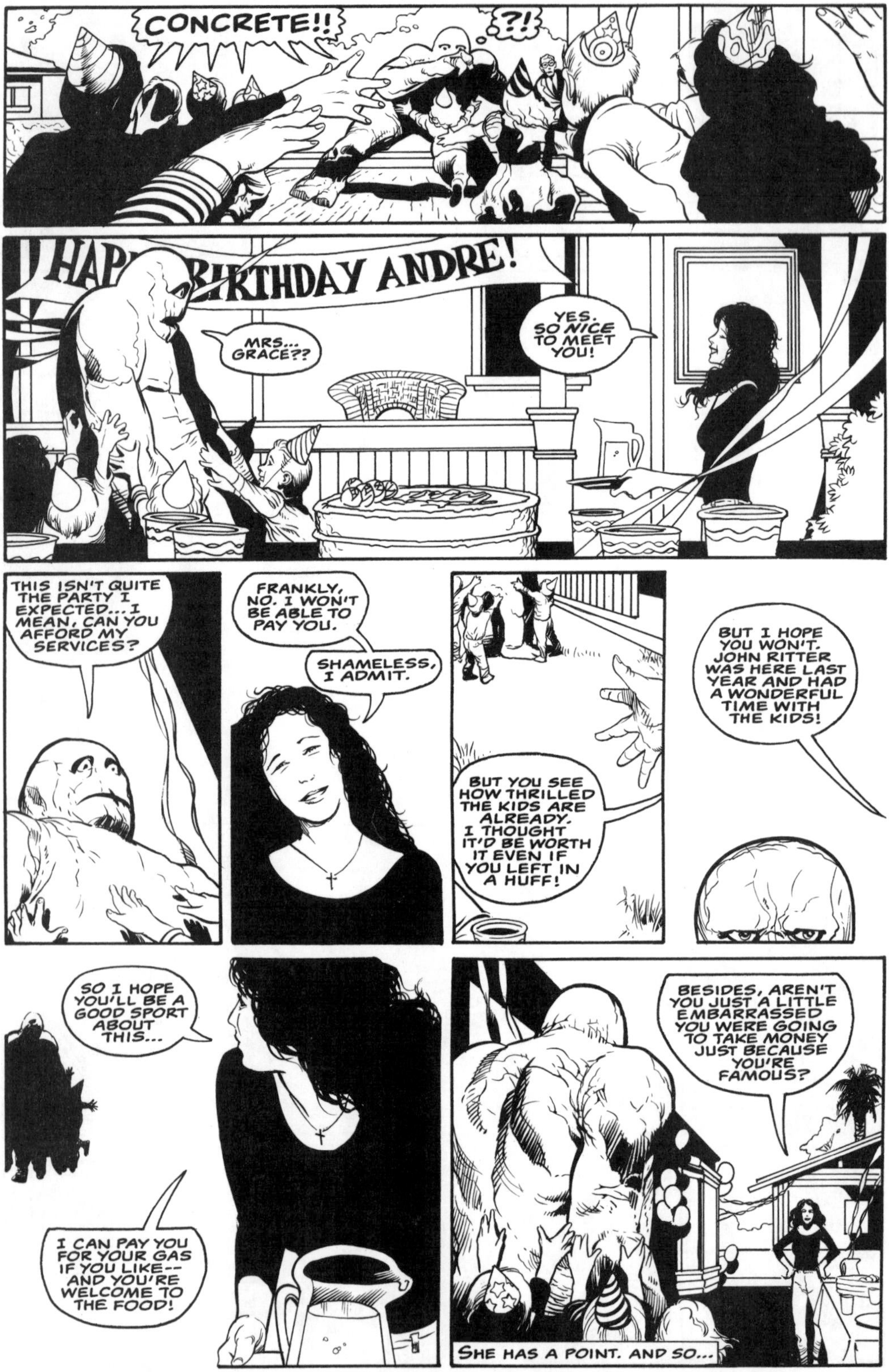
CONCRETE!!
?!
HAPPY BIRTHDAY ANDRE!
MRS... GRACE??
YES. SO NICE TO MEET YOU!
THIS ISN'T QUITE THE PARTY I EXPECTED... I MEAN, CAN YOU AFFORD MY SERVICES?
FRANKLY, NO. I WON'T BE ABLE TO PAY YOU.
SHAMELESS, I ADMIT.
BUT YOU SEE HOW THRILLED THE KIDS ARE ALREADY. I THOUGHT IT'D BE WORTH IT EVEN IF YOU LEFT IN A HUFF!
BUT I HOPE YOU WON'T. JOHN RITTER WAS HERE LAST YEAR AND HAD A WONDERFUL TIME WITH THE KIDS!
SO I HOPE YOU'LL BE A GOOD SPORT ABOUT THIS...
I CAN PAY YOU FOR YOUR GAS IF YOU LIKE-- AND YOU'RE WELCOME TO THE FOOD!
BESIDES, AREN'T YOU JUST A LITTLE EMBARRASSED YOU WERE GOING TO TAKE MONEY JUST BECAUSE YOU'RE FAMOUS?
SHE HAS A POINT. AND SO...

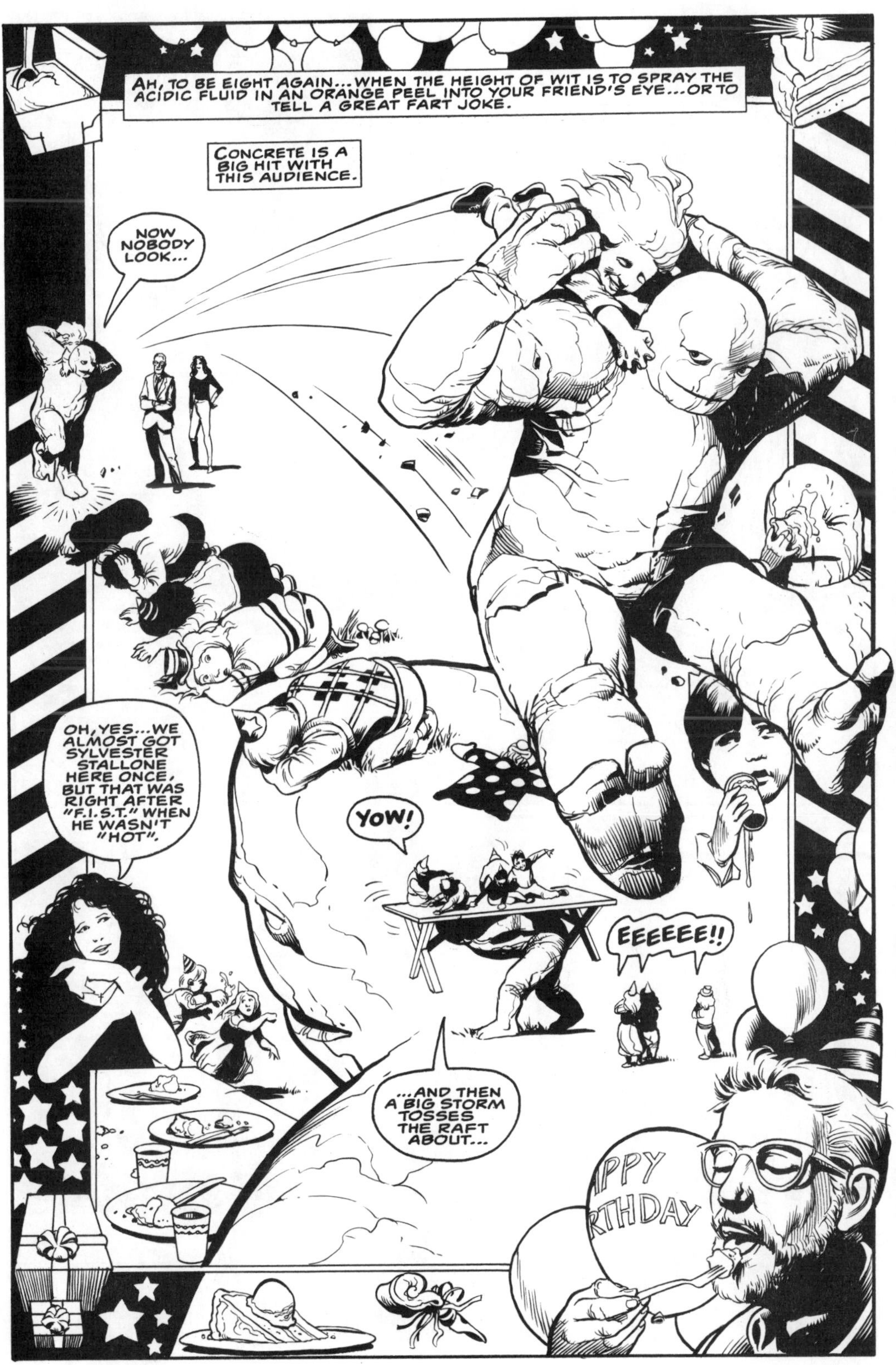
AH, TO BE EIGHT AGAIN... WHEN THE HEIGHT OF WIT IS TO SPRAY THE ACIDIC FLUID IN AN ORANGE PEEL INTO YOUR FRIEND'S EYE... OR TO TELL A GREAT FART JOKE.
CONCRETE IS A BIG HIT WITH THIS AUDIENCE.
NOW NOBODY LOOK...
OH, YES... WE ALMOST GOT SYLVESTER STALLONE HERE ONCE, BUT THAT WAS RIGHT AFTER "F.I.S.T." WHEN HE WASN'T "HOT".
YOW!
EEEEEE!!
...AND THEN A BIG STORM TOSSES THE RAFT ABOUT...
PPY RTHDAY

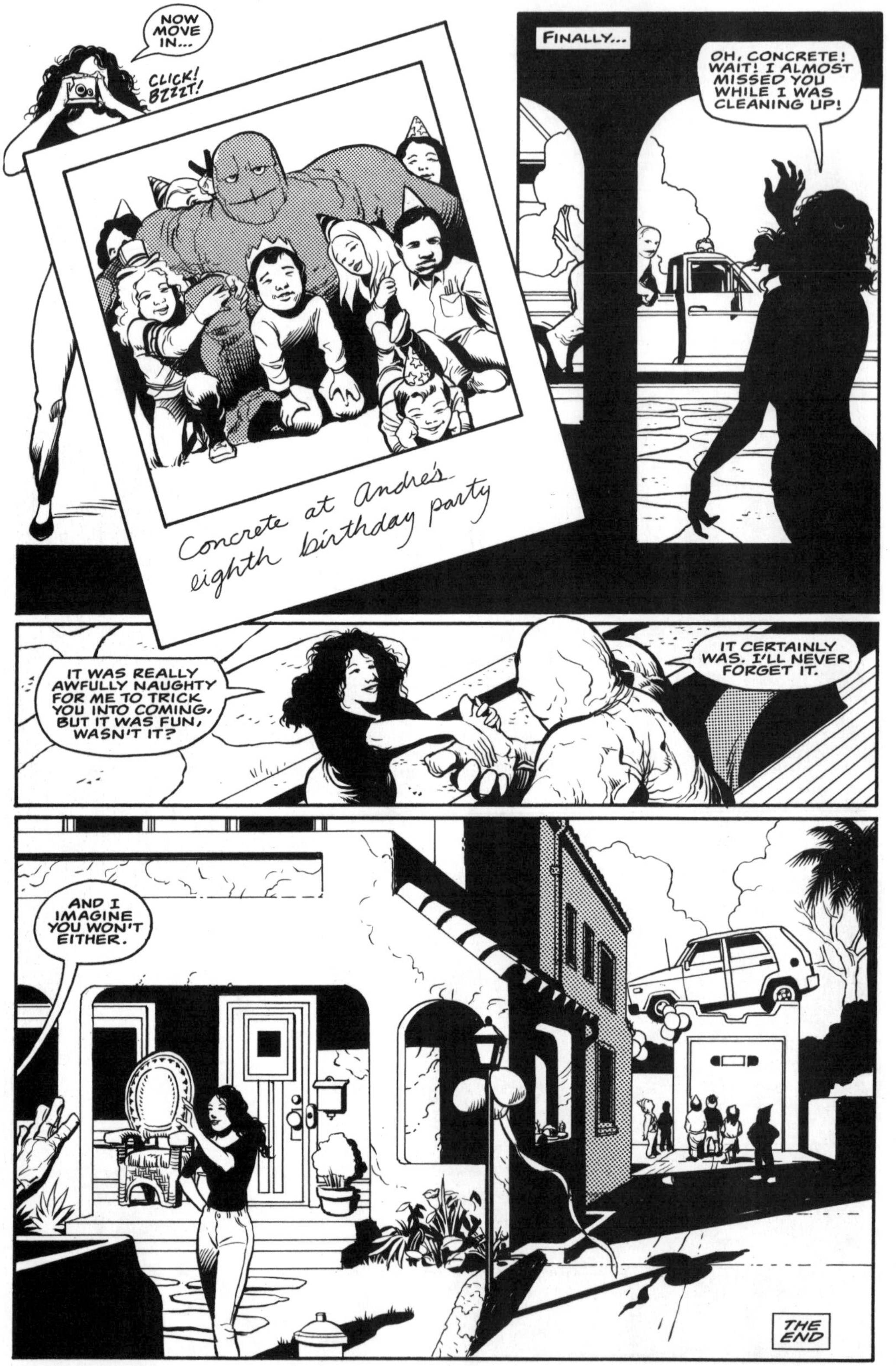
NOW MOVE IN...
CLICK! BZZZT!
Concrete at Andre's eighth birthday party
FINALLY...
OH, CONCRETE! WAIT! I ALMOST MISSED YOU WHILE I WAS CLEANING UP!
IT WAS REALLY AWFULLY NAUGHTY FOR ME TO TRICK YOU INTO COMING, BUT IT WAS FUN, WASN'T IT?
IT CERTAINLY WAS. I'LL NEVER FORGET IT.
AND I IMAGINE YOU WON'T EITHER.
THE END

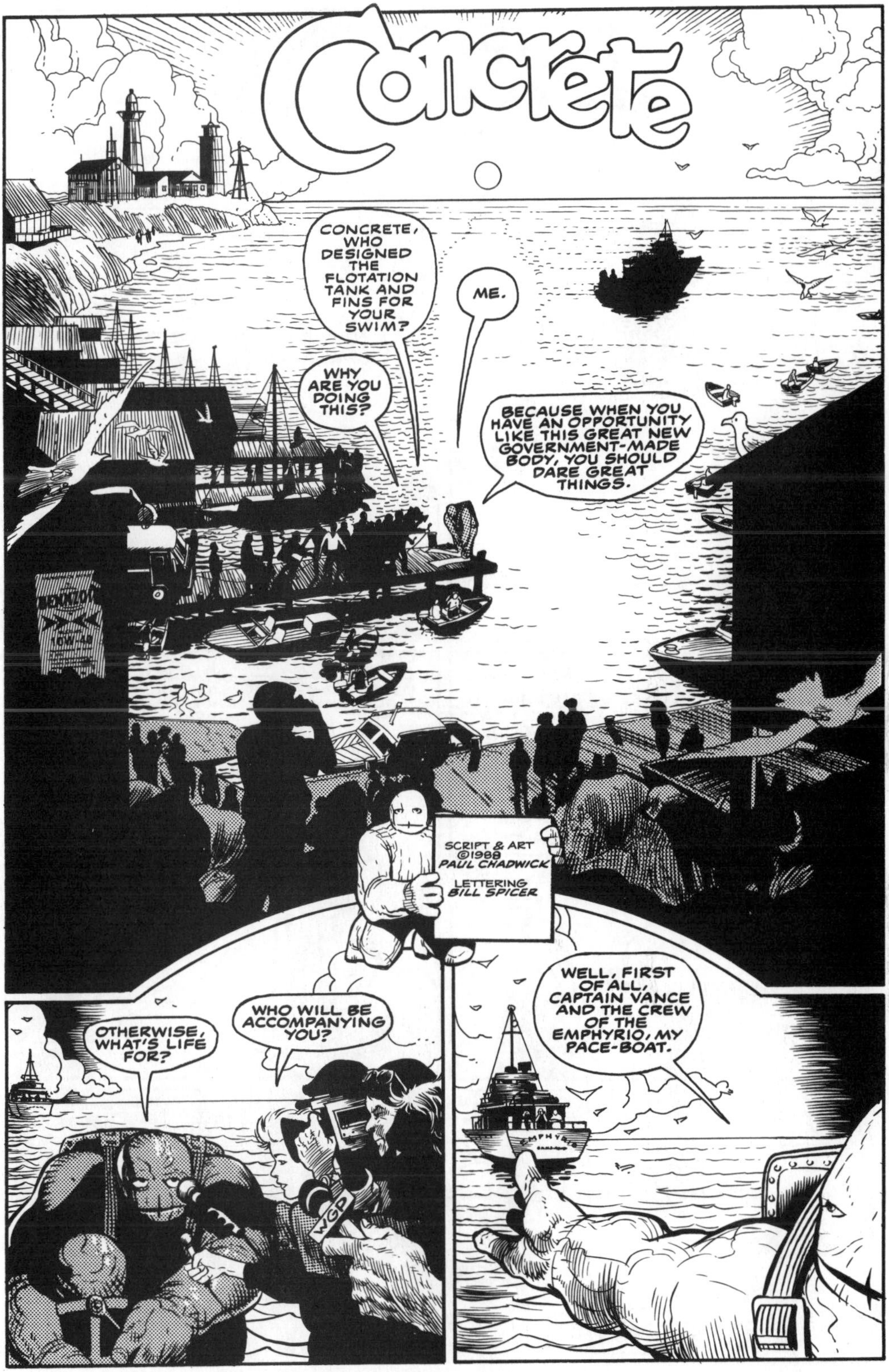
Concrete
CONCRETE, WHO DESIGNED THE FLOTATION TANK AND FINS FOR YOUR SWIM?
ME.
WHY ARE YOU DOING THIS?
BECAUSE WHEN YOU HAVE AN OPPORTUNITY LIKE THIS GREAT NEW GOVERNMENT-MADE BODY, YOU SHOULD DARE GREAT THINGS.
SCRIPT & ART ©1988 PAUL CHADWICK
LETTERING BILL SPICER
OTHERWISE, WHAT'S LIFE FOR?
WHO WILL BE ACCOMPANYING YOU?
WELL, FIRST OF ALL, CAPTAIN VANCE AND THE CREW OF THE EMPHYRIO, MY PACE-BOAT.

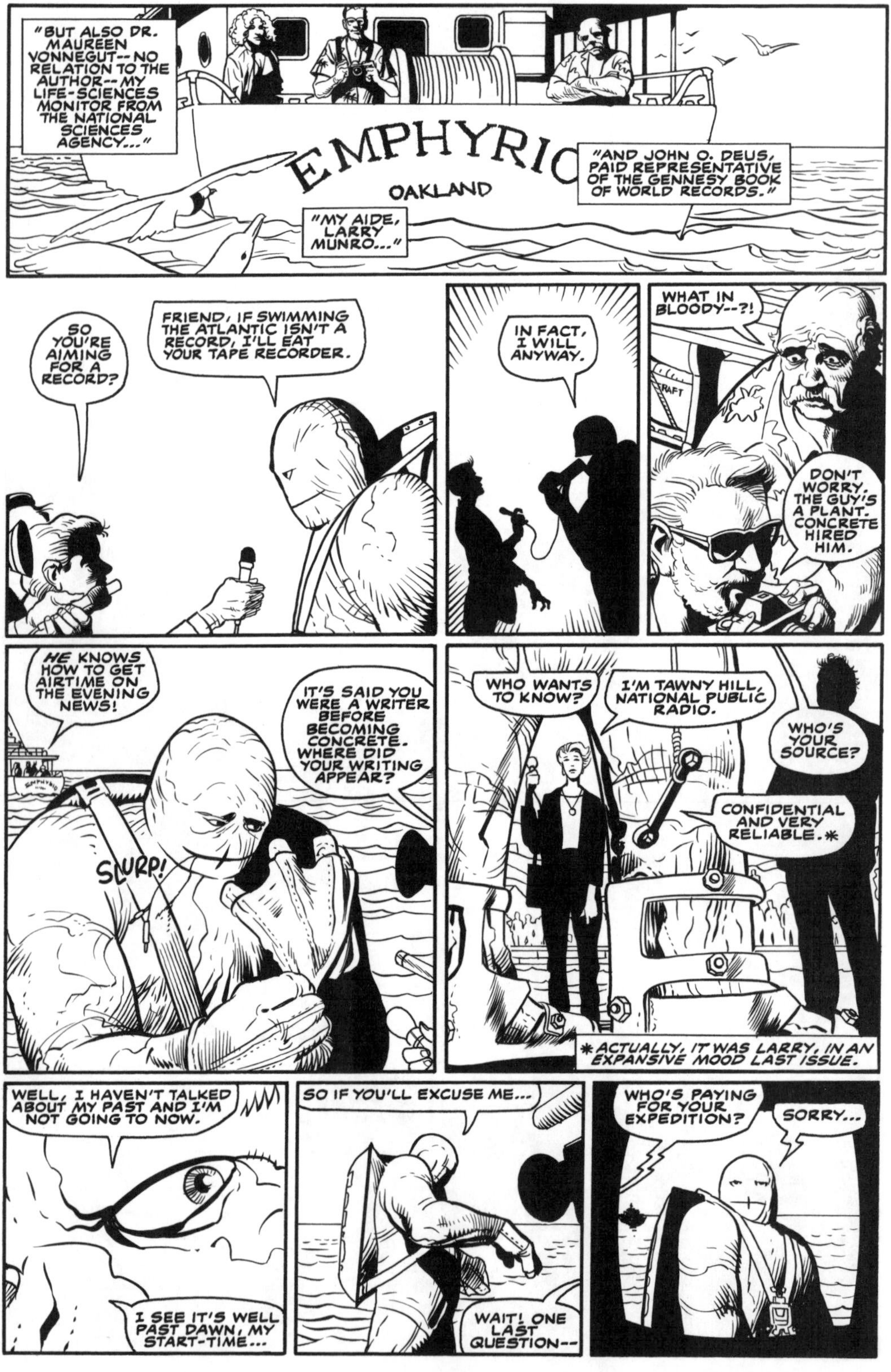
"BUT ALSO DR. MAUREEN VONNEGUT--NO RELATION TO THE AUTHOR--MY LIFE-SCIENCES MONITOR FROM THE NATIONAL SCIENCES AGENCY..."
EMPHYRIO
OAKLAND
"MY AIDE, LARRY MUNRO..."
"AND JOHN O. DEUS, PAID REPRESENTATIVE OF THE GENNESY BOOK OF WORLD RECORDS."
SO YOU'RE AIMING FOR A RECORD?
FRIEND, IF SWIMMING THE ATLANTIC ISN'T A RECORD, I'LL EAT YOUR TAPE RECORDER.
IN FACT, I WILL ANYWAY.
WHAT IN BLOODY--?!
DON'T WORRY. THE GUY'S A PLANT. CONCRETE HIRED HIM.
HE KNOWS HOW TO GET AIRTIME ON THE EVENING NEWS!
IT'S SAID YOU WERE A WRITER BEFORE BECOMING CONCRETE. WHERE DID YOUR WRITING APPEAR?
SLURP!
WHO WANTS TO KNOW?
I'M TAWNY HILL, NATIONAL PUBLIC RADIO.
WHO'S YOUR SOURCE?
CONFIDENTIAL AND VERY RELIABLE.*
*ACTUALLY, IT WAS LARRY, IN AN EXPANSIVE MOOD LAST ISSUE.
WELL, I HAVEN'T TALKED ABOUT MY PAST AND I'M NOT GOING TO NOW.
I SEE IT'S WELL PAST DAWN, MY START-TIME...
SO IF YOU'LL EXCUSE ME...
WAIT! ONE LAST QUESTION--
WHO'S PAYING FOR YOUR EXPEDITION?
SORRY...

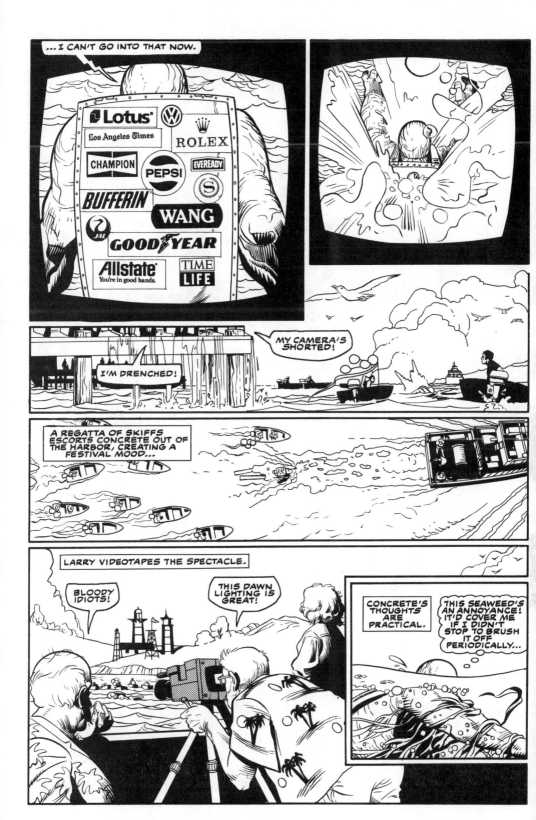

...I CAN'T GO INTO THAT NOW.

Lotus
VW
ROLEX
Los Angeles Times
CHAMPION
PEPSI
EVEREADY
S
BUFFERIN
WANG
JAL
GOODYEAR
Allstate
You're in good hands.
TIME
LIFE

MY CAMERA'S SHORTED!

I'M DRENCHED!

A REGATTA OF SKIFFS ESCORTS CONCRETE OUT OF THE HARBOR, CREATING A FESTIVAL MOOD...

LARRY VIDEOTAPES THE SPECTACLE.

BLOODY IDIOTS!

THIS DAWN LIGHTING IS GREAT!

CONCRETE'S THOUGHTS ARE PRACTICAL.

THIS SEAWEED'S AN ANNOYANCE! IT'D COVER ME IF I DIDN'T STOP TO BRUSH IT OFF PERIODICALLY...

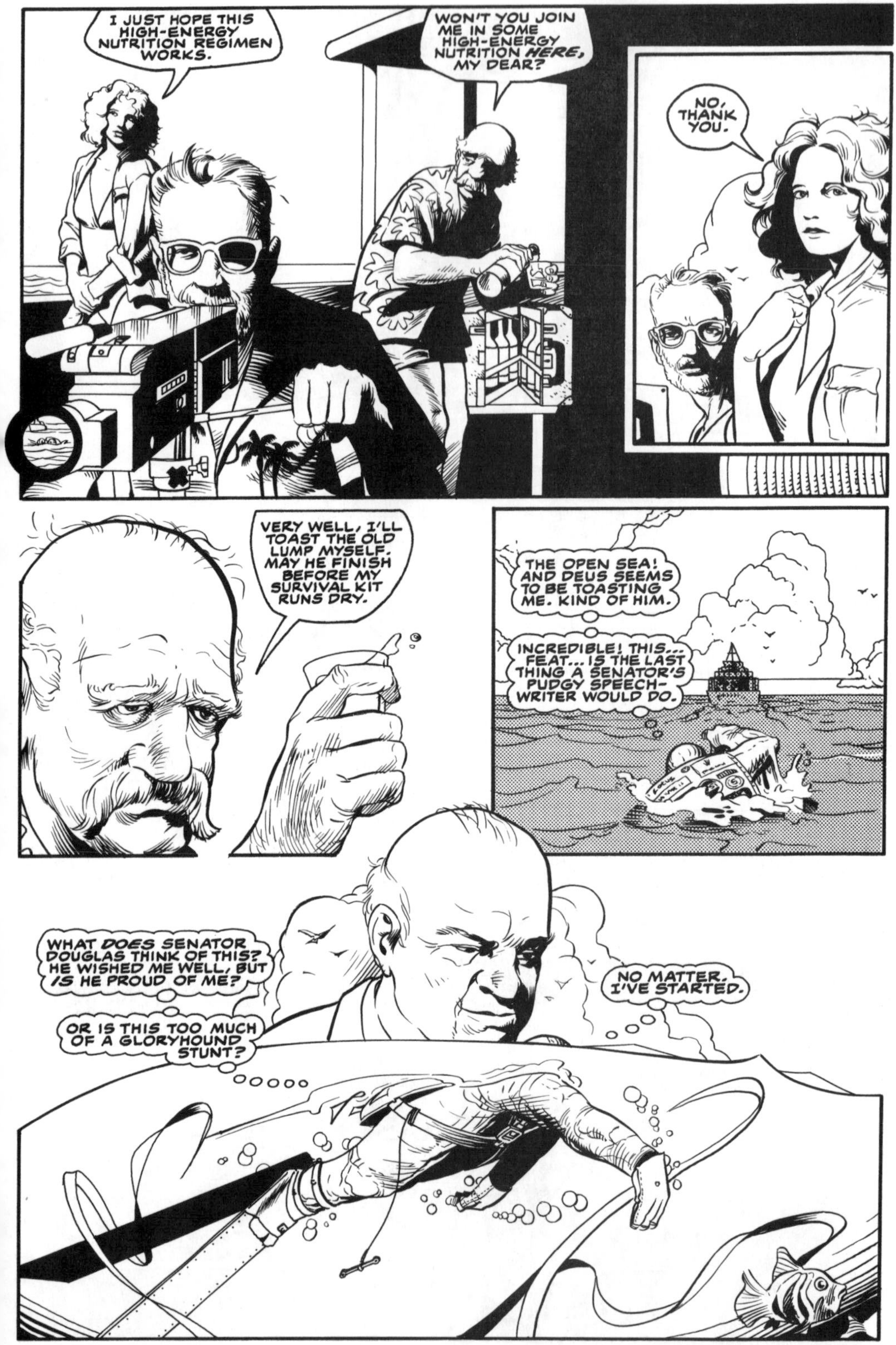
I JUST HOPE THIS HIGH-ENERGY NUTRITION REGIMEN WORKS.
WON'T YOU JOIN ME IN SOME HIGH-ENERGY NUTRITION *HERE,* MY DEAR?
NO, THANK YOU.
VERY WELL, I'LL TOAST THE OLD LUMP MYSELF. MAY HE FINISH BEFORE MY SURVIVAL KIT RUNS DRY.
THE OPEN SEA! AND DEUS SEEMS TO BE TOASTING ME. KIND OF HIM.
INCREDIBLE! THIS... FEAT... IS THE LAST THING A SENATOR'S PUDGY SPEECH-WRITER WOULD DO.
WHAT *DOES* SENATOR DOUGLAS THINK OF THIS? HE WISHED ME WELL, BUT *IS* HE PROUD OF ME?
OR IS THIS TOO MUCH OF A GLORYHOUND STUNT?
NO MATTER. I'VE STARTED.

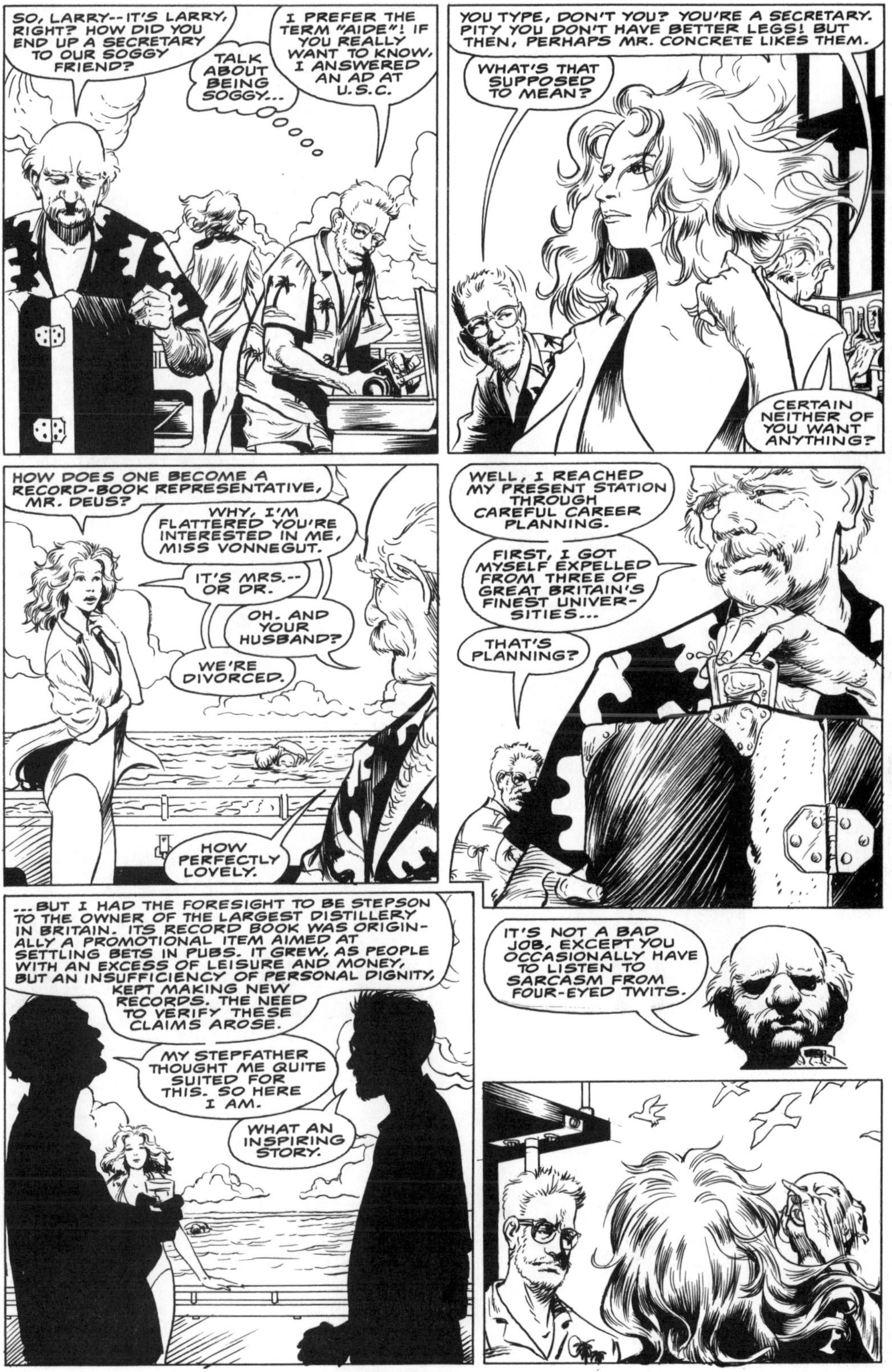
SO, LARRY--IT'S LARRY, RIGHT? HOW DID YOU END UP A SECRETARY TO OUR SOGGY FRIEND?
TALK ABOUT BEING SOGGY...
I PREFER THE TERM "AIDE"! IF YOU REALLY WANT TO KNOW, I ANSWERED AN AD AT U.S.C.
YOU TYPE, DON'T YOU? YOU'RE A SECRETARY. PITY YOU DON'T HAVE BETTER LEGS! BUT THEN, PERHAPS MR. CONCRETE LIKES THEM.
WHAT'S THAT SUPPOSED TO MEAN?
CERTAIN NEITHER OF YOU WANT ANYTHING?
HOW DOES ONE BECOME A RECORD-BOOK REPRESENTATIVE, MR. DEUS?
WHY, I'M FLATTERED YOU'RE INTERESTED IN ME, MISS VONNEGUT.
IT'S MRS.-- OR DR.
OH. AND YOUR HUSBAND?
WE'RE DIVORCED.
HOW PERFECTLY LOVELY.
WELL, I REACHED MY PRESENT STATION THROUGH CAREFUL CAREER PLANNING.
FIRST, I GOT MYSELF EXPELLED FROM THREE OF GREAT BRITAIN'S FINEST UNIVERSITIES...
THAT'S PLANNING?
...BUT I HAD THE FORESIGHT TO BE STEPSON TO THE OWNER OF THE LARGEST DISTILLERY IN BRITAIN. ITS RECORD BOOK WAS ORIGINALLY A PROMOTIONAL ITEM AIMED AT SETTLING BETS IN PUBS. IT GREW, AS PEOPLE WITH AN EXCESS OF LEISURE AND MONEY, BUT AN INSUFFICIENCY OF PERSONAL DIGNITY, KEPT MAKING NEW RECORDS. THE NEED TO VERIFY THESE CLAIMS AROSE.
MY STEPFATHER THOUGHT ME QUITE SUITED FOR THIS. SO HERE I AM.
WHAT AN INSPIRING STORY.
IT'S NOT A BAD JOB, EXCEPT YOU OCCASIONALLY HAVE TO LISTEN TO SARCASM FROM FOUR-EYED TWITS.

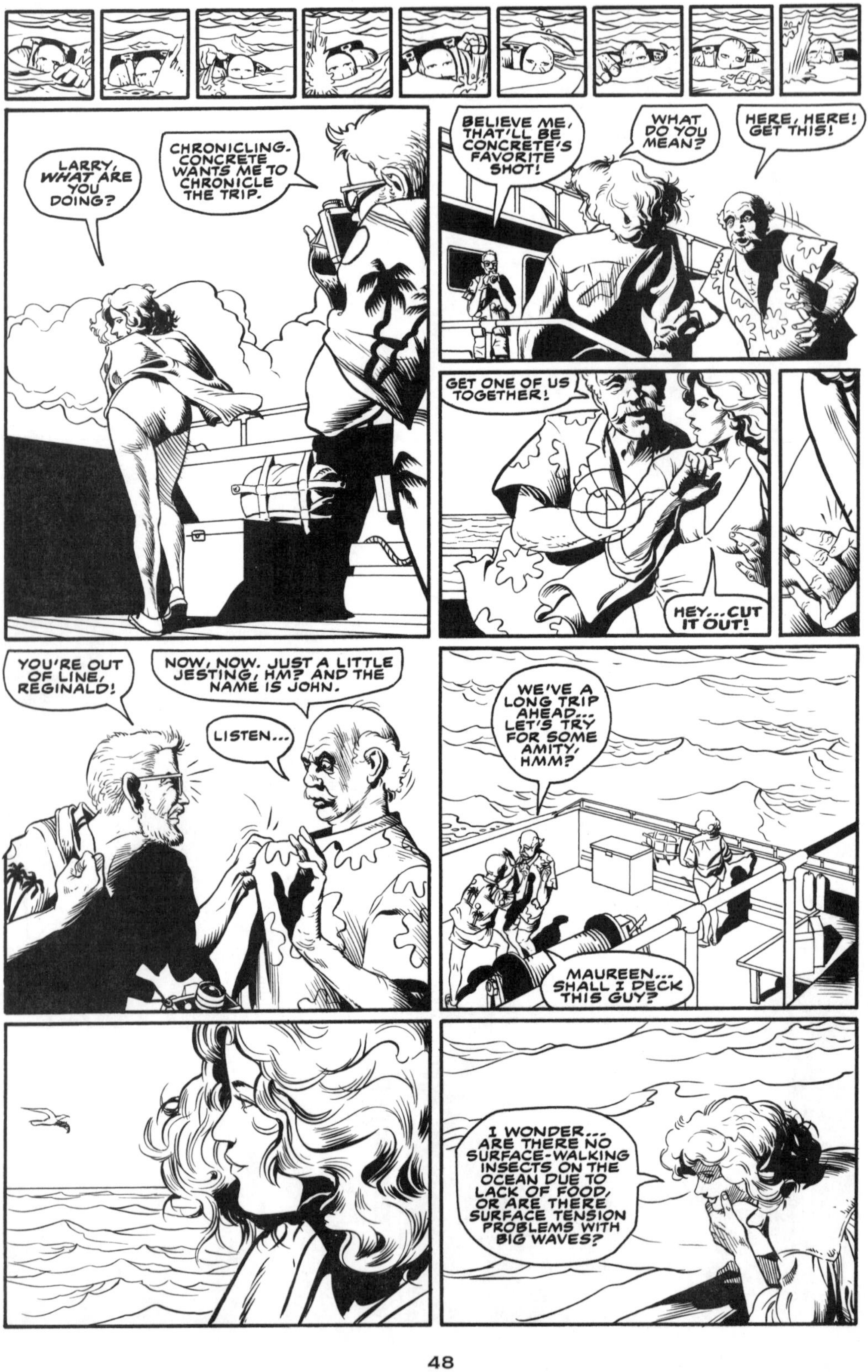
LARRY, *WHAT* ARE YOU DOING?
CHRONICLING. CONCRETE WANTS ME TO CHRONICLE THE TRIP.
BELIEVE ME, THAT'LL BE CONCRETE'S FAVORITE SHOT!
WHAT DO YOU MEAN?
HERE, HERE! GET THIS!
GET ONE OF US TOGETHER!
HEY...CUT IT OUT!
YOU'RE OUT OF LINE, REGINALD!
NOW, NOW. JUST A LITTLE JESTING, HM? AND THE NAME IS JOHN.
LISTEN...
WE'VE A LONG TRIP AHEAD... LET'S TRY FOR SOME AMITY, HMM?
MAUREEN... SHALL I DECK THIS GUY?
I WONDER... ARE THERE NO SURFACE-WALKING INSECTS ON THE OCEAN DUE TO LACK OF FOOD, OR ARE THERE SURFACE TENSION PROBLEMS WITH BIG WAVES?

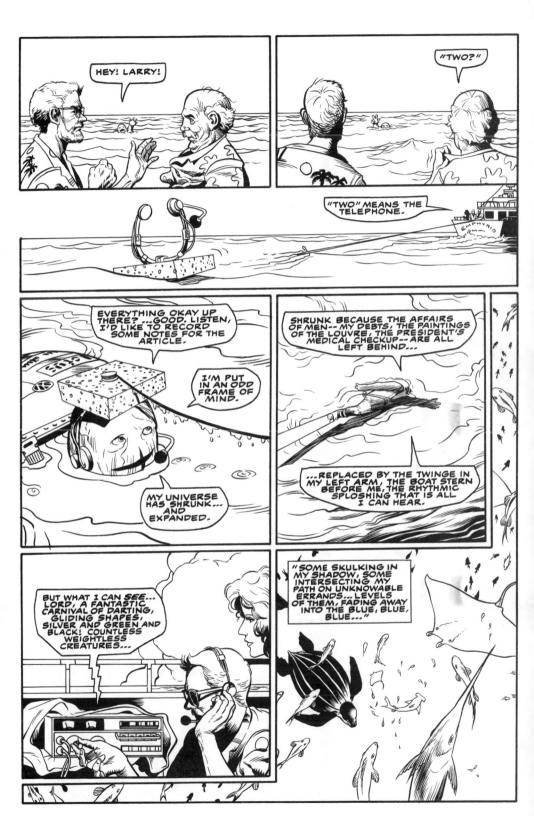

HEY! LARRY!

"TWO?"

"TWO" MEANS THE TELEPHONE.

EMPHYRIO

EVERYTHING OKAY UP THERE? ...GOOD. LISTEN, I'D LIKE TO RECORD SOME NOTES FOR THE ARTICLE.

I'M PUT IN AN ODD FRAME OF MIND.

MY UNIVERSE HAS SHRUNK... AND EXPANDED.

SHRUNK BECAUSE THE AFFAIRS OF MEN-- MY DEBTS, THE PAINTINGS OF THE LOUVRE, THE PRESIDENT'S MEDICAL CHECKUP-- ARE ALL LEFT BEHIND...

...REPLACED BY THE TWINGE IN MY LEFT ARM, THE BOAT STERN BEFORE ME, THE RHYTHMIC SPLOSHING THAT IS ALL I CAN HEAR.

BUT WHAT I CAN SEE... LORD, A FANTASTIC CARNIVAL OF DARTING, GLIDING SHAPES, SILVER AND GREEN AND BLACK! COUNTLESS WEIGHTLESS CREATURES...

"SOME SKULKING IN MY SHADOW, SOME INTERSECTING MY PATH ON UNKNOWABLE ERRANDS... LEVELS OF THEM, FADING AWAY INTO THE BLUE, BLUE, BLUE..."

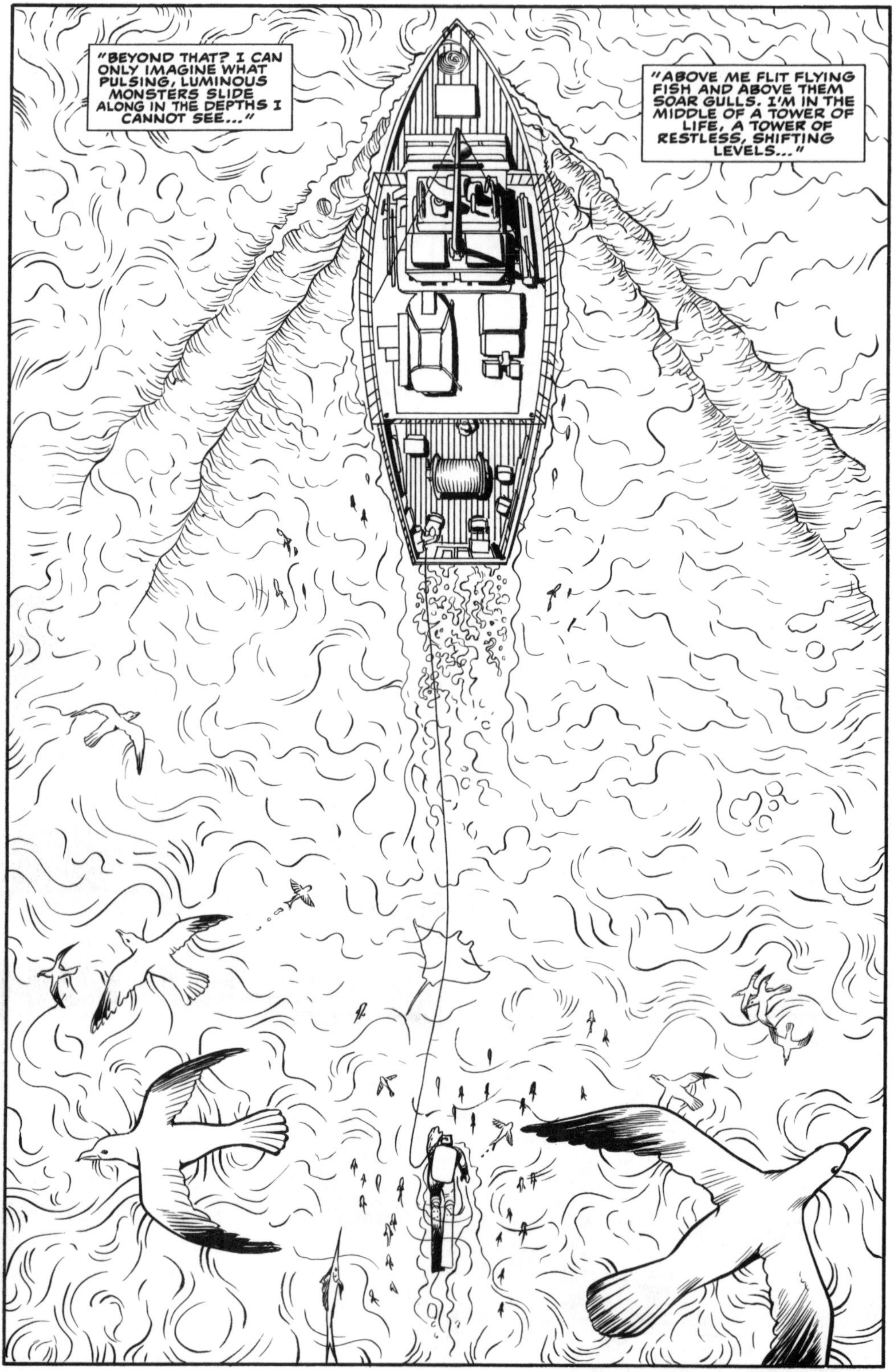
"BEYOND THAT? I CAN ONLY IMAGINE WHAT PULSING, LUMINOUS MONSTERS SLIDE ALONG IN THE DEPTHS I CANNOT SEE..."
"ABOVE ME FLIT FLYING FISH AND ABOVE THEM SOAR GULLS. I'M IN THE MIDDLE OF A TOWER OF LIFE, A TOWER OF RESTLESS, SHIFTING LEVELS..."

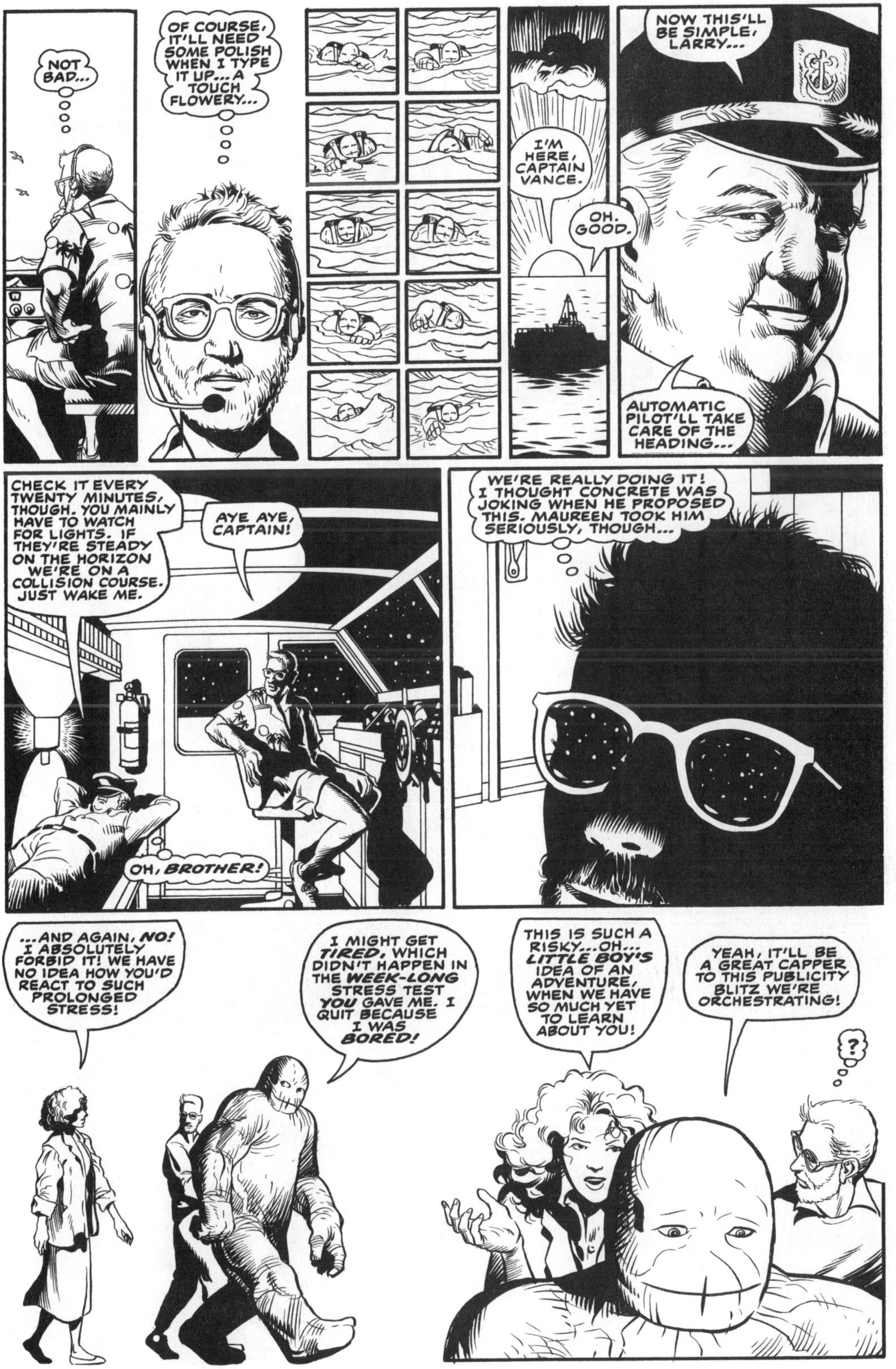
NOT BAD...
OF COURSE, IT'LL NEED SOME POLISH WHEN I TYPE IT UP... A TOUCH FLOWERY...
I'M HERE, CAPTAIN VANCE.
OH. GOOD.
NOW THIS'LL BE SIMPLE, LARRY...
AUTOMATIC PILOT'LL TAKE CARE OF THE HEADING...
CHECK IT EVERY TWENTY MINUTES, THOUGH. YOU MAINLY HAVE TO WATCH FOR LIGHTS. IF THEY'RE STEADY ON THE HORIZON WE'RE ON A COLLISION COURSE. JUST WAKE ME.
AYE AYE, CAPTAIN!
OH, BROTHER!
WE'RE REALLY DOING IT! I THOUGHT CONCRETE WAS JOKING WHEN HE PROPOSED THIS. MAUREEN TOOK HIM SERIOUSLY, THOUGH...
...AND AGAIN, NO! I ABSOLUTELY FORBID IT! WE HAVE NO IDEA HOW YOU'D REACT TO SUCH PROLONGED STRESS!
I MIGHT GET TIRED, WHICH DIDN'T HAPPEN IN THE WEEK-LONG STRESS TEST YOU GAVE ME. I QUIT BECAUSE I WAS BORED!
THIS IS SUCH A RISKY...OH... LITTLE BOY'S IDEA OF AN ADVENTURE, WHEN WE HAVE SO MUCH YET TO LEARN ABOUT YOU!
YEAH, IT'LL BE A GREAT CAPPER TO THIS PUBLICITY BLITZ WE'RE ORCHESTRATING!
?

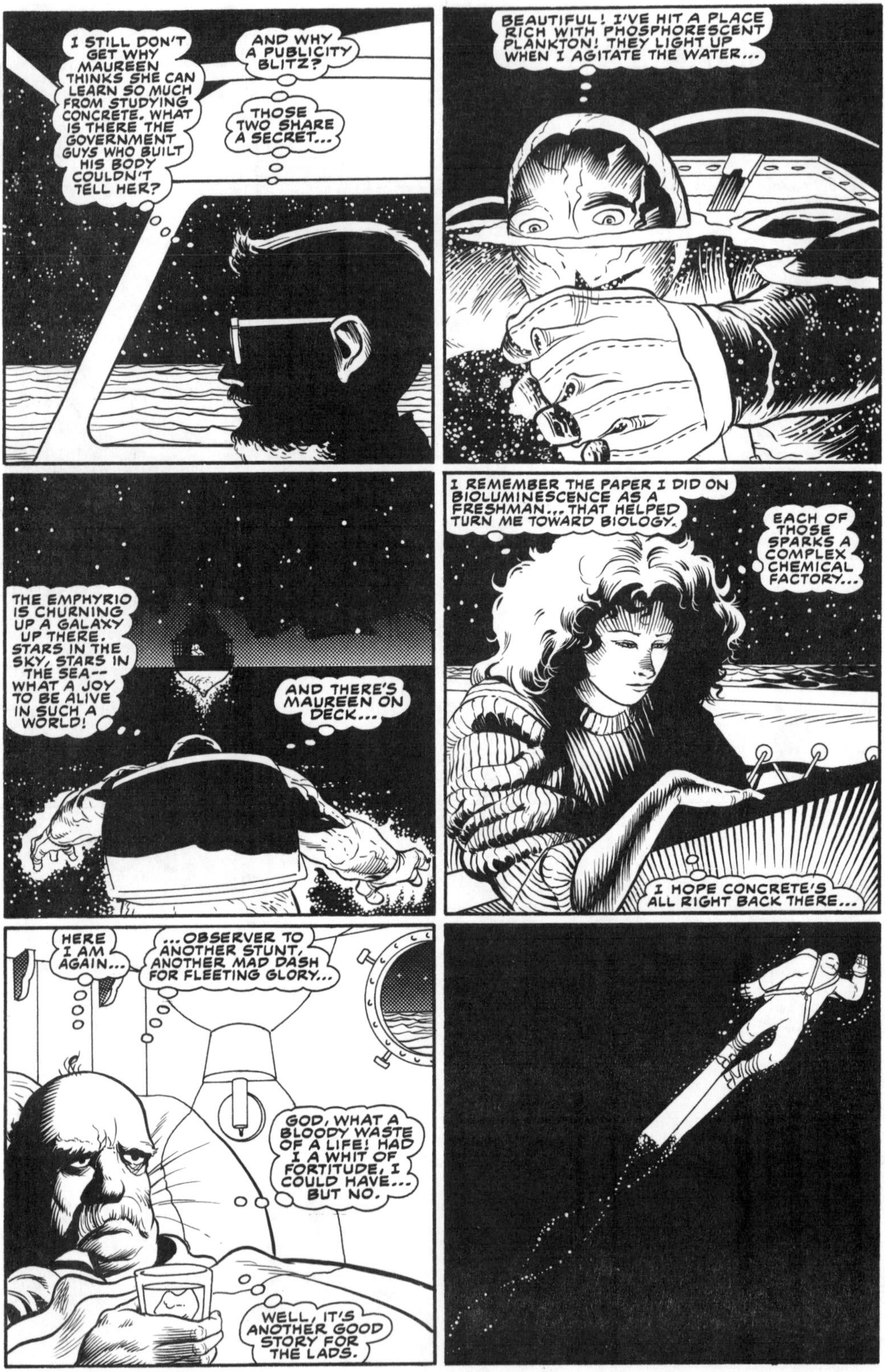
I STILL DON'T GET WHY MAUREEN THINKS SHE CAN LEARN SO MUCH FROM STUDYING CONCRETE. WHAT IS THERE THE GOVERNMENT GUYS WHO BUILT HIS BODY COULDN'T TELL HER?
AND WHY A PUBLICITY BLITZ?
THOSE TWO SHARE A SECRET...
BEAUTIFUL! I'VE HIT A PLACE RICH WITH PHOSPHORESCENT PLANKTON! THEY LIGHT UP WHEN I AGITATE THE WATER...
THE EMPHYRIO IS CHURNING UP A GALAXY UP THERE. STARS IN THE SKY, STARS IN THE SEA-- WHAT A JOY TO BE ALIVE IN SUCH A WORLD!
AND THERE'S MAUREEN ON DECK...
I REMEMBER THE PAPER I DID ON BIOLUMINESCENCE AS A FRESHMAN... THAT HELPED TURN ME TOWARD BIOLOGY.
EACH OF THOSE SPARKS A COMPLEX CHEMICAL FACTORY...
I HOPE CONCRETE'S ALL RIGHT BACK THERE...
HERE I AM AGAIN...
...OBSERVER TO ANOTHER STUNT, ANOTHER MAD DASH FOR FLEETING GLORY...
GOD, WHAT A BLOODY WASTE OF A LIFE! HAD I A WHIT OF FORTITUDE, I COULD HAVE... BUT NO.
WELL, IT'S ANOTHER GOOD STORY FOR THE LADS.

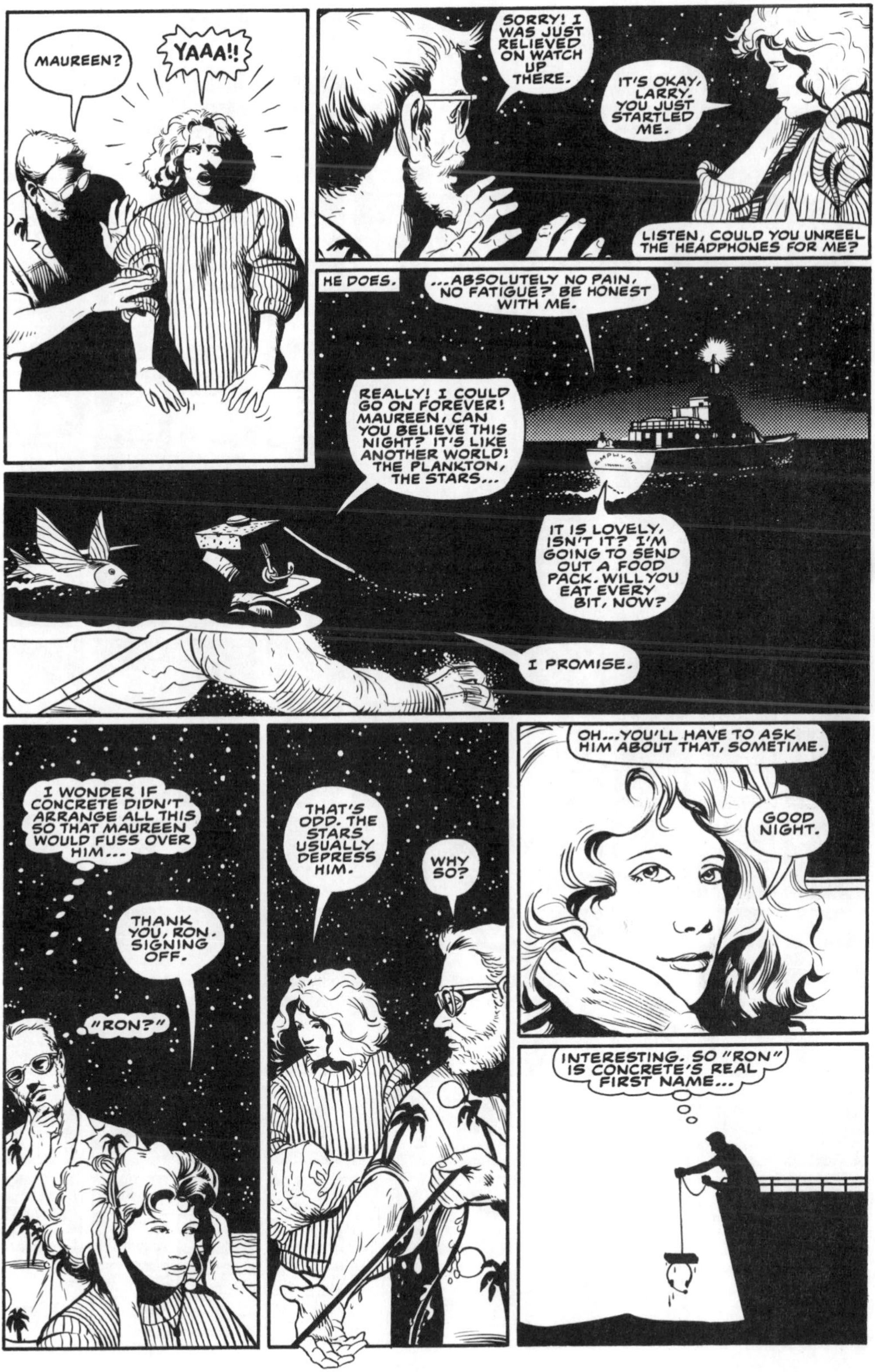
MAUREEN?
YAAA!!
SORRY! I WAS JUST RELIEVED ON WATCH UP THERE.
IT'S OKAY, LARRY. YOU JUST STARTLED ME.
LISTEN, COULD YOU UNREEL THE HEADPHONES FOR ME?
HE DOES.
...ABSOLUTELY NO PAIN, NO FATIGUE? BE HONEST WITH ME.
REALLY! I COULD GO ON FOREVER! MAUREEN, CAN YOU BELIEVE THIS NIGHT? IT'S LIKE ANOTHER WORLD! THE PLANKTON, THE STARS...
IT IS LOVELY, ISN'T IT? I'M GOING TO SEND OUT A FOOD PACK. WILL YOU EAT EVERY BIT, NOW?
I PROMISE.
I WONDER IF CONCRETE DIDN'T ARRANGE ALL THIS SO THAT MAUREEN WOULD FUSS OVER HIM...
THANK YOU, RON. SIGNING OFF.
"RON?"
THAT'S ODD. THE STARS USUALLY DEPRESS HIM.
WHY SO?
OH...YOU'LL HAVE TO ASK HIM ABOUT THAT, SOMETIME.
GOOD NIGHT.
INTERESTING. SO "RON" IS CONCRETE'S REAL FIRST NAME...

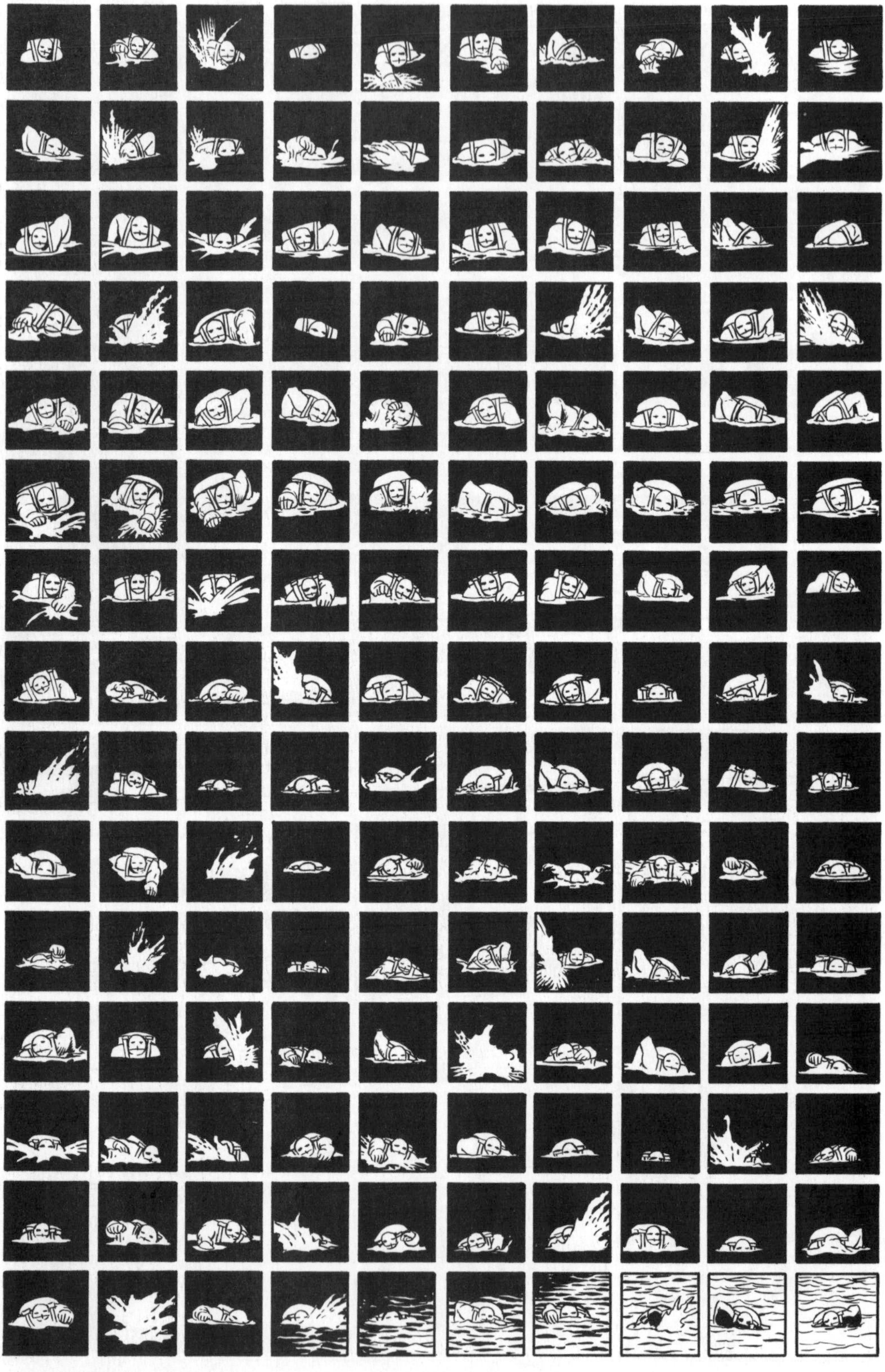

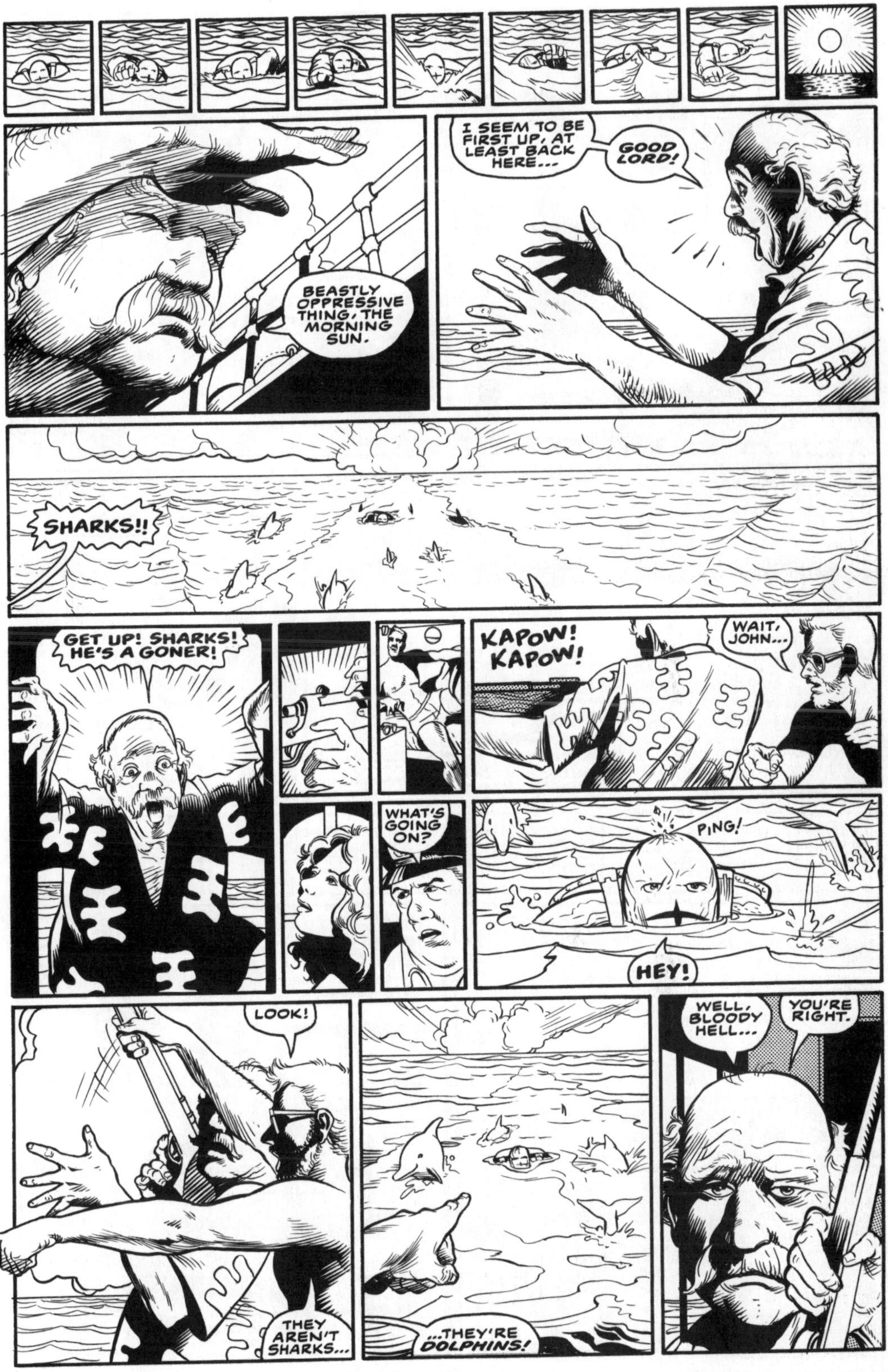
BEASTLY OPPRESSIVE THING, THE MORNING SUN.
I SEEM TO BE FIRST UP, AT LEAST BACK HERE...
GOOD LORD!
SHARKS!!
GET UP! SHARKS! HE'S A GONER!
KAPOW! KAPOW!
WAIT, JOHN...
WHAT'S GOING ON?
PING!
HEY!
LOOK!
THEY AREN'T SHARKS...
...THEY'RE DOLPHINS!
WELL, BLOODY HELL...
YOU'RE RIGHT.

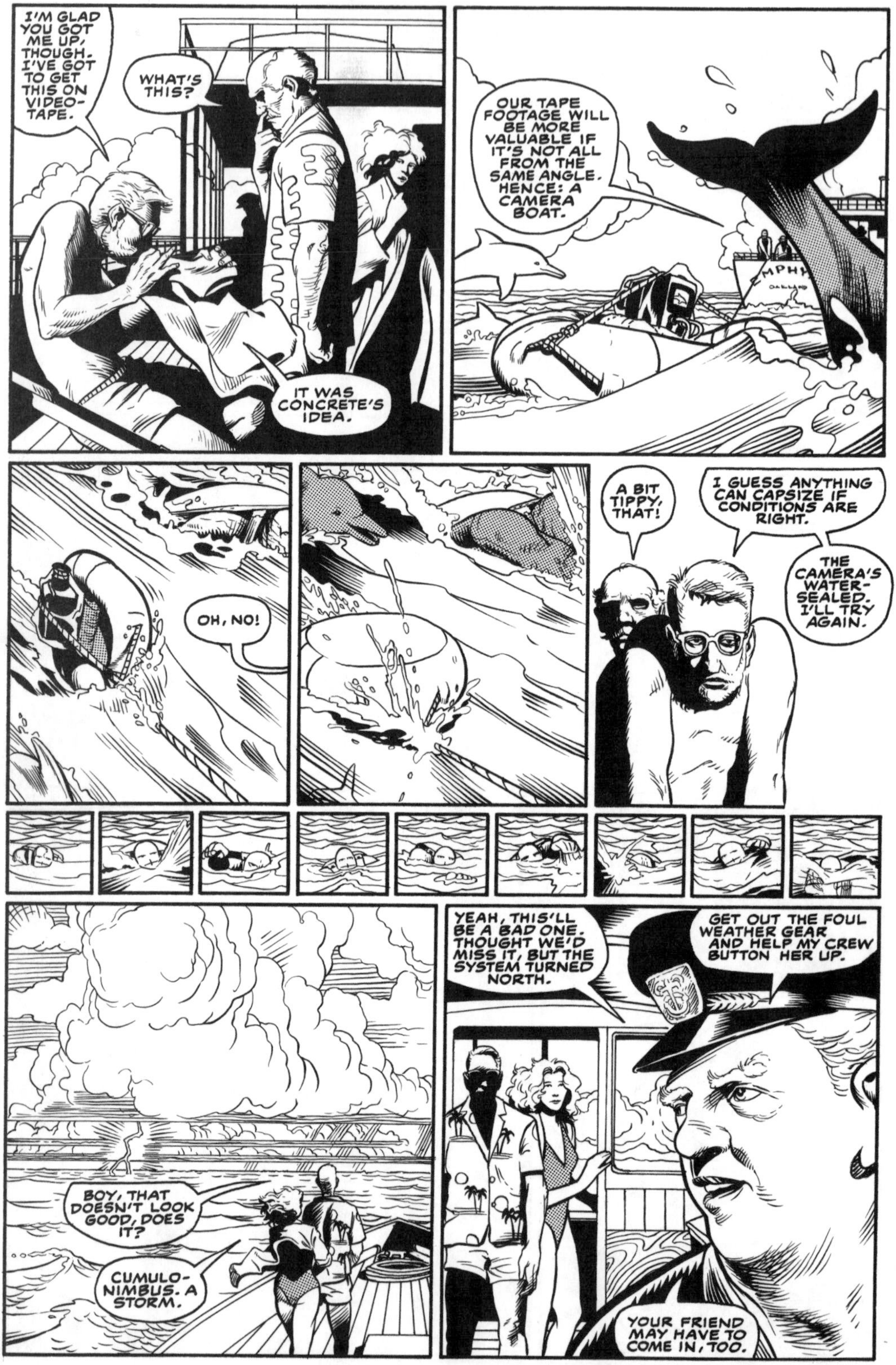

I'M GLAD YOU GOT ME UP, THOUGH. I'VE GOT TO GET THIS ON VIDEO-TAPE.
WHAT'S THIS?
IT WAS CONCRETE'S IDEA.
OUR TAPE FOOTAGE WILL BE MORE VALUABLE IF IT'S NOT ALL FROM THE SAME ANGLE. HENCE: A CAMERA BOAT.
OH, NO!
A BIT TIPPY, THAT!
I GUESS ANYTHING CAN CAPSIZE IF CONDITIONS ARE RIGHT.
THE CAMERA'S WATER-SEALED. I'LL TRY AGAIN.
BOY, THAT DOESN'T LOOK GOOD, DOES IT?
CUMULO-NIMBUS. A STORM.
YEAH, THIS'LL BE A BAD ONE. THOUGHT WE'D MISS IT, BUT THE SYSTEM TURNED NORTH.
GET OUT THE FOUL WEATHER GEAR AND HELP MY CREW BUTTON HER UP.
YOUR FRIEND MAY HAVE TO COME IN, TOO.

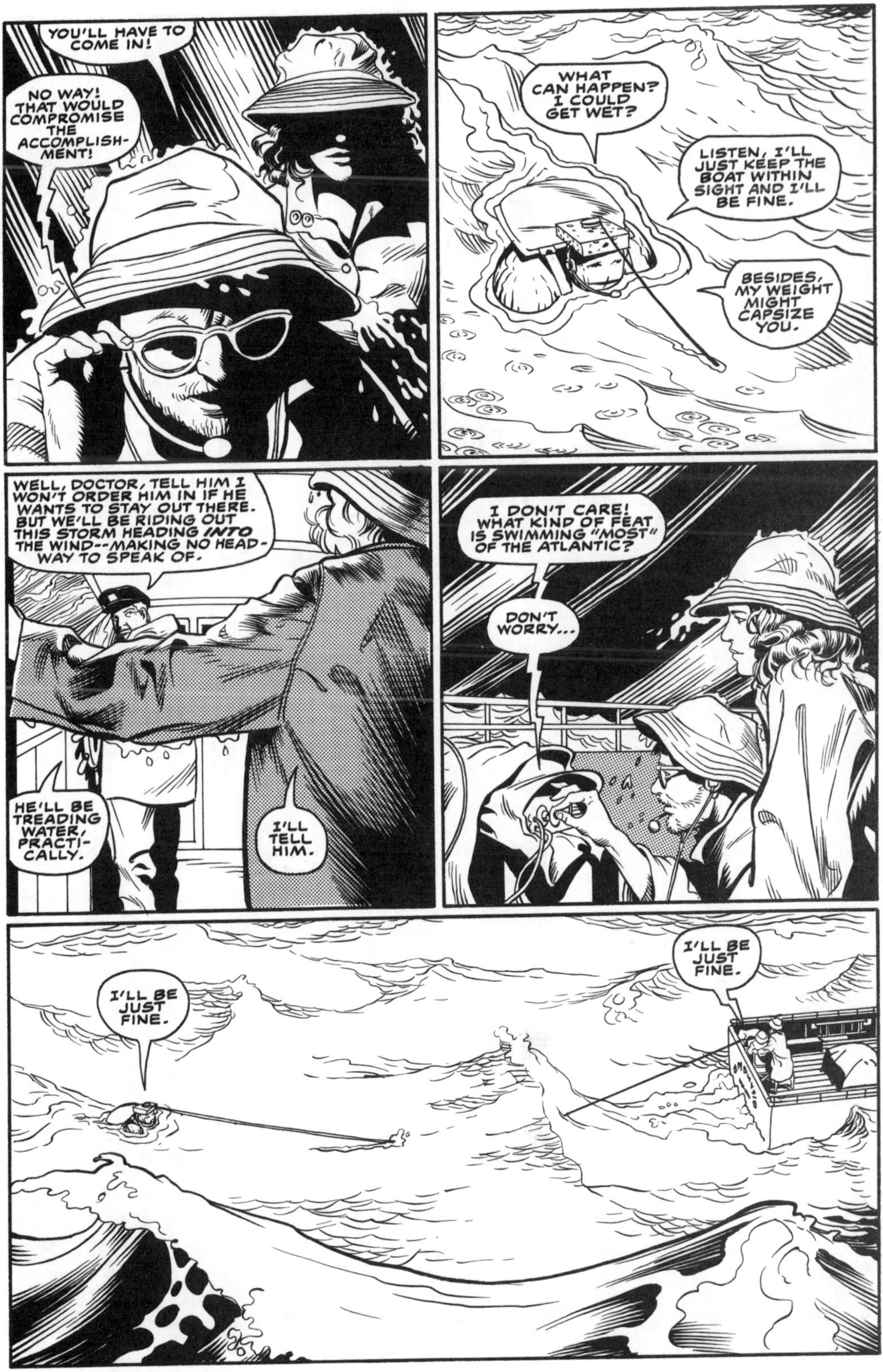
YOU'LL HAVE TO COME IN!
NO WAY! THAT WOULD COMPROMISE THE ACCOMPLISHMENT!
WHAT CAN HAPPEN? I COULD GET WET?
LISTEN, I'LL JUST KEEP THE BOAT WITHIN SIGHT AND I'LL BE FINE.
BESIDES, MY WEIGHT MIGHT CAPSIZE YOU.
WELL, DOCTOR, TELL HIM I WON'T ORDER HIM IN IF HE WANTS TO STAY OUT THERE. BUT WE'LL BE RIDING OUT THIS STORM HEADING *INTO* THE WIND--MAKING NO HEADWAY TO SPEAK OF.
HE'LL BE TREADING WATER, PRACTICALLY.
I'LL TELL HIM.
I DON'T CARE! WHAT KIND OF FEAT IS SWIMMING "MOST" OF THE ATLANTIC?
DON'T WORRY...
I'LL BE JUST FINE.
I'LL BE JUST FINE.

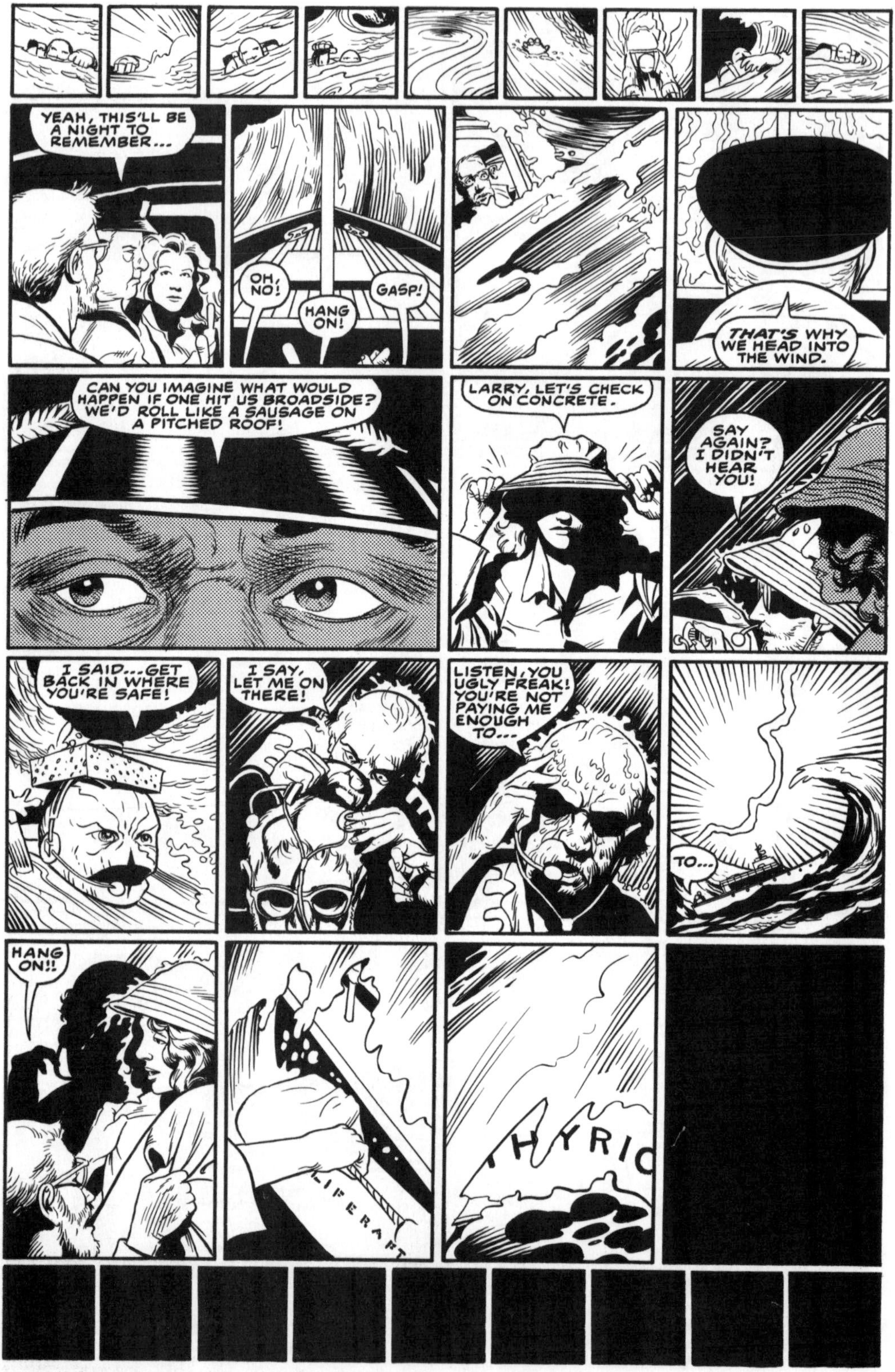
YEAH, THIS'LL BE A NIGHT TO REMEMBER...
OH, NO!
HANG ON!
GASP!
THAT'S WHY WE HEAD INTO THE WIND.
CAN YOU IMAGINE WHAT WOULD HAPPEN IF ONE HIT US BROADSIDE? WE'D ROLL LIKE A SAUSAGE ON A PITCHED ROOF!
LARRY, LET'S CHECK ON CONCRETE.
SAY AGAIN? I DIDN'T HEAR YOU!
I SAID...GET BACK IN WHERE YOU'RE SAFE!
I SAY, LET ME ON THERE!
LISTEN, YOU UGLY FREAK! YOU'RE NOT PAYING ME ENOUGH TO...
TO...
HANG ON!!
LIFERAFT
THYRIC

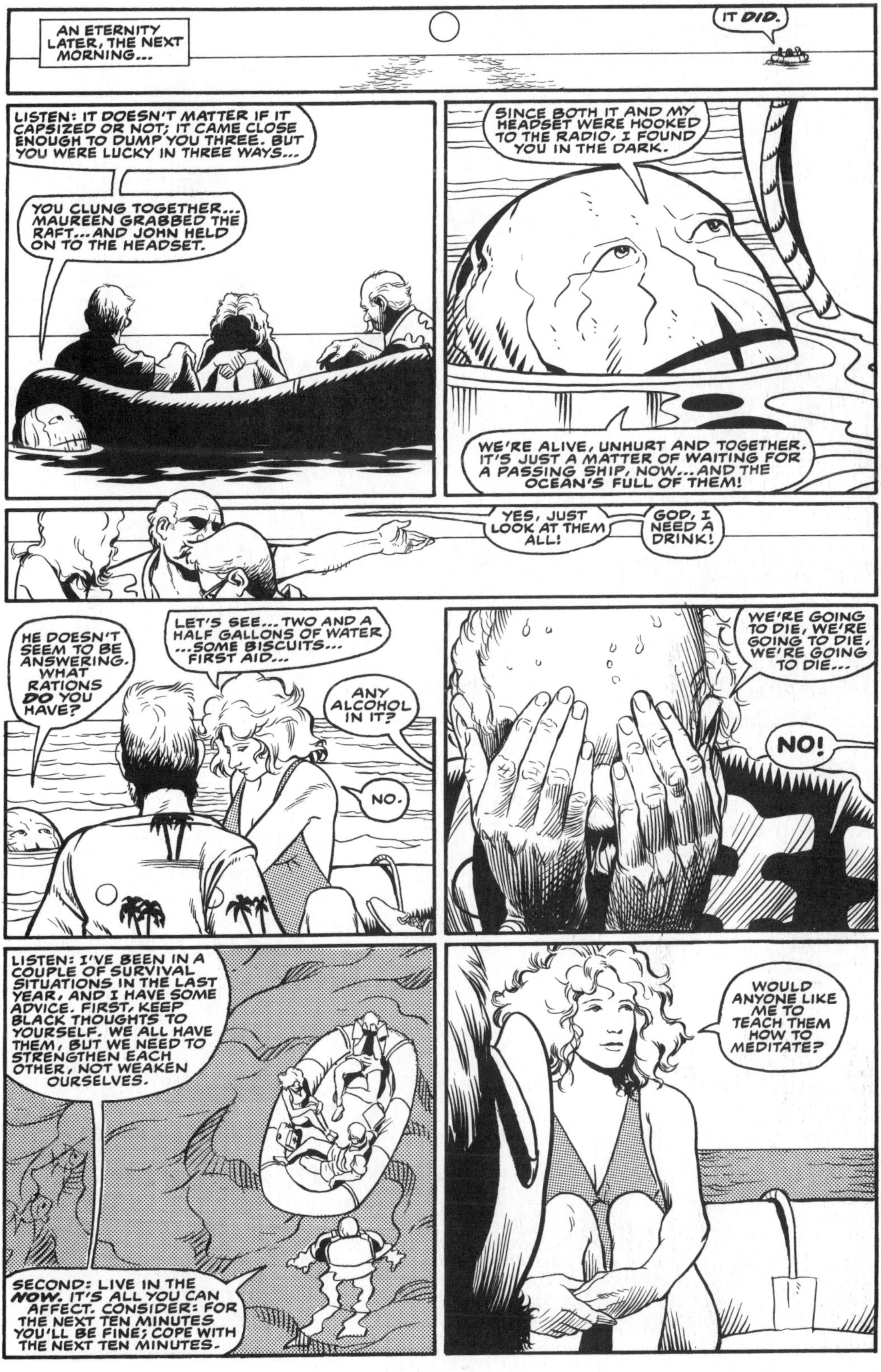
AN ETERNITY LATER, THE NEXT MORNING...
IT DID.
LISTEN: IT DOESN'T MATTER IF IT CAPSIZED OR NOT; IT CAME CLOSE ENOUGH TO DUMP YOU THREE. BUT YOU WERE LUCKY IN THREE WAYS...
YOU CLUNG TOGETHER... MAUREEN GRABBED THE RAFT... AND JOHN HELD ON TO THE HEADSET.
SINCE BOTH IT AND MY HEADSET WERE HOOKED TO THE RADIO, I FOUND YOU IN THE DARK.
WE'RE ALIVE, UNHURT AND TOGETHER. IT'S JUST A MATTER OF WAITING FOR A PASSING SHIP, NOW... AND THE OCEAN'S FULL OF THEM!
YES, JUST LOOK AT THEM ALL!
GOD, I NEED A DRINK!
HE DOESN'T SEEM TO BE ANSWERING. WHAT RATIONS DO YOU HAVE?
LET'S SEE... TWO AND A HALF GALLONS OF WATER ...SOME BISCUITS... FIRST AID...
ANY ALCOHOL IN IT?
NO.
WE'RE GOING TO DIE, WE'RE GOING TO DIE, WE'RE GOING TO DIE...
NO!
LISTEN: I'VE BEEN IN A COUPLE OF SURVIVAL SITUATIONS IN THE LAST YEAR, AND I HAVE SOME ADVICE. FIRST, KEEP BLACK THOUGHTS TO YOURSELF. WE ALL HAVE THEM, BUT WE NEED TO STRENGTHEN EACH OTHER, NOT WEAKEN OURSELVES.
SECOND: LIVE IN THE NOW. IT'S ALL YOU CAN AFFECT. CONSIDER: FOR THE NEXT TEN MINUTES YOU'LL BE FINE; COPE WITH THE NEXT TEN MINUTES.
WOULD ANYONE LIKE ME TO TEACH THEM HOW TO MEDITATE?

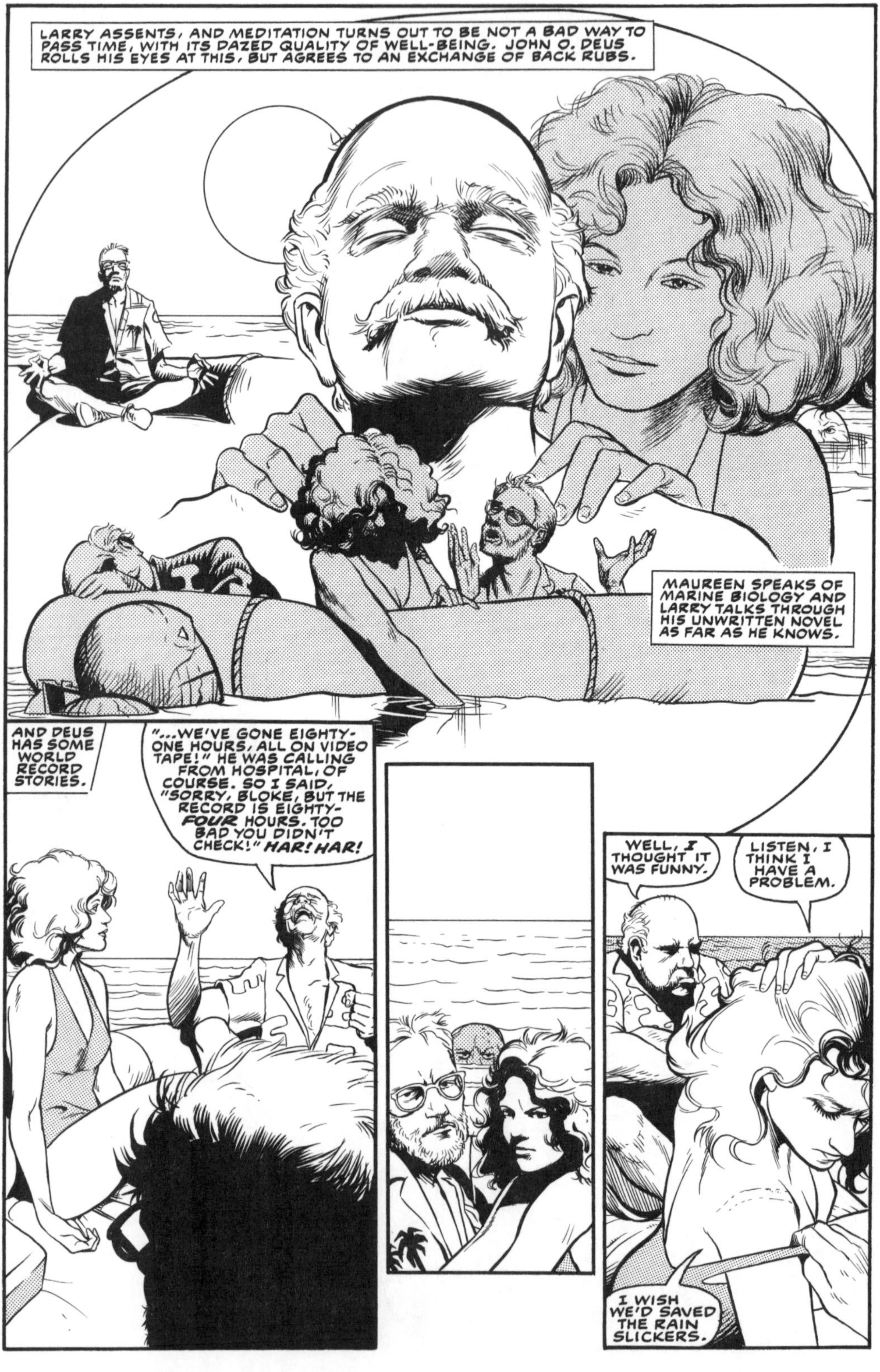
LARRY ASSENTS, AND MEDITATION TURNS OUT TO BE NOT A BAD WAY TO PASS TIME, WITH ITS DAZED QUALITY OF WELL-BEING. JOHN O. DEUS ROLLS HIS EYES AT THIS, BUT AGREES TO AN EXCHANGE OF BACK RUBS.
MAUREEN SPEAKS OF MARINE BIOLOGY AND LARRY TALKS THROUGH HIS UNWRITTEN NOVEL AS FAR AS HE KNOWS.
AND DEUS HAS SOME WORLD RECORD STORIES.
"...WE'VE GONE EIGHTY-ONE HOURS, ALL ON VIDEO TAPE!" HE WAS CALLING FROM HOSPITAL, OF COURSE. SO I SAID, "SORRY, BLOKE, BUT THE RECORD IS EIGHTY-FOUR HOURS. TOO BAD YOU DIDN'T CHECK!" HAR! HAR!
WELL, I THOUGHT IT WAS FUNNY.
LISTEN, I THINK I HAVE A PROBLEM.
I WISH WE'D SAVED THE RAIN SLICKERS.

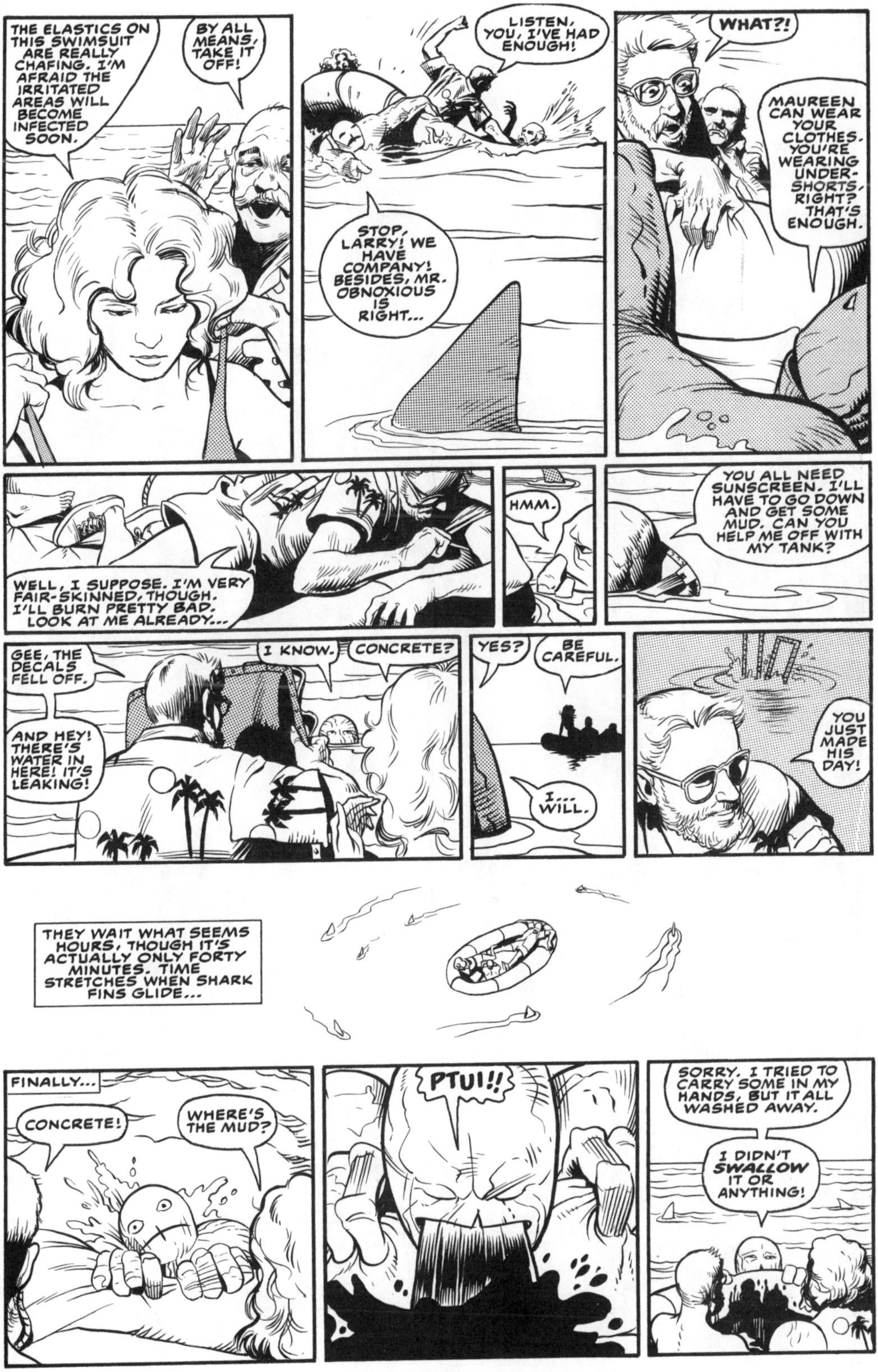
THE ELASTICS ON THIS SWIMSUIT ARE REALLY CHAFING. I'M AFRAID THE IRRITATED AREAS WILL BECOME INFECTED SOON.
BY ALL MEANS, TAKE IT OFF!
LISTEN, YOU, I'VE HAD ENOUGH!
STOP, LARRY! WE HAVE COMPANY! BESIDES, MR. OBNOXIOUS IS RIGHT...
WHAT?!
MAUREEN CAN WEAR YOUR CLOTHES. YOU'RE WEARING UNDER-SHORTS, RIGHT? THAT'S ENOUGH.
WELL, I SUPPOSE. I'M VERY FAIR-SKINNED, THOUGH. I'LL BURN PRETTY BAD. LOOK AT ME ALREADY...
HMM.
YOU ALL NEED SUNSCREEN. I'LL HAVE TO GO DOWN AND GET SOME MUD. CAN YOU HELP ME OFF WITH MY TANK?
GEE, THE DECALS FELL OFF.
I KNOW.
CONCRETE?
AND HEY! THERE'S WATER IN HERE! IT'S LEAKING!
YES?
BE CAREFUL.
I... WILL.
YOU JUST MADE HIS DAY!
THEY WAIT WHAT SEEMS HOURS, THOUGH IT'S ACTUALLY ONLY FORTY MINUTES. TIME STRETCHES WHEN SHARK FINS GLIDE...
FINALLY...
CONCRETE!
WHERE'S THE MUD?
PTUI!!
SORRY. I TRIED TO CARRY SOME IN MY HANDS, BUT IT ALL WASHED AWAY.
I DIDN'T SWALLOW IT OR ANYTHING!

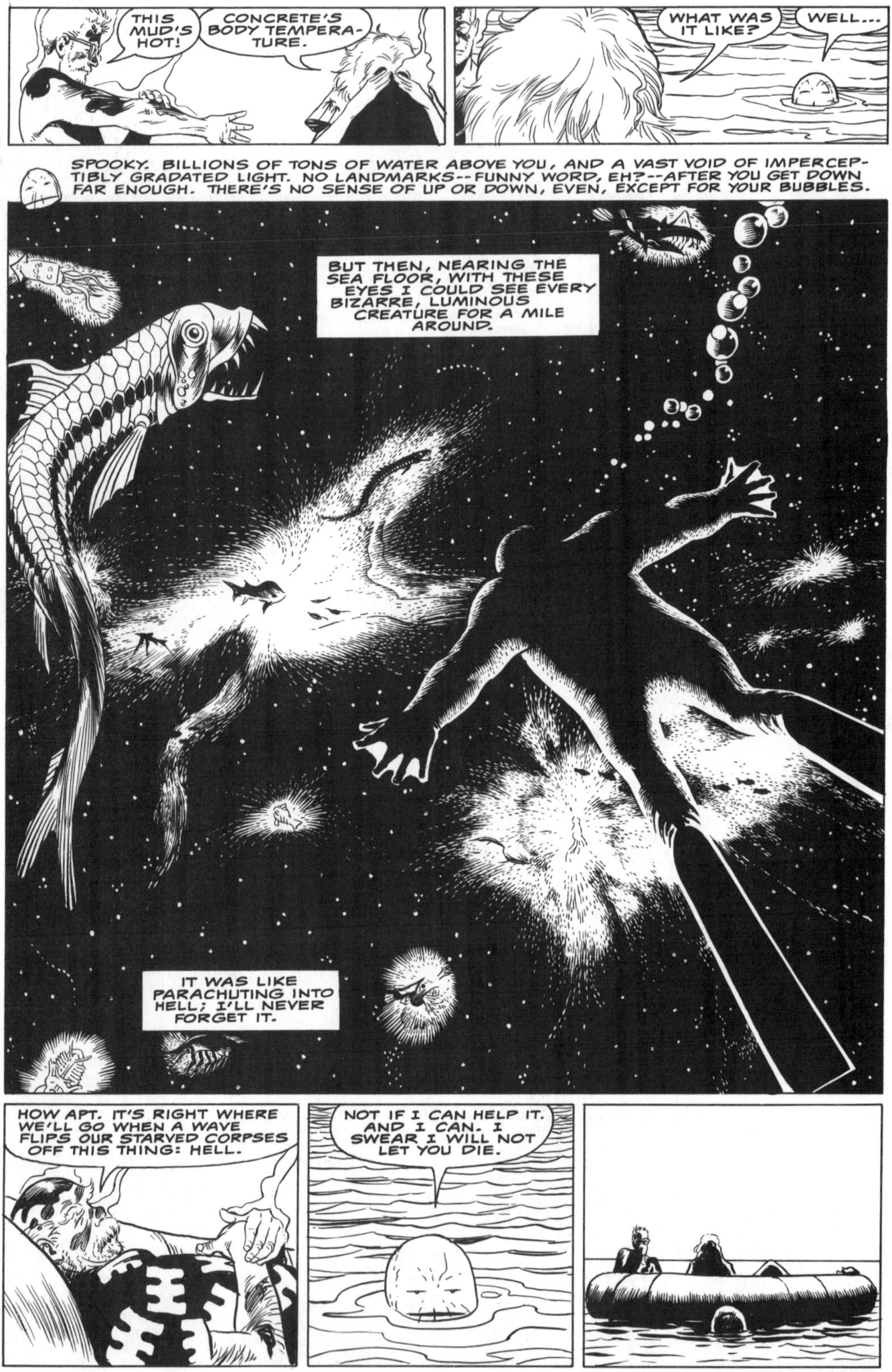

THIS MUD'S HOT!
CONCRETE'S BODY TEMPERATURE.
WHAT WAS IT LIKE?
WELL...
SPOOKY. BILLIONS OF TONS OF WATER ABOVE YOU, AND A VAST VOID OF IMPERCEPTIBLY GRADATED LIGHT. NO LANDMARKS--FUNNY WORD, EH?--AFTER YOU GET DOWN FAR ENOUGH. THERE'S NO SENSE OF UP OR DOWN, EVEN, EXCEPT FOR YOUR BUBBLES.
BUT THEN, NEARING THE SEA FLOOR, WITH THESE EYES I COULD SEE EVERY BIZARRE, LUMINOUS CREATURE FOR A MILE AROUND.
IT WAS LIKE PARACHUTING INTO HELL; I'LL NEVER FORGET IT.
HOW APT. IT'S RIGHT WHERE WE'LL GO WHEN A WAVE FLIPS OUR STARVED CORPSES OFF THIS THING: HELL.
NOT IF I CAN HELP IT. AND I CAN. I SWEAR I WILL NOT LET YOU DIE.

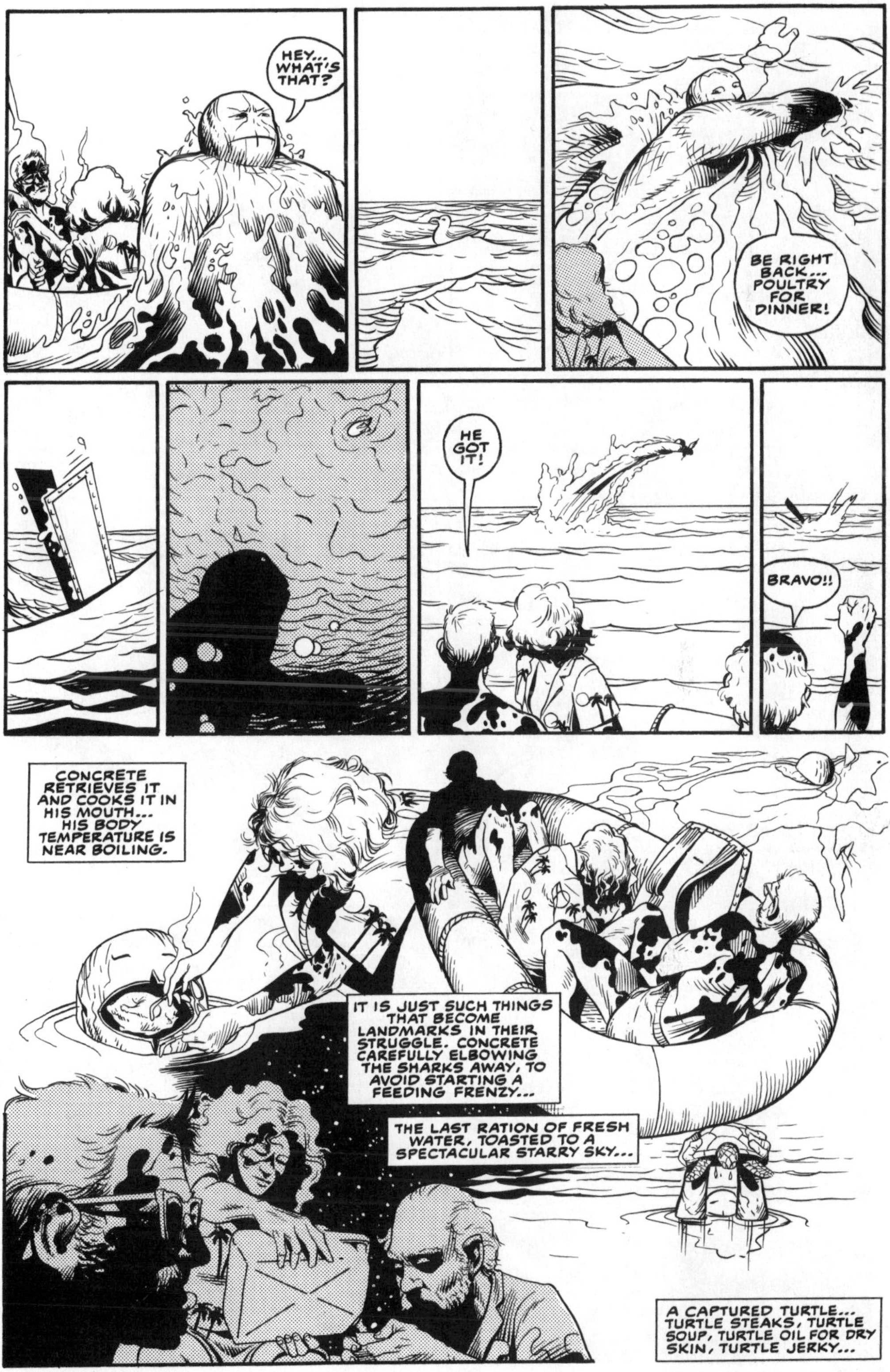
HEY... WHAT'S THAT?
BE RIGHT BACK... POULTRY FOR DINNER!
HE GOT IT!
BRAVO!!
CONCRETE RETRIEVES IT AND COOKS IT IN HIS MOUTH... HIS BODY TEMPERATURE IS NEAR BOILING.
IT IS JUST SUCH THINGS THAT BECOME LANDMARKS IN THEIR STRUGGLE. CONCRETE CAREFULLY ELBOWING THE SHARKS AWAY, TO AVOID STARTING A FEEDING FRENZY...
THE LAST RATION OF FRESH WATER, TOASTED TO A SPECTACULAR STARRY SKY...
A CAPTURED TURTLE... TURTLE STEAKS, TURTLE SOUP, TURTLE OIL FOR DRY SKIN, TURTLE JERKY...

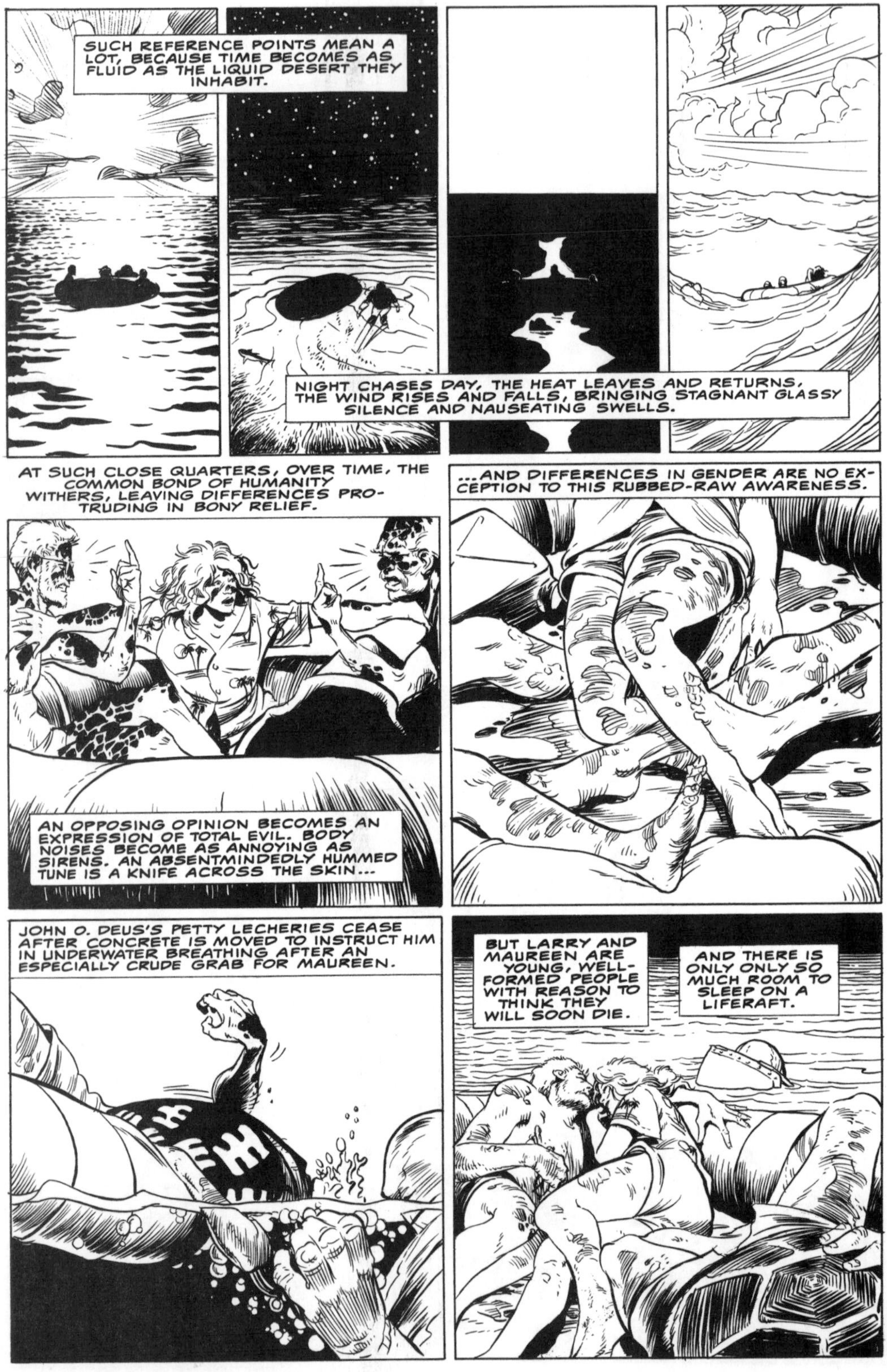
SUCH REFERENCE POINTS MEAN A LOT, BECAUSE TIME BECOMES AS FLUID AS THE LIQUID DESERT THEY INHABIT.
NIGHT CHASES DAY, THE HEAT LEAVES AND RETURNS, THE WIND RISES AND FALLS, BRINGING STAGNANT GLASSY SILENCE AND NAUSEATING SWELLS.
AT SUCH CLOSE QUARTERS, OVER TIME, THE COMMON BOND OF HUMANITY WITHERS, LEAVING DIFFERENCES PROTRUDING IN BONY RELIEF.
AN OPPOSING OPINION BECOMES AN EXPRESSION OF TOTAL EVIL. BODY NOISES BECOME AS ANNOYING AS SIRENS. AN ABSENTMINDEDLY HUMMED TUNE IS A KNIFE ACROSS THE SKIN...
...AND DIFFERENCES IN GENDER ARE NO EXCEPTION TO THIS RUBBED-RAW AWARENESS.
JOHN O. DEUS'S PETTY LECHERIES CEASE AFTER CONCRETE IS MOVED TO INSTRUCT HIM IN UNDERWATER BREATHING AFTER AN ESPECIALLY CRUDE GRAB FOR MAUREEN.
BUT LARRY AND MAUREEN ARE YOUNG, WELL-FORMED PEOPLE WITH REASON TO THINK THEY WILL SOON DIE.
AND THERE IS ONLY ONLY SO MUCH ROOM TO SLEEP ON A LIFERAFT.

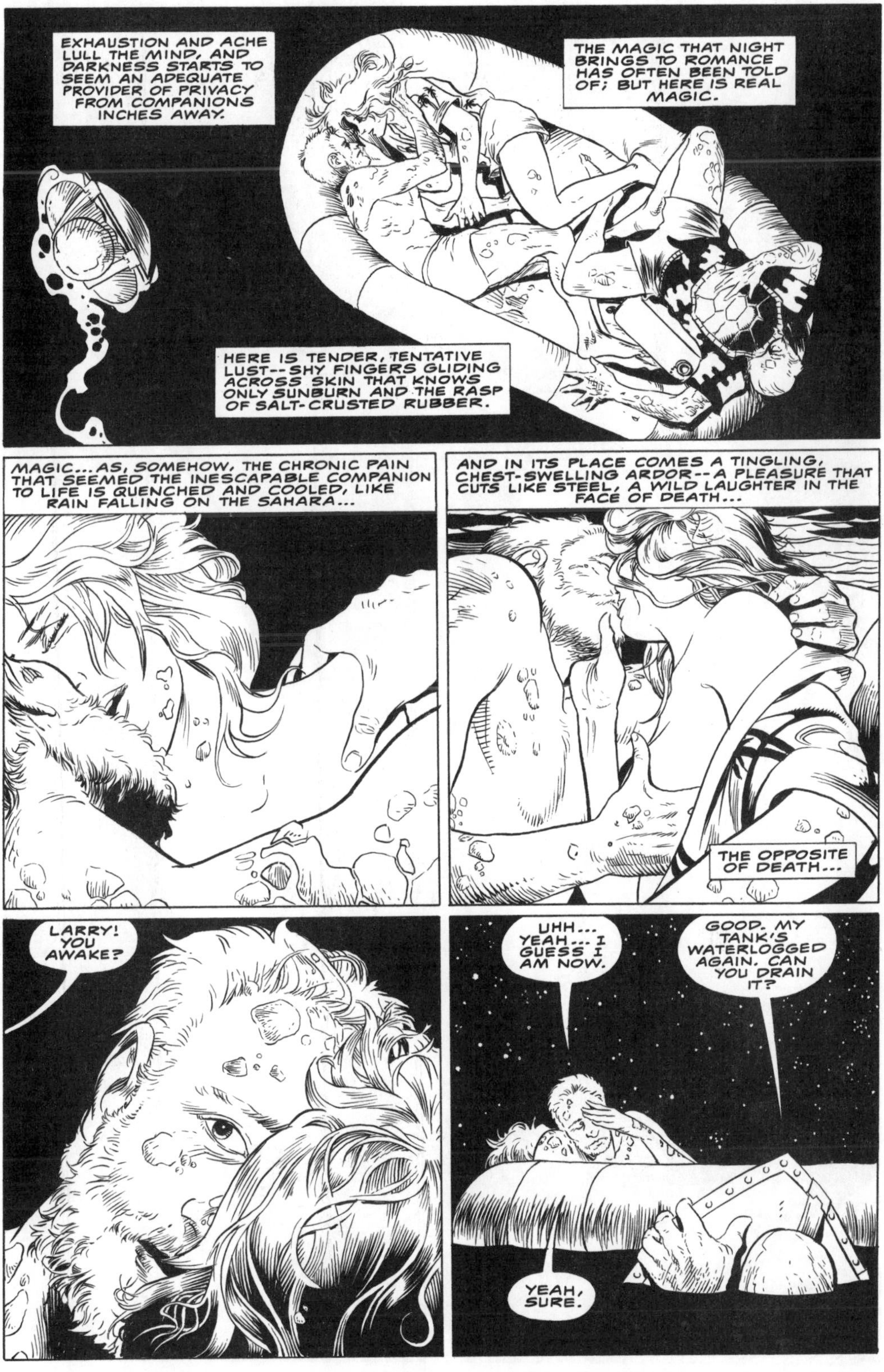
EXHAUSTION AND ACHE LULL THE MIND, AND DARKNESS STARTS TO SEEM AN ADEQUATE PROVIDER OF PRIVACY FROM COMPANIONS INCHES AWAY.
THE MAGIC THAT NIGHT BRINGS TO ROMANCE HAS OFTEN BEEN TOLD OF; BUT HERE IS REAL MAGIC.
HERE IS TENDER, TENTATIVE LUST--SHY FINGERS GLIDING ACROSS SKIN THAT KNOWS ONLY SUNBURN AND THE RASP OF SALT-CRUSTED RUBBER.
MAGIC...AS, SOMEHOW, THE CHRONIC PAIN THAT SEEMED THE INESCAPABLE COMPANION TO LIFE IS QUENCHED AND COOLED, LIKE RAIN FALLING ON THE SAHARA...
AND IN ITS PLACE COMES A TINGLING, CHEST-SWELLING ARDOR--A PLEASURE THAT CUTS LIKE STEEL, A WILD LAUGHTER IN THE FACE OF DEATH...
THE OPPOSITE OF DEATH...
LARRY! YOU AWAKE?
UHH... YEAH... I GUESS I AM NOW.
GOOD. MY TANK'S WATERLOGGED AGAIN. CAN YOU DRAIN IT?
YEAH, SURE.

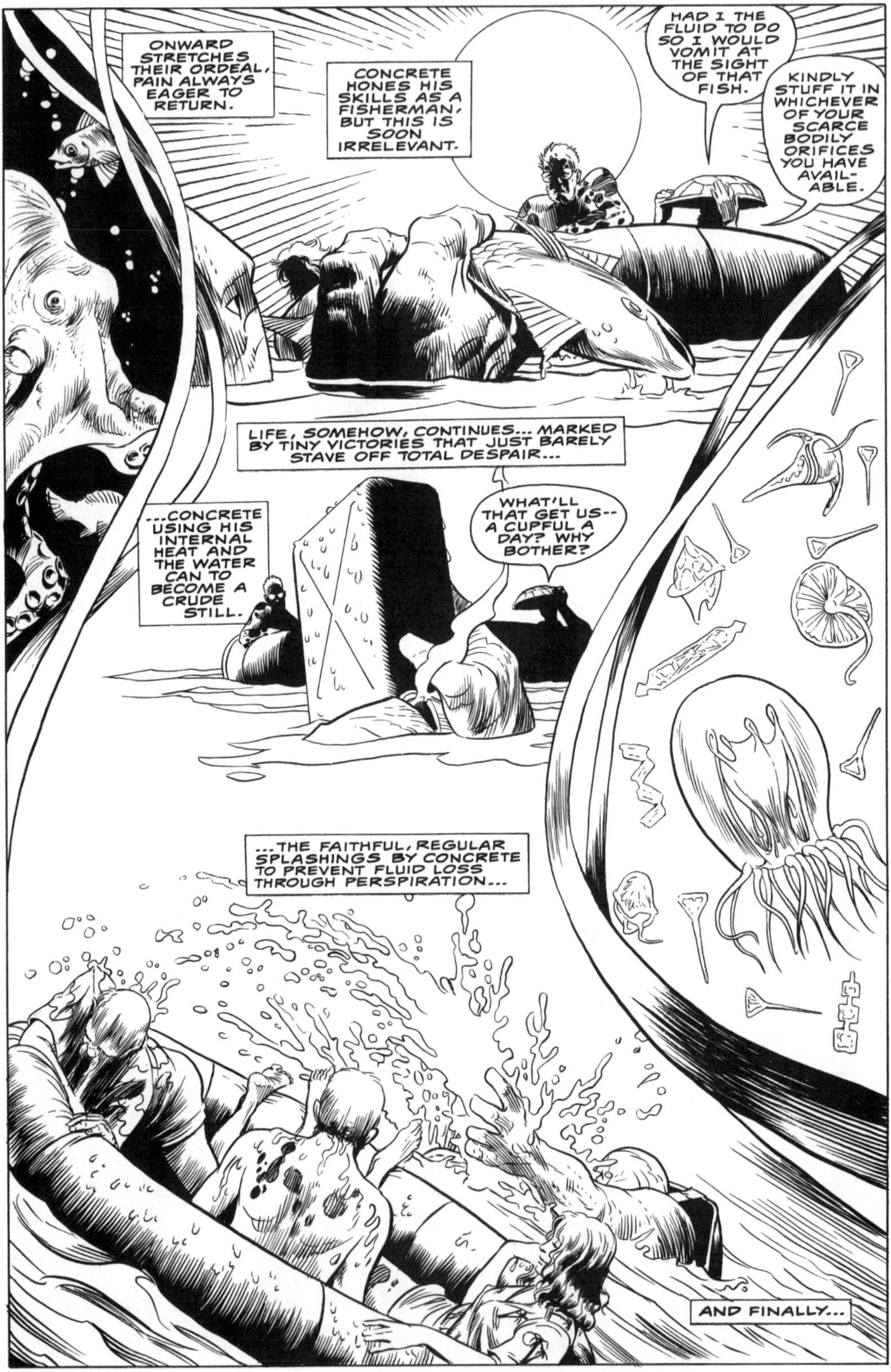
ONWARD STRETCHES THEIR ORDEAL, PAIN ALWAYS EAGER TO RETURN.
CONCRETE HONES HIS SKILLS AS A FISHERMAN, BUT THIS IS SOON IRRELEVANT.
HAD I THE FLUID TO DO SO I WOULD VOMIT AT THE SIGHT OF THAT FISH.
KINDLY STUFF IT IN WHICHEVER OF YOUR SCARCE BODILY ORIFICES YOU HAVE AVAIL-ABLE.
LIFE, SOMEHOW, CONTINUES... MARKED BY TINY VICTORIES THAT JUST BARELY STAVE OFF TOTAL DESPAIR...
...CONCRETE USING HIS INTERNAL HEAT AND THE WATER CAN TO BECOME A CRUDE STILL.
WHAT'LL THAT GET US-- A CUPFUL A DAY? WHY BOTHER?
...THE FAITHFUL, REGULAR SPLASHINGS BY CONCRETE TO PREVENT FLUID LOSS THROUGH PERSPIRATION...
AND FINALLY...

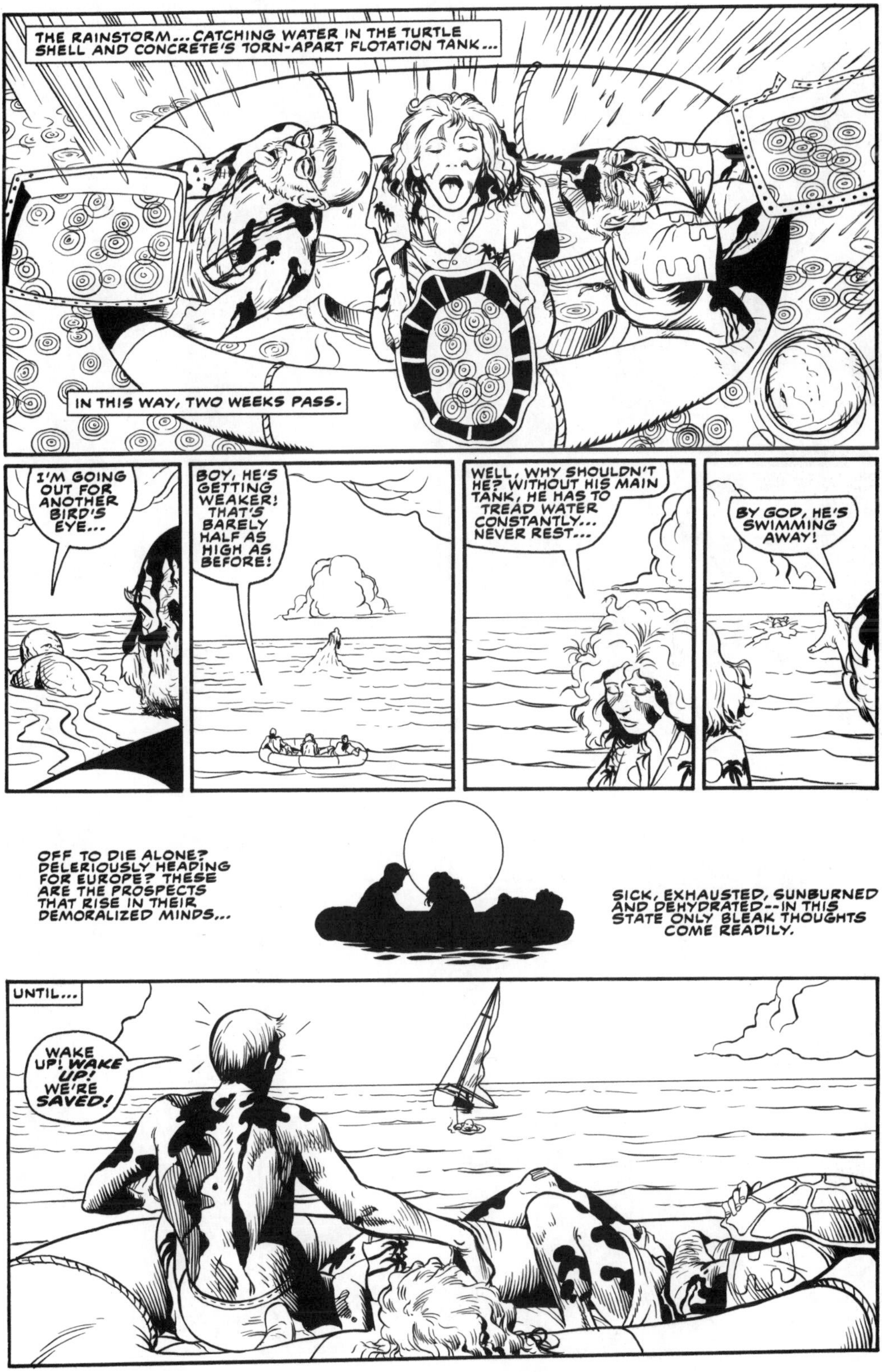
THE RAINSTORM...CATCHING WATER IN THE TURTLE SHELL AND CONCRETE'S TORN-APART FLOTATION TANK...
IN THIS WAY, TWO WEEKS PASS.
I'M GOING OUT FOR ANOTHER BIRD'S EYE...
BOY, HE'S GETTING WEAKER! THAT'S BARELY HALF AS HIGH AS BEFORE!
WELL, WHY SHOULDN'T HE? WITHOUT HIS MAIN TANK, HE HAS TO TREAD WATER CONSTANTLY... NEVER REST...
BY GOD, HE'S SWIMMING AWAY!
OFF TO DIE ALONE? DELERIOUSLY HEADING FOR EUROPE? THESE ARE THE PROSPECTS THAT RISE IN THEIR DEMORALIZED MINDS...
SICK, EXHAUSTED, SUNBURNED AND DEHYDRATED--IN THIS STATE ONLY BLEAK THOUGHTS COME READILY.
UNTIL...
WAKE UP! WAKE UP! WE'RE SAVED!

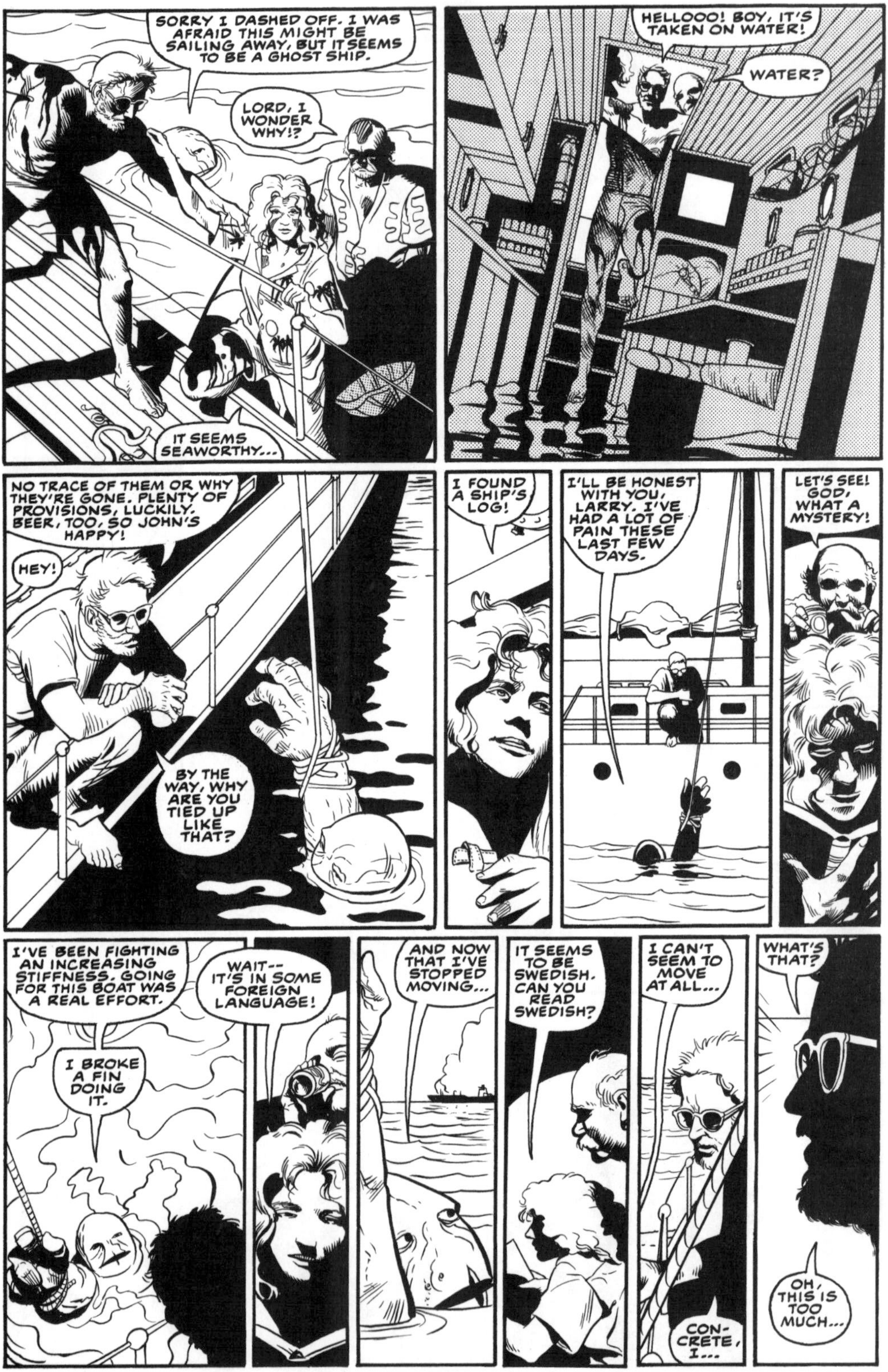
SORRY I DASHED OFF. I WAS AFRAID THIS MIGHT BE SAILING AWAY, BUT IT SEEMS TO BE A GHOST SHIP.
LORD, I WONDER WHY!?
IT SEEMS SEAWORTHY...
HELLOOO! BOY, IT'S TAKEN ON WATER!
WATER?
NO TRACE OF THEM OR WHY THEY'RE GONE. PLENTY OF PROVISIONS, LUCKILY. BEER, TOO, SO JOHN'S HAPPY!
HEY!
BY THE WAY, WHY ARE YOU TIED UP LIKE THAT?
I FOUND A SHIP'S LOG!
I'LL BE HONEST WITH YOU, LARRY. I'VE HAD A LOT OF PAIN THESE LAST FEW DAYS.
LET'S SEE! GOD, WHAT A MYSTERY!
I'VE BEEN FIGHTING AN INCREASING STIFFNESS. GOING FOR THIS BOAT WAS A REAL EFFORT.
I BROKE A FIN DOING IT.
WAIT-- IT'S IN SOME FOREIGN LANGUAGE!
AND NOW THAT I'VE STOPPED MOVING...
IT SEEMS TO BE SWEDISH. CAN YOU READ SWEDISH?
I CAN'T SEEM TO MOVE AT ALL...
CON-CRETE, I...
WHAT'S THAT?
OH, THIS IS TOO MUCH...

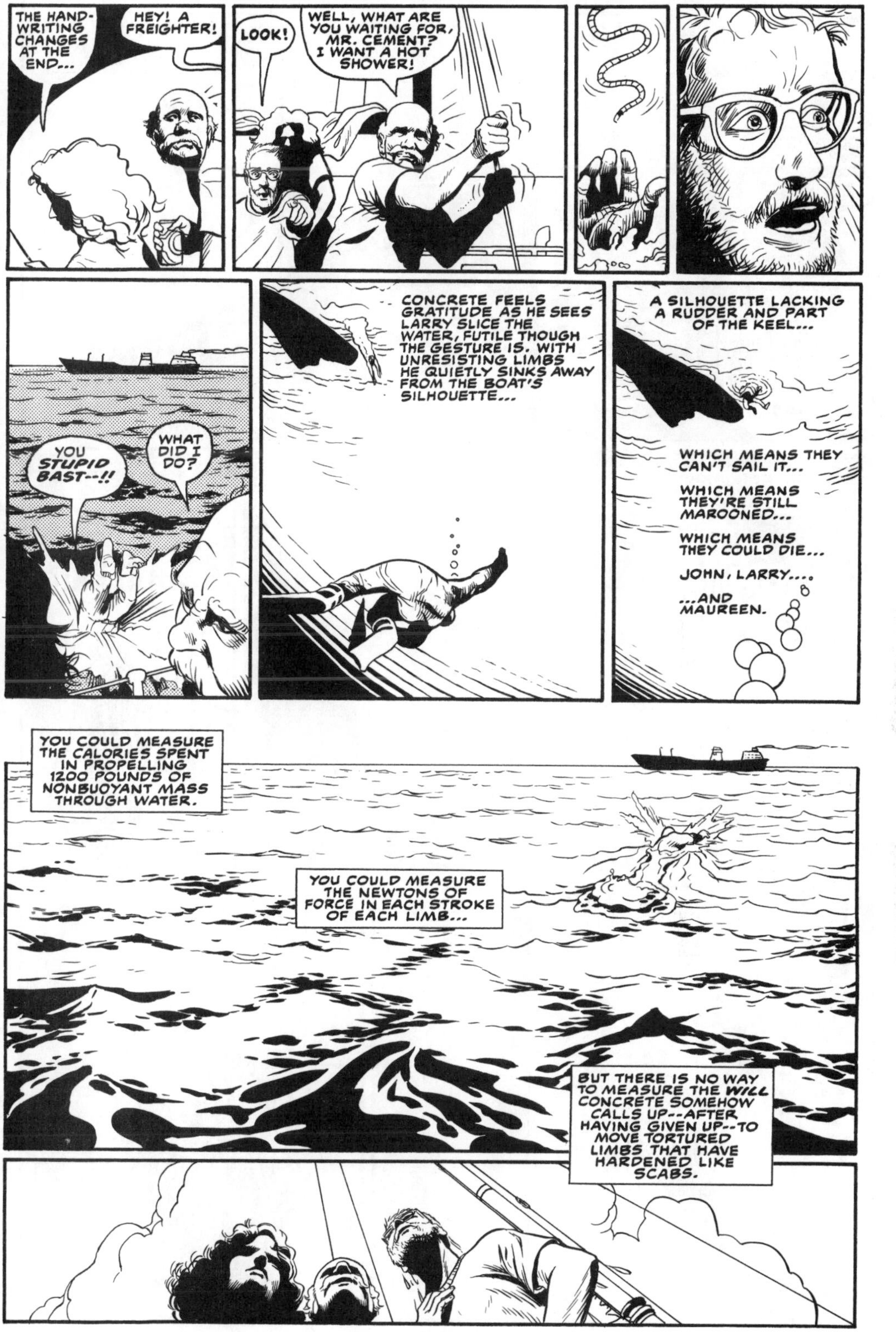
THE HAND-WRITING CHANGES AT THE END...
HEY! A FREIGHTER!
LOOK!
WELL, WHAT ARE YOU WAITING FOR, MR. CEMENT? I WANT A HOT SHOWER!
YOU STUPID BAST--!!
WHAT DID I DO?
CONCRETE FEELS GRATITUDE AS HE SEES LARRY SLICE THE WATER, FUTILE THOUGH THE GESTURE IS. WITH UNRESISTING LIMBS HE QUIETLY SINKS AWAY FROM THE BOAT'S SILHOUETTE...
A SILHOUETTE LACKING A RUDDER AND PART OF THE KEEL...
WHICH MEANS THEY CAN'T SAIL IT...
WHICH MEANS THEY'RE STILL MAROONED...
WHICH MEANS THEY COULD DIE...
JOHN, LARRY....
...AND MAUREEN.
YOU COULD MEASURE THE CALORIES SPENT IN PROPELLING 1200 POUNDS OF NONBUOYANT MASS THROUGH WATER.
YOU COULD MEASURE THE NEWTONS OF FORCE IN EACH STROKE OF EACH LIMB...
BUT THERE IS NO WAY TO MEASURE THE WILL CONCRETE SOMEHOW CALLS UP--AFTER HAVING GIVEN UP--TO MOVE TORTURED LIMBS THAT HAVE HARDENED LIKE SCABS.

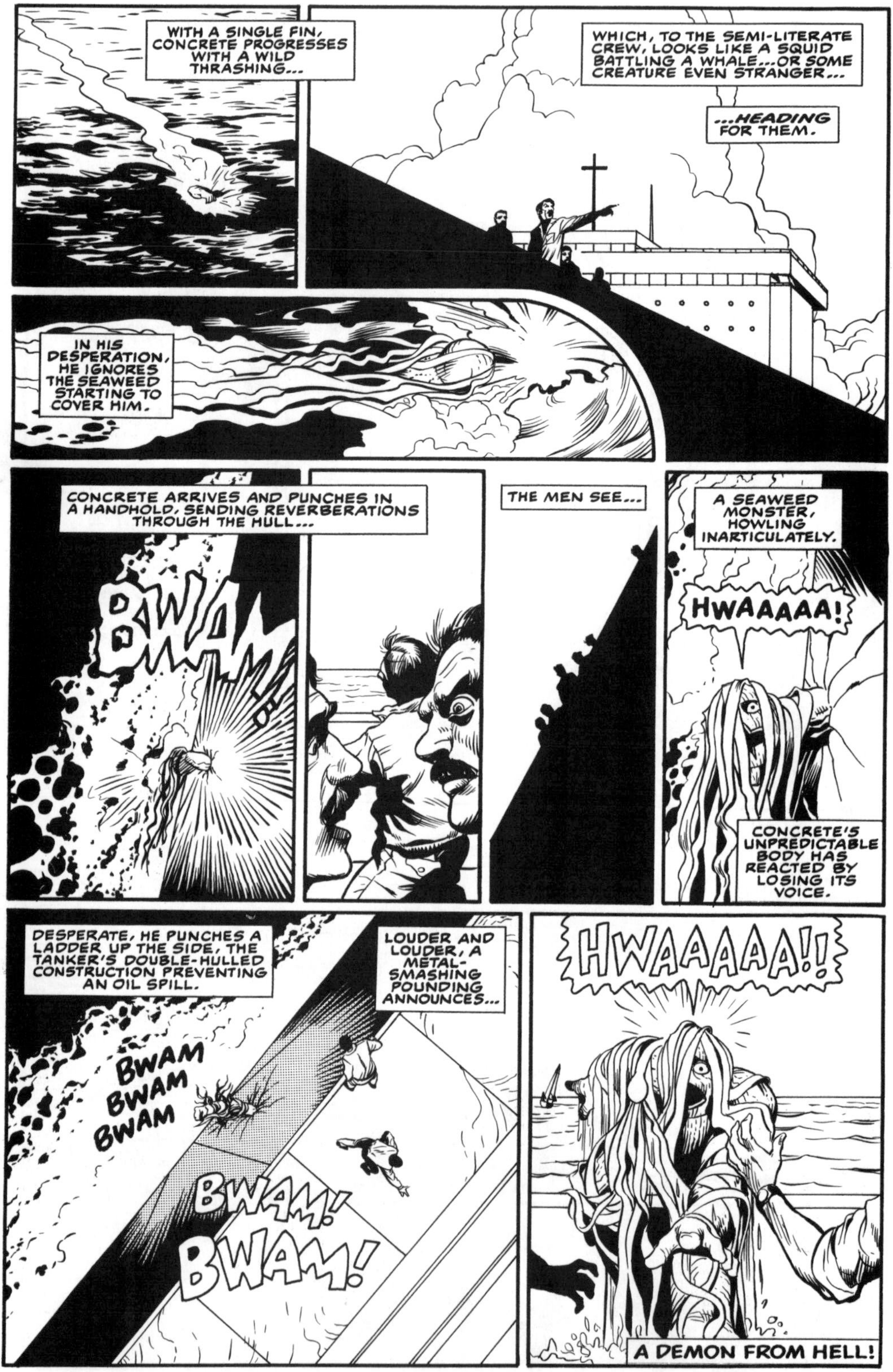
WITH A SINGLE FIN, CONCRETE PROGRESSES WITH A WILD THRASHING...
WHICH, TO THE SEMI-LITERATE CREW, LOOKS LIKE A SQUID BATTLING A WHALE...OR SOME CREATURE EVEN STRANGER...
...HEADING FOR THEM.
IN HIS DESPERATION, HE IGNORES THE SEAWEED STARTING TO COVER HIM.
CONCRETE ARRIVES AND PUNCHES IN A HANDHOLD, SENDING REVERBERATIONS THROUGH THE HULL...
BWAM!
THE MEN SEE...
A SEAWEED MONSTER, HOWLING INARTICULATELY.
HWAAAAA!
CONCRETE'S UNPREDICTABLE BODY HAS REACTED BY LOSING ITS VOICE.
DESPERATE, HE PUNCHES A LADDER UP THE SIDE, THE TANKER'S DOUBLE-HULLED CONSTRUCTION PREVENTING AN OIL SPILL.
LOUDER AND LOUDER, A METAL-SMASHING POUNDING ANNOUNCES...
BWAM BWAM BWAM
BWAM! BWAM!
HWAAAAA!!
A DEMON FROM HELL!

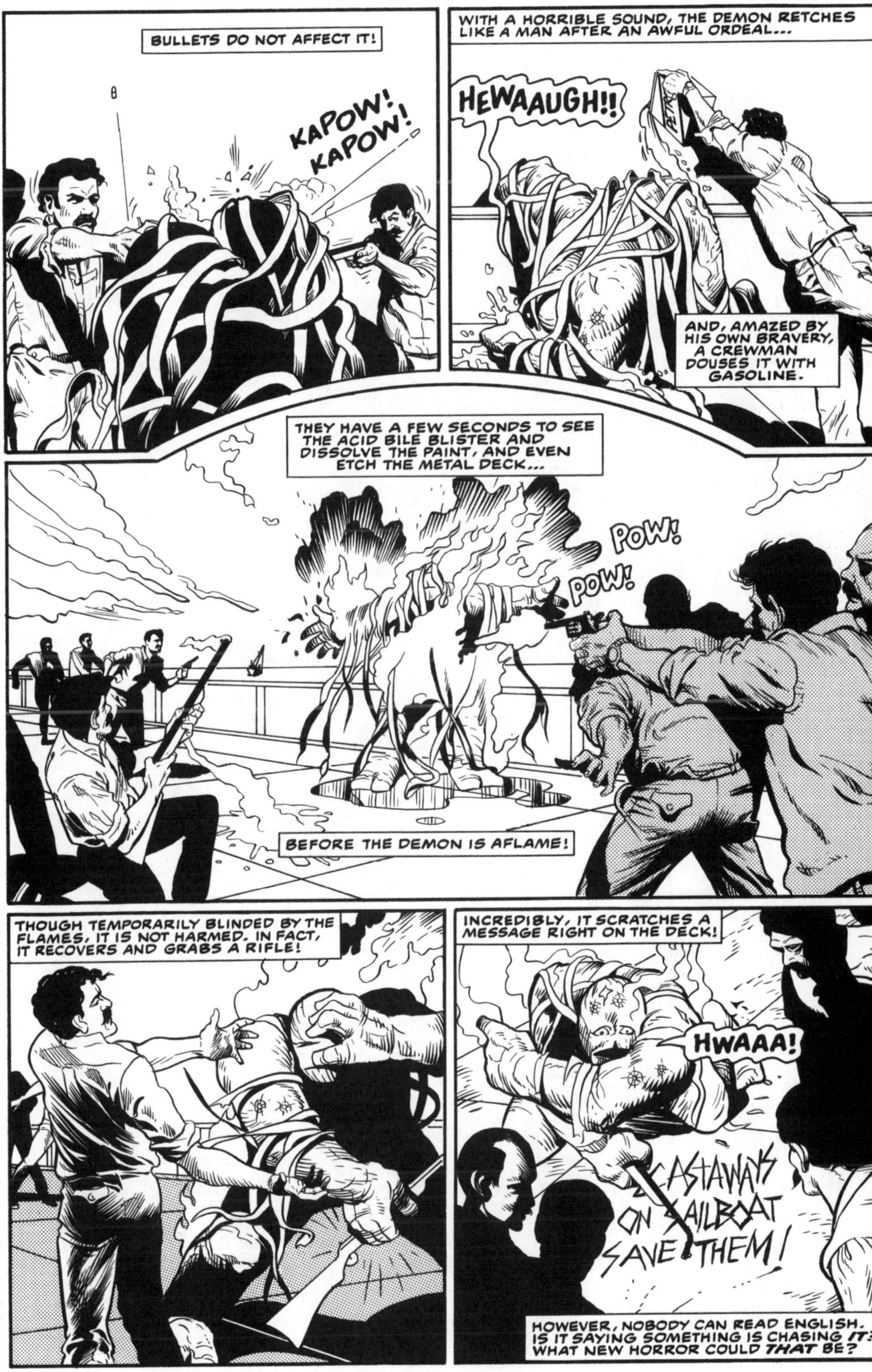
BULLETS DO NOT AFFECT IT!
KAPOW! KAPOW!
WITH A HORRIBLE SOUND, THE DEMON RETCHES LIKE A MAN AFTER AN AWFUL ORDEAL...
HEWAAUGH!!
AND, AMAZED BY HIS OWN BRAVERY, A CREWMAN DOUSES IT WITH GASOLINE.
THEY HAVE A FEW SECONDS TO SEE THE ACID BILE BLISTER AND DISSOLVE THE PAINT, AND EVEN ETCH THE METAL DECK...
POW!
POW!
BEFORE THE DEMON IS AFLAME!
THOUGH TEMPORARILY BLINDED BY THE FLAMES, IT IS NOT HARMED. IN FACT, IT RECOVERS AND GRABS A RIFLE!
INCREDIBLY, IT SCRATCHES A MESSAGE RIGHT ON THE DECK!
HWAAA!
CASTAWAYS ON SAILBOAT SAVE THEM!
HOWEVER, NOBODY CAN READ ENGLISH. IS IT SAYING SOMETHING IS CHASING *IT*? WHAT NEW HORROR COULD *THAT* BE?

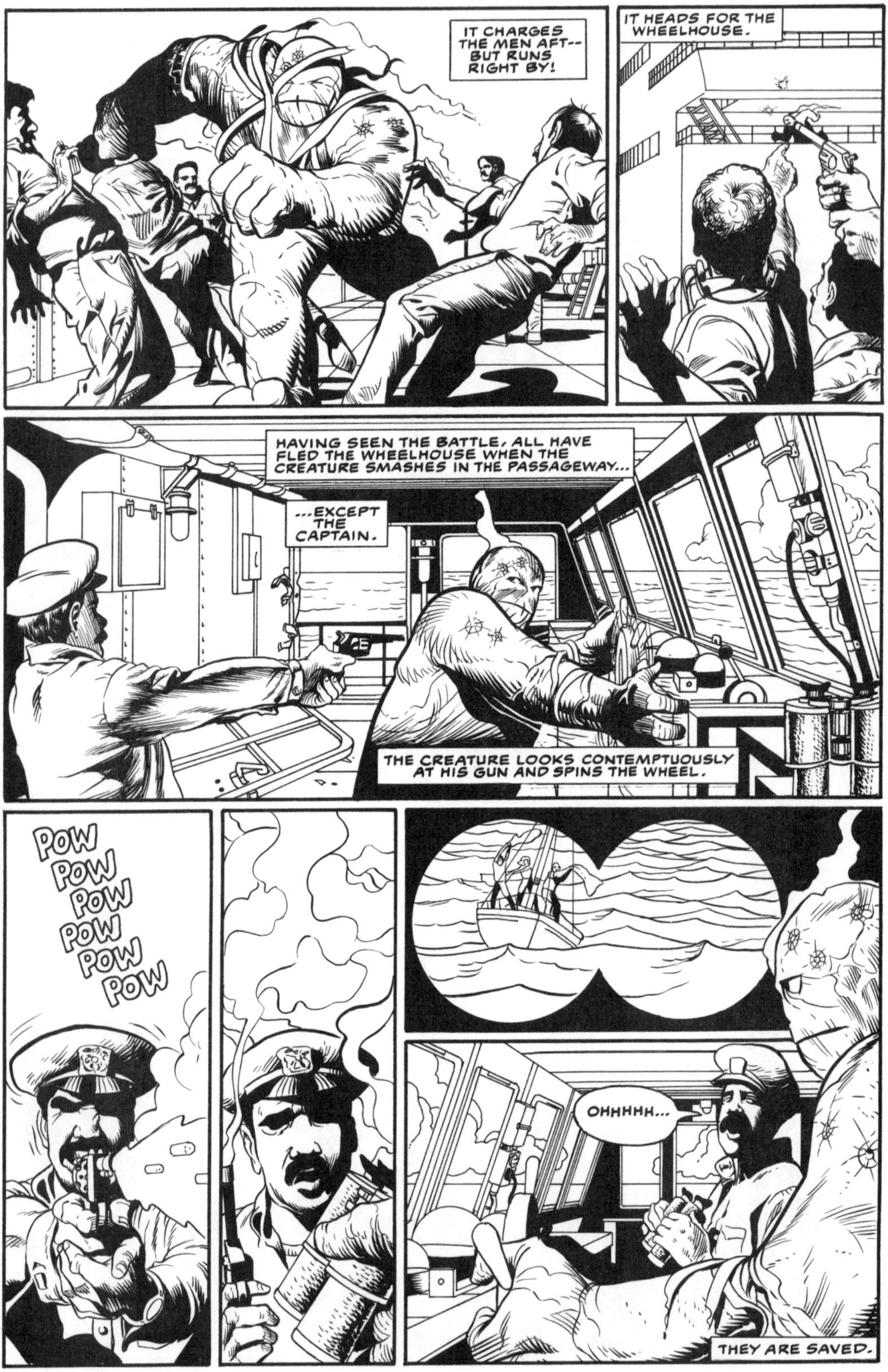
IT CHARGES THE MEN AFT--BUT RUNS RIGHT BY!
IT HEADS FOR THE WHEELHOUSE.
HAVING SEEN THE BATTLE, ALL HAVE FLED THE WHEELHOUSE WHEN THE CREATURE SMASHES IN THE PASSAGEWAY...
...EXCEPT THE CAPTAIN.
THE CREATURE LOOKS CONTEMPTUOUSLY AT HIS GUN AND SPINS THE WHEEL.
POW POW POW POW POW POW
OHHHHH...
THEY ARE SAVED.

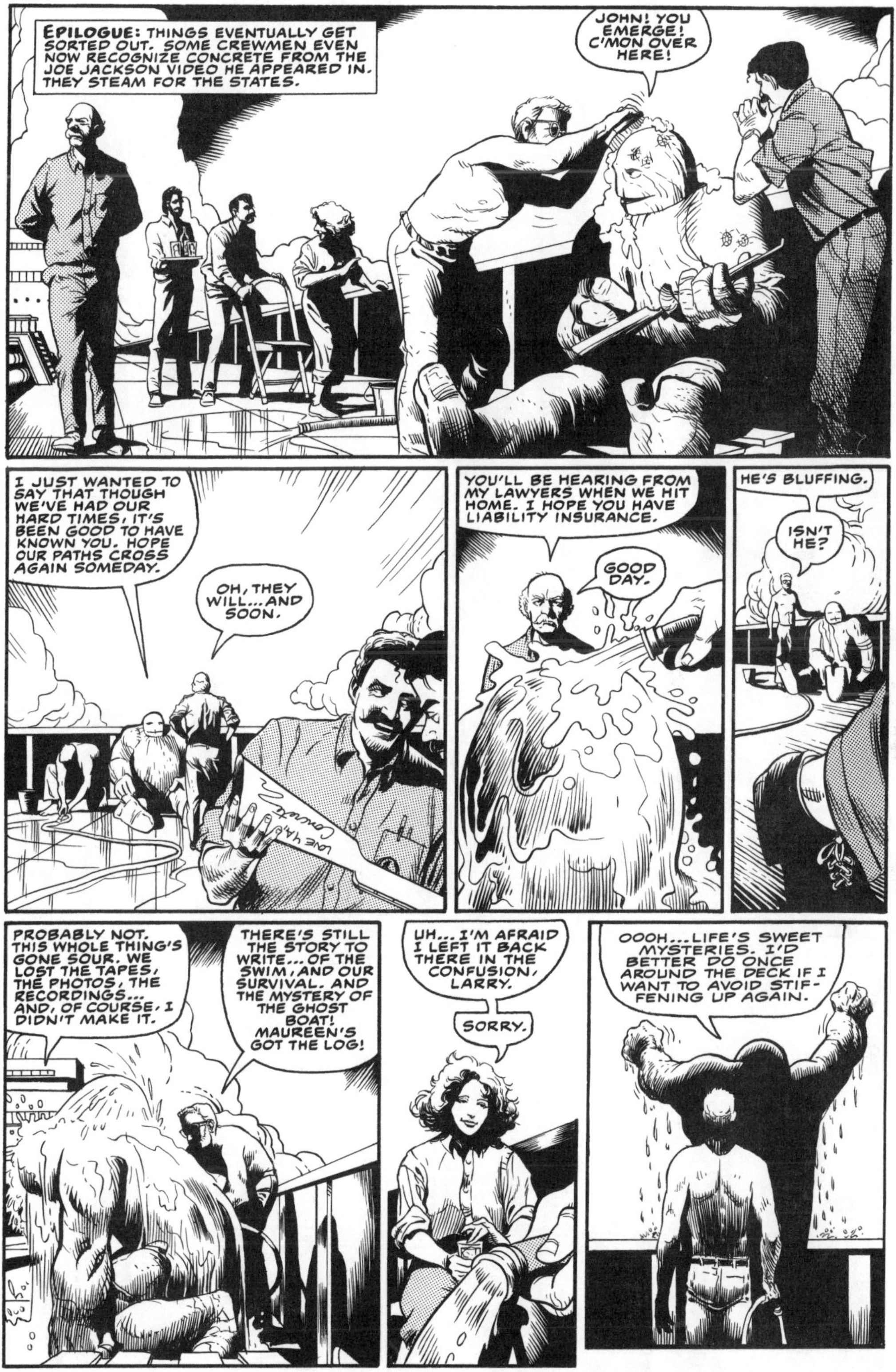
EPILOGUE: THINGS EVENTUALLY GET SORTED OUT. SOME CREWMEN EVEN NOW RECOGNIZE CONCRETE FROM THE JOE JACKSON VIDEO HE APPEARED IN. THEY STEAM FOR THE STATES.
JOHN! YOU EMERGE! C'MON OVER HERE!
I JUST WANTED TO SAY THAT THOUGH WE'VE HAD OUR HARD TIMES, IT'S BEEN GOOD TO HAVE KNOWN YOU. HOPE OUR PATHS CROSS AGAIN SOMEDAY.
OH, THEY WILL... AND SOON.
YOU'LL BE HEARING FROM MY LAWYERS WHEN WE HIT HOME. I HOPE YOU HAVE LIABILITY INSURANCE.
GOOD DAY.
HE'S BLUFFING.
ISN'T HE?
PROBABLY NOT. THIS WHOLE THING'S GONE SOUR. WE LOST THE TAPES, THE PHOTOS, THE RECORDINGS... AND, OF COURSE, I DIDN'T MAKE IT.
THERE'S STILL THE STORY TO WRITE... OF THE SWIM, AND OUR SURVIVAL. AND THE MYSTERY OF THE GHOST BOAT! MAUREEN'S GOT THE LOG!
UH... I'M AFRAID I LEFT IT BACK THERE IN THE CONFUSION, LARRY.
SORRY.
OOOH... LIFE'S SWEET MYSTERIES. I'D BETTER DO ONCE AROUND THE DECK IF I WANT TO AVOID STIF-FENING UP AGAIN.

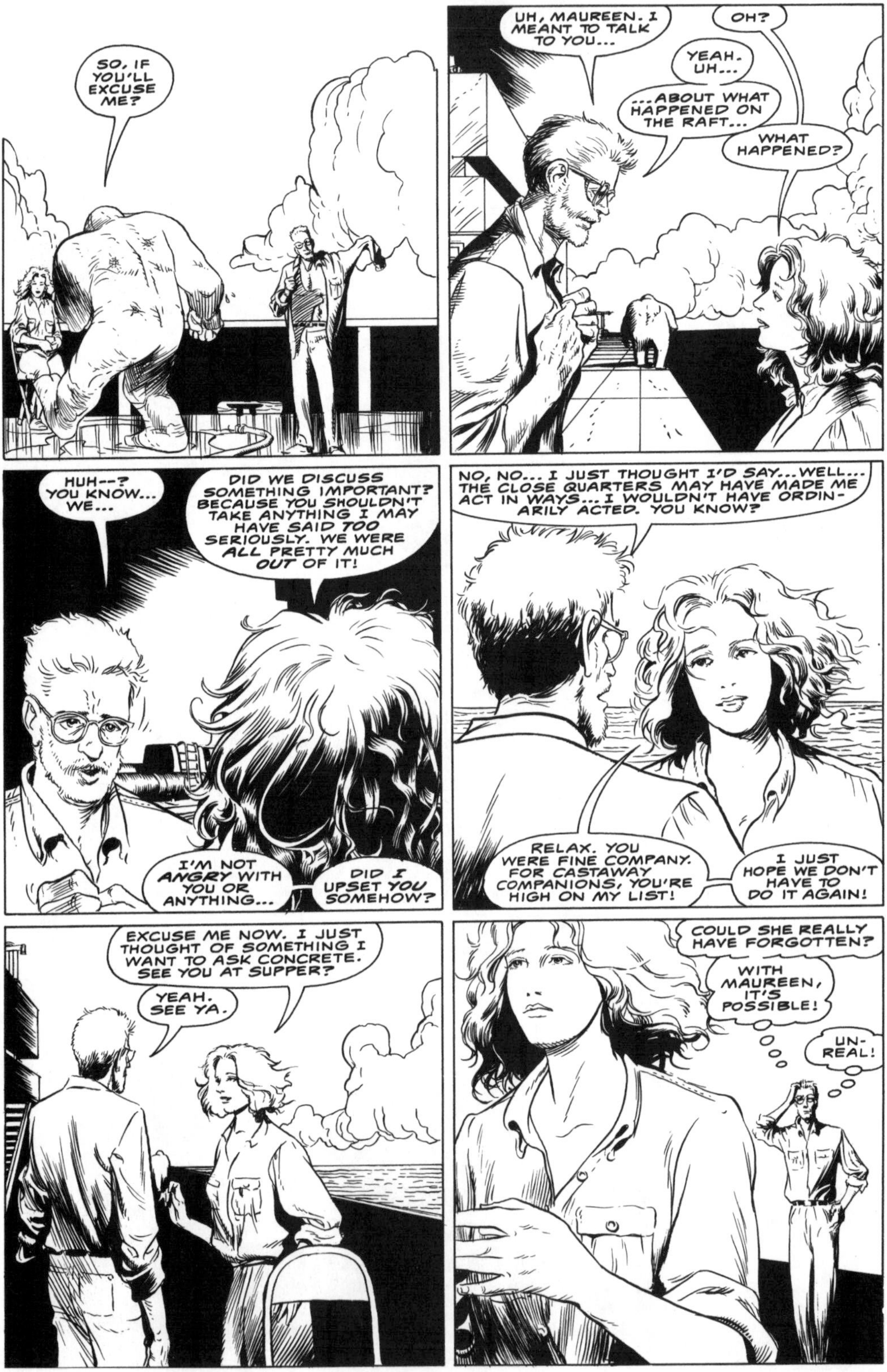
SO, IF YOU'LL EXCUSE ME?
UH, MAUREEN. I MEANT TO TALK TO YOU...
OH?
YEAH. UH...
...ABOUT WHAT HAPPENED ON THE RAFT...
WHAT HAPPENED?
HUH--? YOU KNOW... WE...
DID WE DISCUSS SOMETHING IMPORTANT? BECAUSE YOU SHOULDN'T TAKE ANYTHING I MAY HAVE SAID TOO SERIOUSLY. WE WERE ALL PRETTY MUCH OUT OF IT!
I'M NOT ANGRY WITH YOU OR ANYTHING...
DID I UPSET YOU SOMEHOW?
NO, NO... I JUST THOUGHT I'D SAY... WELL... THE CLOSE QUARTERS MAY HAVE MADE ME ACT IN WAYS... I WOULDN'T HAVE ORDINARILY ACTED. YOU KNOW?
RELAX. YOU WERE FINE COMPANY. FOR CASTAWAY COMPANIONS, YOU'RE HIGH ON MY LIST!
I JUST HOPE WE DON'T HAVE TO DO IT AGAIN!
EXCUSE ME NOW. I JUST THOUGHT OF SOMETHING I WANT TO ASK CONCRETE. SEE YOU AT SUPPER?
YEAH. SEE YA.
COULD SHE REALLY HAVE FORGOTTEN?
WITH MAUREEN, IT'S POSSIBLE!
UN-REAL!

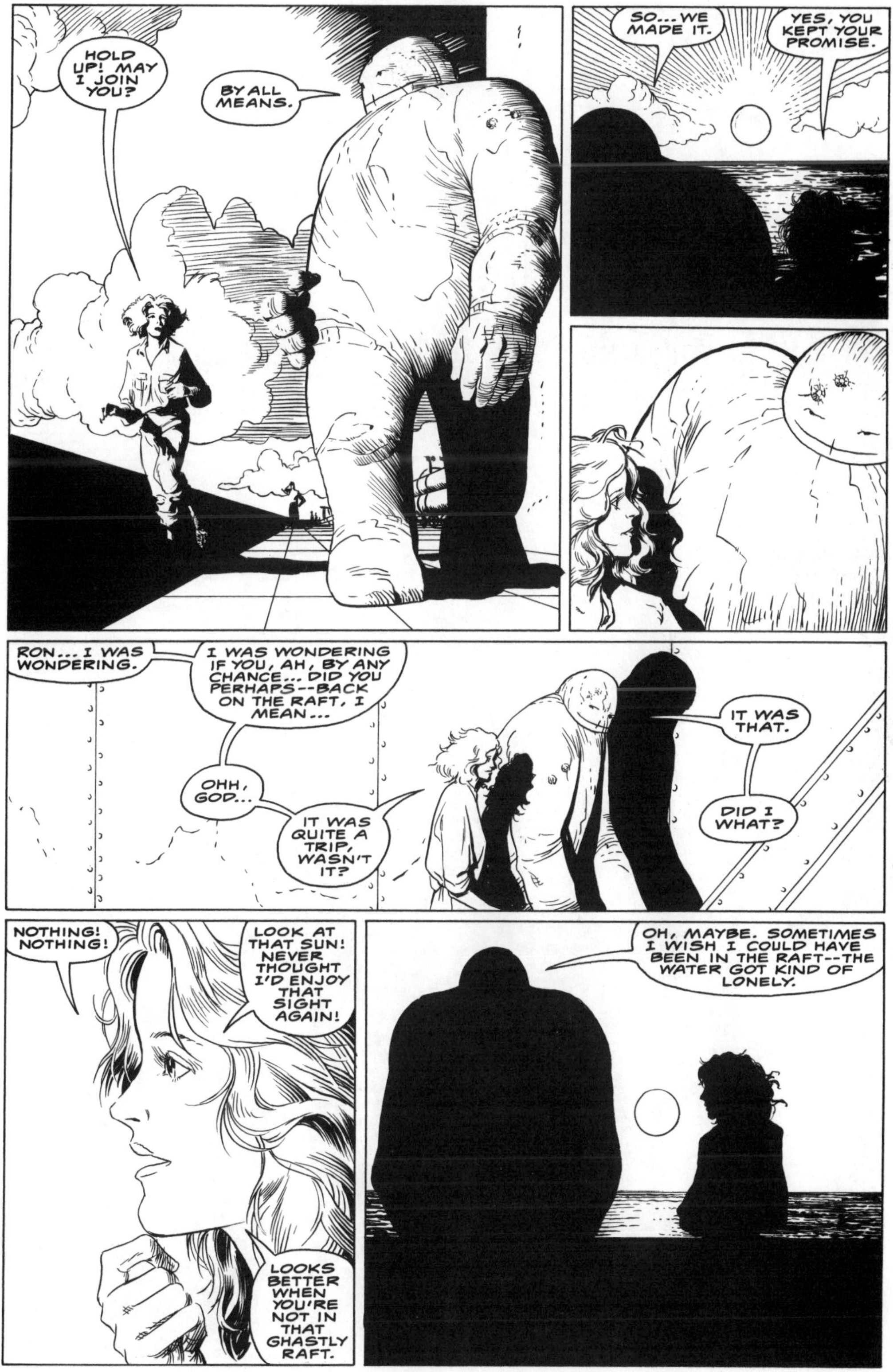
HOLD UP! MAY I JOIN YOU?
BY ALL MEANS.
SO... WE MADE IT.
YES, YOU KEPT YOUR PROMISE.
RON... I WAS WONDERING.
I WAS WONDERING IF YOU, AH, BY ANY CHANCE... DID YOU PERHAPS--BACK ON THE RAFT, I MEAN...
DID I WHAT?
IT WAS THAT.
OHH, GOD...
IT WAS QUITE A TRIP, WASN'T IT?
NOTHING! NOTHING!
LOOK AT THAT SUN! NEVER THOUGHT I'D ENJOY THAT SIGHT AGAIN!
LOOKS BETTER WHEN YOU'RE NOT IN THAT GHASTLY RAFT.
OH, MAYBE. SOMETIMES I WISH I COULD HAVE BEEN IN THE RAFT--THE WATER GOT KIND OF LONELY.

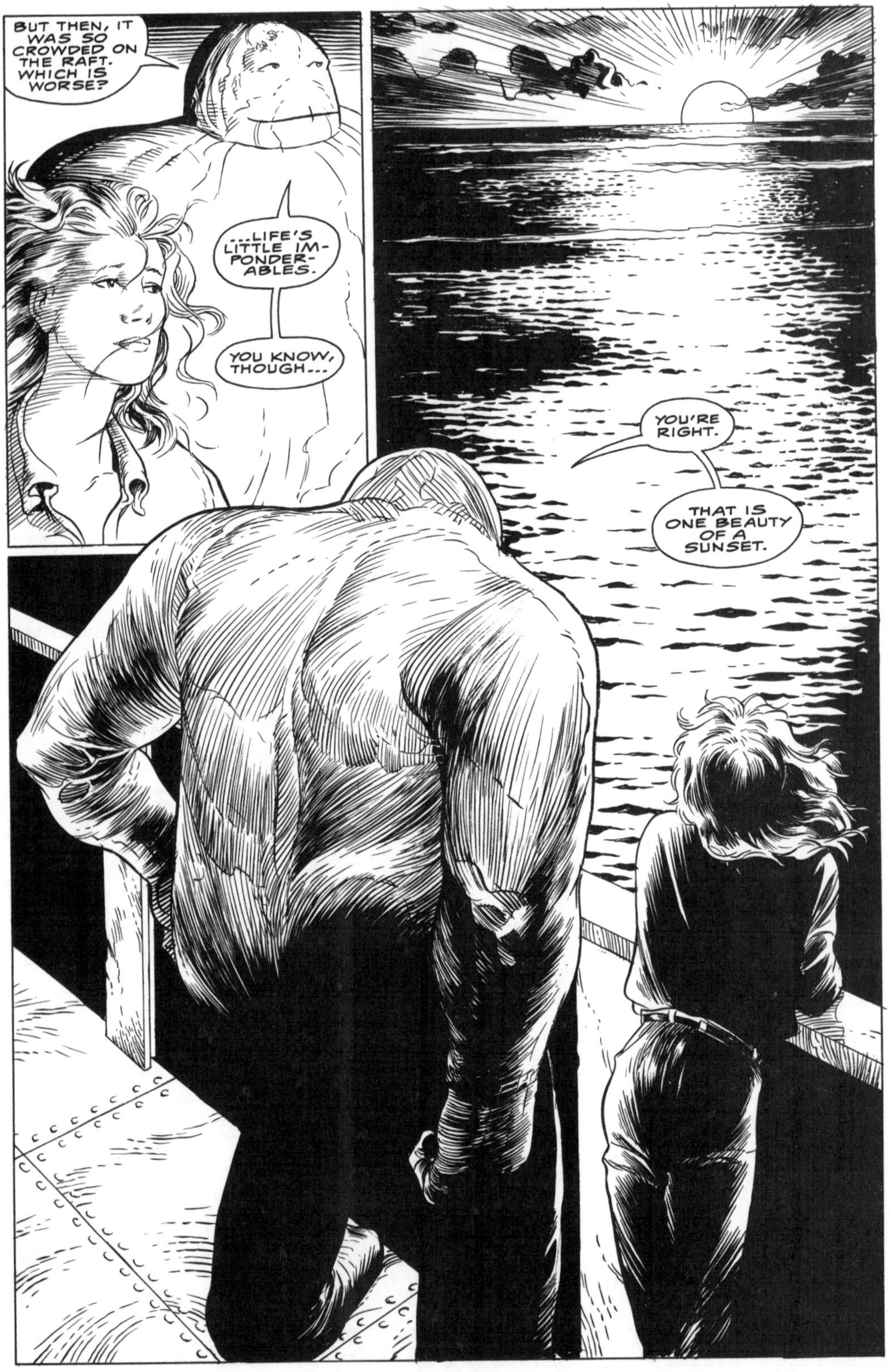
BUT THEN, IT WAS SO CROWDED ON THE RAFT. WHICH IS WORSE?
...LIFE'S LITTLE IMPONDERABLES.
YOU KNOW, THOUGH...
YOU'RE RIGHT.
THAT IS ONE BEAUTY OF A SUNSET.

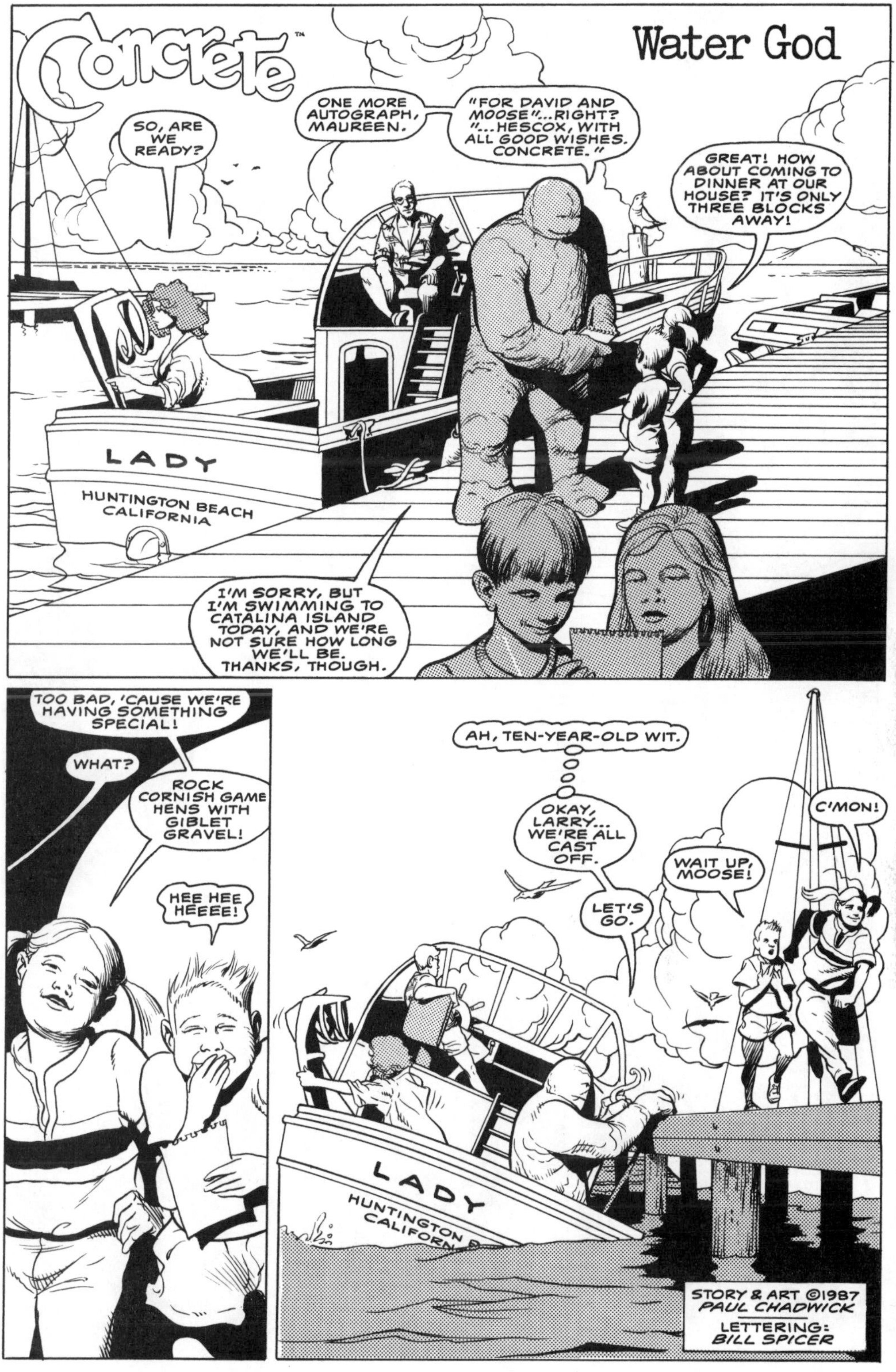
Concrete™
Water God
SO, ARE WE READY?
ONE MORE AUTOGRAPH, MAUREEN.
"FOR DAVID AND MOOSE"...RIGHT? "...HESCOX, WITH ALL GOOD WISHES. CONCRETE."
GREAT! HOW ABOUT COMING TO DINNER AT OUR HOUSE? IT'S ONLY THREE BLOCKS AWAY!
LADY
HUNTINGTON BEACH CALIFORNIA
I'M SORRY, BUT I'M SWIMMING TO CATALINA ISLAND TODAY, AND WE'RE NOT SURE HOW LONG WE'LL BE. THANKS, THOUGH.
TOO BAD, 'CAUSE WE'RE HAVING SOMETHING SPECIAL!
WHAT?
ROCK CORNISH GAME HENS WITH GIBLET GRAVEL!
HEE HEE HEEEE!
AH, TEN-YEAR-OLD WIT.
OKAY, LARRY... WE'RE ALL CAST OFF.
LET'S GO.
WAIT UP, MOOSE!
C'MON!
LADY
STORY & ART ©1987 PAUL CHADWICK
LETTERING: BILL SPICER

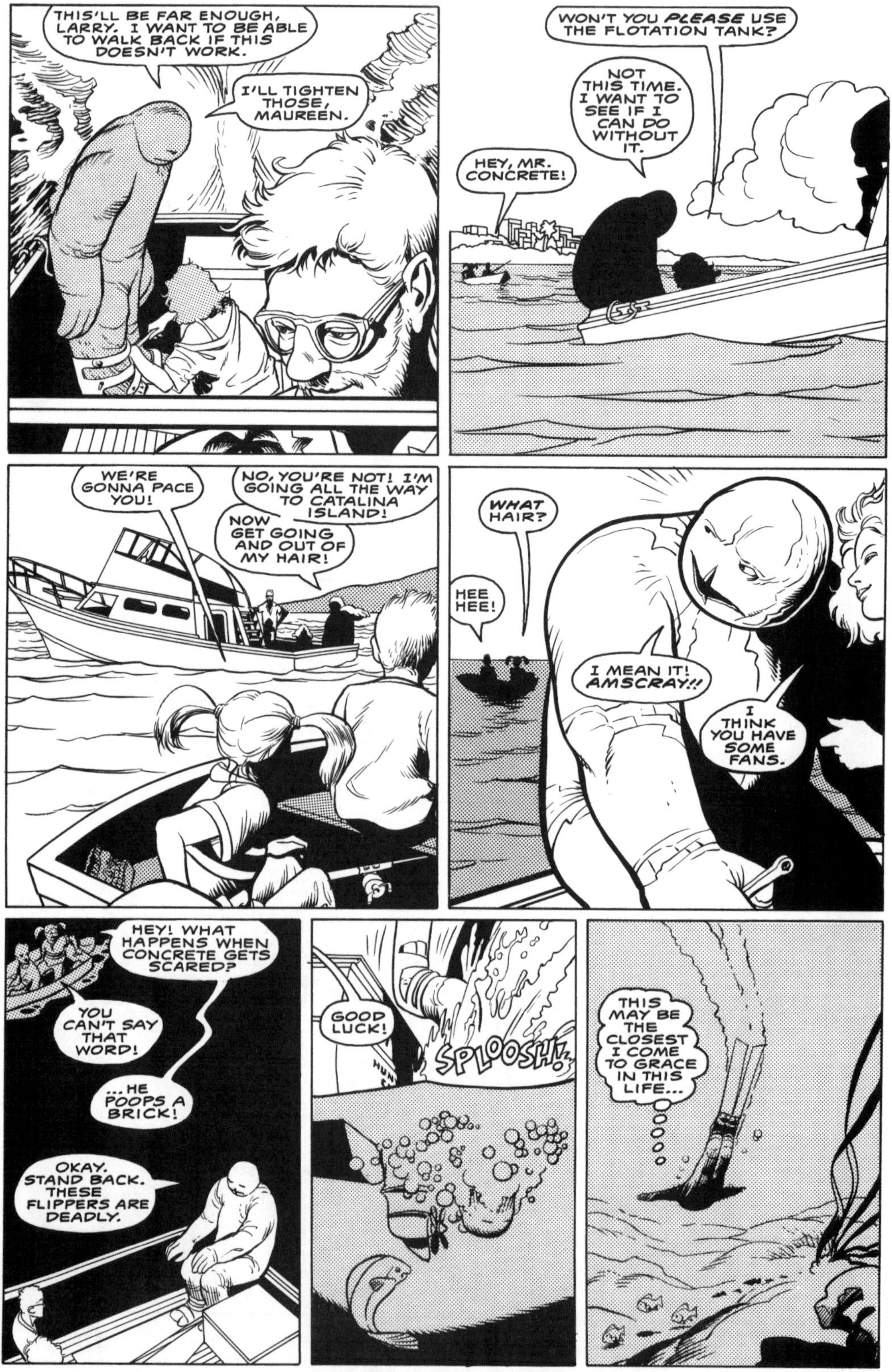
THIS'LL BE FAR ENOUGH, LARRY. I WANT TO BE ABLE TO WALK BACK IF THIS DOESN'T WORK.
I'LL TIGHTEN THOSE, MAUREEN.
WON'T YOU PLEASE USE THE FLOTATION TANK?
NOT THIS TIME. I WANT TO SEE IF I CAN DO WITHOUT IT.
HEY, MR. CONCRETE!
WE'RE GONNA PACE YOU!
NO, YOU'RE NOT! I'M GOING ALL THE WAY TO CATALINA ISLAND!
NOW GET GOING AND OUT OF MY HAIR!
WHAT HAIR?
HEE HEE!
I MEAN IT! AMSCRAY!!
I THINK YOU HAVE SOME FANS.
HEY! WHAT HAPPENS WHEN CONCRETE GETS SCARED?
YOU CAN'T SAY THAT WORD!
...HE POOPS A BRICK!
OKAY. STAND BACK. THESE FLIPPERS ARE DEADLY.
GOOD LUCK!
SPLOOSH!
THIS MAY BE THE CLOSEST I COME TO GRACE IN THIS LIFE...

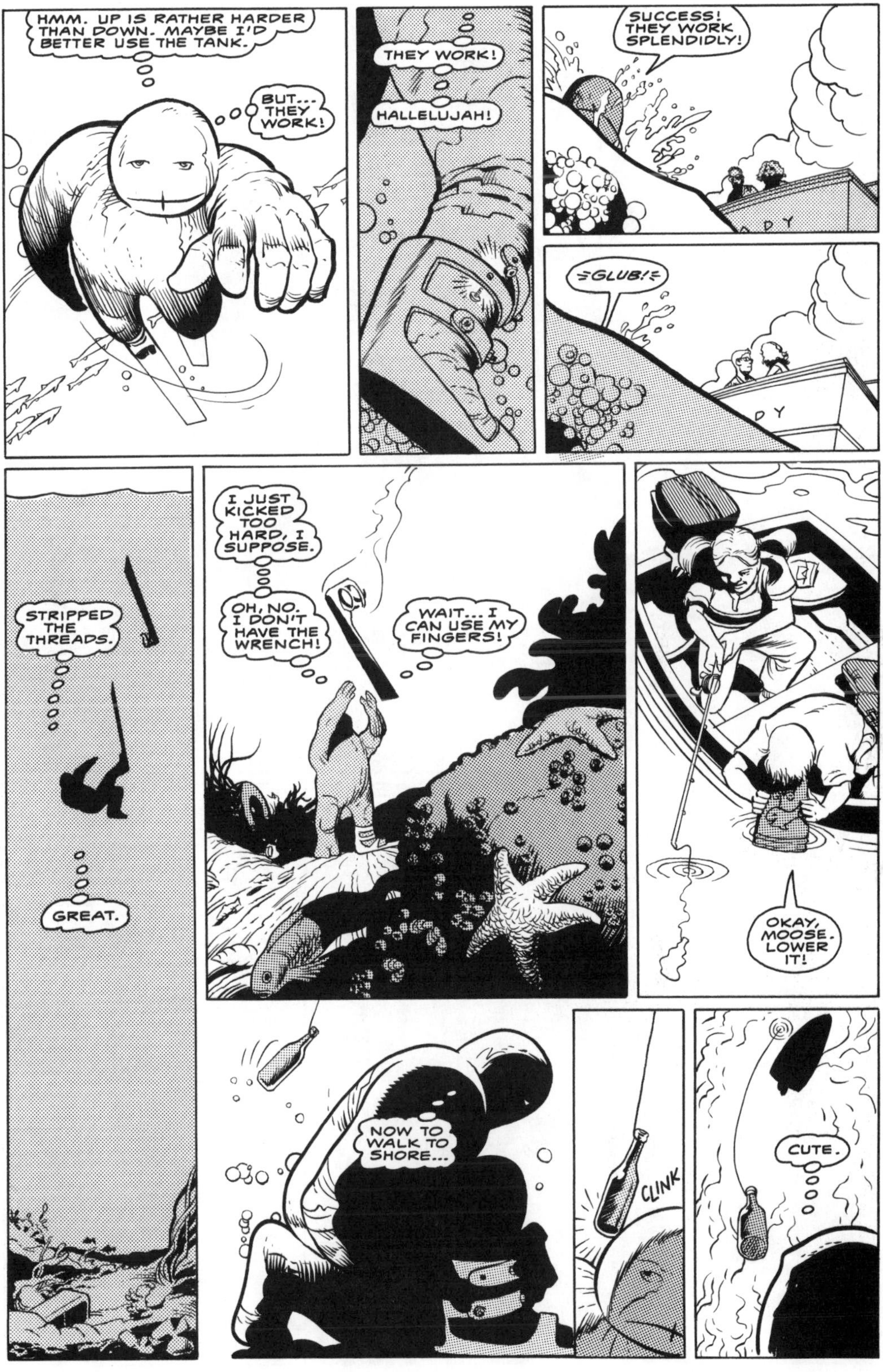
HMM. UP IS RATHER HARDER THAN DOWN. MAYBE I'D BETTER USE THE TANK.
BUT... THEY WORK!
THEY WORK!
HALLELUJAH!
SUCCESS! THEY WORK SPLENDIDLY!
≈GLUB!≈
STRIPPED THE THREADS.
GREAT.
I JUST KICKED TOO HARD, I SUPPOSE.
OH, NO. I DON'T HAVE THE WRENCH!
WAIT... I CAN USE MY FINGERS!
OKAY, MOOSE. LOWER IT!
NOW TO WALK TO SHORE...
CLINK
CUTE.

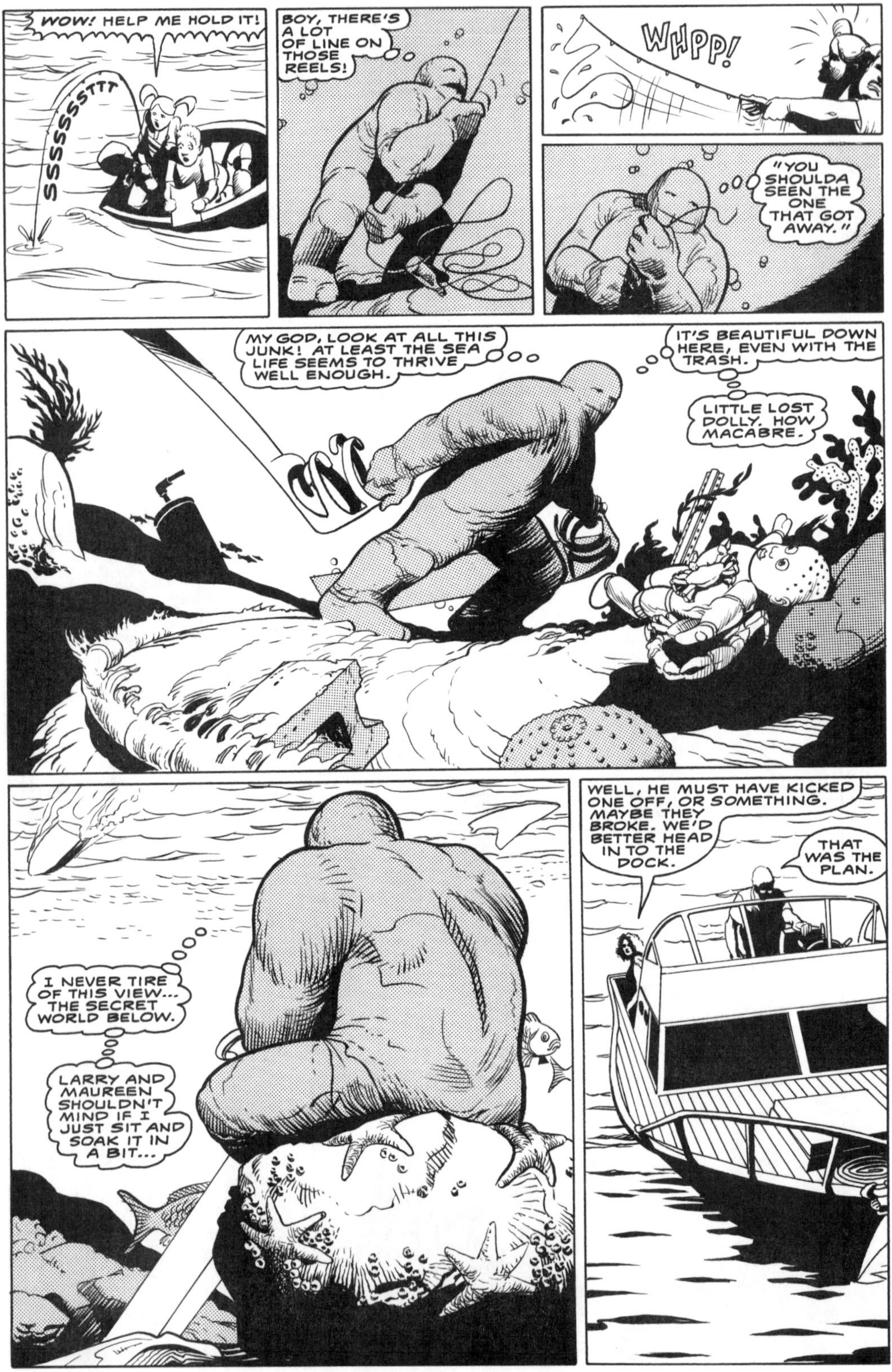
WOW! HELP ME HOLD IT!
SSSSSSSTTT
BOY, THERE'S A LOT OF LINE ON THOSE REELS!
WHPP!
"YOU SHOULDA SEEN THE ONE THAT GOT AWAY."
MY GOD, LOOK AT ALL THIS JUNK! AT LEAST THE SEA LIFE SEEMS TO THRIVE WELL ENOUGH.
IT'S BEAUTIFUL DOWN HERE, EVEN WITH THE TRASH.
LITTLE LOST DOLLY. HOW MACABRE.
I NEVER TIRE OF THIS VIEW... THE SECRET WORLD BELOW.
LARRY AND MAUREEN SHOULDN'T MIND IF I JUST SIT AND SOAK IT IN A BIT...
WELL, HE MUST HAVE KICKED ONE OFF, OR SOMETHING. MAYBE THEY BROKE. WE'D BETTER HEAD IN TO THE DOCK.
THAT WAS THE PLAN.

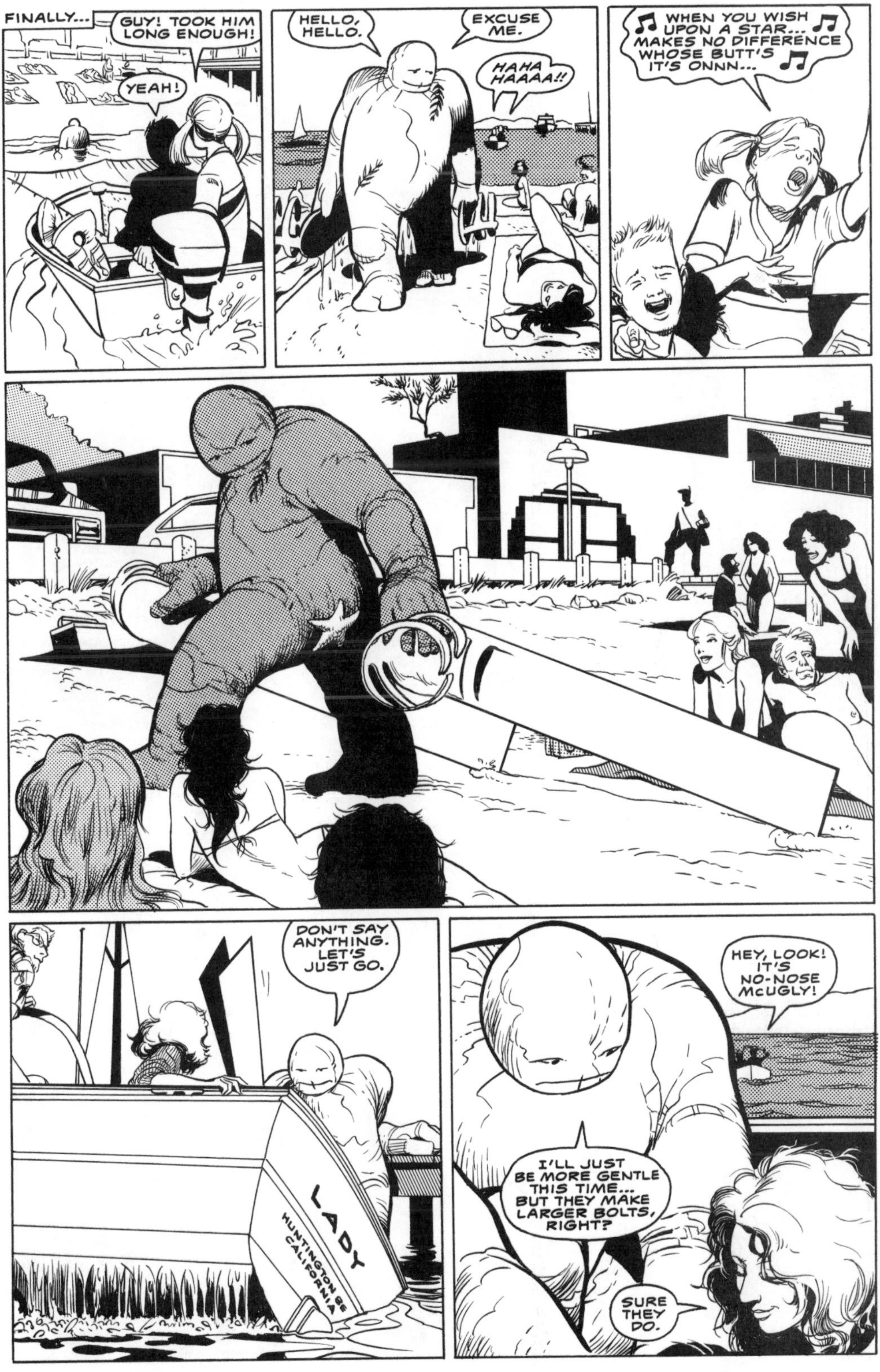
FINALLY...
GUY! TOOK HIM LONG ENOUGH!
YEAH!
HELLO, HELLO.
EXCUSE ME.
HAHA HAAAA!!
WHEN YOU WISH UPON A STAR... MAKES NO DIFFERENCE WHOSE BUTT'S IT'S ONNN...
DON'T SAY ANYTHING. LET'S JUST GO.
LADY
HUNTINGTON BE CALIFORNIA
HEY, LOOK! IT'S NO-NOSE McUGLY!
I'LL JUST BE MORE GENTLE THIS TIME... BUT THEY MAKE LARGER BOLTS, RIGHT?
SURE THEY DO.

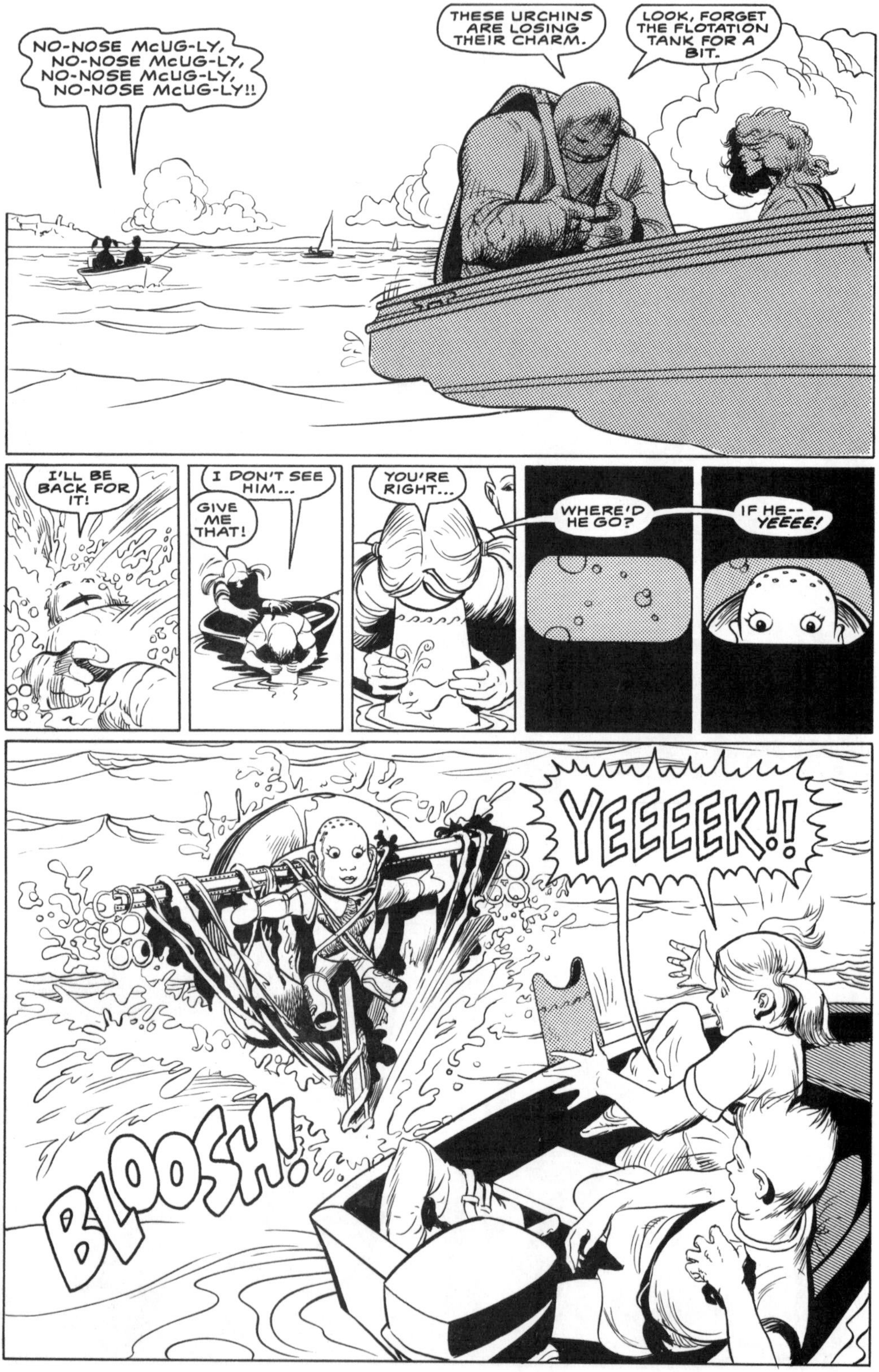

NO-NOSE McUG-LY, NO-NOSE McUG-LY, NO-NOSE McUG-LY, NO-NOSE McUG-LY!!
THESE URCHINS ARE LOSING THEIR CHARM.
LOOK, FORGET THE FLOTATION TANK FOR A BIT.
I'LL BE BACK FOR IT!
I DON'T SEE HIM...
GIVE ME THAT!
YOU'RE RIGHT...
WHERE'D HE GO?
IF HE-- YEEEE!
YEEEEK!!
BLOOSH!

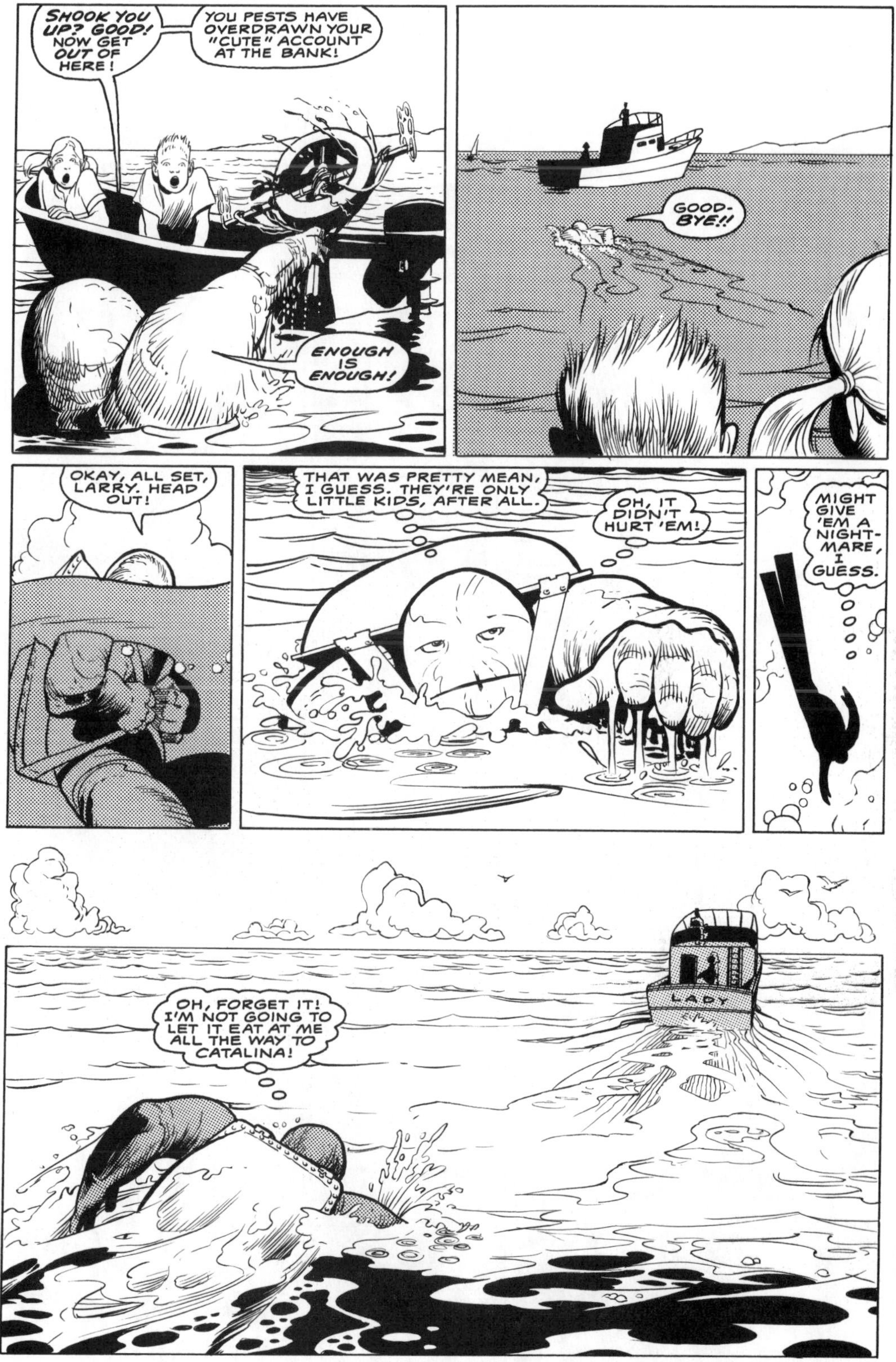
SHOOK YOU UP? GOOD! NOW GET OUT OF HERE!
YOU PESTS HAVE OVERDRAWN YOUR "CUTE" ACCOUNT AT THE BANK!
ENOUGH IS ENOUGH!
GOOD-BYE!!
OKAY, ALL SET, LARRY. HEAD OUT!
THAT WAS PRETTY MEAN, I GUESS. THEY'RE ONLY LITTLE KIDS, AFTER ALL.
OH, IT DIDN'T HURT 'EM!
MIGHT GIVE 'EM A NIGHT-MARE, I GUESS.
LADY
OH, FORGET IT! I'M NOT GOING TO LET IT EAT AT ME ALL THE WAY TO CATALINA!

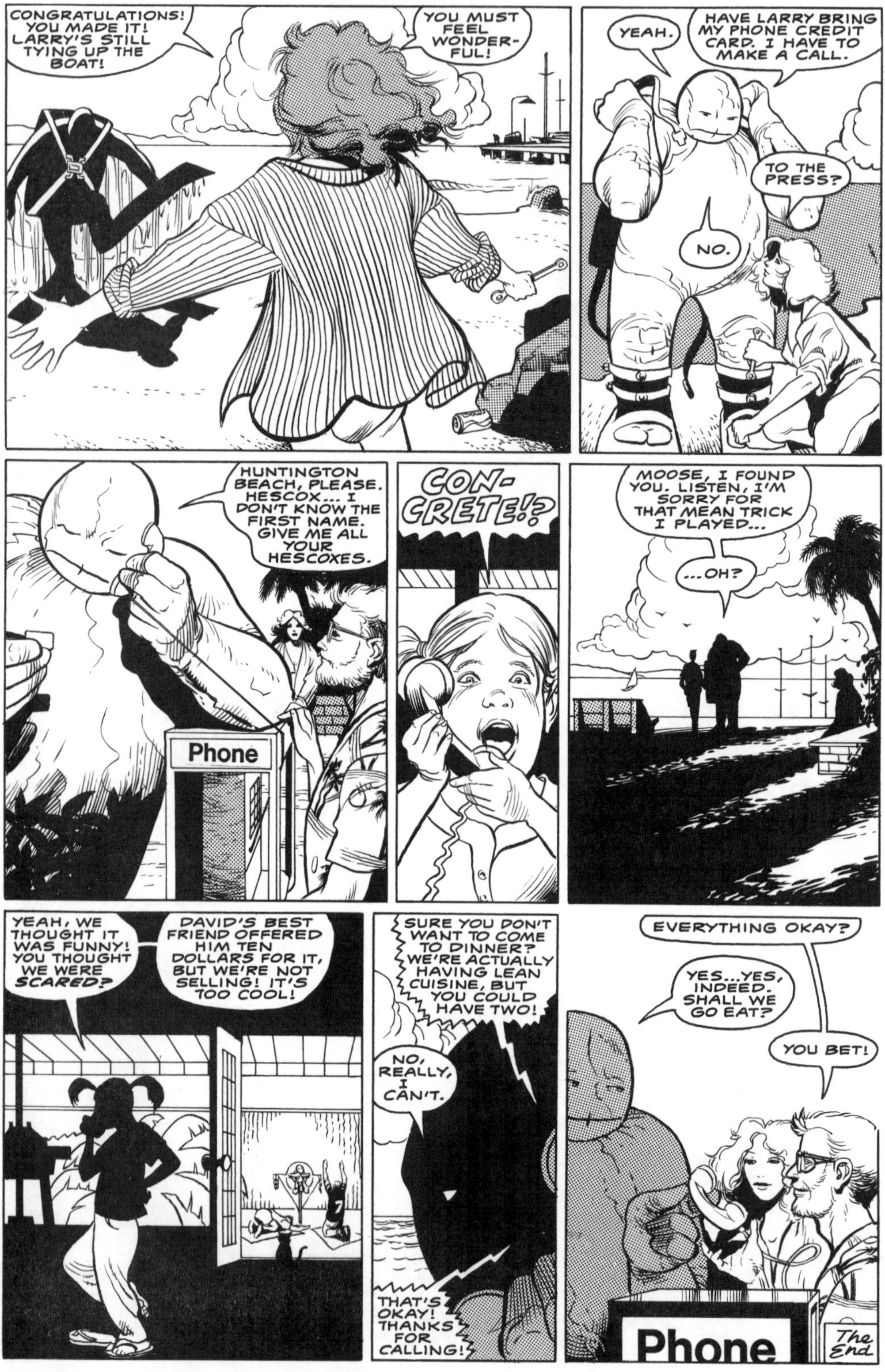
CONGRATULATIONS! YOU MADE IT! LARRY'S STILL TYING UP THE BOAT!
YOU MUST FEEL WONDER-FUL!
YEAH.
HAVE LARRY BRING MY PHONE CREDIT CARD. I HAVE TO MAKE A CALL.
TO THE PRESS?
NO.
HUNTINGTON BEACH, PLEASE. HESCOX... I DON'T KNOW THE FIRST NAME. GIVE ME ALL YOUR HESCOXES.
Phone
CON-CRETE!?
MOOSE, I FOUND YOU. LISTEN, I'M SORRY FOR THAT MEAN TRICK I PLAYED...
...OH?
YEAH, WE THOUGHT IT WAS FUNNY! YOU THOUGHT WE WERE SCARED?
DAVID'S BEST FRIEND OFFERED HIM TEN DOLLARS FOR IT, BUT WE'RE NOT SELLING! IT'S TOO COOL!
SURE YOU DON'T WANT TO COME TO DINNER? WE'RE ACTUALLY HAVING LEAN CUISINE, BUT YOU COULD HAVE TWO!
NO, REALLY, I CAN'T.
THAT'S OKAY! THANKS FOR CALLING!
EVERYTHING OKAY?
YES...YES, INDEED. SHALL WE GO EAT?
YOU BET!
Phone
The End

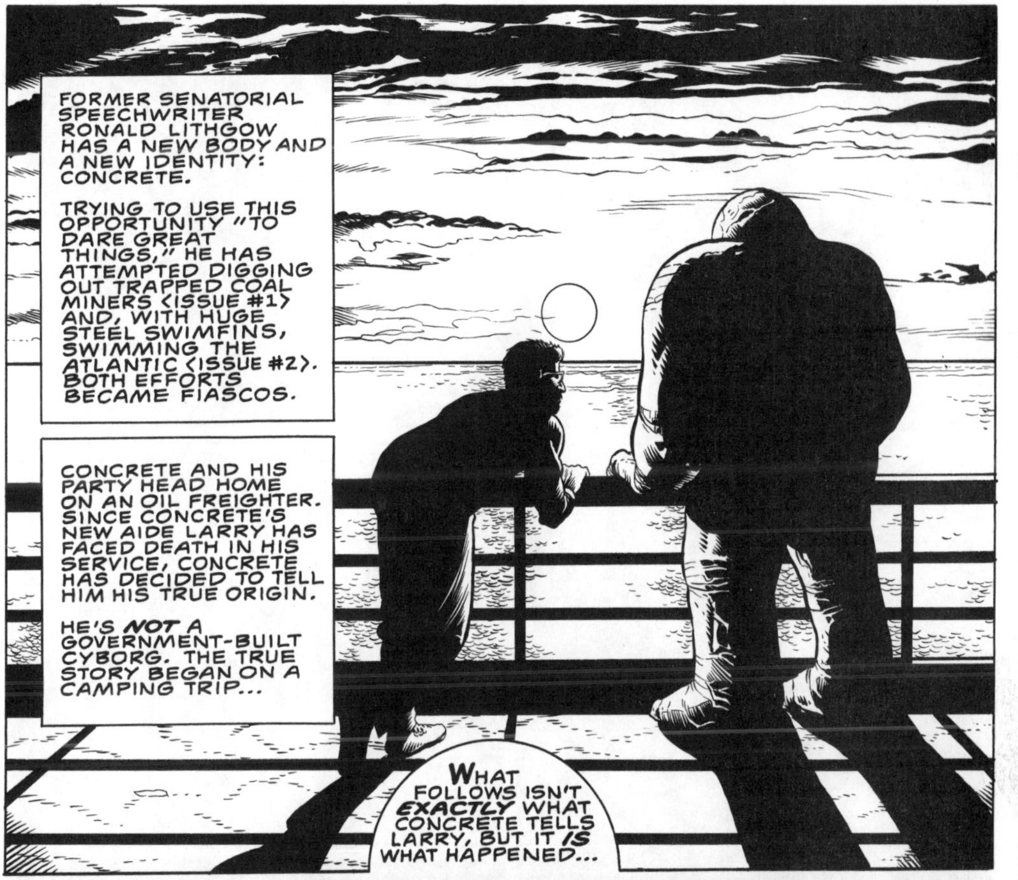
FORMER SENATORIAL SPEECHWRITER RONALD LITHGOW HAS A NEW BODY AND A NEW IDENTITY: CONCRETE.
TRYING TO USE THIS OPPORTUNITY "TO DARE GREAT THINGS," HE HAS ATTEMPTED DIGGING OUT TRAPPED COAL MINERS <ISSUE #1> AND, WITH HUGE STEEL SWIMFINS, SWIMMING THE ATLANTIC <ISSUE #2>. BOTH EFFORTS BECAME FIASCOS.
CONCRETE AND HIS PARTY HEAD HOME ON AN OIL FREIGHTER. SINCE CONCRETE'S NEW AIDE LARRY HAS FACED DEATH IN HIS SERVICE, CONCRETE HAS DECIDED TO TELL HIM HIS TRUE ORIGIN.
HE'S NOT A GOVERNMENT-BUILT CYBORG. THE TRUE STORY BEGAN ON A CAMPING TRIP...
WHAT FOLLOWS ISN'T EXACTLY WHAT CONCRETE TELLS LARRY, BUT IT IS WHAT HAPPENED...

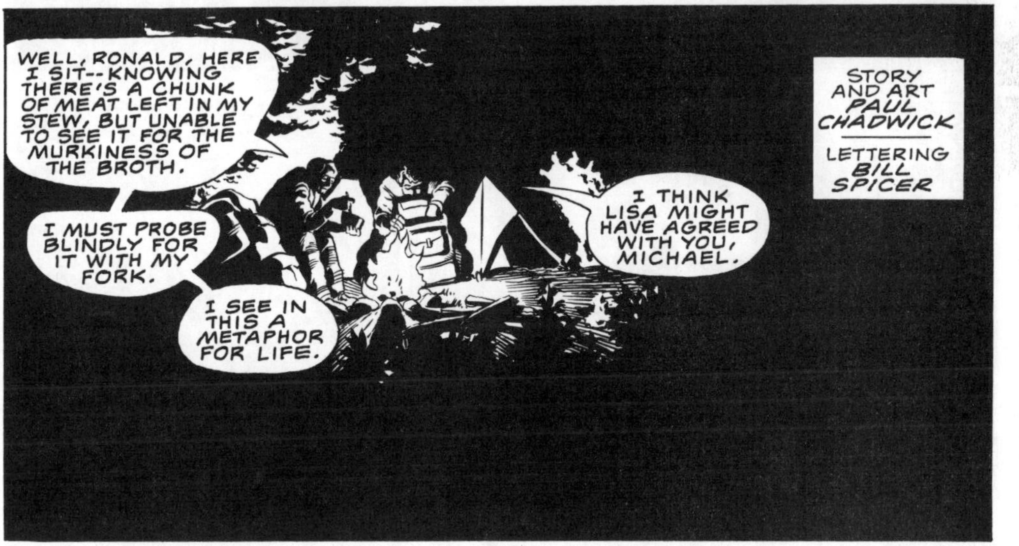
WELL, RONALD, HERE I SIT--KNOWING THERE'S A CHUNK OF MEAT LEFT IN MY STEW, BUT UNABLE TO SEE IT FOR THE MURKINESS OF THE BROTH.
I MUST PROBE BLINDLY FOR IT WITH MY FORK.
I SEE IN THIS A METAPHOR FOR LIFE.
I THINK LISA MIGHT HAVE AGREED WITH YOU, MICHAEL.
STORY AND ART PAUL CHADWICK
LETTERING BILL SPICER

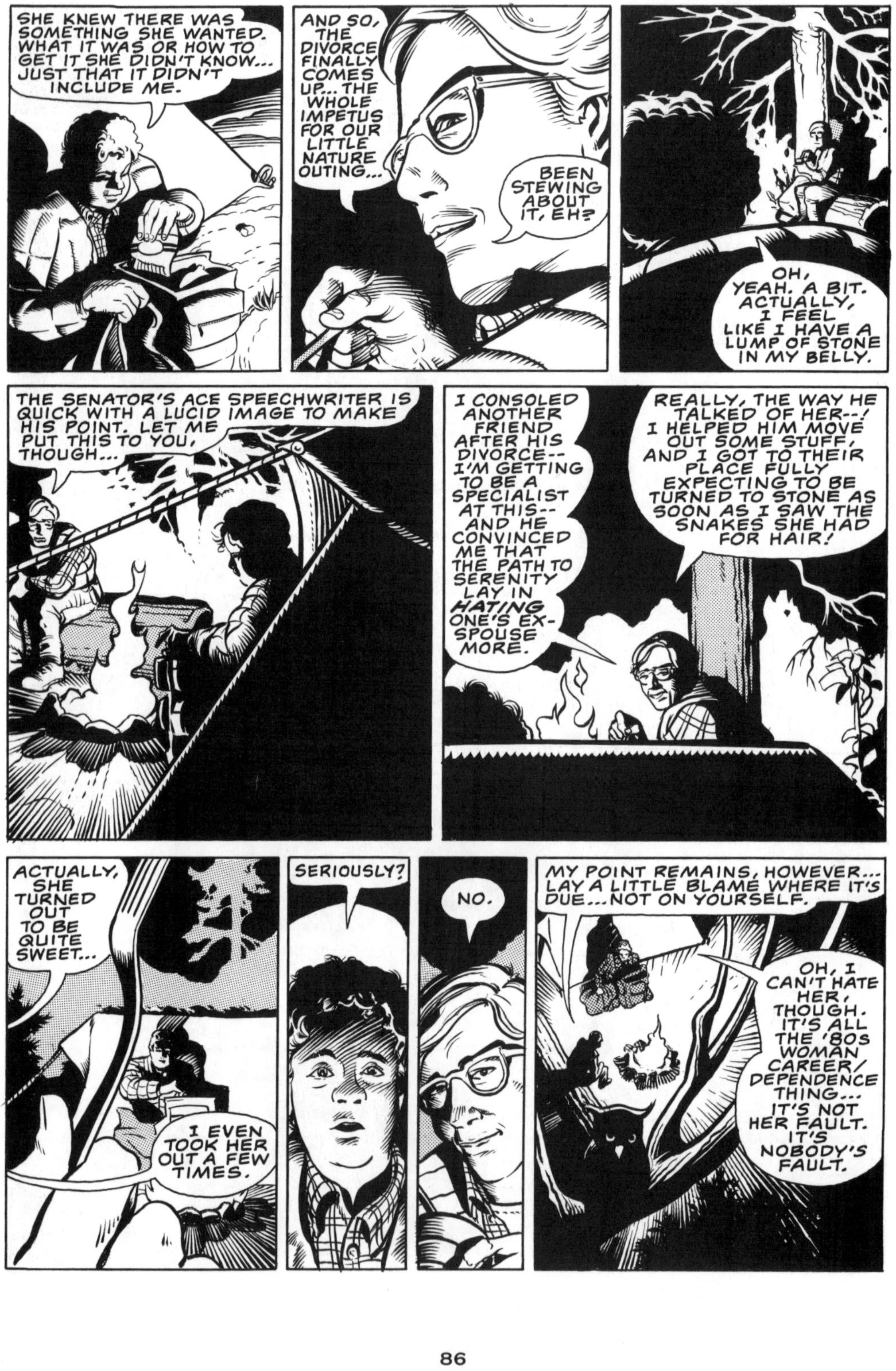

SHE KNEW THERE WAS SOMETHING SHE WANTED. WHAT IT WAS OR HOW TO GET IT SHE DIDN'T KNOW... JUST THAT IT DIDN'T INCLUDE ME.
AND SO, THE DIVORCE FINALLY COMES UP... THE WHOLE IMPETUS FOR OUR LITTLE NATURE OUTING...
BEEN STEWING ABOUT IT, EH?
OH, YEAH. A BIT. ACTUALLY, I FEEL LIKE I HAVE A LUMP OF STONE IN MY BELLY.
THE SENATOR'S ACE SPEECHWRITER IS QUICK WITH A LUCID IMAGE TO MAKE HIS POINT. LET ME PUT THIS TO YOU, THOUGH...
I CONSOLED ANOTHER FRIEND AFTER HIS DIVORCE-- I'M GETTING TO BE A SPECIALIST AT THIS-- AND HE CONVINCED ME THAT THE PATH TO SERENITY LAY IN *HATING* ONE'S EX-SPOUSE MORE.
REALLY, THE WAY HE TALKED OF HER--! I HELPED HIM MOVE OUT SOME STUFF, AND I GOT TO THEIR PLACE FULLY EXPECTING TO BE TURNED TO STONE AS SOON AS I SAW THE SNAKES SHE HAD FOR HAIR!
ACTUALLY, SHE TURNED OUT TO BE QUITE SWEET...
I EVEN TOOK HER OUT A FEW TIMES.
SERIOUSLY?
NO.
MY POINT REMAINS, HOWEVER... LAY A LITTLE BLAME WHERE IT'S DUE... NOT ON YOURSELF.
OH, I CAN'T HATE HER, THOUGH. IT'S ALL THE '80S WOMAN CAREER/DEPENDENCE THING... IT'S NOT HER FAULT. IT'S NOBODY'S FAULT.

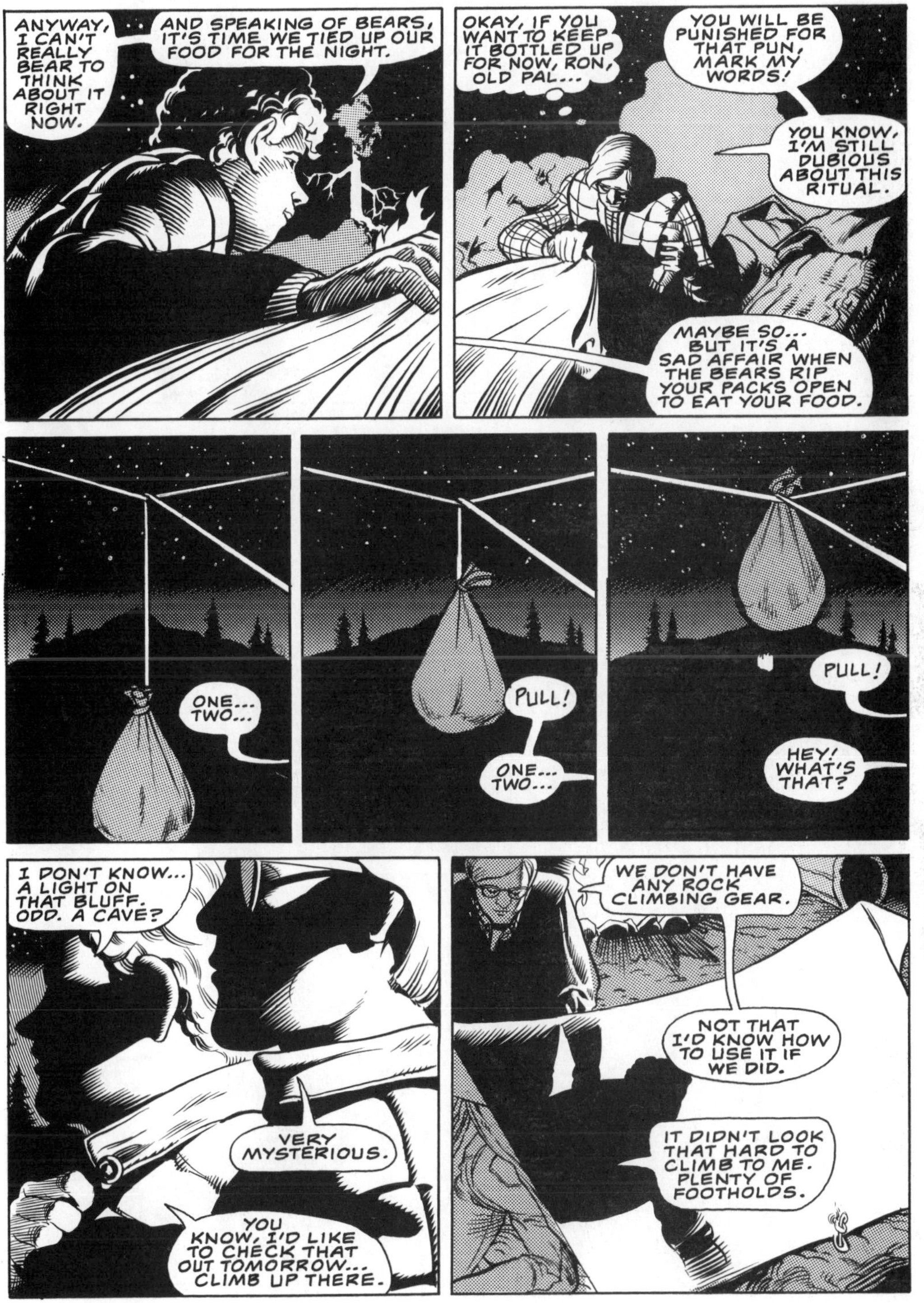
ANYWAY, I CAN'T REALLY BEAR TO THINK ABOUT IT RIGHT NOW.
AND SPEAKING OF BEARS, IT'S TIME WE TIED UP OUR FOOD FOR THE NIGHT.
OKAY, IF YOU WANT TO KEEP IT BOTTLED UP FOR NOW, RON, OLD PAL...
YOU WILL BE PUNISHED FOR THAT PUN, MARK MY WORDS!
YOU KNOW, I'M STILL DUBIOUS ABOUT THIS RITUAL.
MAYBE SO... BUT IT'S A SAD AFFAIR WHEN THE BEARS RIP YOUR PACKS OPEN TO EAT YOUR FOOD.
ONE... TWO...
PULL!
ONE... TWO...
PULL!
HEY! WHAT'S THAT?
I DON'T KNOW... A LIGHT ON THAT BLUFF. ODD. A CAVE?
VERY MYSTERIOUS.
YOU KNOW, I'D LIKE TO CHECK THAT OUT TOMORROW... CLIMB UP THERE.
WE DON'T HAVE ANY ROCK CLIMBING GEAR.
NOT THAT I'D KNOW HOW TO USE IT IF WE DID.
IT DIDN'T LOOK THAT HARD TO CLIMB TO ME. PLENTY OF FOOTHOLDS.

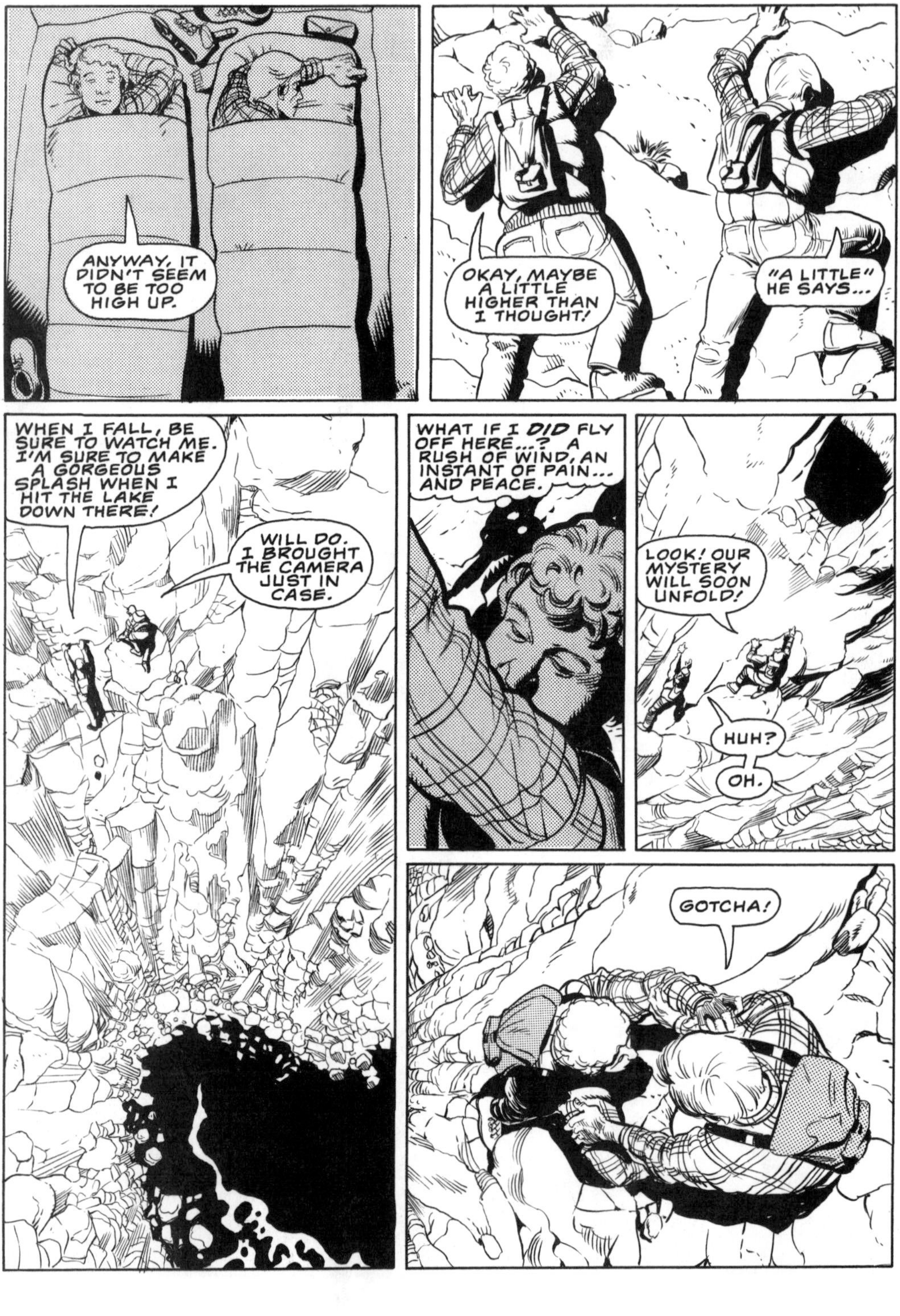

ANYWAY, IT DIDN'T SEEM TO BE TOO HIGH UP.
OKAY, MAYBE A LITTLE HIGHER THAN I THOUGHT!
"A LITTLE" HE SAYS...
WHEN I FALL, BE SURE TO WATCH ME. I'M SURE TO MAKE A GORGEOUS SPLASH WHEN I HIT THE LAKE DOWN THERE!
WILL DO. I BROUGHT THE CAMERA JUST IN CASE.
WHAT IF I DID FLY OFF HERE...? A RUSH OF WIND, AN INSTANT OF PAIN... AND PEACE.
LOOK! OUR MYSTERY WILL SOON UNFOLD!
HUH?
OH.
GOTCHA!

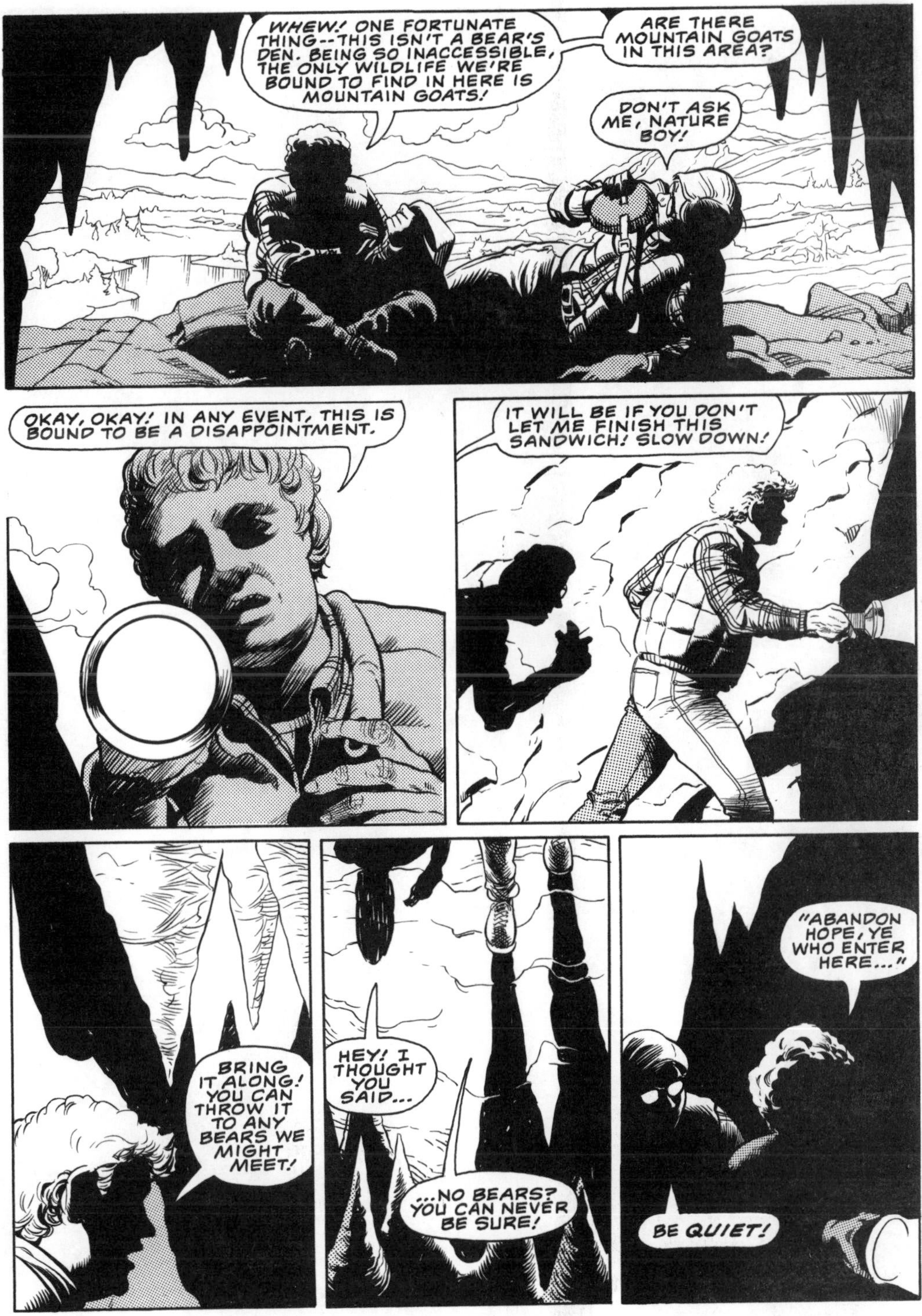
WHEW! ONE FORTUNATE THING--THIS ISN'T A BEAR'S DEN. BEING SO INACCESSIBLE, THE ONLY WILDLIFE WE'RE BOUND TO FIND IN HERE IS MOUNTAIN GOATS!
ARE THERE MOUNTAIN GOATS IN THIS AREA?
DON'T ASK ME, NATURE BOY!
OKAY, OKAY! IN ANY EVENT, THIS IS BOUND TO BE A DISAPPOINTMENT.
IT WILL BE IF YOU DON'T LET ME FINISH THIS SANDWICH! SLOW DOWN!
BRING IT ALONG! YOU CAN THROW IT TO ANY BEARS WE MIGHT MEET!
HEY! I THOUGHT YOU SAID...
...NO BEARS? YOU CAN NEVER BE SURE!
"ABANDON HOPE, YE WHO ENTER HERE..."
BE QUIET!

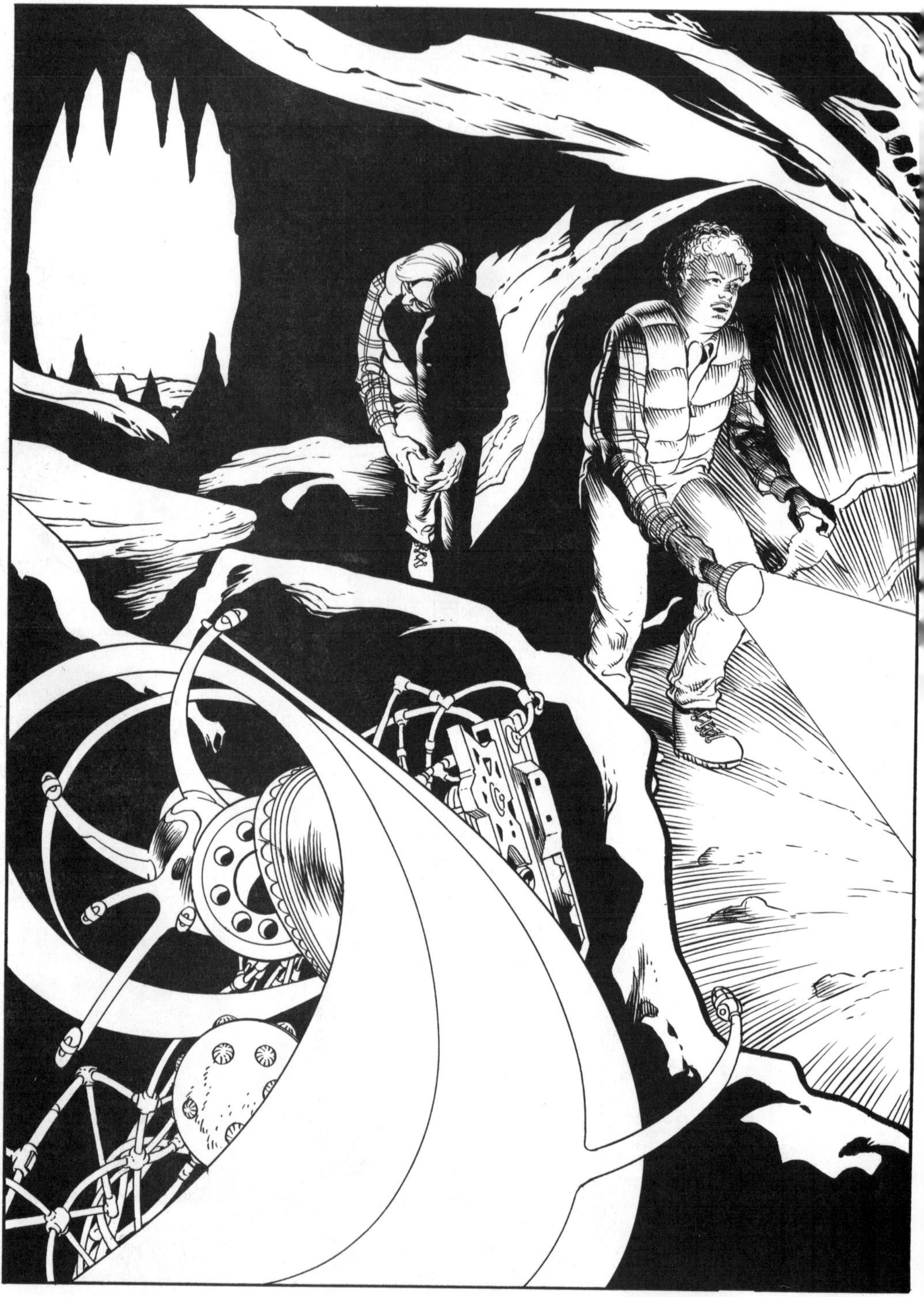

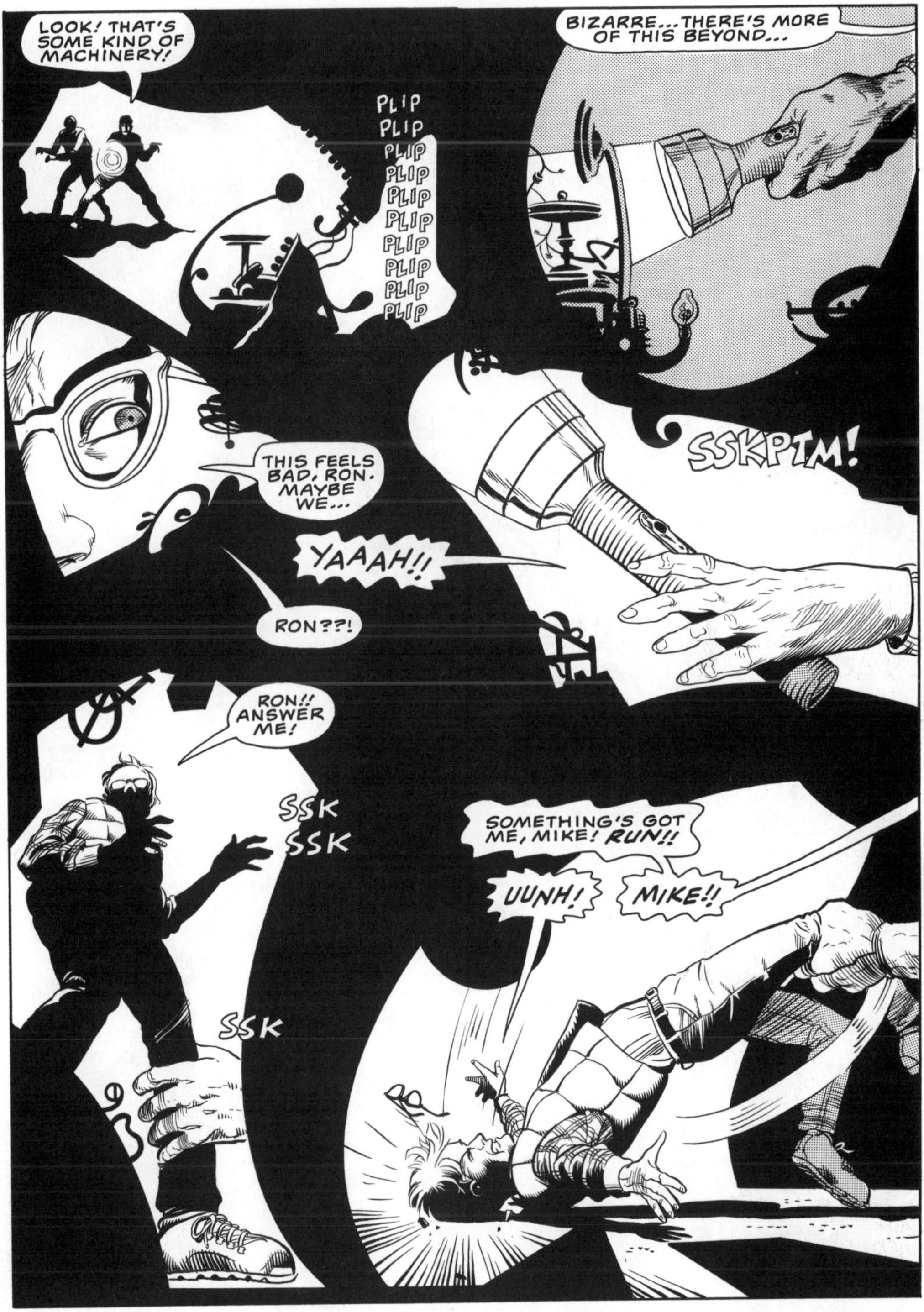
LOOK! THAT'S SOME KIND OF MACHINERY!
PLIP
PLIP
PLIP
PLIP
PLIP
PLIP
PLIP
PLIP
PLIP
PLIP
BIZARRE... THERE'S MORE OF THIS BEYOND...
THIS FEELS BAD, RON. MAYBE WE...
SSKPTM!
YAAAH!!
RON??!
RON!! ANSWER ME!
SSK
SSK
SSK
SOMETHING'S GOT ME, MIKE! RUN!!
UUNH!
MIKE!!

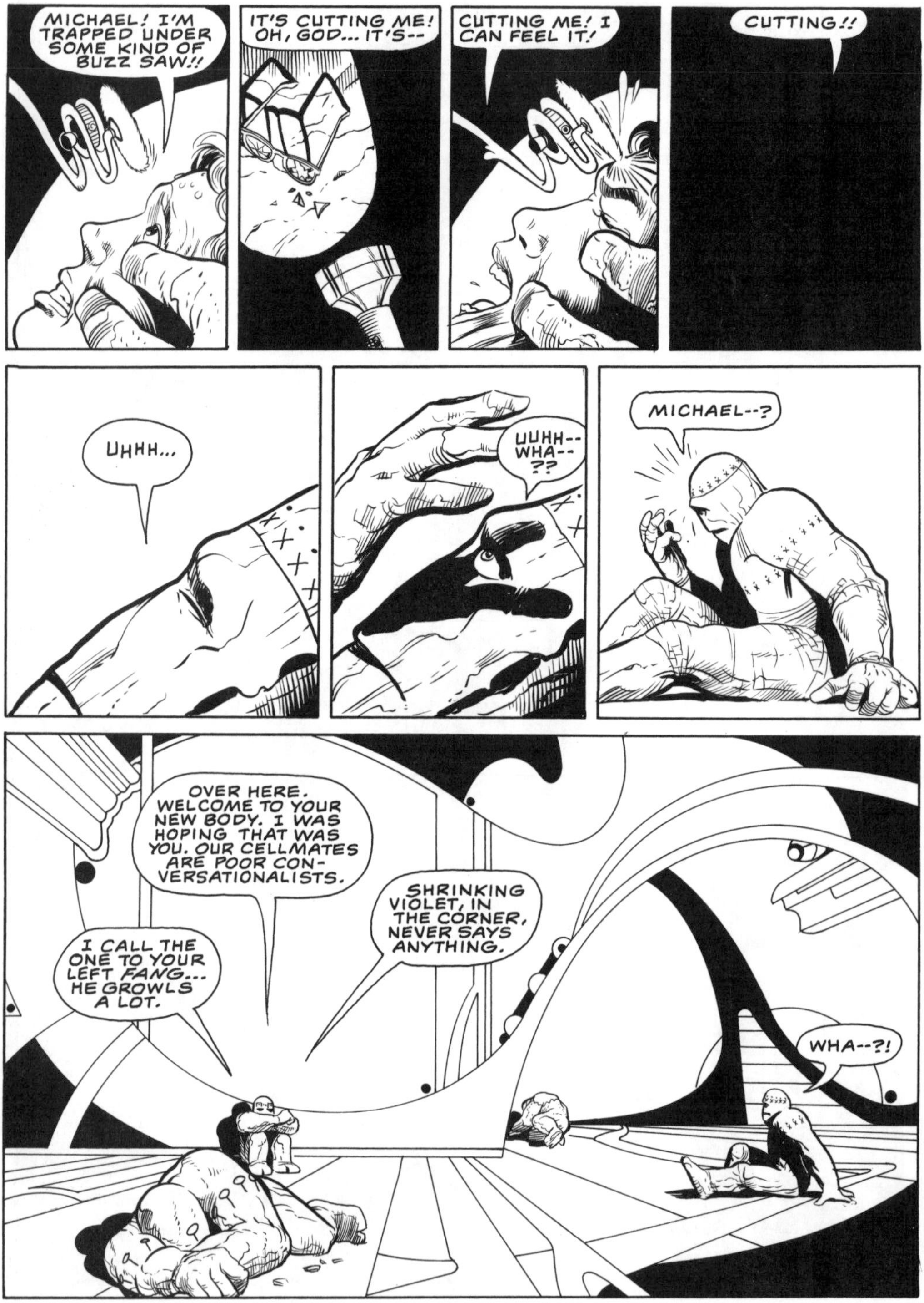
MICHAEL! I'M TRAPPED UNDER SOME KIND OF BUZZ SAW!!
IT'S CUTTING ME! OH, GOD... IT'S--
CUTTING ME! I CAN FEEL IT!
CUTTING!!
UHHH...
UUHH-- WHA-- ??
MICHAEL--?
OVER HERE. WELCOME TO YOUR NEW BODY. I WAS HOPING THAT WAS YOU. OUR CELLMATES ARE POOR CONVERSATIONALISTS.
I CALL THE ONE TO YOUR LEFT FANG... HE GROWLS A LOT.
SHRINKING VIOLET, IN THE CORNER, NEVER SAYS ANYTHING.
WHA--?!

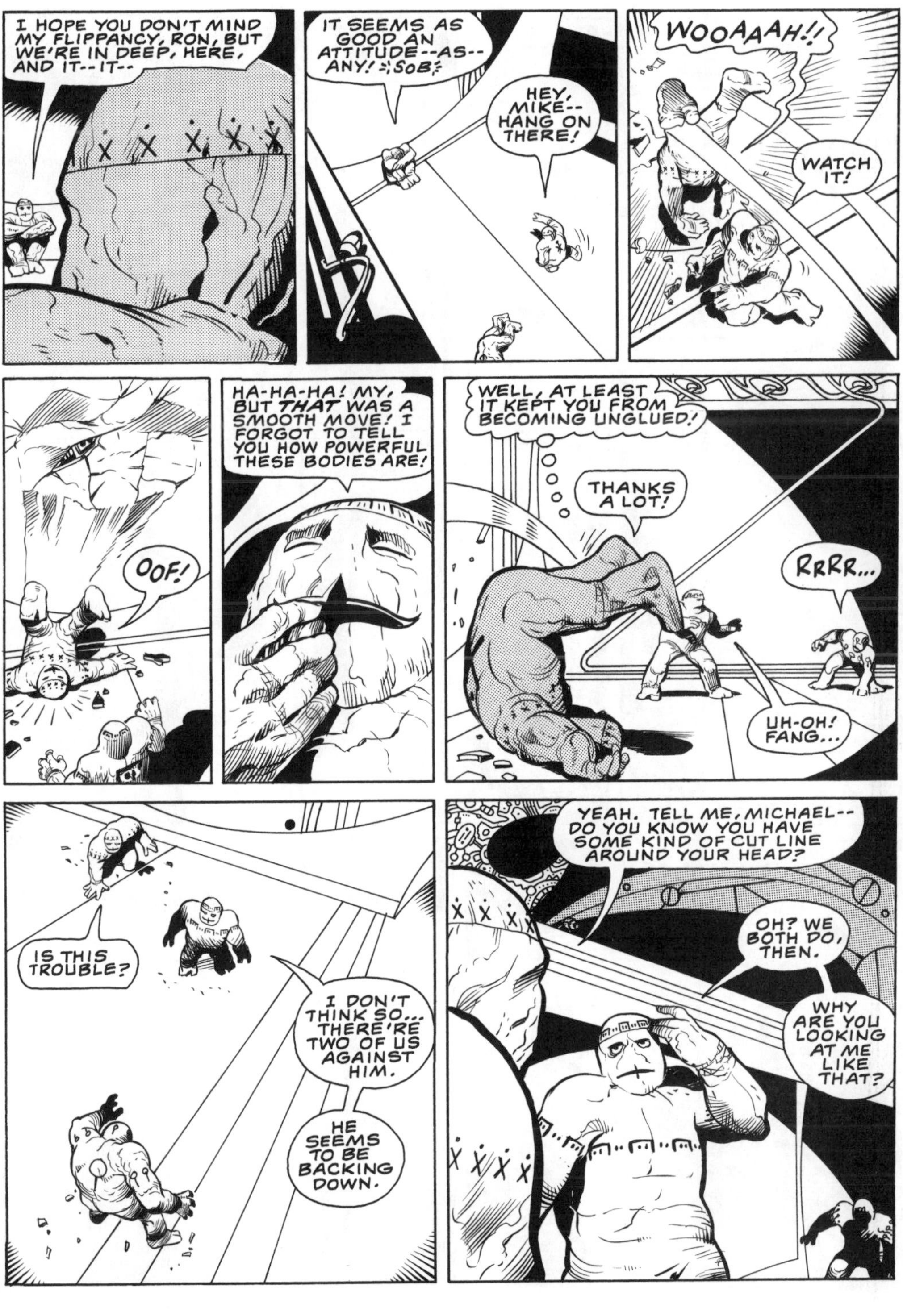
I HOPE YOU DON'T MIND MY FLIPPANCY, RON, BUT WE'RE IN DEEP, HERE, AND IT--IT--
IT SEEMS AS GOOD AN ATTITUDE--AS--ANY! SOB
HEY, MIKE--HANG ON THERE!
WOOAAAH!!
WATCH IT!
OOF!
HA-HA-HA! MY, BUT THAT WAS A SMOOTH MOVE! I FORGOT TO TELL YOU HOW POWERFUL THESE BODIES ARE!
WELL, AT LEAST IT KEPT YOU FROM BECOMING UNGLUED!
THANKS A LOT!
RRRR...
UH-OH! FANG...
IS THIS TROUBLE?
I DON'T THINK SO... THERE'RE TWO OF US AGAINST HIM.
HE SEEMS TO BE BACKING DOWN.
YEAH. TELL ME, MICHAEL--DO YOU KNOW YOU HAVE SOME KIND OF CUT LINE AROUND YOUR HEAD?
OH? WE BOTH DO, THEN.
WHY ARE YOU LOOKING AT ME LIKE THAT?

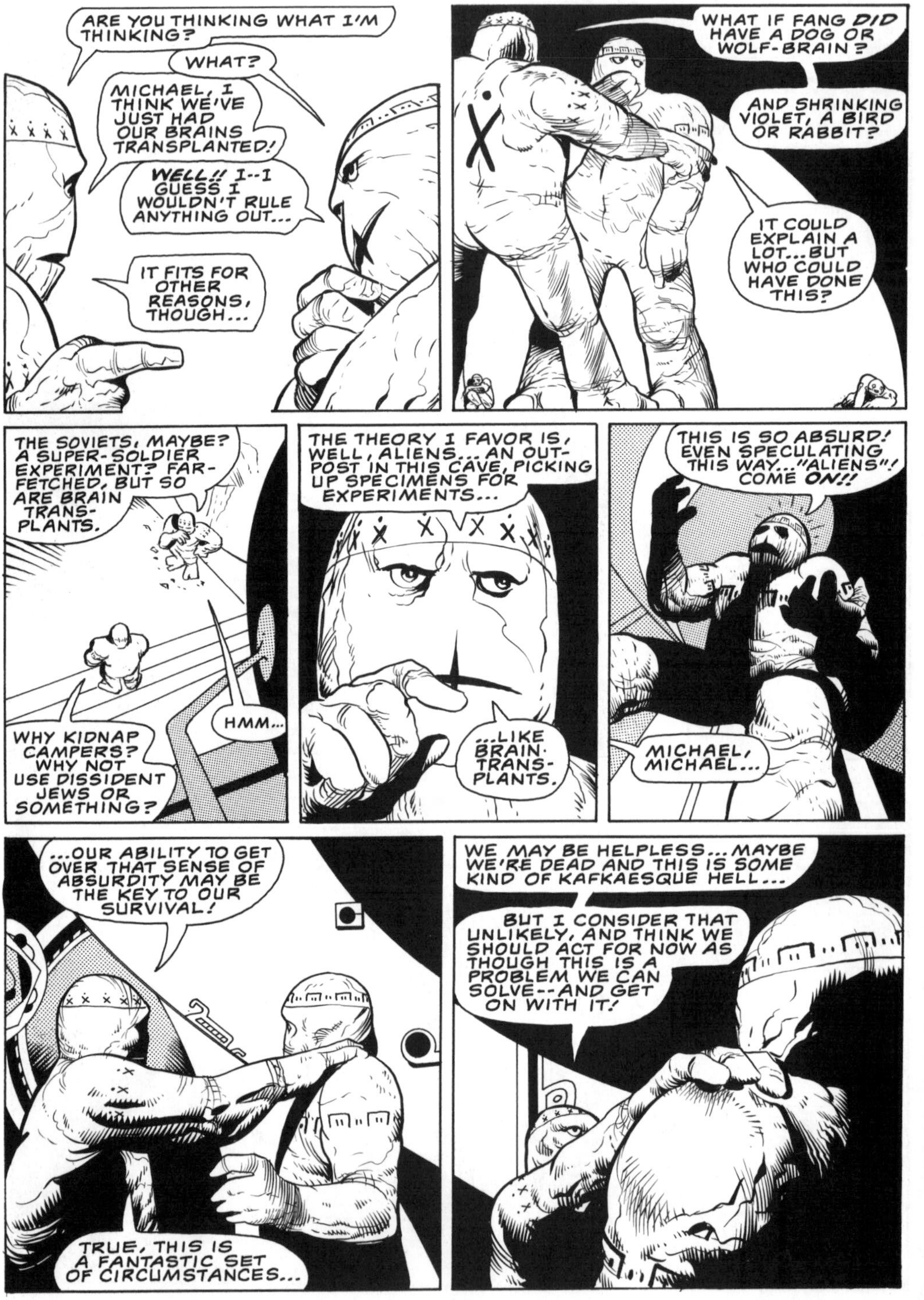
ARE YOU THINKING WHAT I'M THINKING?
WHAT?
MICHAEL, I THINK WE'VE JUST HAD OUR BRAINS TRANSPLANTED!
WELL!! I--I GUESS I WOULDN'T RULE ANYTHING OUT...
IT FITS FOR OTHER REASONS, THOUGH...
WHAT IF FANG DID HAVE A DOG OR WOLF-BRAIN?
AND SHRINKING VIOLET, A BIRD OR RABBIT?
IT COULD EXPLAIN A LOT... BUT WHO COULD HAVE DONE THIS?
THE SOVIETS, MAYBE? A SUPER-SOLDIER EXPERIMENT? FAR-FETCHED, BUT SO ARE BRAIN TRANS-PLANTS.
WHY KIDNAP CAMPERS? WHY NOT USE DISSIDENT JEWS OR SOMETHING?
HMM...
THE THEORY I FAVOR IS, WELL, ALIENS... AN OUT-POST IN THIS CAVE, PICKING UP SPECIMENS FOR EXPERIMENTS...
...LIKE BRAIN-TRANS-PLANTS.
THIS IS SO ABSURD! EVEN SPECULATING THIS WAY... "ALIENS"! COME ON!!
MICHAEL, MICHAEL...
...OUR ABILITY TO GET OVER THAT SENSE OF ABSURDITY MAY BE THE KEY TO OUR SURVIVAL!
TRUE, THIS IS A FANTASTIC SET OF CIRCUMSTANCES...
WE MAY BE HELPLESS... MAYBE WE'RE DEAD AND THIS IS SOME KIND OF KAFKAESQUE HELL...
BUT I CONSIDER THAT UNLIKELY, AND THINK WE SHOULD ACT FOR NOW AS THOUGH THIS IS A PROBLEM WE CAN SOLVE--AND GET ON WITH IT!

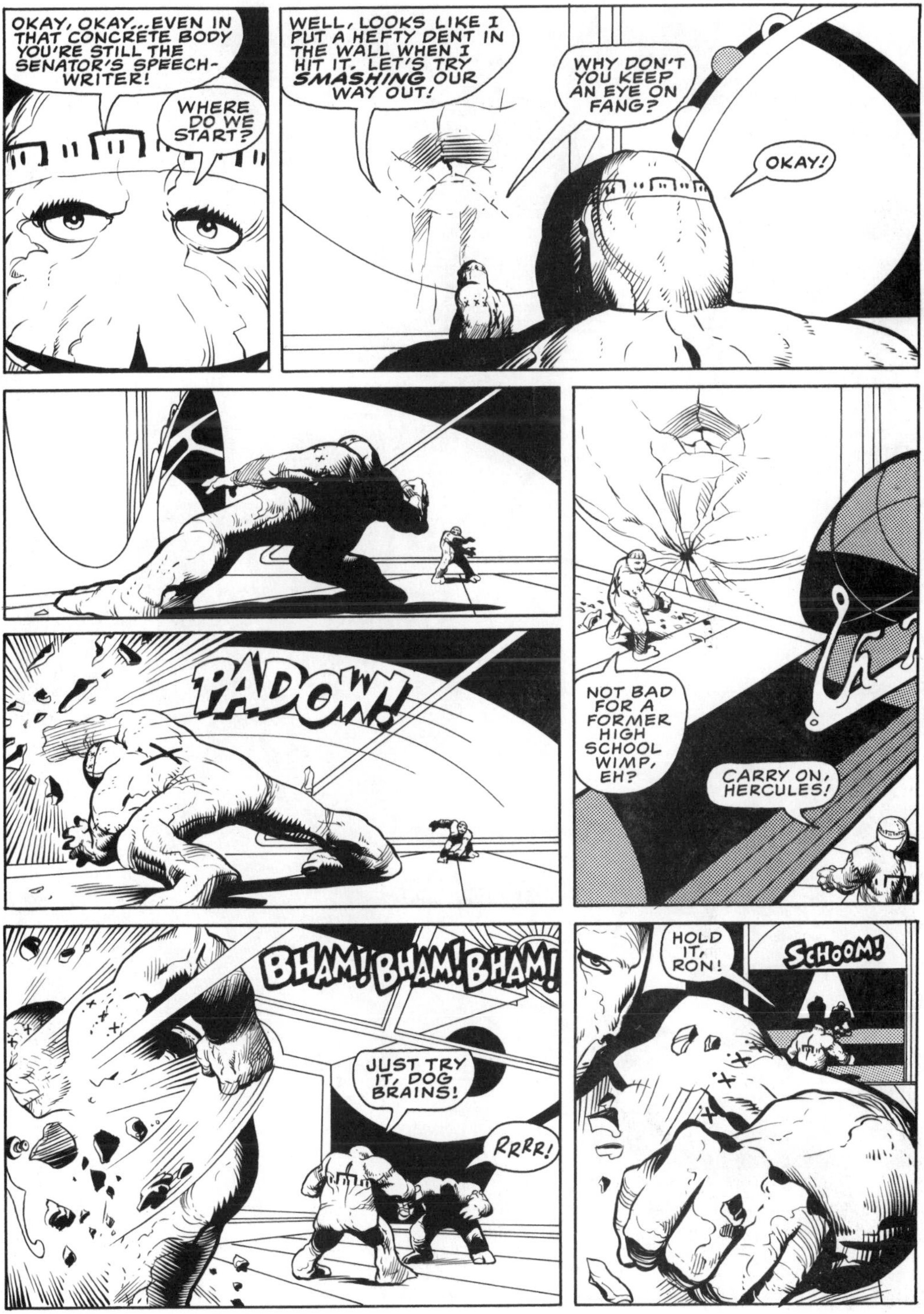
OKAY, OKAY...EVEN IN THAT CONCRETE BODY YOU'RE STILL THE SENATOR'S SPEECH-WRITER!
WHERE DO WE START?
WELL, LOOKS LIKE I PUT A HEFTY DENT IN THE WALL WHEN I HIT IT. LET'S TRY SMASHING OUR WAY OUT!
WHY DON'T YOU KEEP AN EYE ON FANG?
OKAY!
PADOW!
NOT BAD FOR A FORMER HIGH SCHOOL WIMP, EH?
CARRY ON, HERCULES!
BHAM! BHAM! BHAM!
JUST TRY IT, DOG BRAINS!
RRRR!
HOLD IT, RON!
SCHOOM!

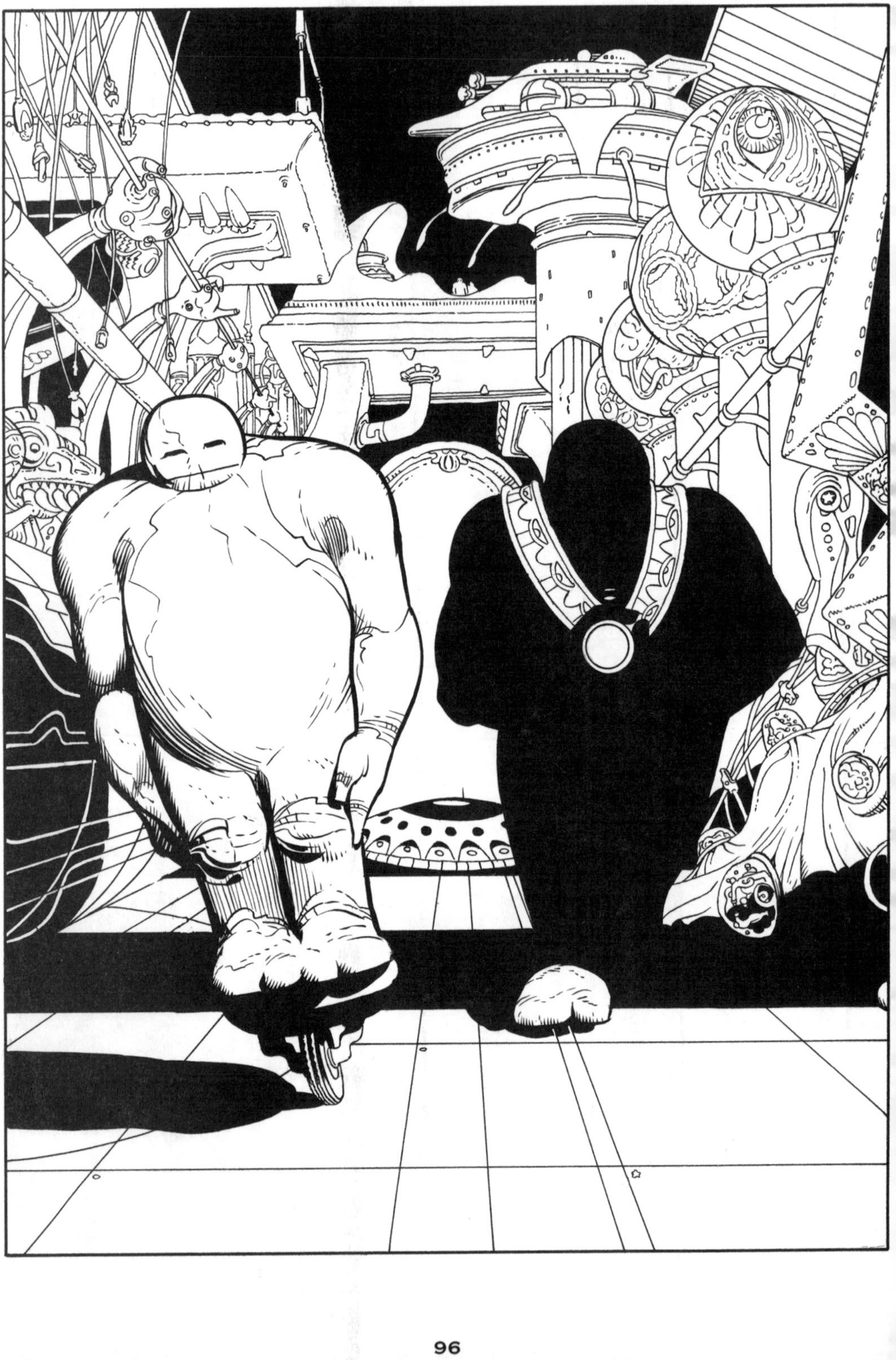

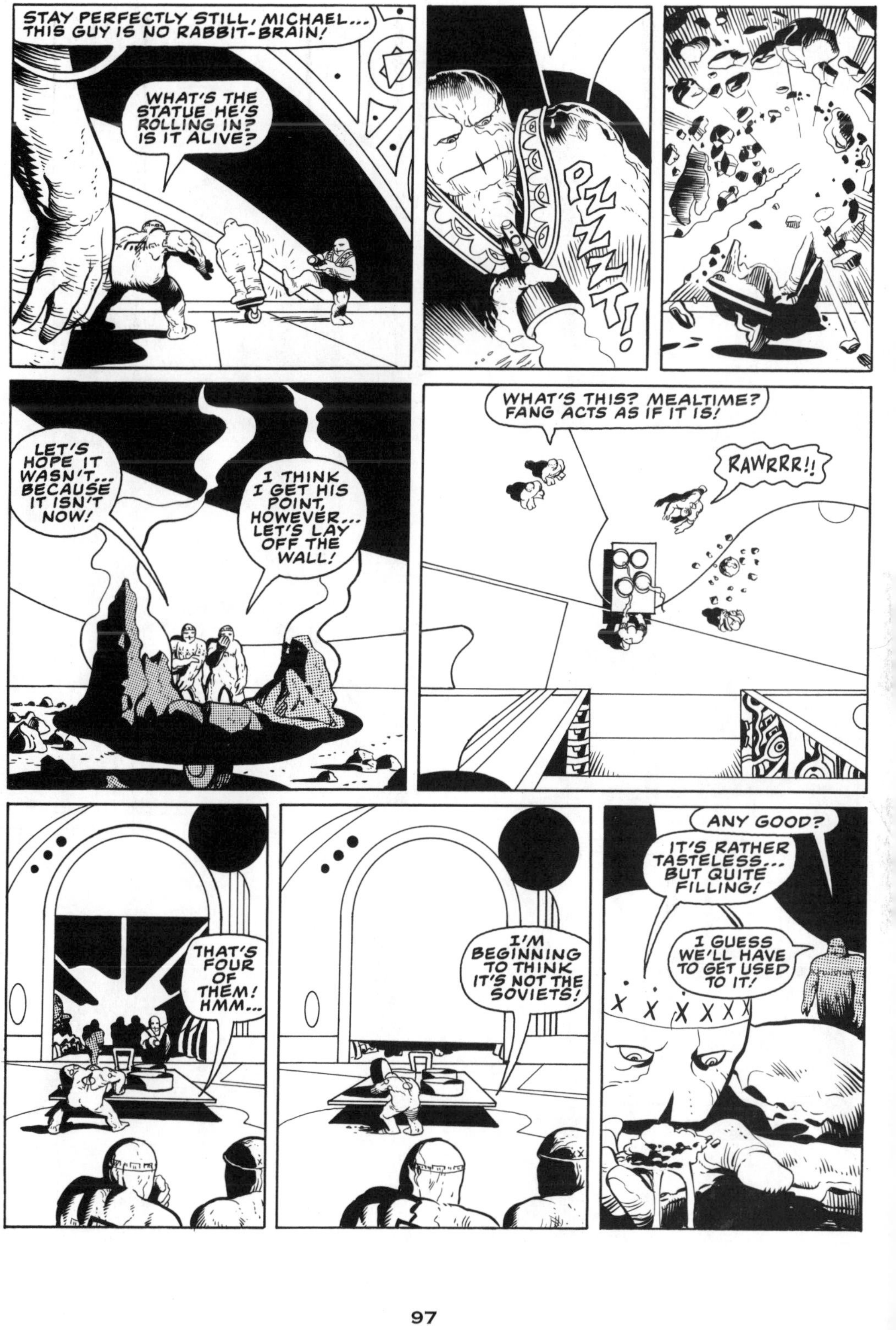
STAY PERFECTLY STILL, MICHAEL... THIS GUY IS NO RABBIT-BRAIN!
WHAT'S THE STATUE HE'S ROLLING IN? IS IT ALIVE?
PZZNT!
LET'S HOPE IT WASN'T... BECAUSE IT ISN'T NOW!
I THINK I GET HIS POINT, HOWEVER... LET'S LAY OFF THE WALL!
WHAT'S THIS? MEALTIME? FANG ACTS AS IF IT IS!
RAWRRR!!
THAT'S FOUR OF THEM! HMM...
I'M BEGINNING TO THINK IT'S NOT THE SOVIETS!
ANY GOOD?
IT'S RATHER TASTELESS... BUT QUITE FILLING!
I GUESS WE'LL HAVE TO GET USED TO IT!

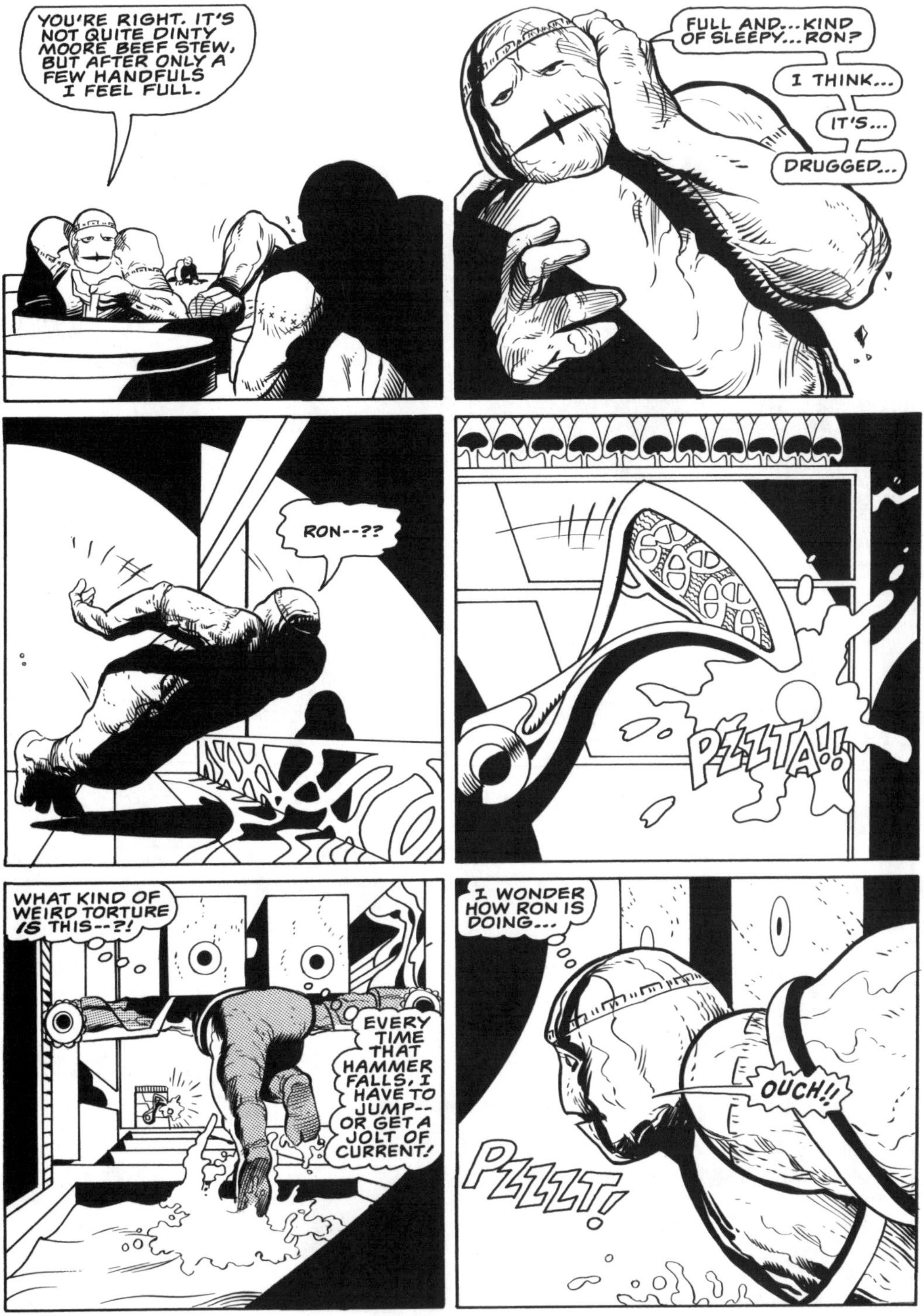
YOU'RE RIGHT. IT'S NOT QUITE DINTY MOORE BEEF STEW, BUT AFTER ONLY A FEW HANDFULS I FEEL FULL.
FULL AND...KIND OF SLEEPY...RON?
I THINK...
IT'S...
DRUGGED...
RON--??
PZZTA!!
WHAT KIND OF WEIRD TORTURE IS THIS--?!
EVERY TIME THAT HAMMER FALLS, I HAVE TO JUMP-- OR GET A JOLT OF CURRENT!
I WONDER HOW RON IS DOING...
OUCH!!
PZZZT!

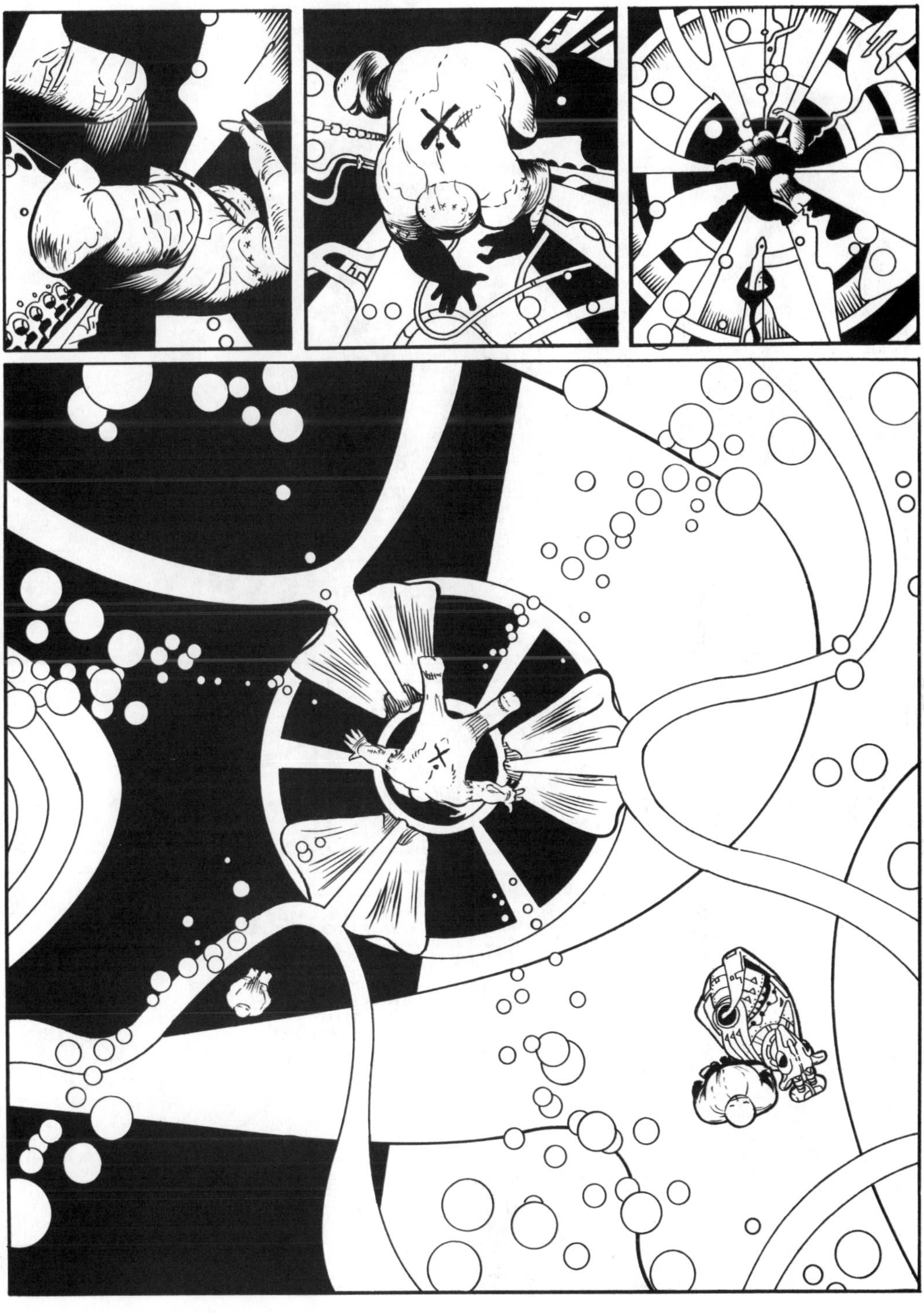

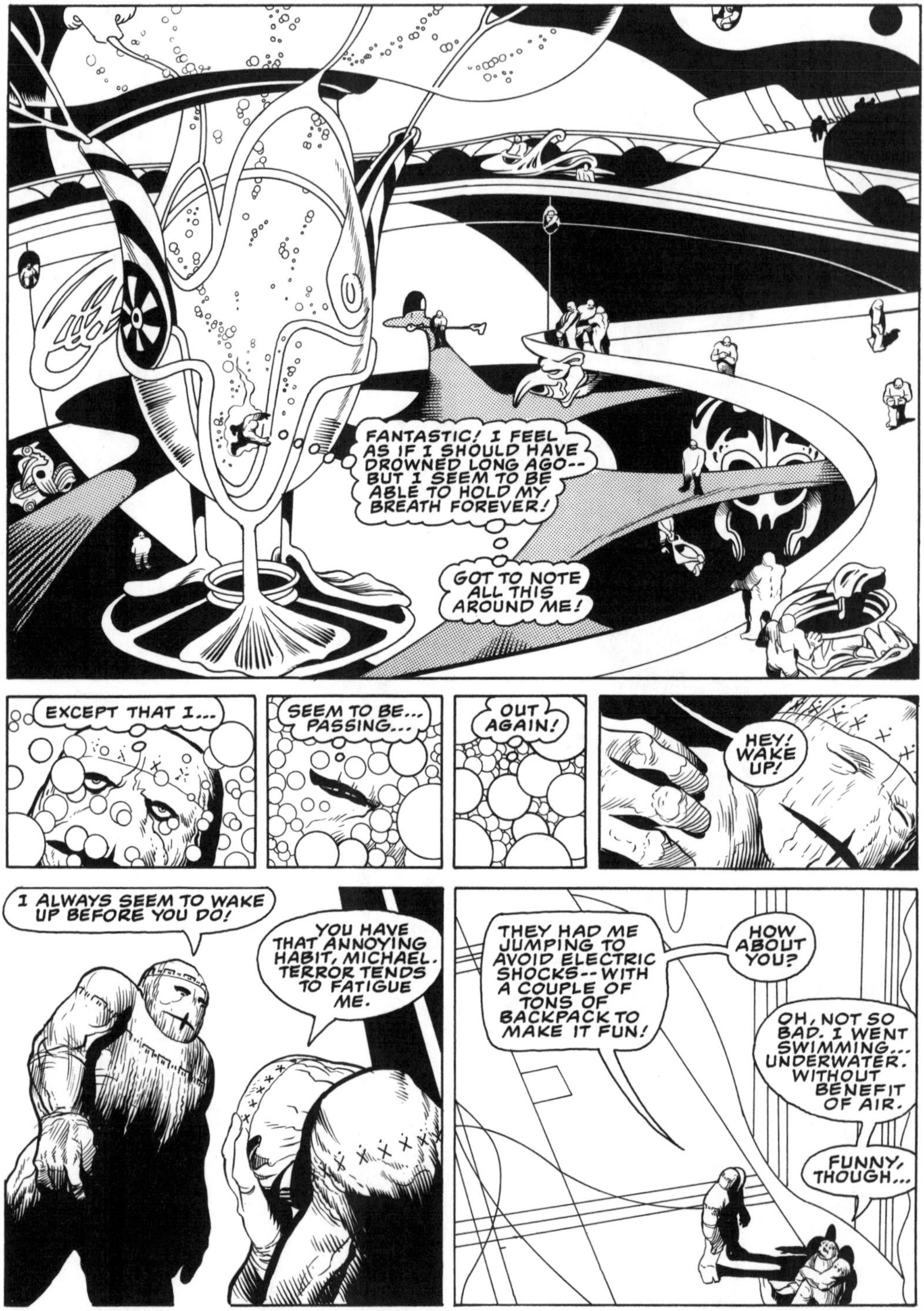
FANTASTIC! I FEEL AS IF I SHOULD HAVE DROWNED LONG AGO-- BUT I SEEM TO BE ABLE TO HOLD MY BREATH FOREVER!
GOT TO NOTE ALL THIS AROUND ME!
EXCEPT THAT I...
SEEM TO BE... PASSING...
OUT AGAIN!
HEY! WAKE UP!
I ALWAYS SEEM TO WAKE UP BEFORE YOU DO!
YOU HAVE THAT ANNOYING HABIT, MICHAEL. TERROR TENDS TO FATIGUE ME.
THEY HAD ME JUMPING TO AVOID ELECTRIC SHOCKS--WITH A COUPLE OF TONS OF BACKPACK TO MAKE IT FUN!
HOW ABOUT YOU?
OH, NOT SO BAD. I WENT SWIMMING... UNDERWATER. WITHOUT BENEFIT OF AIR.
FUNNY, THOUGH...

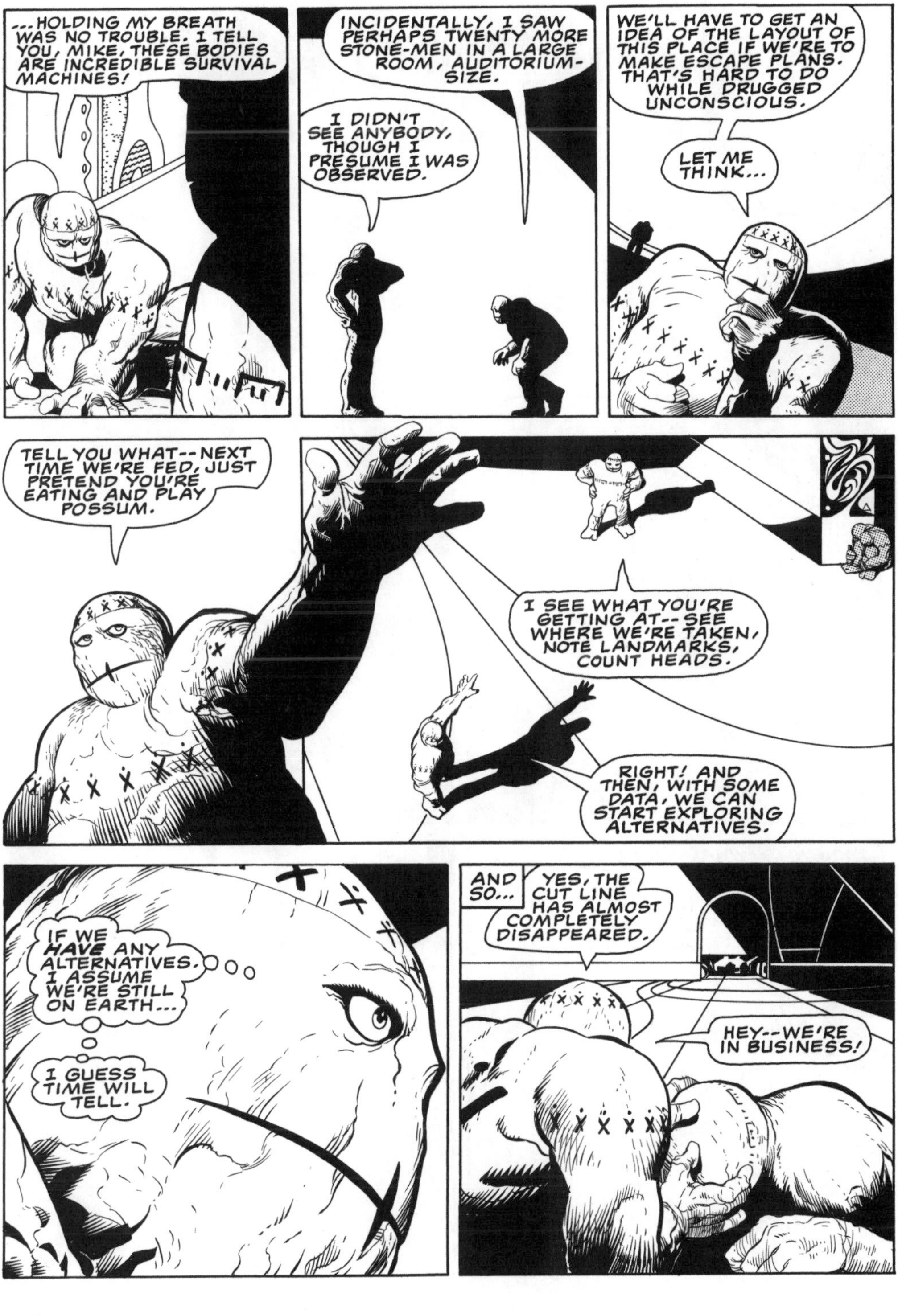
...HOLDING MY BREATH WAS NO TROUBLE. I TELL YOU, MIKE, THESE BODIES ARE INCREDIBLE SURVIVAL MACHINES!
INCIDENTALLY, I SAW PERHAPS TWENTY MORE STONE-MEN IN A LARGE ROOM, AUDITORIUM-SIZE.
I DIDN'T SEE ANYBODY, THOUGH I PRESUME I WAS OBSERVED.
WE'LL HAVE TO GET AN IDEA OF THE LAYOUT OF THIS PLACE IF WE'RE TO MAKE ESCAPE PLANS. THAT'S HARD TO DO WHILE DRUGGED UNCONSCIOUS.
LET ME THINK...
TELL YOU WHAT--NEXT TIME WE'RE FED, JUST PRETEND YOU'RE EATING AND PLAY POSSUM.
I SEE WHAT YOU'RE GETTING AT--SEE WHERE WE'RE TAKEN, NOTE LANDMARKS, COUNT HEADS.
RIGHT! AND THEN, WITH SOME DATA, WE CAN START EXPLORING ALTERNATIVES.
IF WE *HAVE* ANY ALTERNATIVES. I ASSUME WE'RE STILL ON EARTH...
I GUESS TIME WILL TELL.
AND SO...
YES, THE CUT LINE HAS ALMOST COMPLETELY DISAPPEARED.
HEY--WE'RE IN BUSINESS!

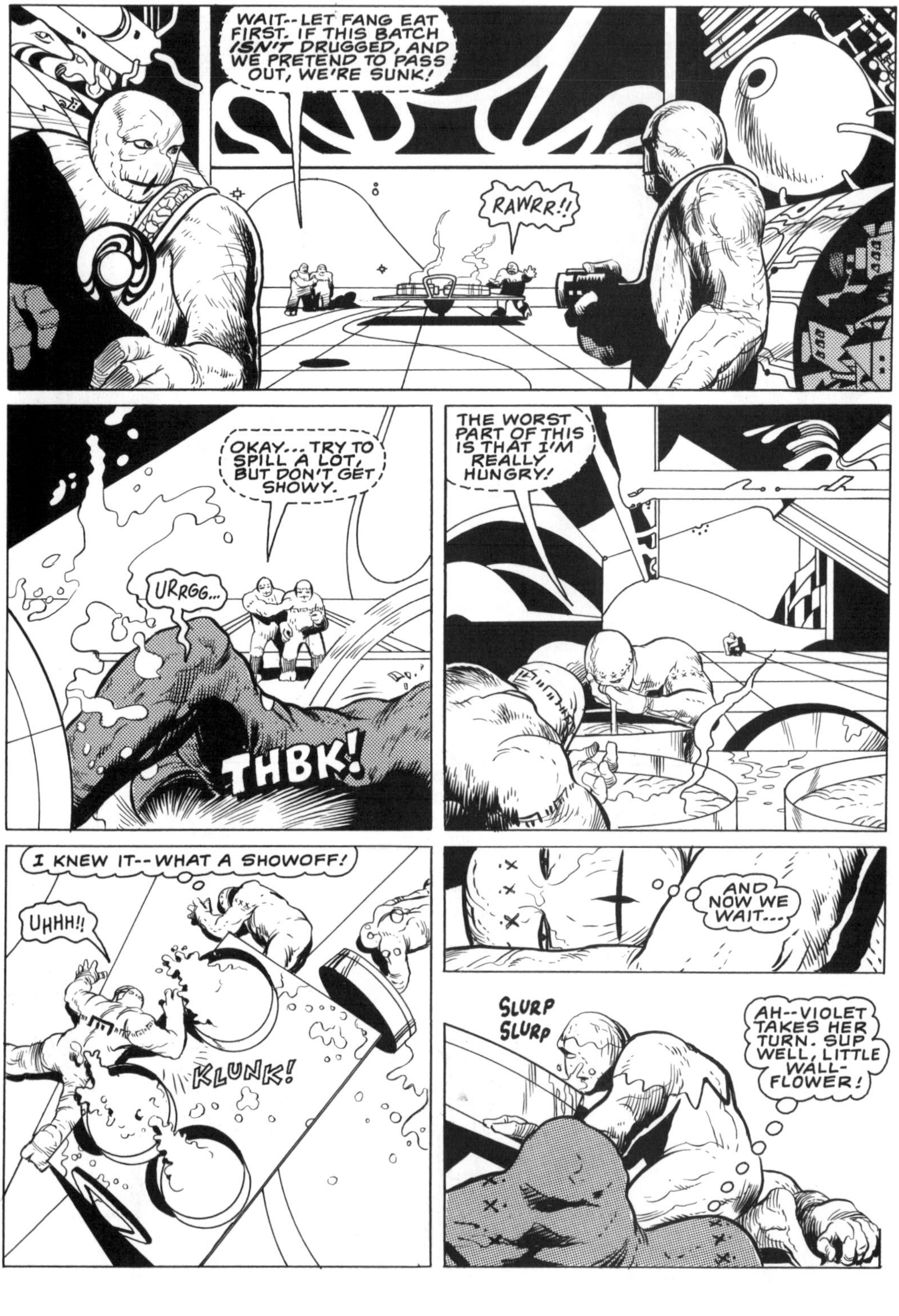
WAIT--LET FANG EAT FIRST. IF THIS BATCH ISN'T DRUGGED, AND WE PRETEND TO PASS OUT, WE'RE SUNK!
RAWRR!!
OKAY... TRY TO SPILL A LOT, BUT DON'T GET SHOWY.
URRGG...
THBK!
THE WORST PART OF THIS IS THAT I'M REALLY HUNGRY!
I KNEW IT--WHAT A SHOWOFF!
UHHH!!
KLUNK!
AND NOW WE WAIT...
SLURP SLURP
AH--VIOLET TAKES HER TURN. SUP WELL, LITTLE WALL-FLOWER!

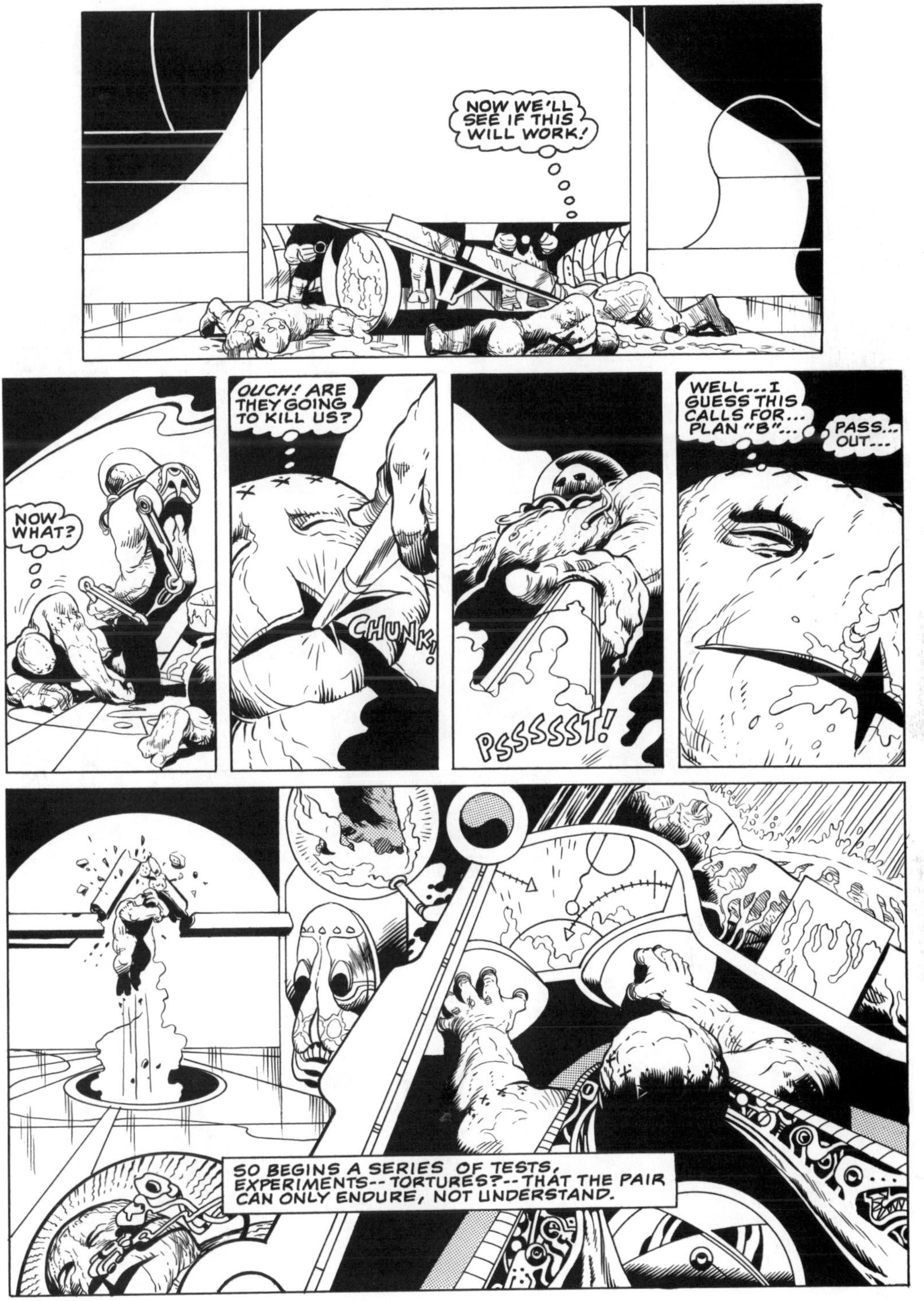
NOW WE'LL SEE IF THIS WILL WORK!
NOW WHAT?
OUCH! ARE THEY GOING TO KILL US?
CHUNK!
PSSSSST!
WELL... I GUESS THIS CALLS FOR... PLAN "B"...
PASS... OUT...
SO BEGINS A SERIES OF TESTS, EXPERIMENTS-- TORTURES?-- THAT THE PAIR CAN ONLY ENDURE, NOT UNDERSTAND.

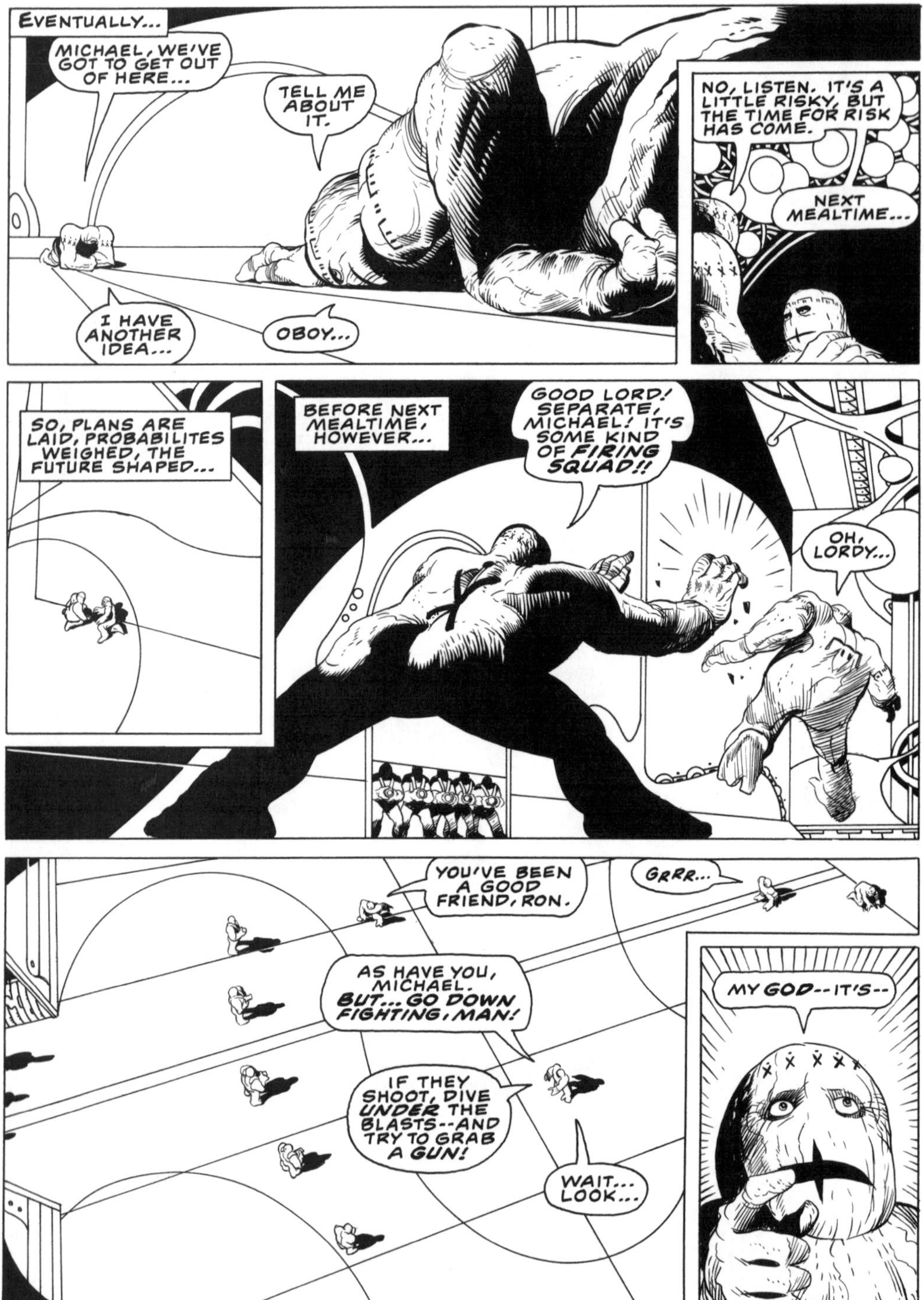
EVENTUALLY...
MICHAEL, WE'VE GOT TO GET OUT OF HERE...
TELL ME ABOUT IT.
I HAVE ANOTHER IDEA...
OBOY...
NO, LISTEN. IT'S A LITTLE RISKY, BUT THE TIME FOR RISK HAS COME.
NEXT MEALTIME...
SO, PLANS ARE LAID, PROBABILITES WEIGHED, THE FUTURE SHAPED...
BEFORE NEXT MEALTIME, HOWEVER...
GOOD LORD! SEPARATE, MICHAEL! IT'S SOME KIND OF FIRING SQUAD!!
OH, LORDY...
YOU'VE BEEN A GOOD FRIEND, RON.
GRRR...
AS HAVE YOU, MICHAEL. BUT...GO DOWN FIGHTING, MAN!
IF THEY SHOOT, DIVE UNDER THE BLASTS--AND TRY TO GRAB A GUN!
WAIT... LOOK...
MY GOD--IT'S--

US!!

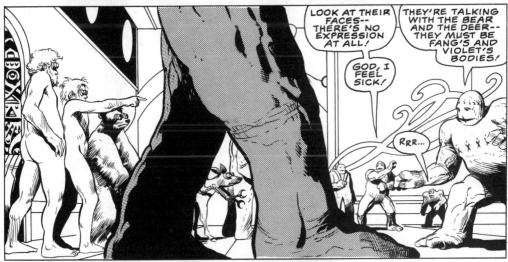

LOOK AT THEIR FACES-- THERE'S NO EXPRESSION AT ALL!

GOD, I FEEL SICK!

THEY'RE TALKING WITH THE BEAR AND THE DEER-- THEY MUST BE FANG'S AND VIOLET'S BODIES!

RRR...

RON-- I FEEL LIKE I HAVE TO VOMIT, BUT I CAN'T! IT'S SOME KIND OF ULTIMATE VIOLATION...

A PERMANENT RAPE...

HANG ON!

AT LEAST WE KNOW OUR BODIES STILL EXIST-- MAYBE THEY'LL TRANSPLANT US BACK!

FANG'S ATTACKING! HIT THE FLOOR!!

RAWRRR!!

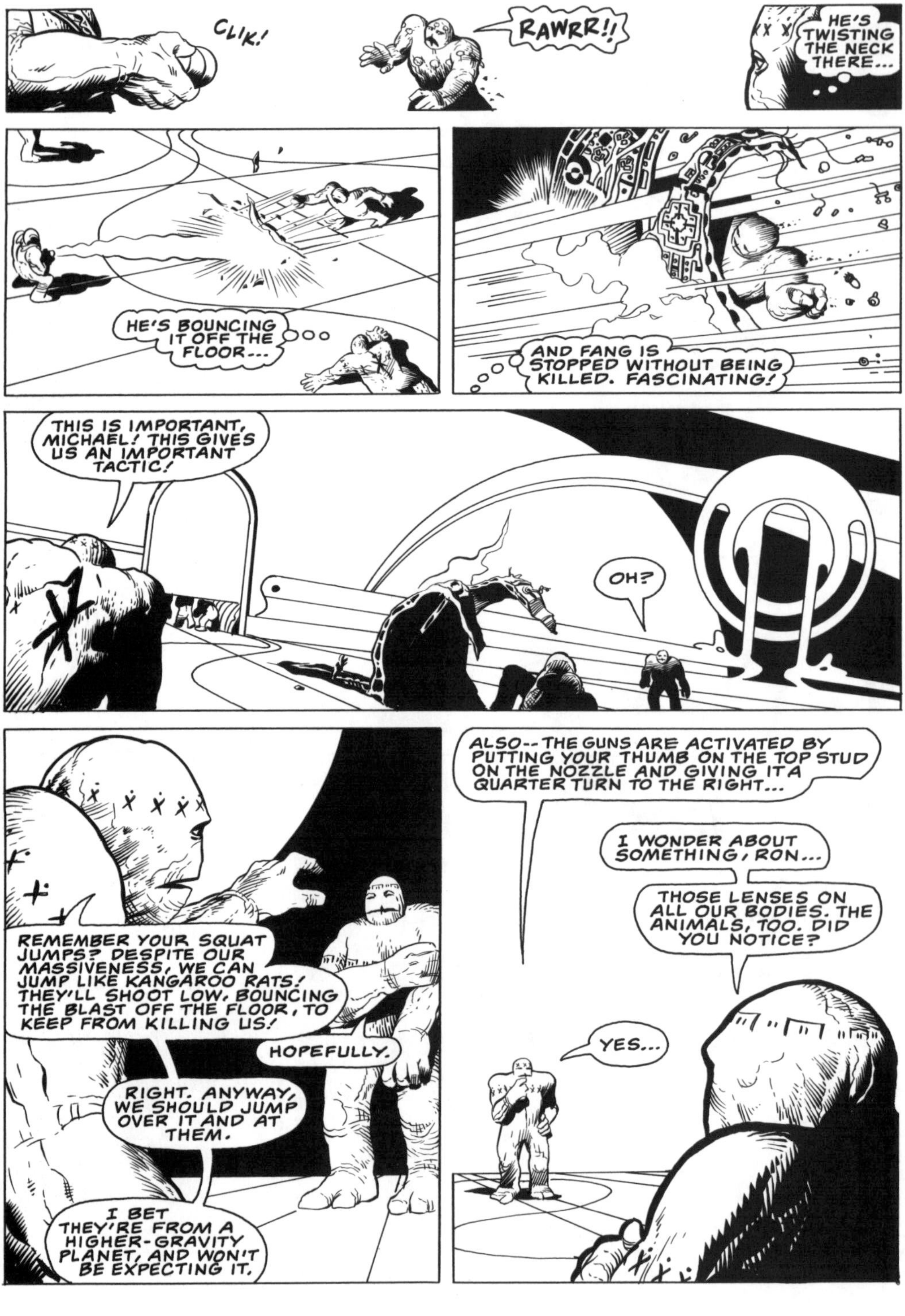
CLIK!
RAWRR!!
HE'S TWISTING THE NECK THERE...
HE'S BOUNCING IT OFF THE FLOOR...
AND FANG IS STOPPED WITHOUT BEING KILLED. FASCINATING!
THIS IS IMPORTANT, MICHAEL! THIS GIVES US AN IMPORTANT TACTIC!
OH?
REMEMBER YOUR SQUAT JUMPS? DESPITE OUR MASSIVENESS, WE CAN JUMP LIKE KANGAROO RATS! THEY'LL SHOOT LOW, BOUNCING THE BLAST OFF THE FLOOR, TO KEEP FROM KILLING US!
HOPEFULLY.
RIGHT. ANYWAY, WE SHOULD JUMP OVER IT AND AT THEM.
I BET THEY'RE FROM A HIGHER-GRAVITY PLANET, AND WON'T BE EXPECTING IT.
ALSO-- THE GUNS ARE ACTIVATED BY PUTTING YOUR THUMB ON THE TOP STUD ON THE NOZZLE AND GIVING IT A QUARTER TURN TO THE RIGHT...
I WONDER ABOUT SOMETHING, RON...
THOSE LENSES ON ALL OUR BODIES. THE ANIMALS, TOO. DID YOU NOTICE?
YES...

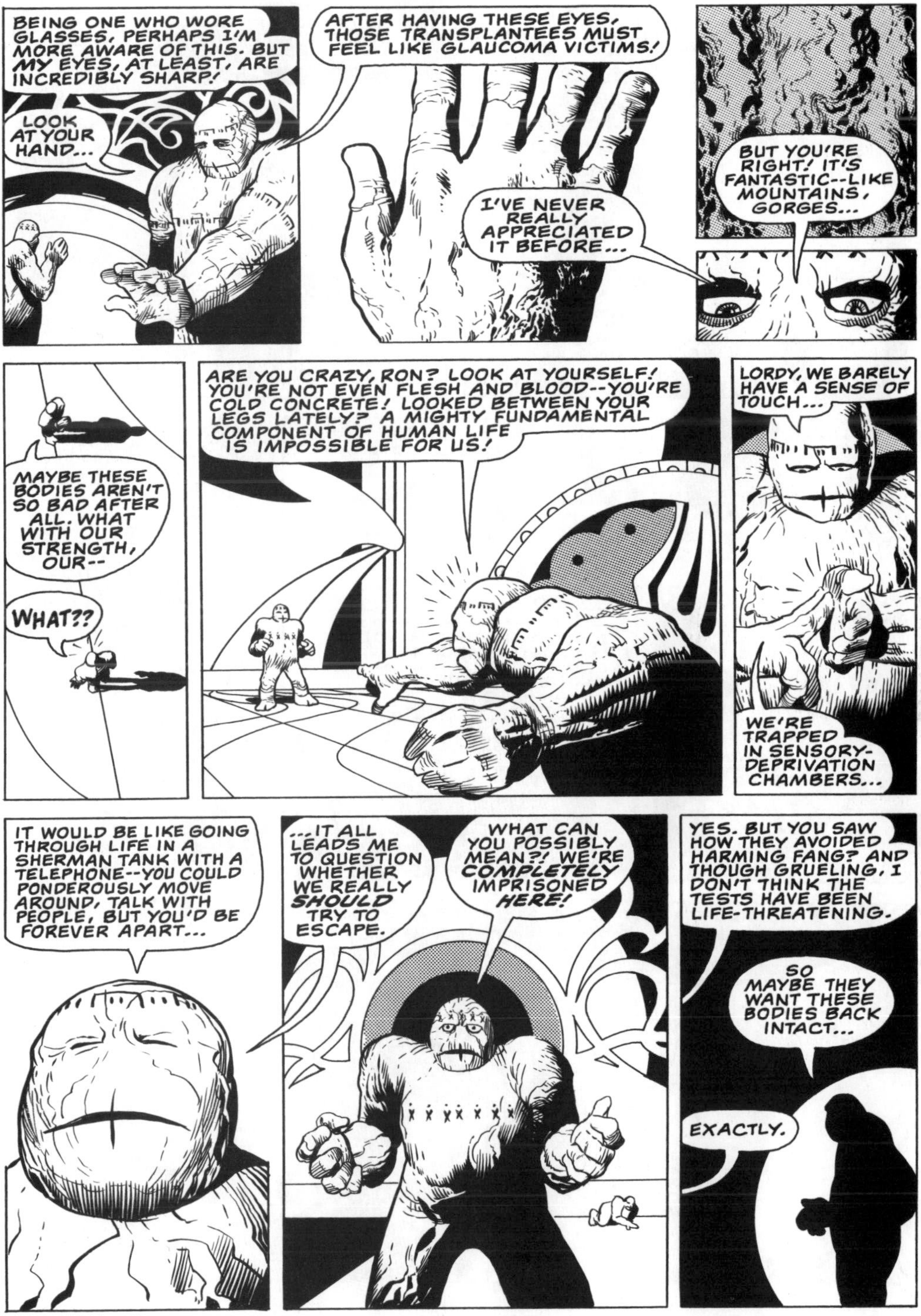

BEING ONE WHO WORE GLASSES, PERHAPS I'M MORE AWARE OF THIS. BUT MY EYES, AT LEAST, ARE INCREDIBLY SHARP!
LOOK AT YOUR HAND...
AFTER HAVING THESE EYES, THOSE TRANSPLANTEES MUST FEEL LIKE GLAUCOMA VICTIMS!
I'VE NEVER REALLY APPRECIATED IT BEFORE...
BUT YOU'RE RIGHT! IT'S FANTASTIC--LIKE MOUNTAINS, GORGES...
MAYBE THESE BODIES AREN'T SO BAD AFTER ALL. WHAT WITH OUR STRENGTH, OUR--
WHAT??
ARE YOU CRAZY, RON? LOOK AT YOURSELF! YOU'RE NOT EVEN FLESH AND BLOOD--YOU'RE COLD CONCRETE! LOOKED BETWEEN YOUR LEGS LATELY? A MIGHTY FUNDAMENTAL COMPONENT OF HUMAN LIFE IS IMPOSSIBLE FOR US!
LORDY, WE BARELY HAVE A SENSE OF TOUCH...
WE'RE TRAPPED IN SENSORY-DEPRIVATION CHAMBERS...
IT WOULD BE LIKE GOING THROUGH LIFE IN A SHERMAN TANK WITH A TELEPHONE--YOU COULD PONDEROUSLY MOVE AROUND, TALK WITH PEOPLE, BUT YOU'D BE FOREVER APART...
...IT ALL LEADS ME TO QUESTION WHETHER WE REALLY SHOULD TRY TO ESCAPE.
WHAT CAN YOU POSSIBLY MEAN?! WE'RE COMPLETELY IMPRISONED HERE!
YES. BUT YOU SAW HOW THEY AVOIDED HARMING FANG? AND THOUGH GRUELING, I DON'T THINK THE TESTS HAVE BEEN LIFE-THREATENING.
SO MAYBE THEY WANT THESE BODIES BACK INTACT...
EXACTLY.

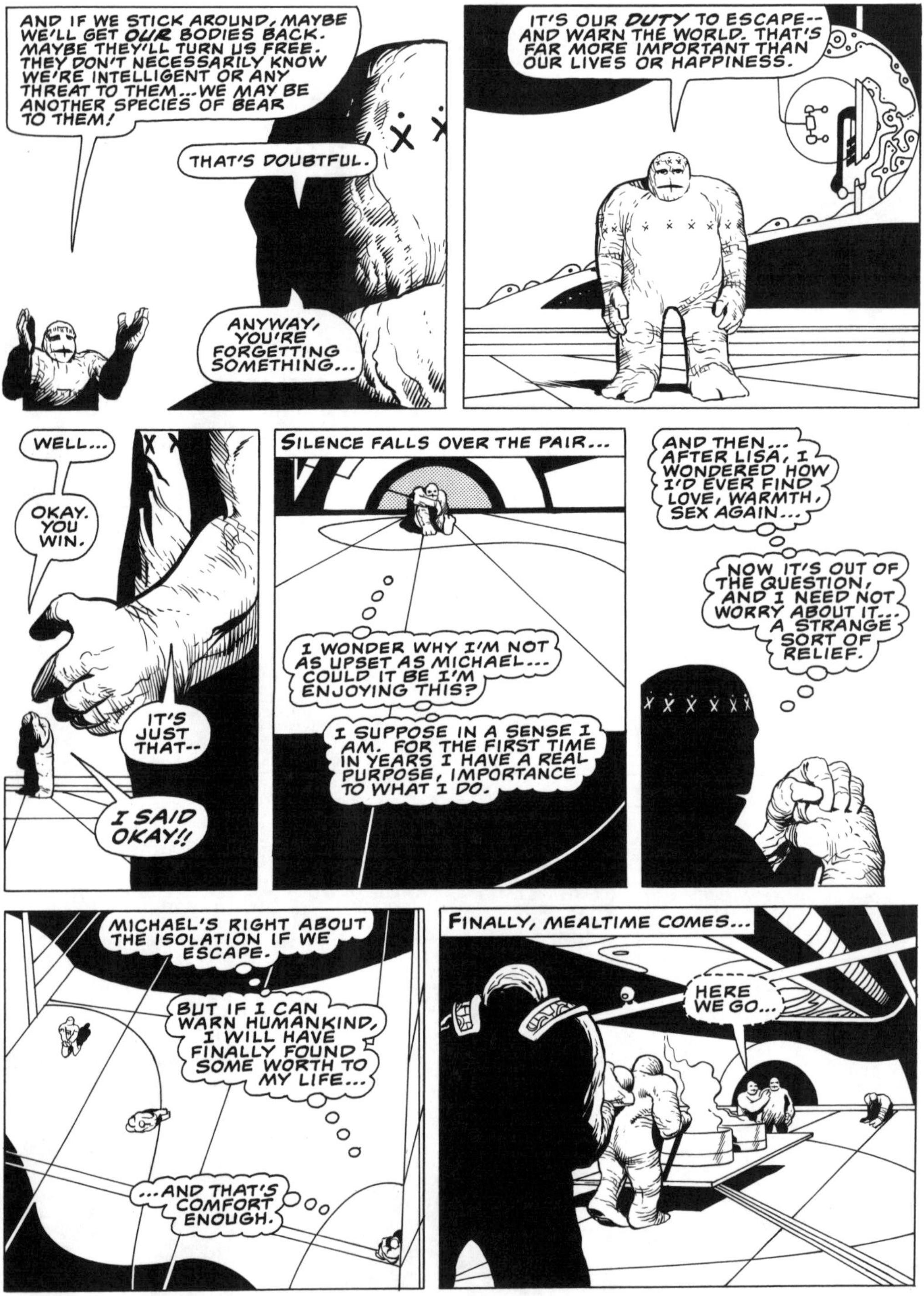
AND IF WE STICK AROUND, MAYBE WE'LL GET OUR BODIES BACK. MAYBE THEY'LL TURN US FREE. THEY DON'T NECESSARILY KNOW WE'RE INTELLIGENT OR ANY THREAT TO THEM... WE MAY BE ANOTHER SPECIES OF BEAR TO THEM!
THAT'S DOUBTFUL.
ANYWAY, YOU'RE FORGETTING SOMETHING...
IT'S OUR DUTY TO ESCAPE-- AND WARN THE WORLD. THAT'S FAR MORE IMPORTANT THAN OUR LIVES OR HAPPINESS.
WELL...
OKAY. YOU WIN.
IT'S JUST THAT--
I SAID OKAY!!
SILENCE FALLS OVER THE PAIR...
I WONDER WHY I'M NOT AS UPSET AS MICHAEL... COULD IT BE I'M ENJOYING THIS?
I SUPPOSE IN A SENSE I AM. FOR THE FIRST TIME IN YEARS I HAVE A REAL PURPOSE, IMPORTANCE TO WHAT I DO.
AND THEN... AFTER LISA, I WONDERED HOW I'D EVER FIND LOVE, WARMTH, SEX AGAIN...
NOW IT'S OUT OF THE QUESTION, AND I NEED NOT WORRY ABOUT IT... A STRANGE SORT OF RELIEF.
MICHAEL'S RIGHT ABOUT THE ISOLATION IF WE ESCAPE.
BUT IF I CAN WARN HUMANKIND, I WILL HAVE FINALLY FOUND SOME WORTH TO MY LIFE...
...AND THAT'S COMFORT ENOUGH.
FINALLY, MEALTIME COMES...
HERE WE GO...

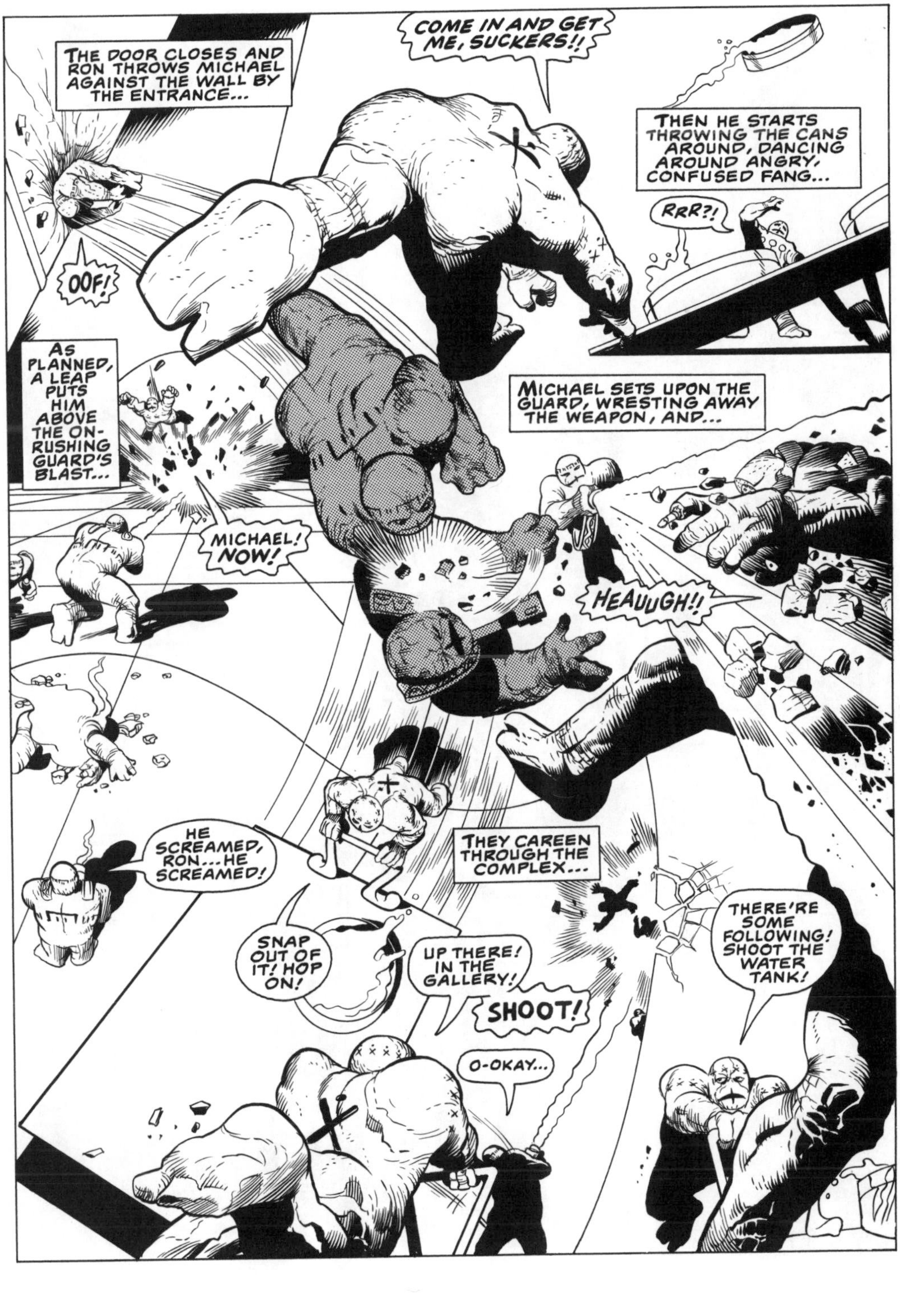
THE DOOR CLOSES AND RON THROWS MICHAEL AGAINST THE WALL BY THE ENTRANCE...
OOF!
COME IN AND GET ME, SUCKERS!!
THEN HE STARTS THROWING THE CANS AROUND, DANCING AROUND ANGRY, CONFUSED FANG...
RRR?!
AS PLANNED, A LEAP PUTS HIM ABOVE THE ON-RUSHING GUARD'S BLAST...
MICHAEL! NOW!
MICHAEL SETS UPON THE GUARD, WRESTING AWAY THE WEAPON, AND...
HEAUUGH!!
HE SCREAMED, RON...HE SCREAMED!
THEY CAREEN THROUGH THE COMPLEX...
SNAP OUT OF IT! HOP ON!
UP THERE! IN THE GALLERY!
SHOOT!
O-OKAY...
THERE'RE SOME FOLLOWING! SHOOT THE WATER TANK!

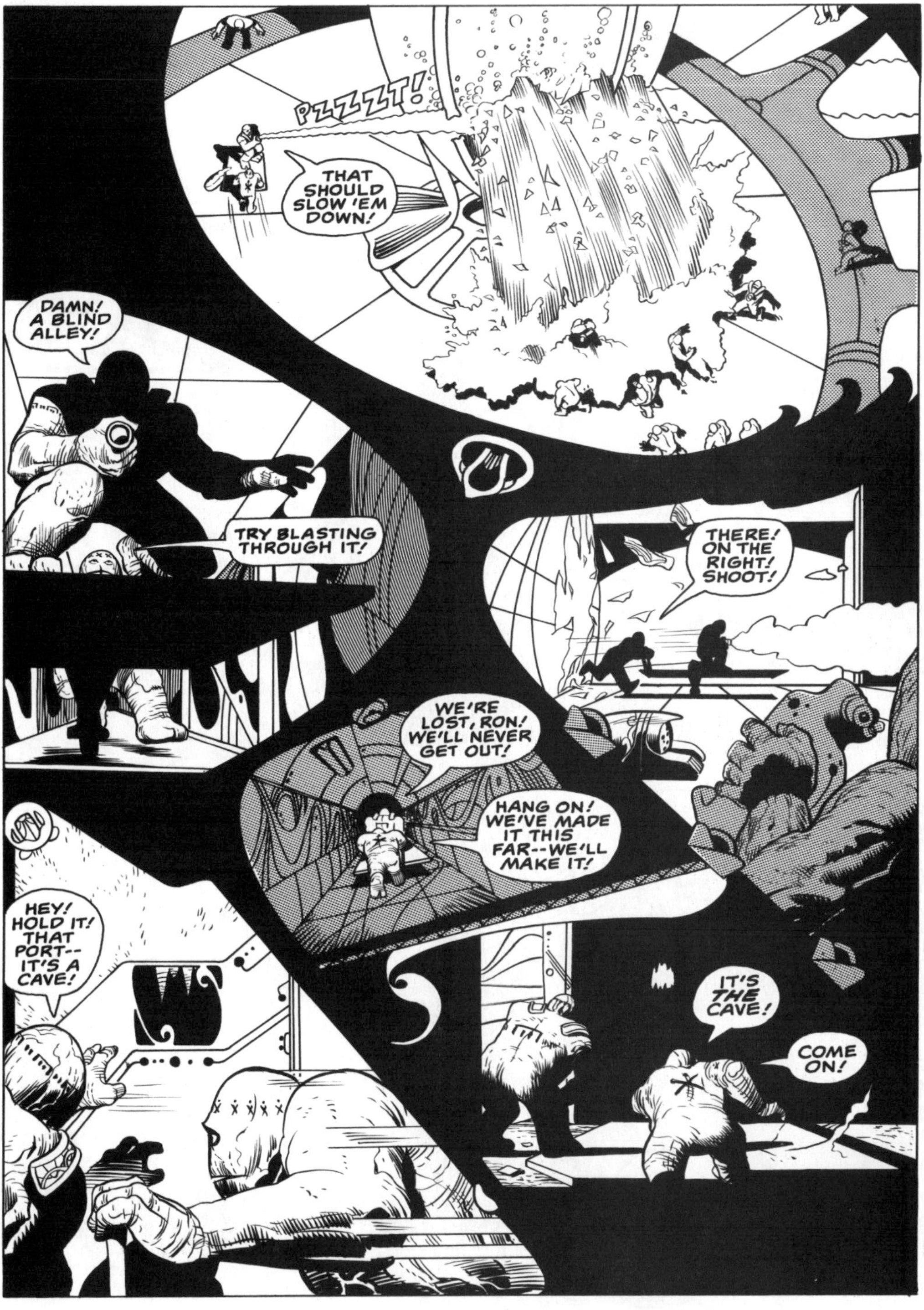
PZZZZT!
THAT SHOULD SLOW 'EM DOWN!
DAMN! A BLIND ALLEY!
TRY BLASTING THROUGH IT!
THERE! ON THE RIGHT! SHOOT!
WE'RE LOST, RON! WE'LL NEVER GET OUT!
HANG ON! WE'VE MADE IT THIS FAR--WE'LL MAKE IT!
HEY! HOLD IT! THAT PORT-- IT'S A CAVE!
IT'S THE CAVE!
COME ON!

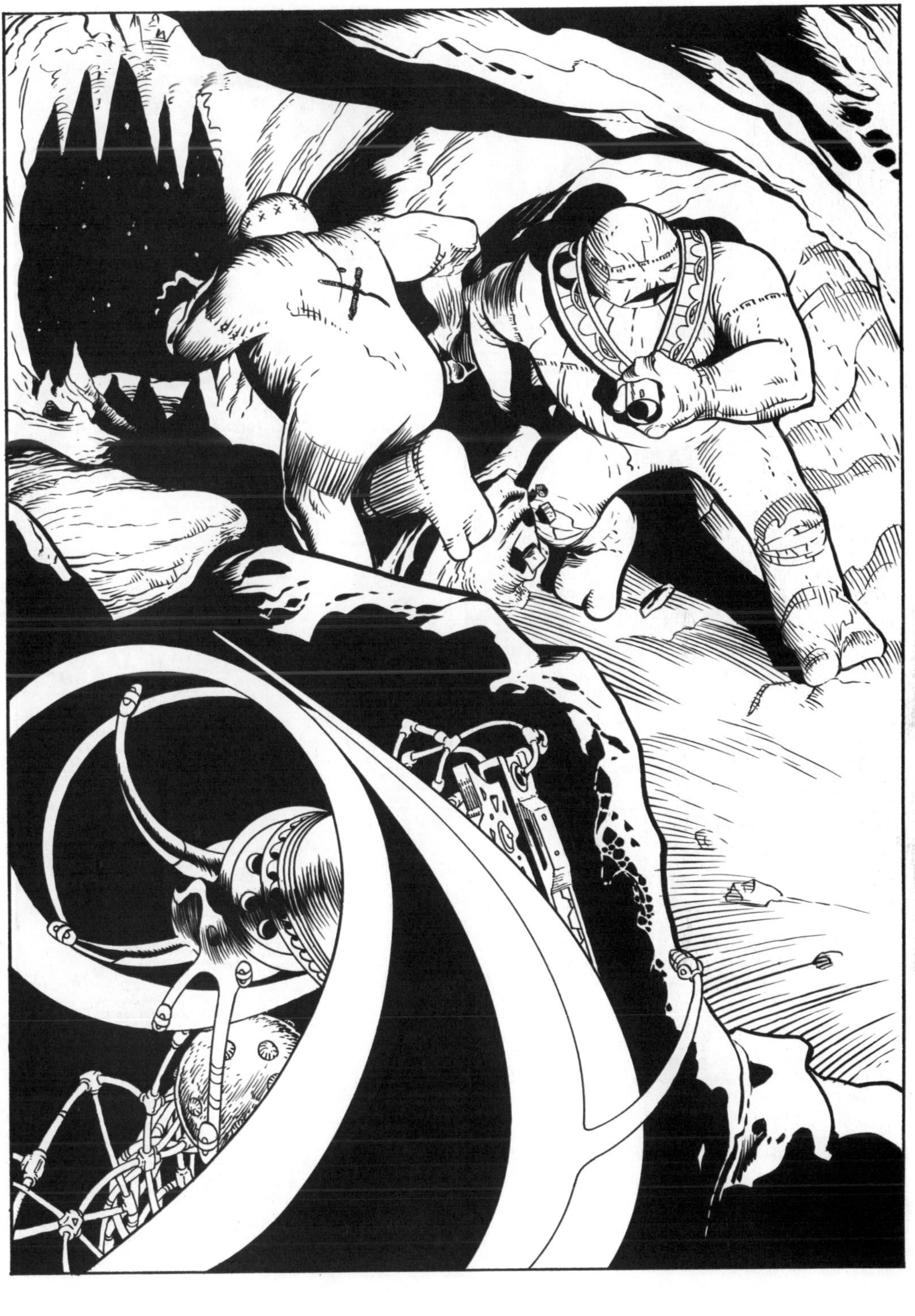

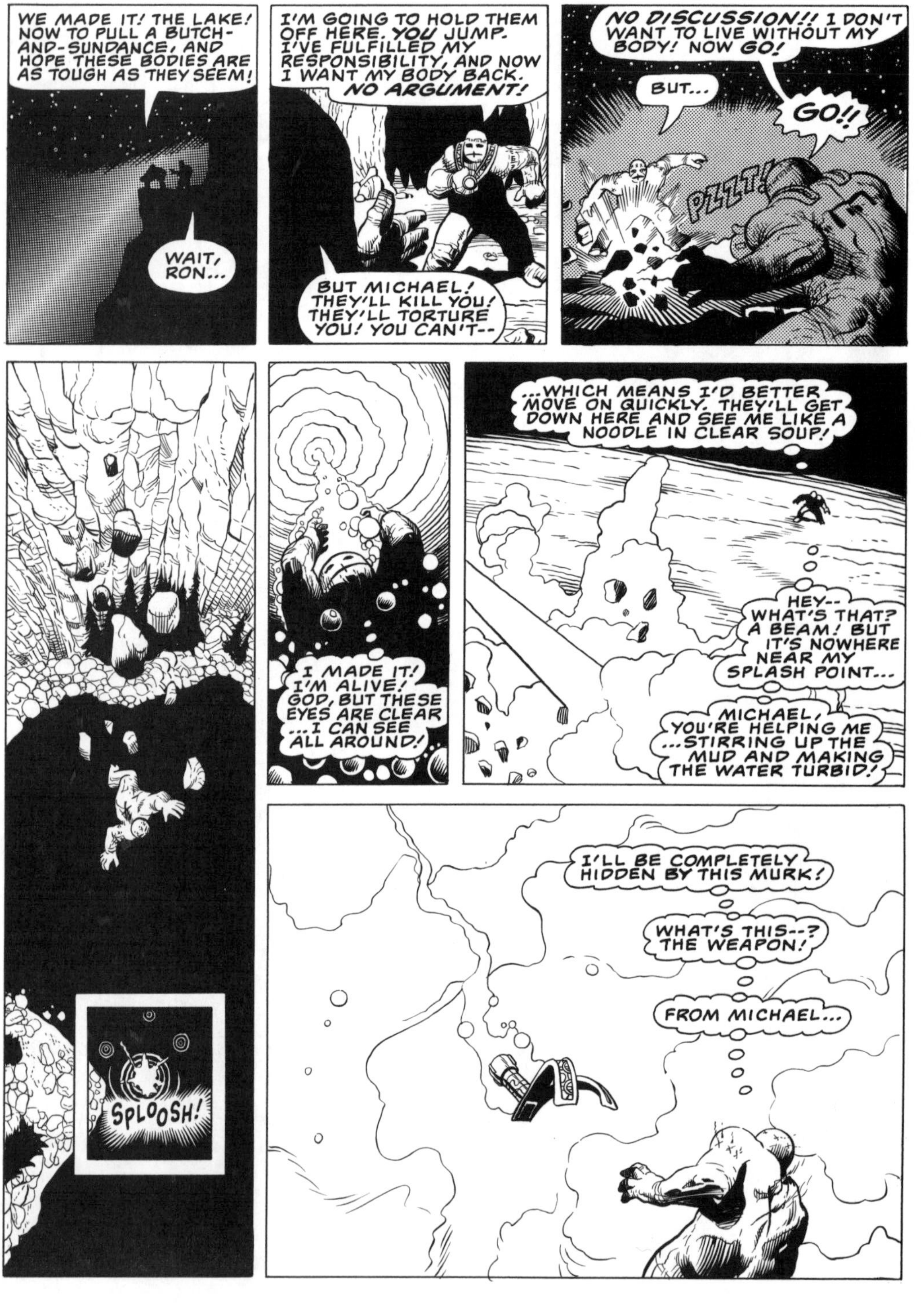
WE MADE IT! THE LAKE! NOW TO PULL A BUTCH-AND-SUNDANCE, AND HOPE THESE BODIES ARE AS TOUGH AS THEY SEEM!
WAIT, RON...
I'M GOING TO HOLD THEM OFF HERE. YOU JUMP. I'VE FULFILLED MY RESPONSIBILITY, AND NOW I WANT MY BODY BACK. NO ARGUMENT!
BUT MICHAEL! THEY'LL KILL YOU! THEY'LL TORTURE YOU! YOU CAN'T--
NO DISCUSSION!! I DON'T WANT TO LIVE WITHOUT MY BODY! NOW GO!
BUT...
GO!!
PZZZT!
SPLOOSH!
I MADE IT! I'M ALIVE! GOD, BUT THESE EYES ARE CLEAR ...I CAN SEE ALL AROUND!
...WHICH MEANS I'D BETTER MOVE ON QUICKLY. THEY'LL GET DOWN HERE AND SEE ME LIKE A NOODLE IN CLEAR SOUP!
HEY-- WHAT'S THAT? A BEAM! BUT IT'S NOWHERE NEAR MY SPLASH POINT...
MICHAEL, YOU'RE HELPING ME ...STIRRING UP THE MUD AND MAKING THE WATER TURBID!
I'LL BE COMPLETELY HIDDEN BY THIS MURK!
WHAT'S THIS--? THE WEAPON!
FROM MICHAEL...

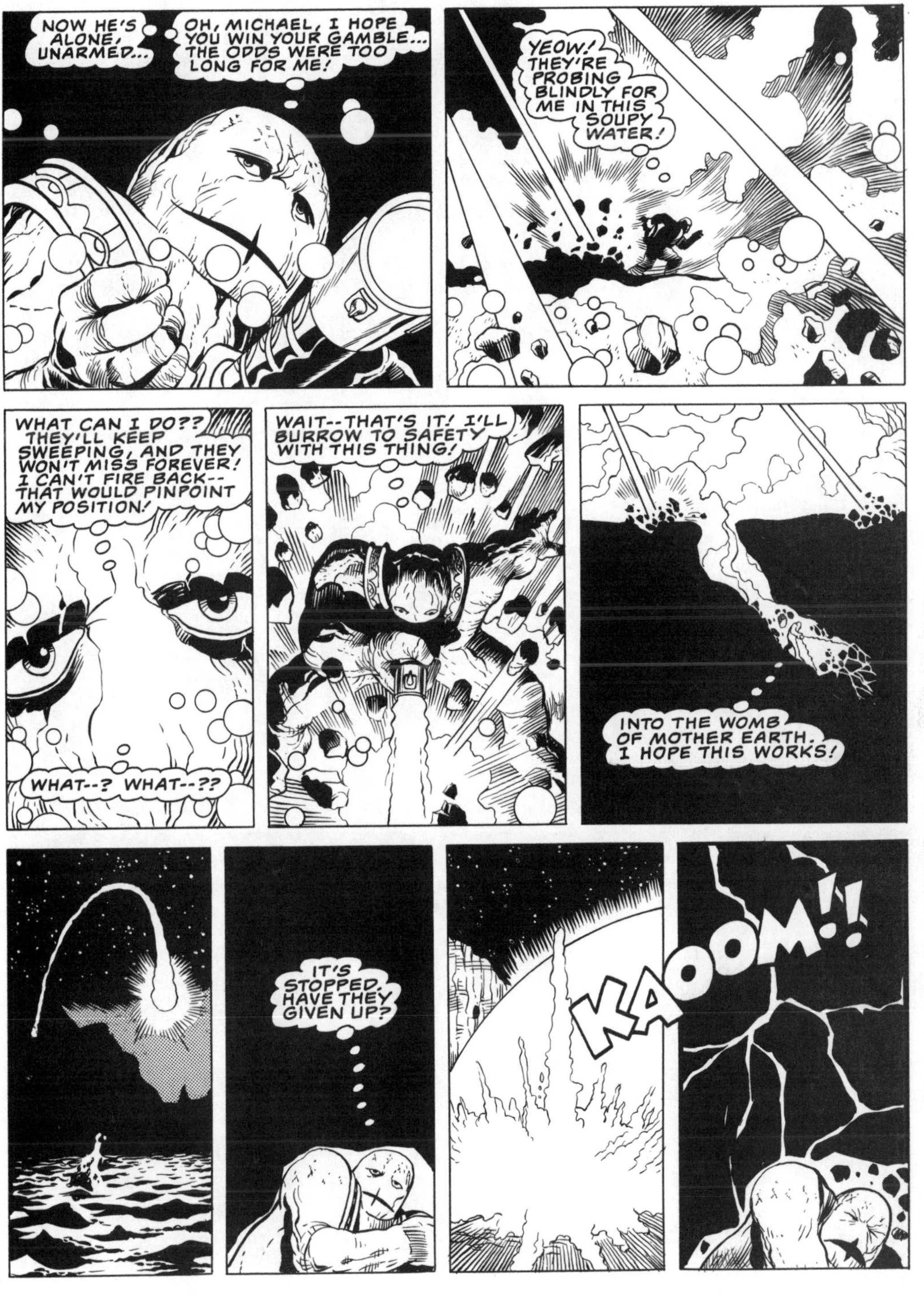

NOW HE'S ALONE, UNARMED...
OH, MICHAEL, I HOPE YOU WIN YOUR GAMBLE... THE ODDS WERE TOO LONG FOR ME!
YEOW! THEY'RE PROBING BLINDLY FOR ME IN THIS SOUPY WATER!
WHAT CAN I DO?? THEY'LL KEEP SWEEPING, AND THEY WON'T MISS FOREVER! I CAN'T FIRE BACK-- THAT WOULD PINPOINT MY POSITION!
WHAT--? WHAT--??
WAIT--THAT'S IT! I'LL BURROW TO SAFETY WITH THIS THING!
INTO THE WOMB OF MOTHER EARTH. I HOPE THIS WORKS!
IT'S STOPPED. HAVE THEY GIVEN UP?
KAOOM!!

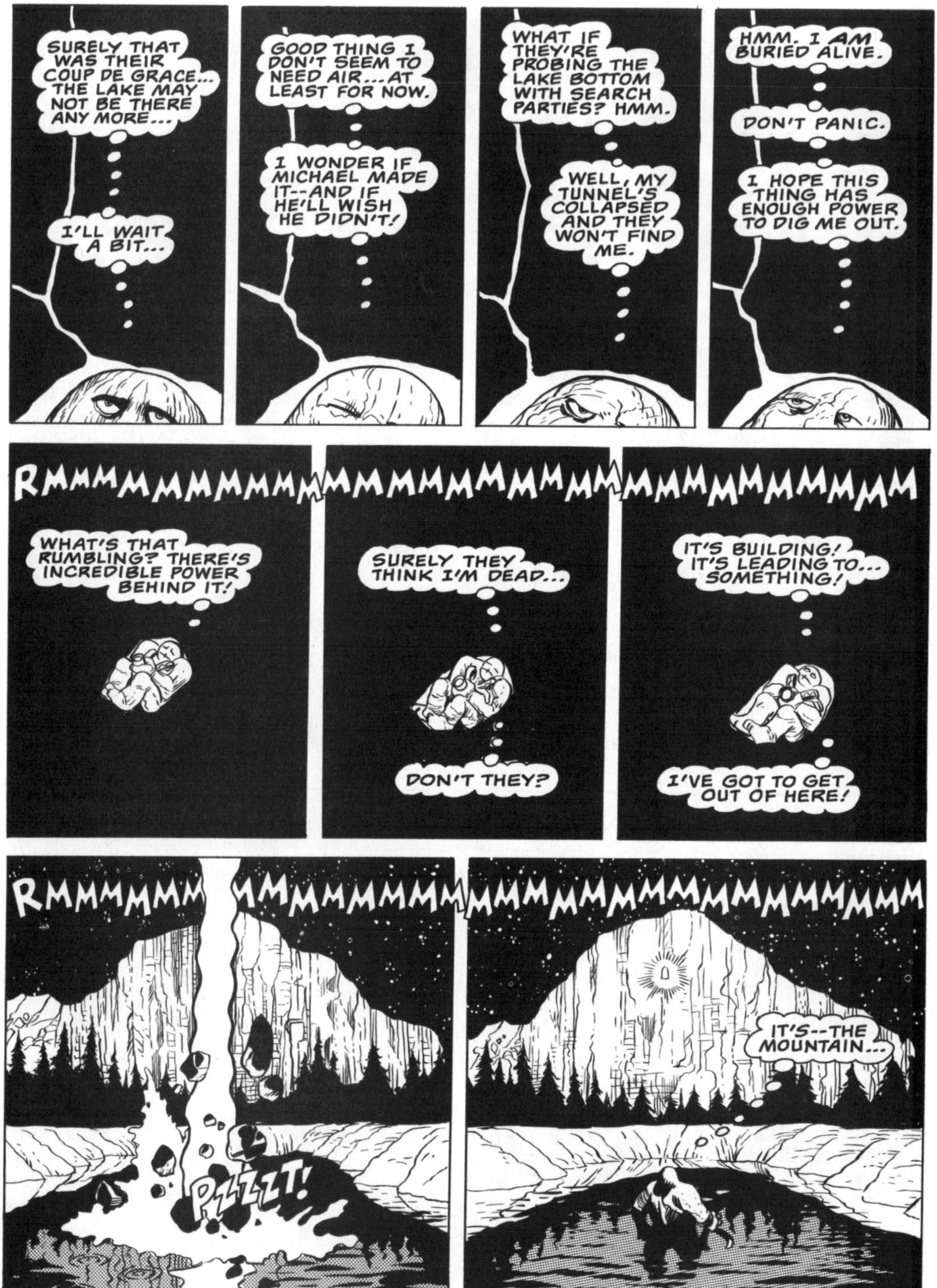
SURELY THAT WAS THEIR COUP DE GRACE... THE LAKE MAY NOT BE THERE ANY MORE...
I'LL WAIT A BIT...
GOOD THING I DON'T SEEM TO NEED AIR... AT LEAST FOR NOW.
I WONDER IF MICHAEL MADE IT--AND IF HE'LL WISH HE DIDN'T!
WHAT IF THEY'RE PROBING THE LAKE BOTTOM WITH SEARCH PARTIES? HMM.
WELL, MY TUNNEL'S COLLAPSED AND THEY WON'T FIND ME.
HMM. I AM BURIED ALIVE.
DON'T PANIC.
I HOPE THIS THING HAS ENOUGH POWER TO DIG ME OUT.
RMMMMMMMMMMMMMMMMMMMMMMMMMMMMMMMMMMMM
WHAT'S THAT RUMBLING? THERE'S INCREDIBLE POWER BEHIND IT!
SURELY THEY THINK I'M DEAD...
DON'T THEY?
IT'S BUILDING! IT'S LEADING TO... SOMETHING!
I'VE GOT TO GET OUT OF HERE!
RMMMMMMMMMMMMMMMMMMMMMMMMMMMMMMMMMMMMMMMMMMMM
PZZZZT!
IT'S--THE MOUNTAIN...

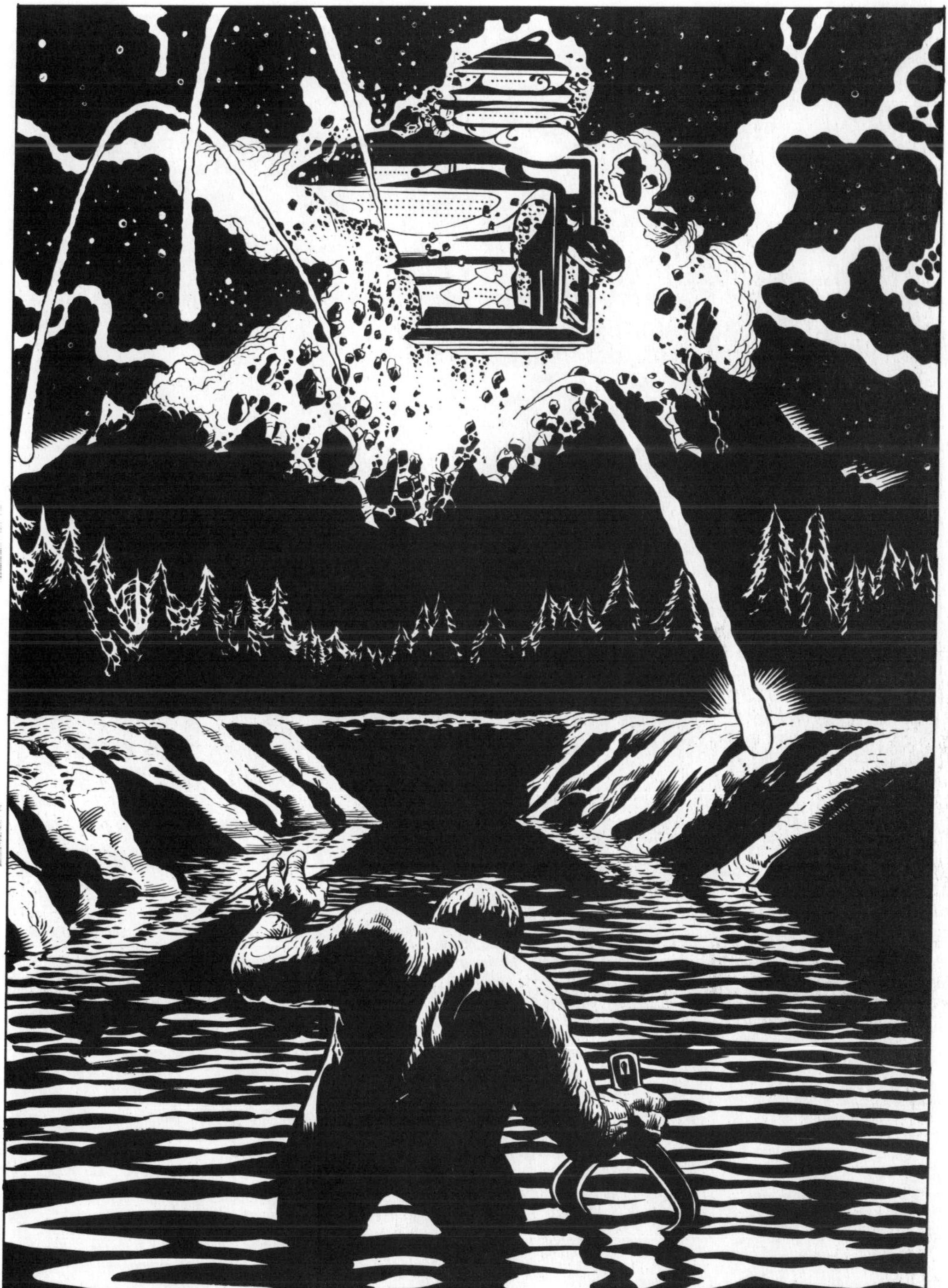

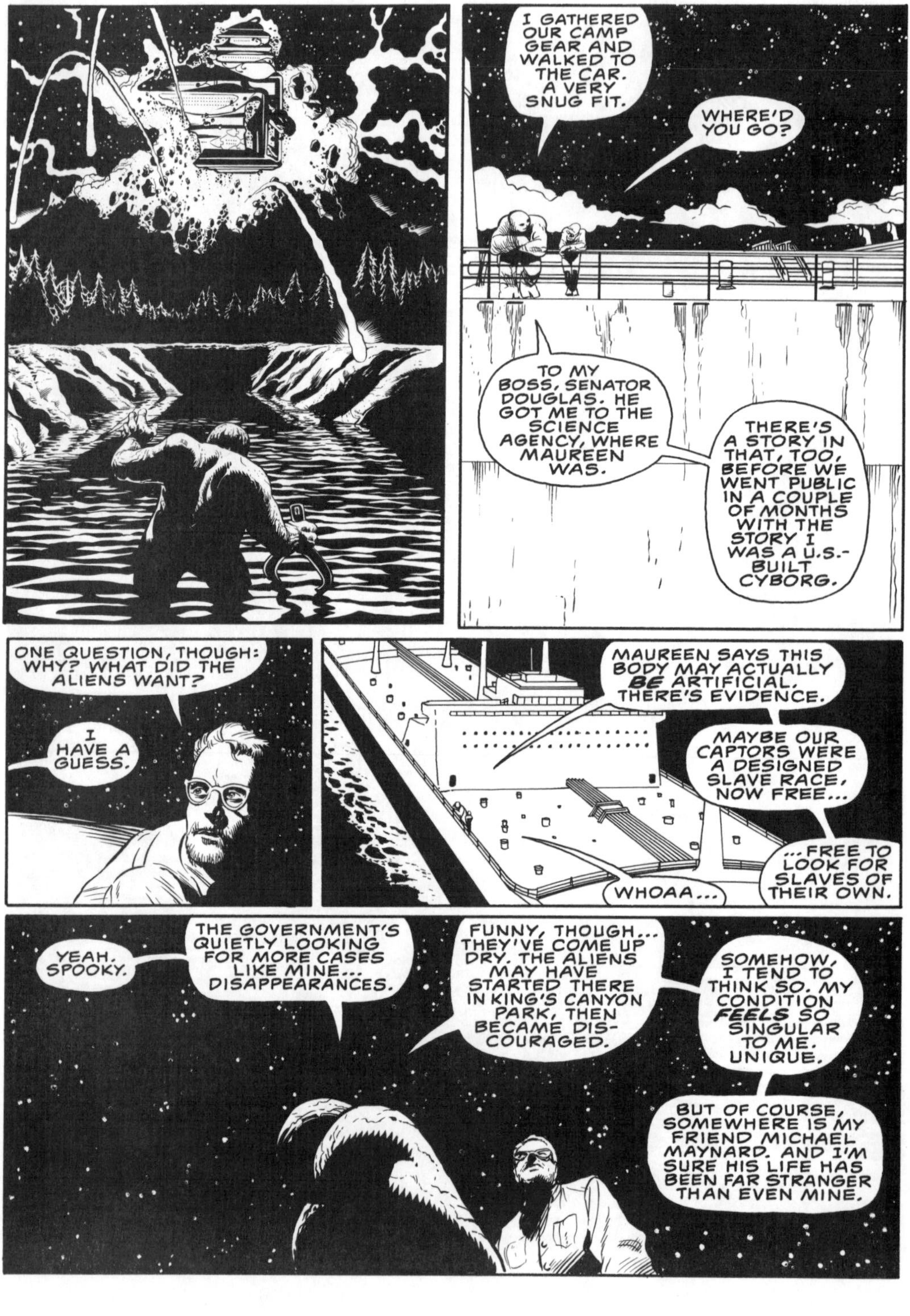

I GATHERED OUR CAMP GEAR AND WALKED TO THE CAR. A VERY SNUG FIT.
WHERE'D YOU GO?
TO MY BOSS, SENATOR DOUGLAS. HE GOT ME TO THE SCIENCE AGENCY, WHERE MAUREEN WAS.
THERE'S A STORY IN THAT, TOO, BEFORE WE WENT PUBLIC IN A COUPLE OF MONTHS WITH THE STORY I WAS A U.S.-BUILT CYBORG.
ONE QUESTION, THOUGH: WHY? WHAT DID THE ALIENS WANT?
I HAVE A GUESS.
MAUREEN SAYS THIS BODY MAY ACTUALLY *BE* ARTIFICIAL. THERE'S EVIDENCE.
MAYBE OUR CAPTORS WERE A DESIGNED SLAVE RACE, NOW FREE...
...FREE TO LOOK FOR SLAVES OF THEIR OWN.
WHOAA...
YEAH. SPOOKY.
THE GOVERNMENT'S QUIETLY LOOKING FOR MORE CASES LIKE MINE... DISAPPEARANCES.
FUNNY, THOUGH... THEY'VE COME UP DRY. THE ALIENS MAY HAVE STARTED THERE IN KING'S CANYON PARK, THEN BECAME DIS-COURAGED.
SOMEHOW, I TEND TO THINK SO. MY CONDITION *FEELS* SO SINGULAR TO ME. UNIQUE.
BUT OF COURSE, SOMEWHERE IS MY FRIEND MICHAEL MAYNARD. AND I'M SURE HIS LIFE HAS BEEN FAR STRANGER THAN EVEN MINE.

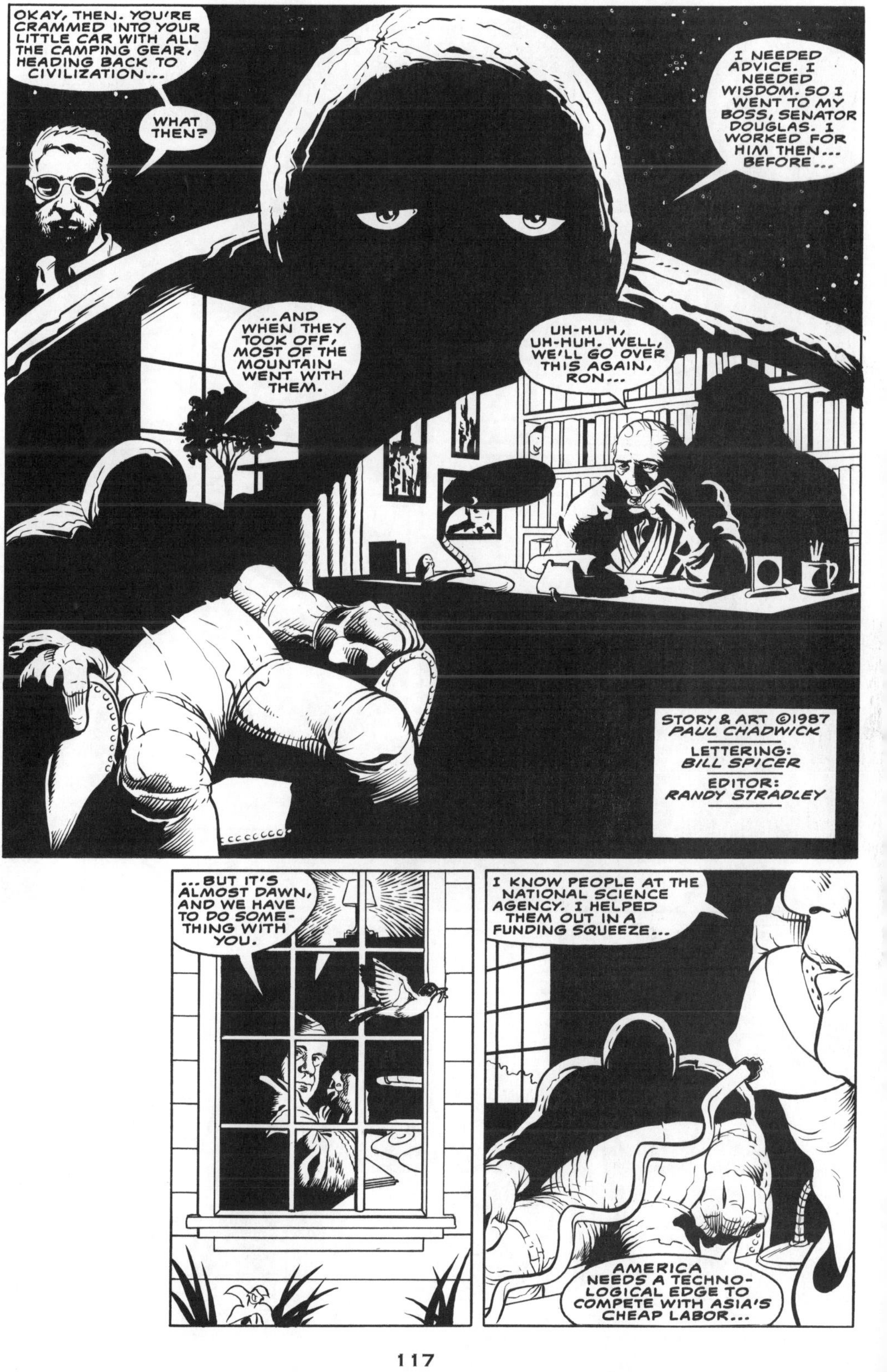
OKAY, THEN. YOU'RE CRAMMED INTO YOUR LITTLE CAR WITH ALL THE CAMPING GEAR, HEADING BACK TO CIVILIZATION...
WHAT THEN?
I NEEDED ADVICE. I NEEDED WISDOM. SO I WENT TO MY BOSS, SENATOR DOUGLAS. I WORKED FOR HIM THEN... BEFORE...
...AND WHEN THEY TOOK OFF, MOST OF THE MOUNTAIN WENT WITH THEM.
UH-HUH, UH-HUH. WELL, WE'LL GO OVER THIS AGAIN, RON...
STORY & ART ©1987 PAUL CHADWICK
LETTERING: BILL SPICER
EDITOR: RANDY STRADLEY
...BUT IT'S ALMOST DAWN, AND WE HAVE TO DO SOMETHING WITH YOU.
I KNOW PEOPLE AT THE NATIONAL SCIENCE AGENCY. I HELPED THEM OUT IN A FUNDING SQUEEZE...
AMERICA NEEDS A TECHNOLOGICAL EDGE TO COMPETE WITH ASIA'S CHEAP LABOR...

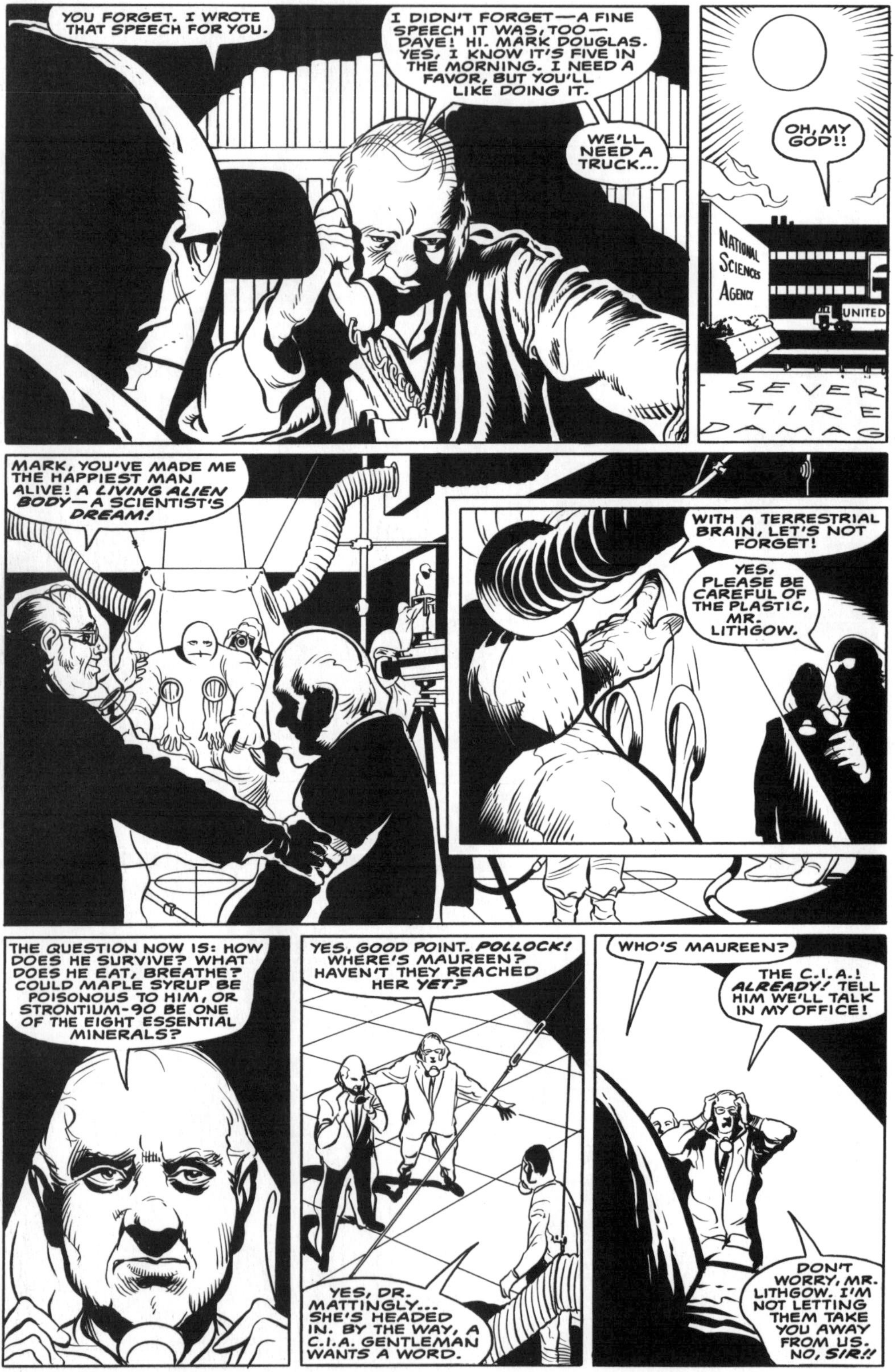
YOU FORGET. I WROTE THAT SPEECH FOR YOU.
I DIDN'T FORGET—A FINE SPEECH IT WAS, TOO—DAVE! HI. MARK DOUGLAS. YES, I KNOW IT'S FIVE IN THE MORNING. I NEED A FAVOR, BUT YOU'LL LIKE DOING IT.
WE'LL NEED A TRUCK...
OH, MY GOD!!
NATIONAL SCIENCES AGENCY
UNITED
SEVER TIRE DAMAG
MARK, YOU'VE MADE ME THE HAPPIEST MAN ALIVE! A LIVING ALIEN BODY—A SCIENTIST'S DREAM!
WITH A TERRESTRIAL BRAIN, LET'S NOT FORGET!
YES, PLEASE BE CAREFUL OF THE PLASTIC, MR. LITHGOW.
THE QUESTION NOW IS: HOW DOES HE SURVIVE? WHAT DOES HE EAT, BREATHE? COULD MAPLE SYRUP BE POISONOUS TO HIM, OR STRONTIUM-90 BE ONE OF THE EIGHT ESSENTIAL MINERALS?
YES, GOOD POINT. POLLOCK! WHERE'S MAUREEN? HAVEN'T THEY REACHED HER YET?
YES, DR. MATTINGLY... SHE'S HEADED IN. BY THE WAY, A C.I.A. GENTLEMAN WANTS A WORD.
WHO'S MAUREEN?
THE C.I.A.! ALREADY! TELL HIM WE'LL TALK IN MY OFFICE!
DON'T WORRY, MR. LITHGOW. I'M NOT LETTING THEM TAKE YOU AWAY FROM US. NO, SIR!!

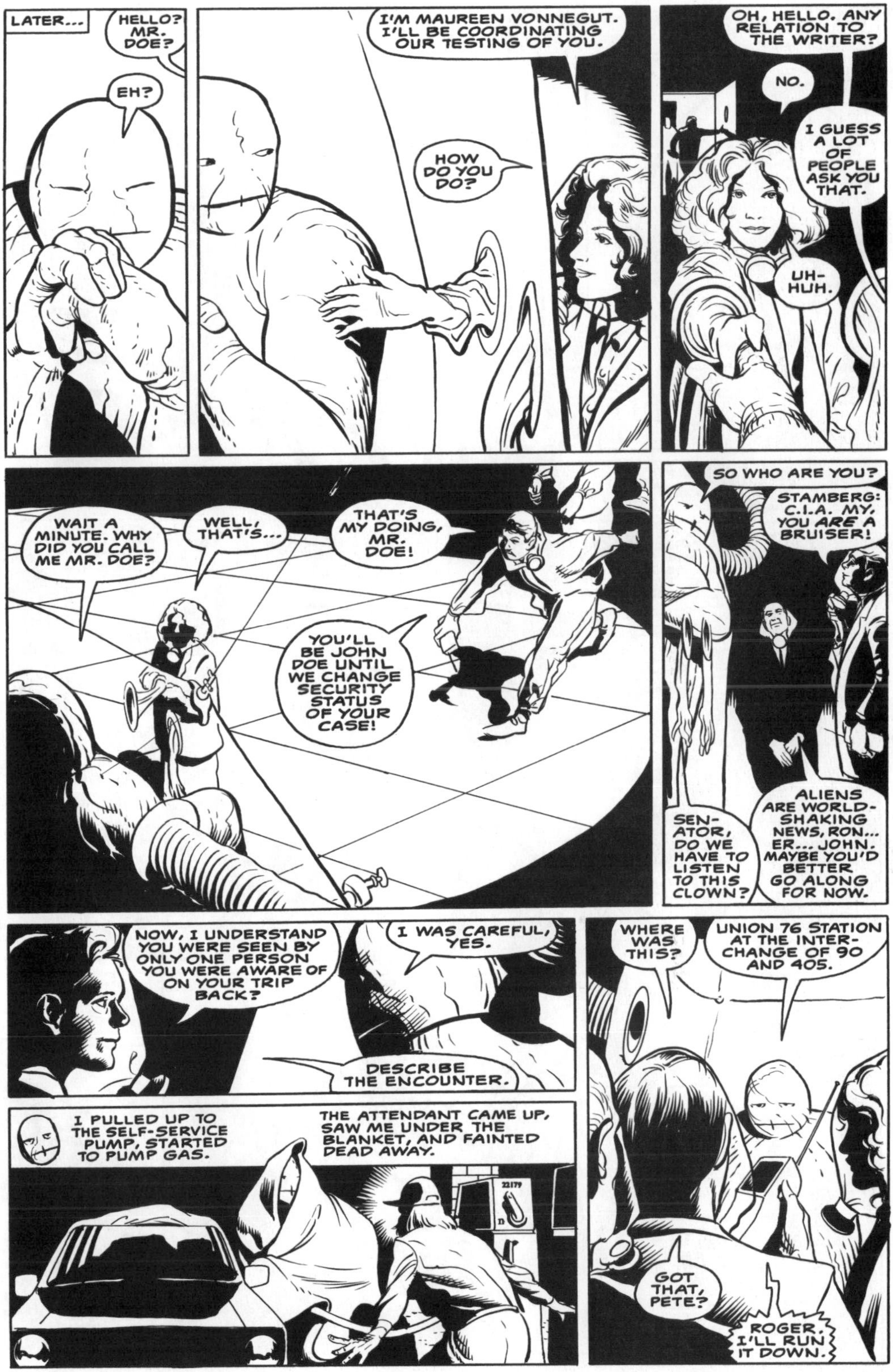

LATER...
HELLO? MR. DOE?
EH?
I'M MAUREEN VONNEGUT. I'LL BE COORDINATING OUR TESTING OF YOU.
HOW DO YOU DO?
OH, HELLO. ANY RELATION TO THE WRITER?
NO.
I GUESS A LOT OF PEOPLE ASK YOU THAT.
UH-HUH.
WAIT A MINUTE. WHY DID YOU CALL ME MR. DOE?
WELL, THAT'S...
THAT'S MY DOING, MR. DOE!
YOU'LL BE JOHN DOE UNTIL WE CHANGE SECURITY STATUS OF YOUR CASE!
SO WHO ARE YOU?
STAMBERG: C.I.A. MY, YOU ARE A BRUISER!
SENATOR, DO WE HAVE TO LISTEN TO THIS CLOWN?
ALIENS ARE WORLD-SHAKING NEWS, RON... ER... JOHN. MAYBE YOU'D BETTER GO ALONG FOR NOW.
NOW, I UNDERSTAND YOU WERE SEEN BY ONLY ONE PERSON YOU WERE AWARE OF ON YOUR TRIP BACK?
I WAS CAREFUL, YES.
DESCRIBE THE ENCOUNTER.
I PULLED UP TO THE SELF-SERVICE PUMP, STARTED TO PUMP GAS.
THE ATTENDANT CAME UP, SAW ME UNDER THE BLANKET, AND FAINTED DEAD AWAY.
WHERE WAS THIS?
UNION 76 STATION AT THE INTER-CHANGE OF 90 AND 405.
GOT THAT, PETE?
ROGER. I'LL RUN IT DOWN.

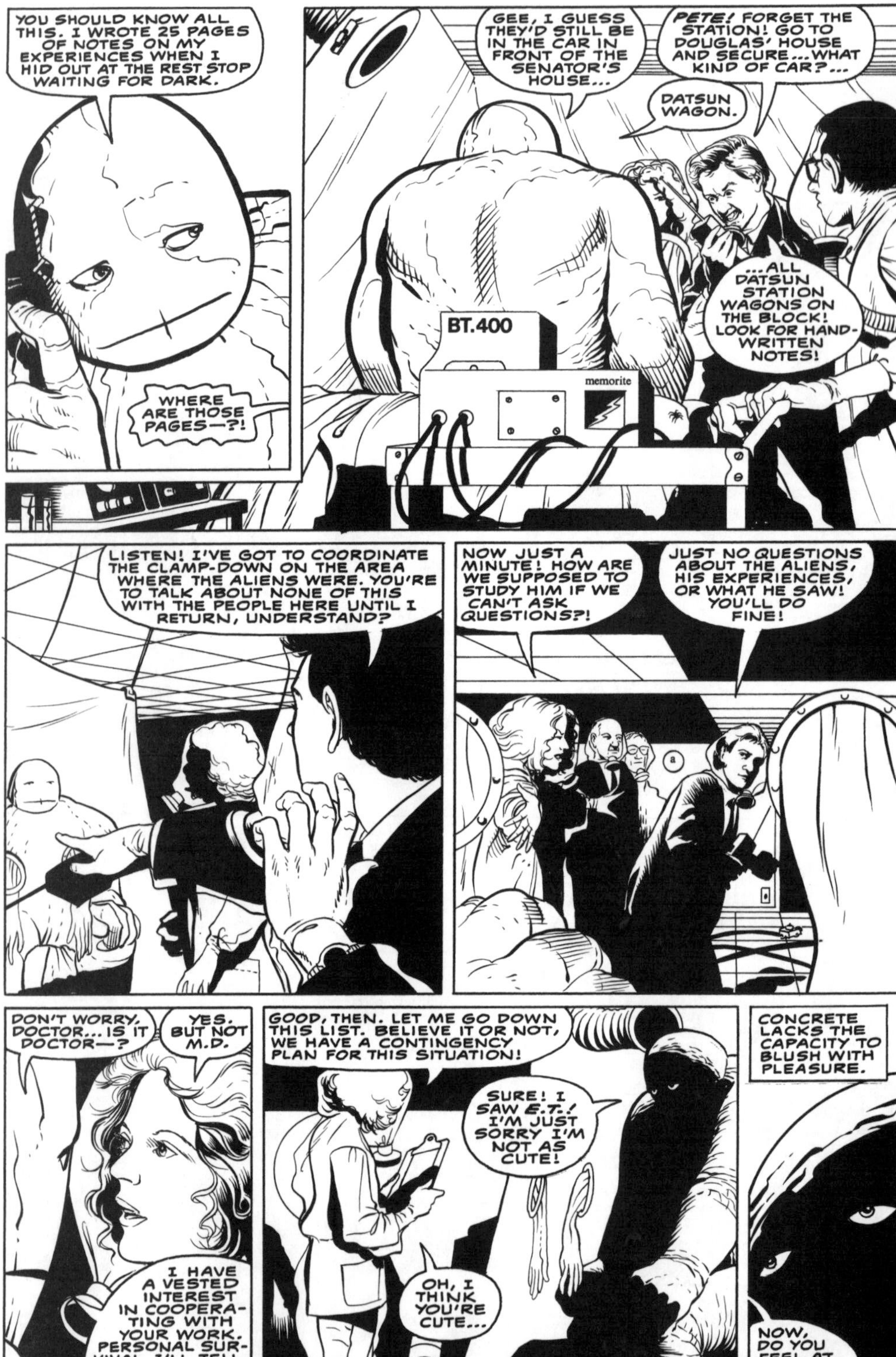
YOU SHOULD KNOW ALL THIS. I WROTE 25 PAGES OF NOTES ON MY EXPERIENCES WHEN I HID OUT AT THE REST STOP WAITING FOR DARK.
WHERE ARE THOSE PAGES—?!
GEE, I GUESS THEY'D STILL BE IN THE CAR IN FRONT OF THE SENATOR'S HOUSE...
PETE! FORGET THE STATION! GO TO DOUGLAS' HOUSE AND SECURE... WHAT KIND OF CAR?...
DATSUN WAGON.
...ALL DATSUN STATION WAGONS ON THE BLOCK! LOOK FOR HAND-WRITTEN NOTES!
BT.400
memorite
LISTEN! I'VE GOT TO COORDINATE THE CLAMP-DOWN ON THE AREA WHERE THE ALIENS WERE. YOU'RE TO TALK ABOUT NONE OF THIS WITH THE PEOPLE HERE UNTIL I RETURN, UNDERSTAND?
NOW JUST A MINUTE! HOW ARE WE SUPPOSED TO STUDY HIM IF WE CAN'T ASK QUESTIONS?!
JUST NO QUESTIONS ABOUT THE ALIENS, HIS EXPERIENCES, OR WHAT HE SAW! YOU'LL DO FINE!
DON'T WORRY, DOCTOR... IS IT DOCTOR—?
YES. BUT NOT M.D.
I HAVE A VESTED INTEREST IN COOPERATING WITH YOUR WORK. PERSONAL SURVIVAL. I'LL TELL YOU WHAT YOU NEED TO KNOW.
GOOD, THEN. LET ME GO DOWN THIS LIST. BELIEVE IT OR NOT, WE HAVE A CONTINGENCY PLAN FOR THIS SITUATION!
SURE! I SAW E.T.! I'M JUST SORRY I'M NOT AS CUTE!
OH, I THINK YOU'RE CUTE...
CONCRETE LACKS THE CAPACITY TO BLUSH WITH PLEASURE.
NOW, DO YOU FEEL AT ALL DEHYDRATED?

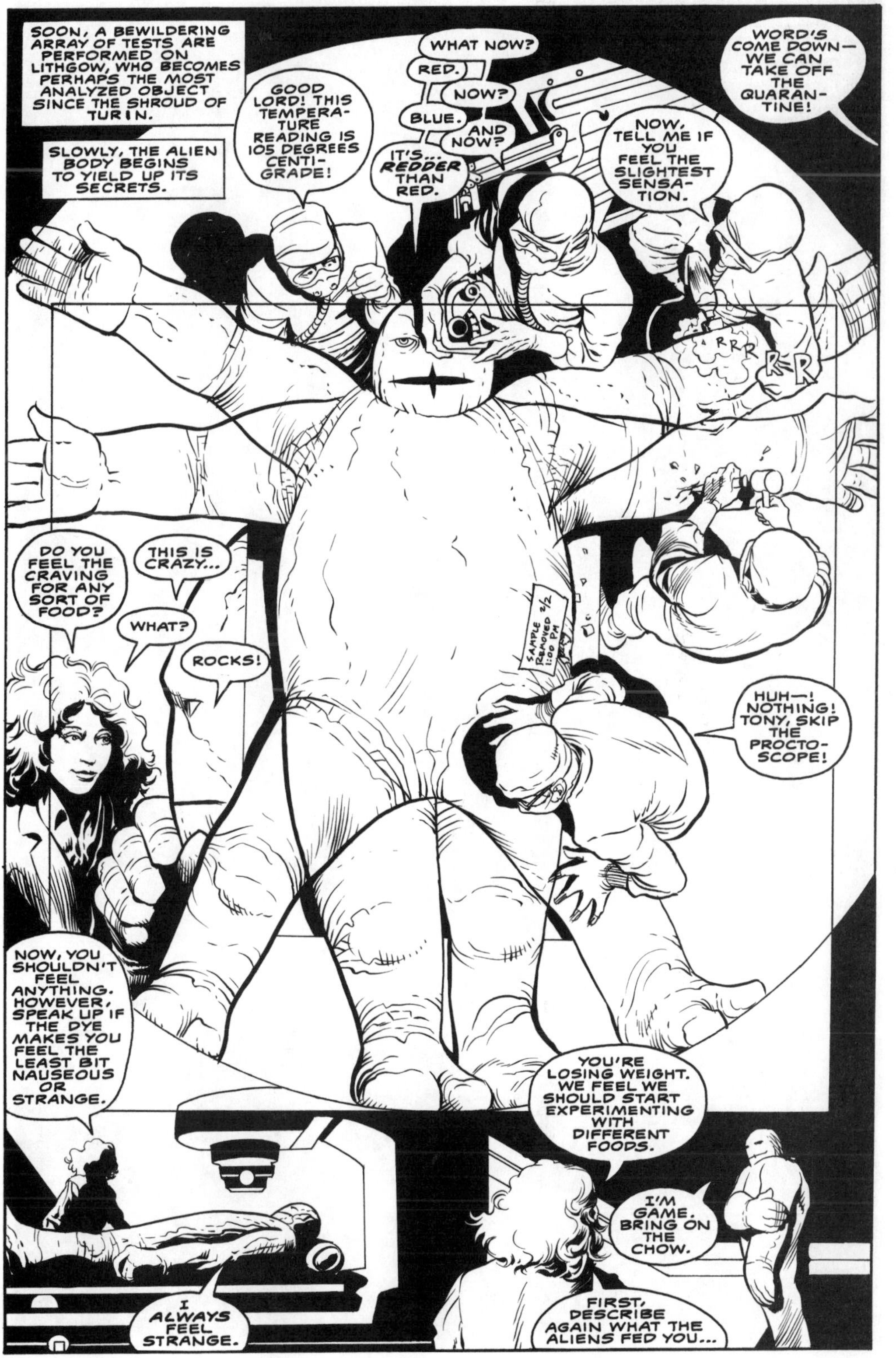
SOON, A BEWILDERING ARRAY OF TESTS ARE PERFORMED ON LITHGOW, WHO BECOMES PERHAPS THE MOST ANALYZED OBJECT SINCE THE SHROUD OF TURIN.
SLOWLY, THE ALIEN BODY BEGINS TO YIELD UP ITS SECRETS.
GOOD LORD! THIS TEMPERATURE READING IS 105 DEGREES CENTIGRADE!
WHAT NOW?
RED.
NOW?
BLUE.
AND NOW?
IT'S... REDDER THAN RED.
NOW, TELL ME IF YOU FEEL THE SLIGHTEST SENSATION.
WORD'S COME DOWN— WE CAN TAKE OFF THE QUARANTINE!
RRRRR
DO YOU FEEL THE CRAVING FOR ANY SORT OF FOOD?
THIS IS CRAZY...
WHAT?
ROCKS!
SAMPLE REMOVED 2/2 1:00 PM
HUH—! NOTHING! TONY, SKIP THE PROCTOSCOPE!
NOW, YOU SHOULDN'T FEEL ANYTHING. HOWEVER, SPEAK UP IF THE DYE MAKES YOU FEEL THE LEAST BIT NAUSEOUS OR STRANGE.
I ALWAYS FEEL STRANGE.
YOU'RE LOSING WEIGHT. WE FEEL WE SHOULD START EXPERIMENTING WITH DIFFERENT FOODS.
I'M GAME. BRING ON THE CHOW.
FIRST, DESCRIBE AGAIN WHAT THE ALIENS FED YOU...

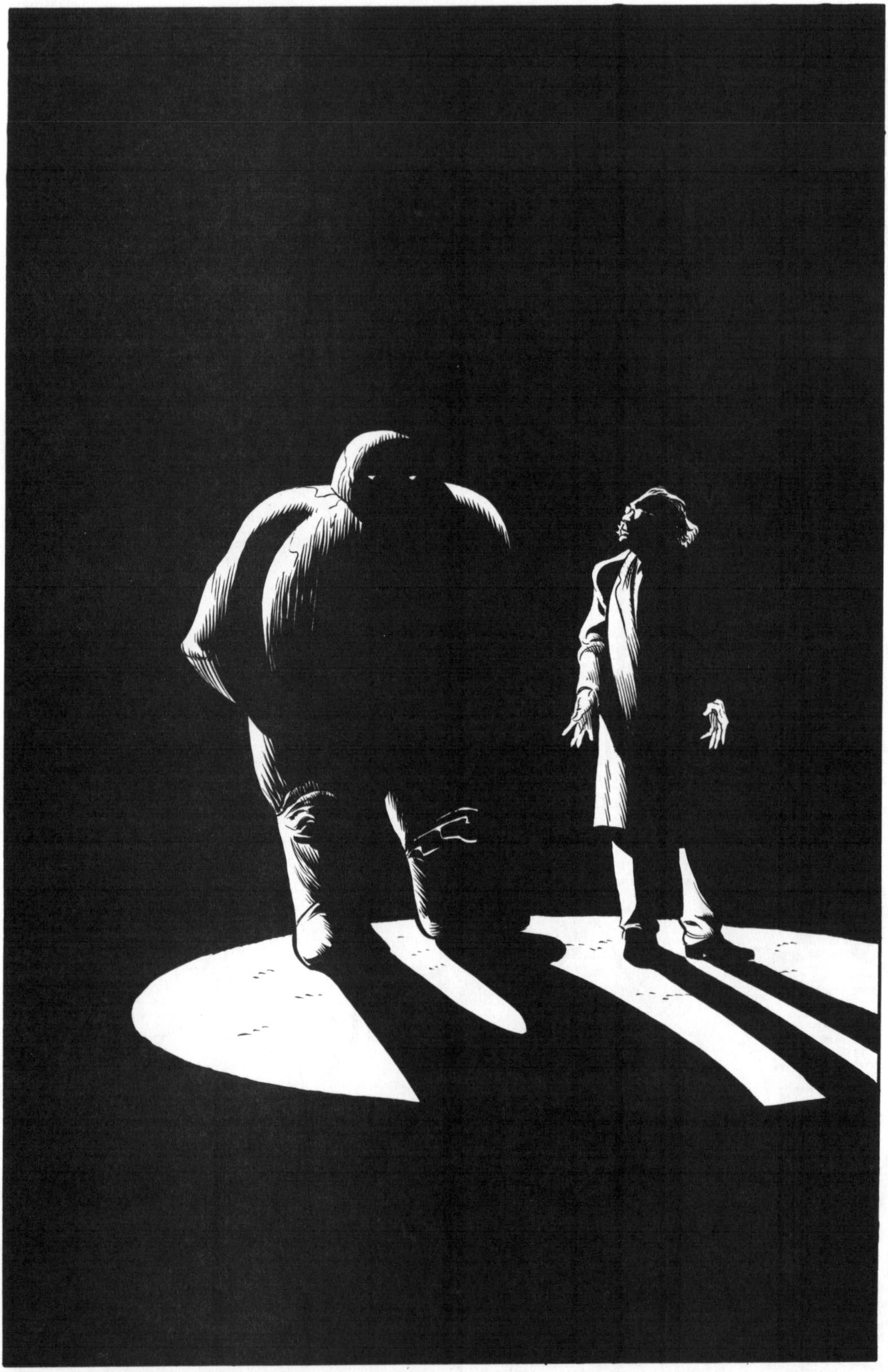

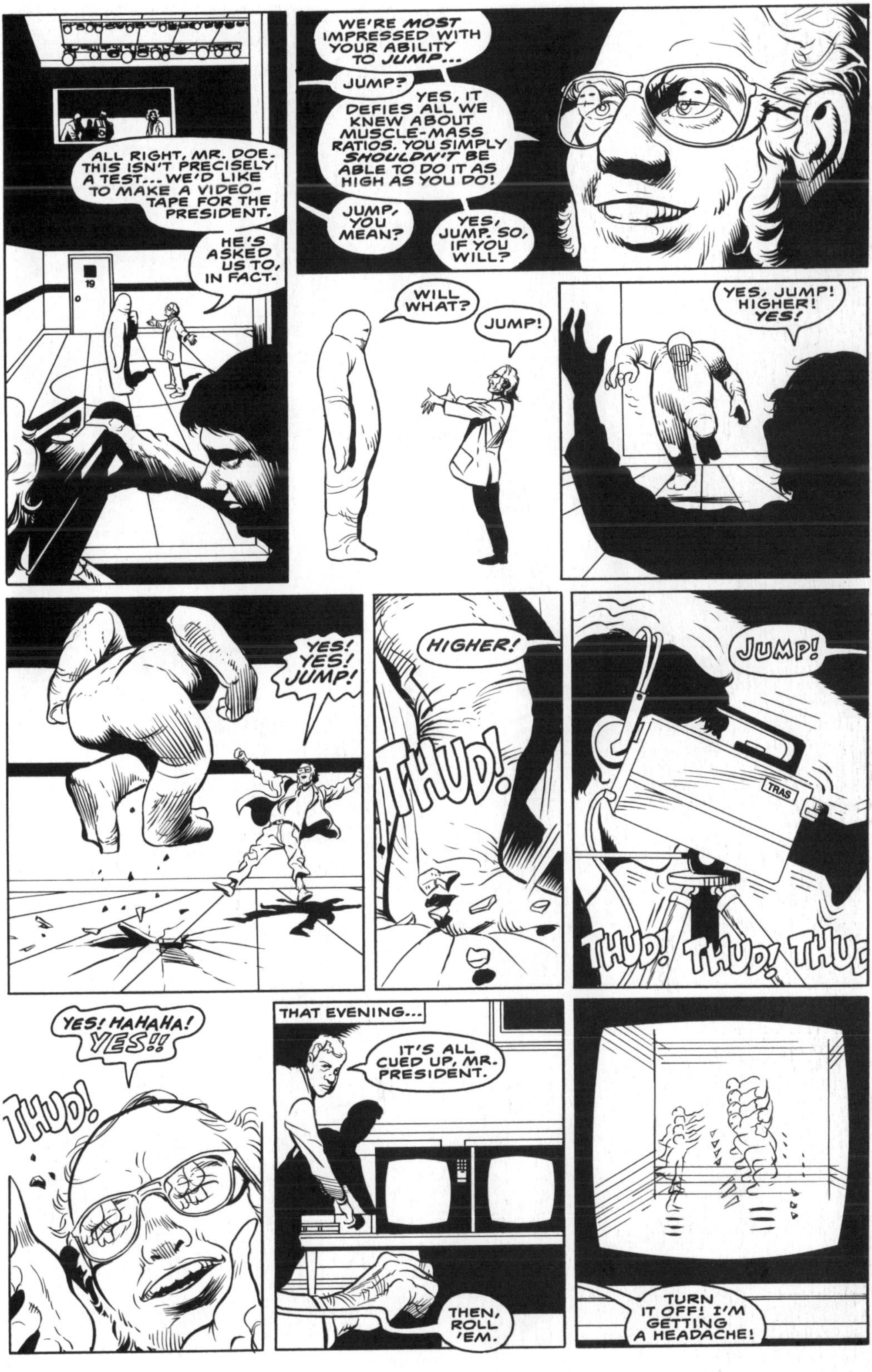
ALL RIGHT, MR. DOE. THIS ISN'T PRECISELY A TEST... WE'D LIKE TO MAKE A VIDEO-TAPE FOR THE PRESIDENT.
HE'S ASKED US TO, IN FACT.
19
WE'RE MOST IMPRESSED WITH YOUR ABILITY TO JUMP...
JUMP?
YES, IT DEFIES ALL WE KNEW ABOUT MUSCLE-MASS RATIOS. YOU SIMPLY SHOULDN'T BE ABLE TO DO IT AS HIGH AS YOU DO!
JUMP, YOU MEAN?
YES, JUMP. SO, IF YOU WILL?
WILL WHAT?
JUMP!
YES, JUMP! HIGHER! YES!
YES! YES! JUMP!
HIGHER!
THUD!
JUMP!
TRAS
THUD! THUD! THUD
YES! HAHAHA! YES!!
THUD!
THAT EVENING...
IT'S ALL CUED UP, MR. PRESIDENT.
THEN, ROLL 'EM.
TURN IT OFF! I'M GETTING A HEADACHE!

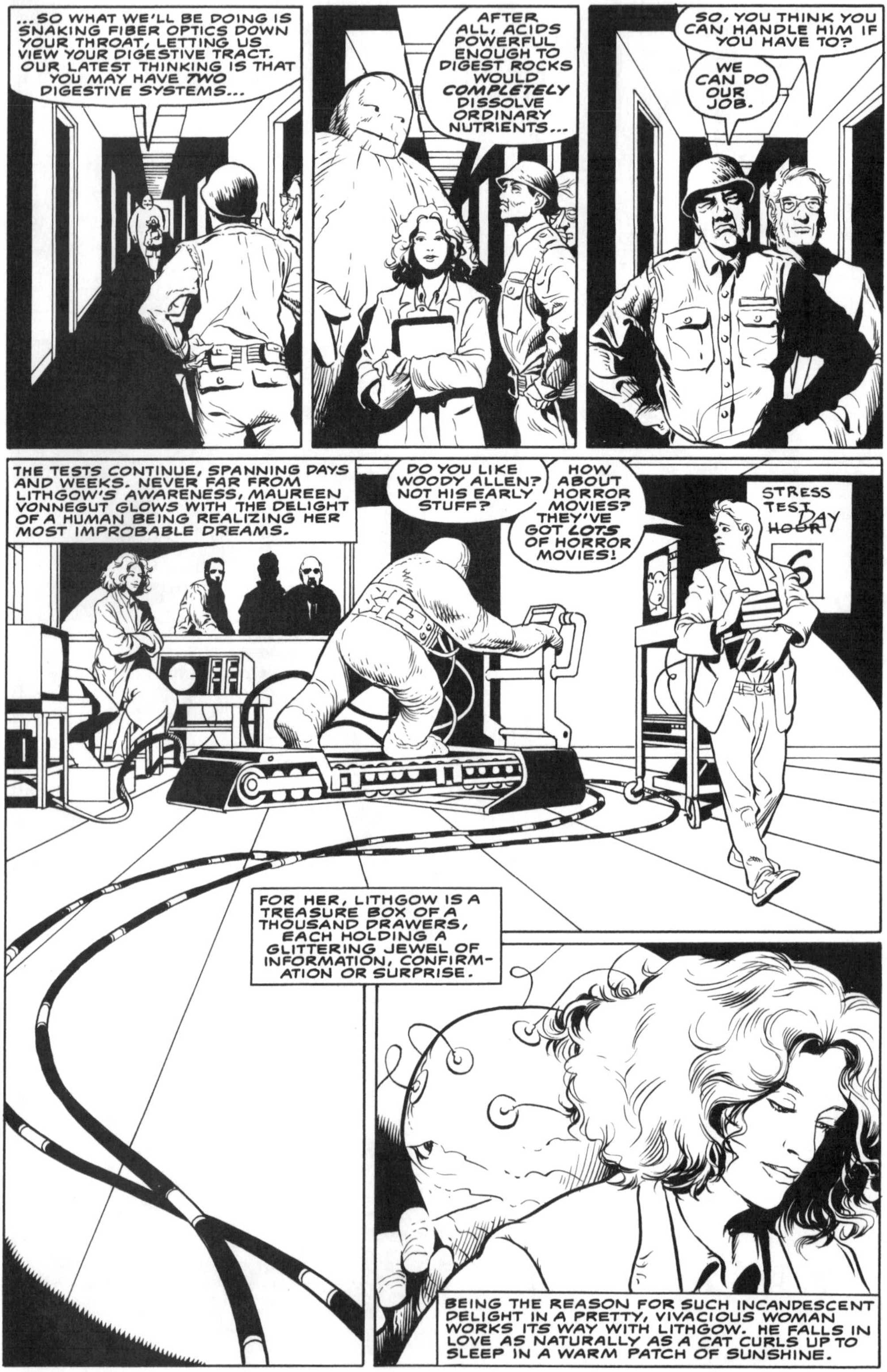
...SO WHAT WE'LL BE DOING IS SNAKING FIBER OPTICS DOWN YOUR THROAT, LETTING US VIEW YOUR DIGESTIVE TRACT. OUR LATEST THINKING IS THAT YOU MAY HAVE TWO DIGESTIVE SYSTEMS...
AFTER ALL, ACIDS POWERFUL ENOUGH TO DIGEST ROCKS WOULD COMPLETELY DISSOLVE ORDINARY NUTRIENTS...
SO, YOU THINK YOU CAN HANDLE HIM IF YOU HAVE TO?
WE CAN DO OUR JOB.
THE TESTS CONTINUE, SPANNING DAYS AND WEEKS. NEVER FAR FROM LITHGOW'S AWARENESS, MAUREEN VONNEGUT GLOWS WITH THE DELIGHT OF A HUMAN BEING REALIZING HER MOST IMPROBABLE DREAMS.
DO YOU LIKE WOODY ALLEN? NOT HIS EARLY STUFF?
HOW ABOUT HORROR MOVIES? THEY'VE GOT LOTS OF HORROR MOVIES!
STRESS TEST HOUR DAY
6
FOR HER, LITHGOW IS A TREASURE BOX OF A THOUSAND DRAWERS, EACH HOLDING A GLITTERING JEWEL OF INFORMATION, CONFIRMATION OR SURPRISE.
BEING THE REASON FOR SUCH INCANDESCENT DELIGHT IN A PRETTY, VIVACIOUS WOMAN WORKS ITS WAY WITH LITHGOW. HE FALLS IN LOVE AS NATURALLY AS A CAT CURLS UP TO SLEEP IN A WARM PATCH OF SUNSHINE.

SO MAUREEN WAS INVOLVED IN YOUR EARLY TESTING... THAT'S WHERE YOU MET HER?

YES, SHE WAS ONE OF THEM.

MAUREEN'S A WONDERFUL PERSON. DID YOU REALIZE THAT THEN?

YEAH, SHE WAS OKAY.

ANYWAY, THESE TESTS WERE BECOMING PRETTY BLOODY TEDIOUS, AND I'D BEGUN TO THINK ABOUT WHAT THE REST OF MY LIFE WOULD BE LIKE.

SENATOR DOUGLAS AND I TALKED IT OVER.

MY LIFE IS SHATTERED AND WAITING TO BE RE-ASSEMBLED IN A NEW WAY, SENATOR DOUGLAS.

I FIND MYSELF RETURNING TO MY EARLIEST DREAMS.

OH?

WHEN I WAS YOUNG— HIGH SCHOOL AGE— I IDOLIZED, WELL, ADVENTURERS... MEN WHO WENT TO THE WILDEST PARTS OF THE PLANET AND PUT THEMSELVES AT RISK FOR THE SHEER ZEST OF IT.

THIS DOESN'T SOUND LIKE YOU AT ALL, RON.

BELIEVE ME, I REALIZE THAT!

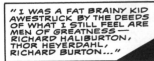

"I WAS A FAT BRAINY KID AWESTRUCK BY THE DEEDS OF WHAT I STILL FEEL ARE MEN OF GREATNESS— RICHARD HALIBURTON, THOR HEYERDAHL, RICHARD BURTON..."

"I PRACTICALLY INHALED BOOKS BY THESE GUYS... EXOTIC TALES OF GENUINE DANGER AND GLORY— AND TRUE, BY GOD!"

WHO ARE THESE FELLOWS? SOME OF THEIR NAMES RING A BELL...

WELL, HALIBURTON WAS SORT OF A GLORY-HUNTING GLOBETROTTER WHO WROTE BESTSELLERS OF HIS ADVENTURES IN AFRICA AND ASIA IN THE '20s.

HEYERDAHL'S STILL ALIVE, I THINK. HE'D BUILD AND SAIL RECON-STRUCTIONS OF ANCIENT BOATS OUT OF ORIGINAL MATERIALS—BALSA OR PAPYRUS, FOR EXAMPLE—TO TEST THE PLAUSIBILITY OF HIS THEORIES ON HUMAN MIGRATION.

BURTON, THOUGH— HE WAS MY HERO. THIS RICHARD BURTON WASN'T AN ACTOR, BUT A VICTORIAN-AGE ENGLISHMAN, AN EXPLORER AND SCHOLAR AND SWORDSMAN.

LORDY, WHAT A CHARACTER...

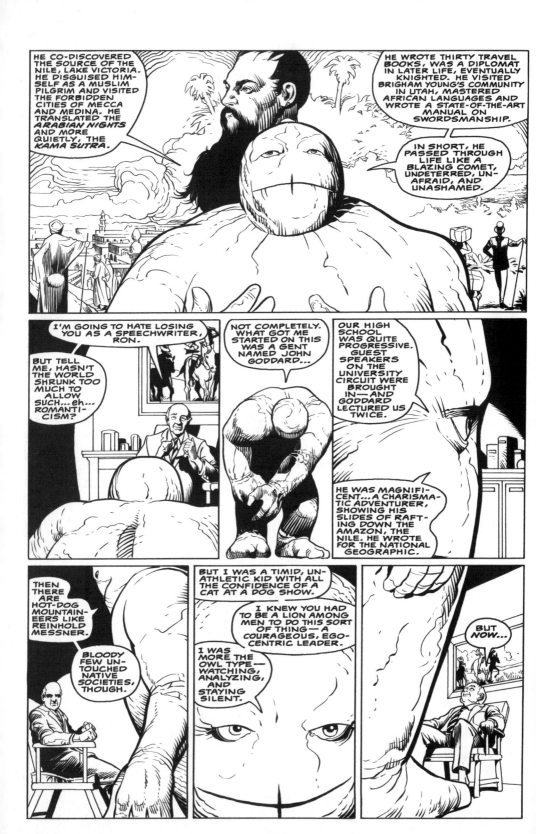

HE CO-DISCOVERED THE SOURCE OF THE NILE, LAKE VICTORIA. HE DISGUISED HIMSELF AS A MUSLIM PILGRIM AND VISITED THE FORBIDDEN CITIES OF MECCA AND MEDINA. HE TRANSLATED THE *ARABIAN NIGHTS* AND MORE QUIETLY, THE *KAMA SUTRA*.

HE WROTE THIRTY TRAVEL BOOKS, WAS A DIPLOMAT IN LATER LIFE, EVENTUALLY KNIGHTED. HE VISITED BRIGHAM YOUNG'S COMMUNITY IN UTAH, MASTERED AFRICAN LANGUAGES AND WROTE A STATE-OF-THE-ART MANUAL ON SWORDSMANSHIP.

IN SHORT, HE PASSED THROUGH LIFE LIKE A BLAZING COMET, UNDETERRED, UNAFRAID, AND UNASHAMED.

I'M GOING TO HATE LOSING YOU AS A SPEECHWRITER, RON.

BUT TELL ME, HASN'T THE WORLD SHRUNK TOO MUCH TO ALLOW SUCH... EH... ROMANTICISM?

NOT COMPLETELY. WHAT GOT ME STARTED ON THIS WAS A GENT NAMED JOHN GODDARD...

OUR HIGH SCHOOL WAS QUITE PROGRESSIVE. GUEST SPEAKERS ON THE UNIVERSITY CIRCUIT WERE BROUGHT IN—AND GODDARD LECTURED US TWICE.

HE WAS MAGNIFICENT... A CHARISMATIC ADVENTURER, SHOWING HIS SLIDES OF RAFTING DOWN THE AMAZON, THE NILE. HE WROTE FOR THE NATIONAL GEOGRAPHIC.

THEN THERE ARE HOT-DOG MOUNTAINEERS LIKE REINHOLD MESSNER.

BLOODY FEW UNTOUCHED NATIVE SOCIETIES, THOUGH.

BUT I WAS A TIMID, UNATHLETIC KID WITH ALL THE CONFIDENCE OF A CAT AT A DOG SHOW.

I KNEW YOU HAD TO BE A LION AMONG MEN TO DO THIS SORT OF THING—A COURAGEOUS, EGOCENTRIC LEADER.

I WAS MORE THE OWL TYPE— WATCHING, ANALYZING, AND STAYING SILENT.

BUT NOW...

126

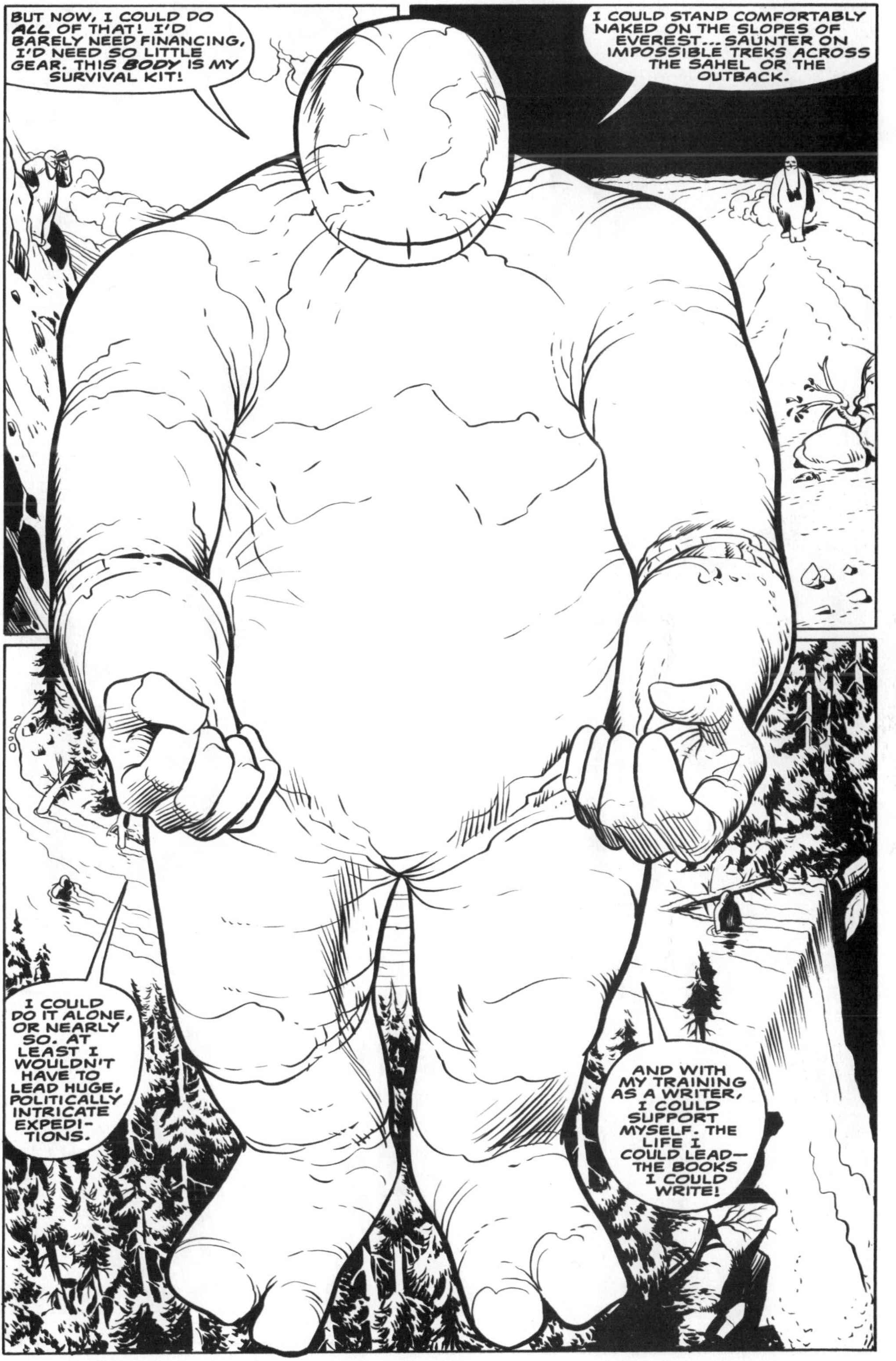
BUT NOW, I COULD DO *ALL* OF THAT! I'D BARELY NEED FINANCING, I'D NEED SO LITTLE GEAR. THIS *BODY* IS MY SURVIVAL KIT!
I COULD STAND COMFORTABLY NAKED ON THE SLOPES OF EVEREST... SAUNTER ON IMPOSSIBLE TREKS ACROSS THE SAHEL OR THE OUTBACK.
I COULD DO IT ALONE, OR NEARLY SO. AT LEAST I WOULDN'T HAVE TO LEAD HUGE, POLITICALLY INTRICATE EXPEDITIONS.
AND WITH MY TRAINING AS A WRITER, I COULD SUPPORT MYSELF. THE LIFE I COULD LEAD— THE BOOKS I COULD WRITE!

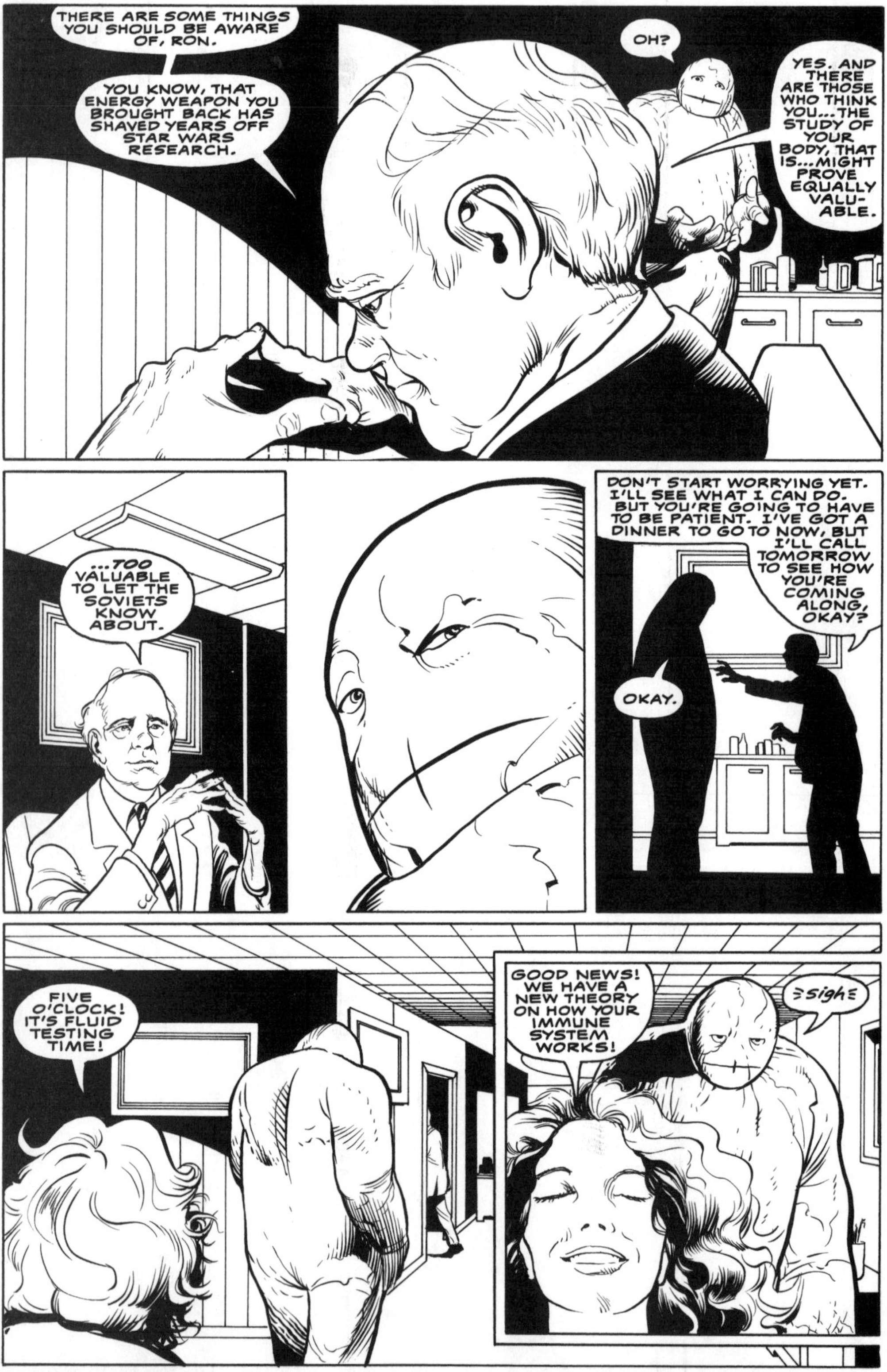
THERE ARE SOME THINGS YOU SHOULD BE AWARE OF, RON.
OH?
YOU KNOW, THAT ENERGY WEAPON YOU BROUGHT BACK HAS SHAVED YEARS OFF STAR WARS RESEARCH.
YES. AND THERE ARE THOSE WHO THINK YOU...THE STUDY OF YOUR BODY, THAT IS...MIGHT PROVE EQUALLY VALUABLE.
...TOO VALUABLE TO LET THE SOVIETS KNOW ABOUT.
DON'T START WORRYING YET. I'LL SEE WHAT I CAN DO. BUT YOU'RE GOING TO HAVE TO BE PATIENT. I'VE GOT A DINNER TO GO TO NOW, BUT I'LL CALL TOMORROW TO SEE HOW YOU'RE COMING ALONG, OKAY?
OKAY.
FIVE O'CLOCK! IT'S FLUID TESTING TIME!
GOOD NEWS! WE HAVE A NEW THEORY ON HOW YOUR IMMUNE SYSTEM WORKS!
sigh

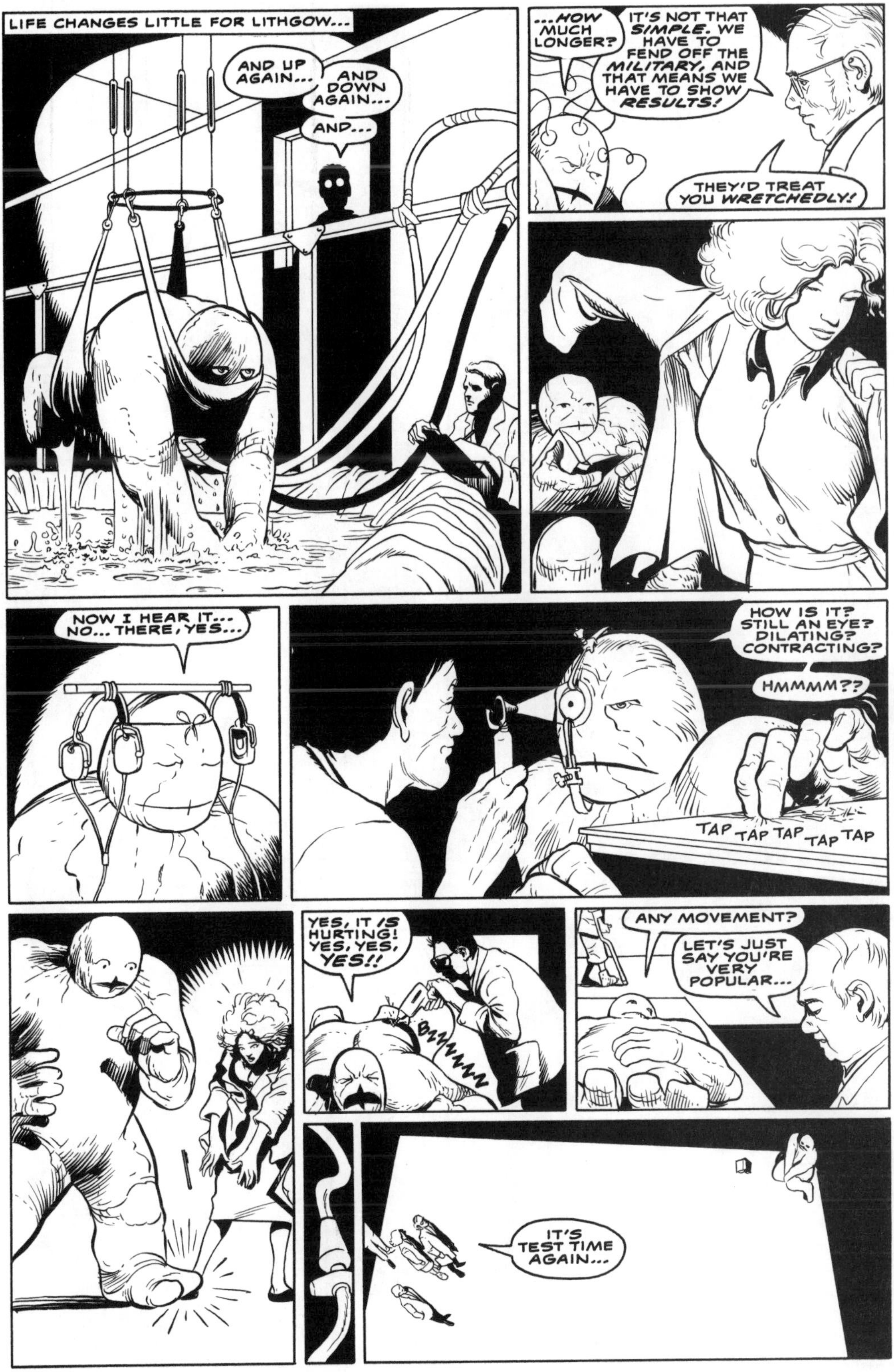

LIFE CHANGES LITTLE FOR LITHGOW...
AND UP AGAIN...
AND DOWN AGAIN...
AND...
...HOW MUCH LONGER?
IT'S NOT THAT SIMPLE. WE HAVE TO FEND OFF THE MILITARY, AND THAT MEANS WE HAVE TO SHOW RESULTS!
THEY'D TREAT YOU WRETCHEDLY!
NOW I HEAR IT... NO... THERE, YES...
HOW IS IT? STILL AN EYE? DILATING? CONTRACTING?
HMMMM??
TAP TAP TAP TAP TAP
YES, IT IS HURTING! YES, YES, YES!!
BZZZNNNN
ANY MOVEMENT?
LET'S JUST SAY YOU'RE VERY POPULAR...
IT'S TEST TIME AGAIN...

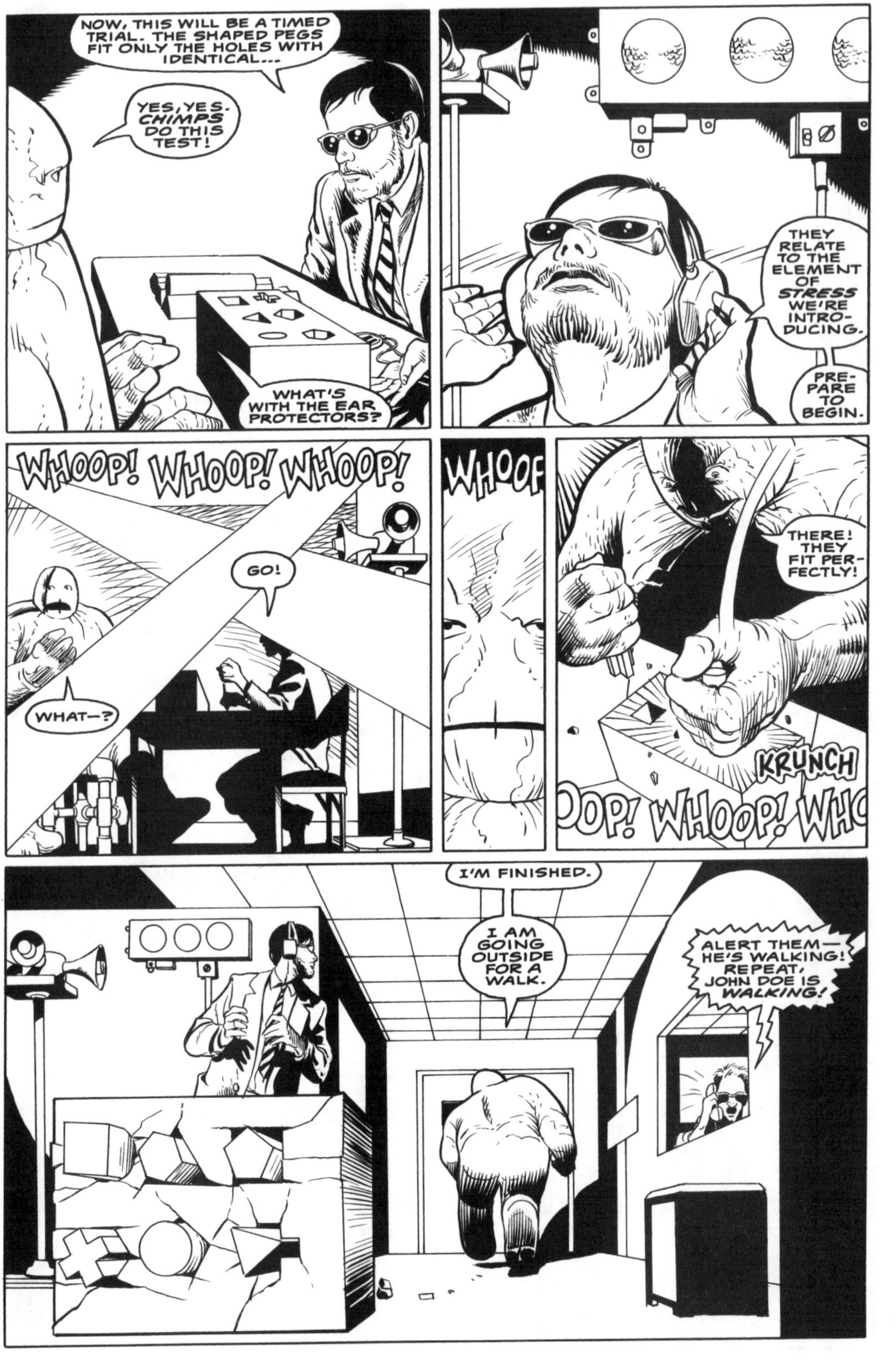
NOW, THIS WILL BE A TIMED TRIAL. THE SHAPED PEGS FIT ONLY THE HOLES WITH IDENTICAL...
YES, YES. CHIMPS DO THIS TEST!
WHAT'S WITH THE EAR PROTECTORS?
THEY RELATE TO THE ELEMENT OF STRESS WE'RE INTRODUCING.
PREPARE TO BEGIN.
WHOOP! WHOOP! WHOOP!
GO!
WHAT—?
WHOOF
THERE! THEY FIT PERFECTLY!
KRUNCH
OOP! WHOOP! WHO
I'M FINISHED.
I AM GOING OUTSIDE FOR A WALK.
ALERT THEM— HE'S WALKING! REPEAT, JOHN DOE IS WALKING!

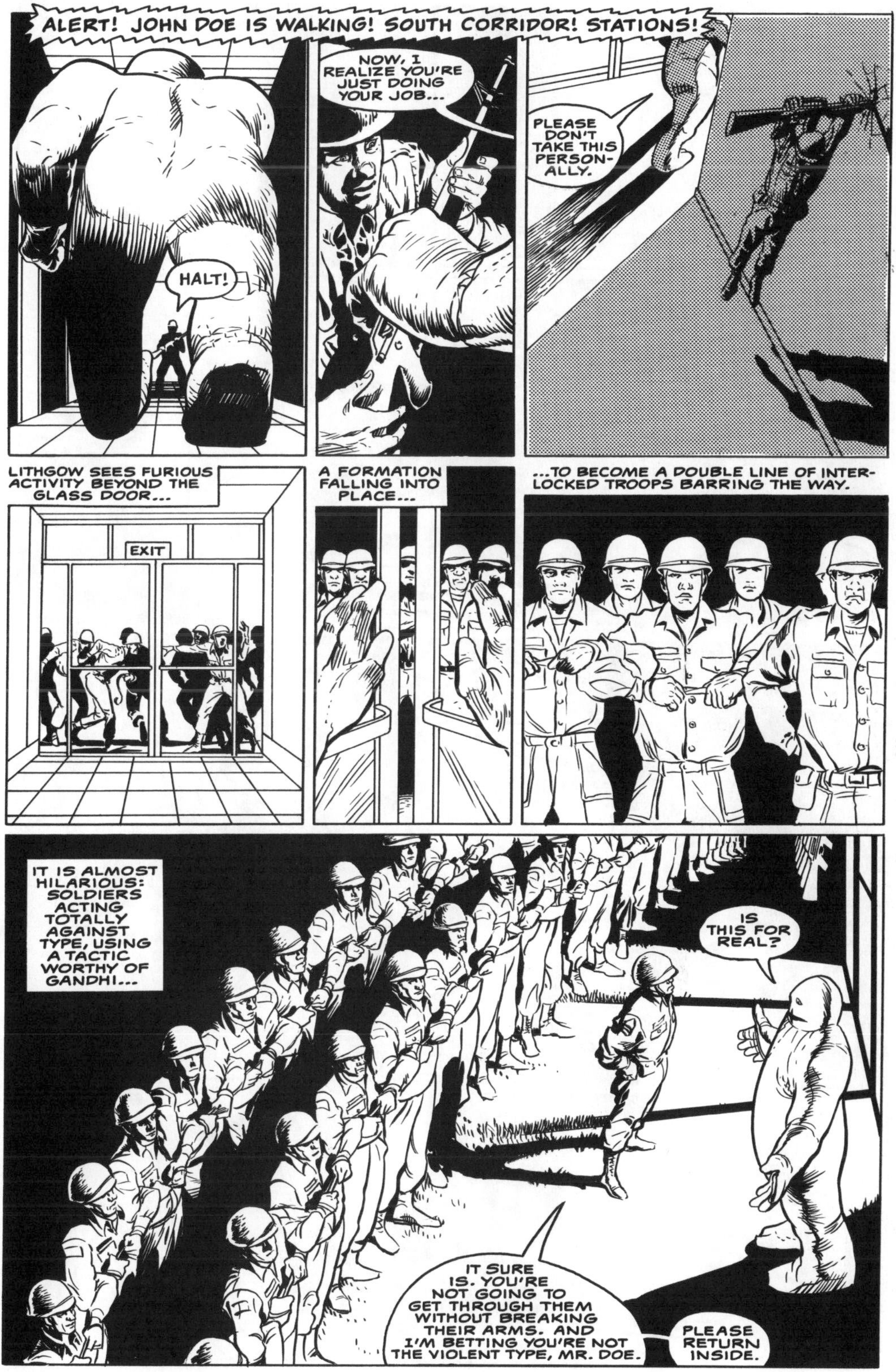
ALERT! JOHN DOE IS WALKING! SOUTH CORRIDOR! STATIONS!
HALT!
NOW, I REALIZE YOU'RE JUST DOING YOUR JOB...
PLEASE DON'T TAKE THIS PERSON-ALLY.
LITHGOW SEES FURIOUS ACTIVITY BEYOND THE GLASS DOOR...
EXIT
A FORMATION FALLING INTO PLACE...
...TO BECOME A DOUBLE LINE OF INTER-LOCKED TROOPS BARRING THE WAY.
IT IS ALMOST HILARIOUS: SOLDIERS ACTING TOTALLY AGAINST TYPE, USING A TACTIC WORTHY OF GANDHI...
IS THIS FOR REAL?
IT SURE IS. YOU'RE NOT GOING TO GET THROUGH THEM WITHOUT BREAKING THEIR ARMS. AND I'M BETTING YOU'RE NOT THE VIOLENT TYPE, MR. DOE.
PLEASE RETURN INSIDE.

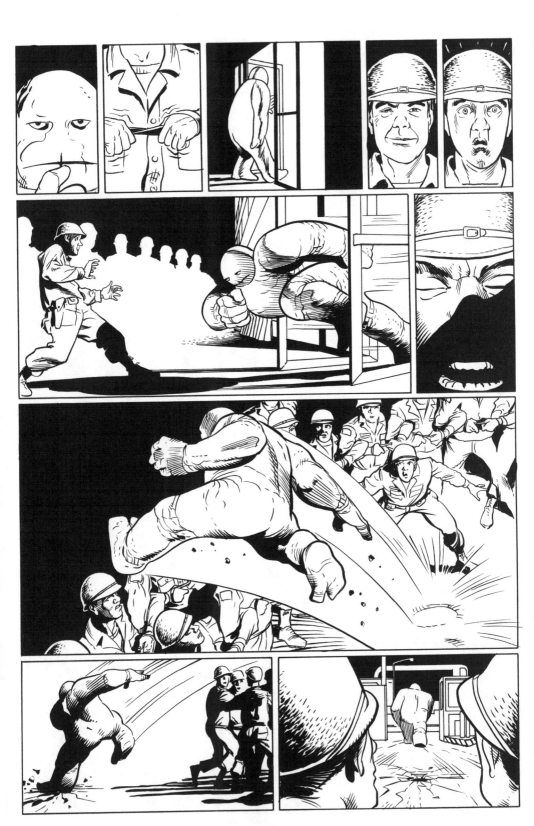

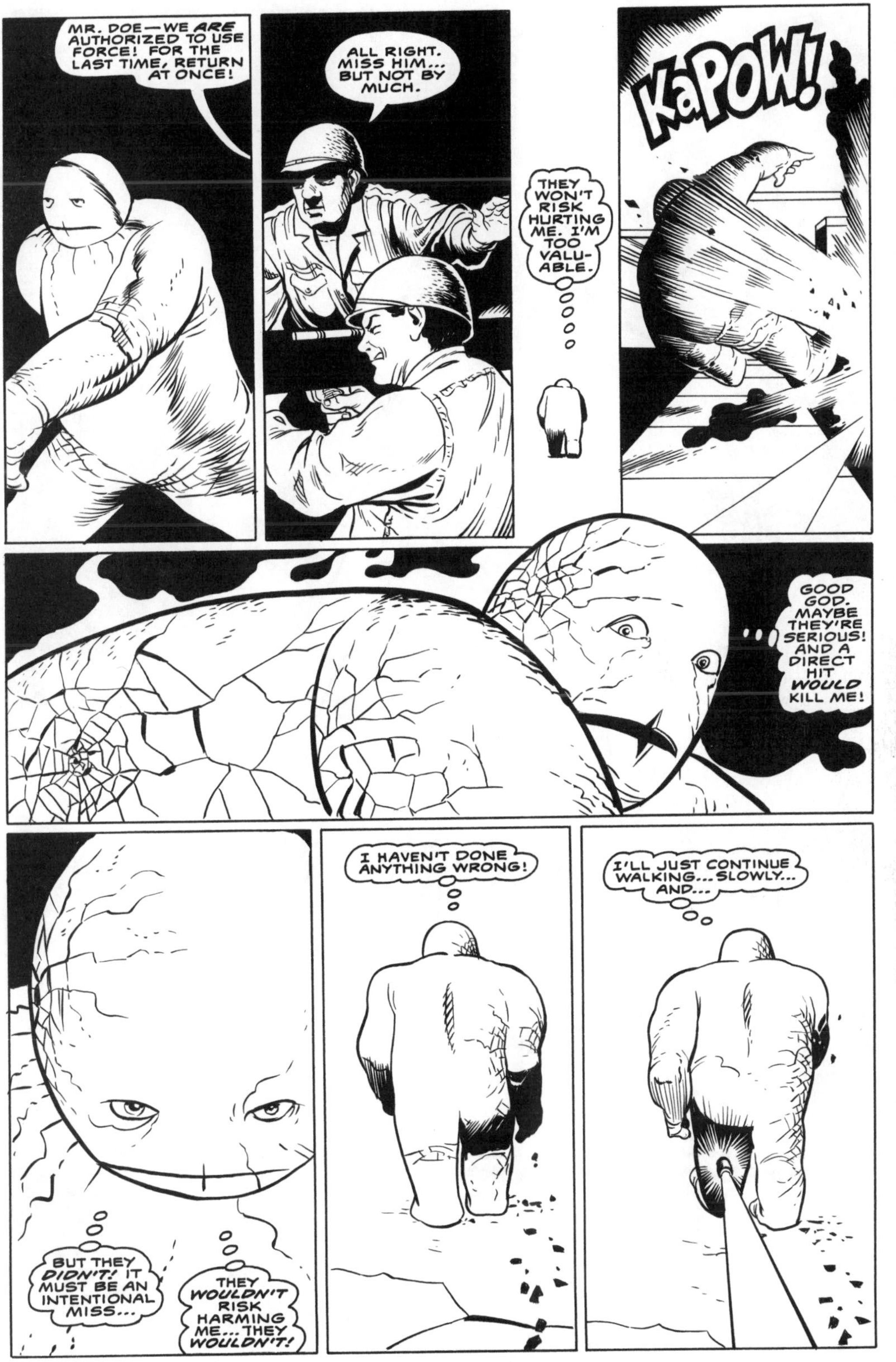
MR. DOE—WE ARE AUTHORIZED TO USE FORCE! FOR THE LAST TIME, RETURN AT ONCE!
ALL RIGHT. MISS HIM... BUT NOT BY MUCH.
THEY WON'T RISK HURTING ME. I'M TOO VALUABLE.
KaPOW!
GOOD GOD. MAYBE THEY'RE SERIOUS! AND A DIRECT HIT WOULD KILL ME!
BUT THEY DIDN'T! IT MUST BE AN INTENTIONAL MISS...
THEY WOULDN'T RISK HARMING ME... THEY WOULDN'T!
I HAVEN'T DONE ANYTHING WRONG!
I'LL JUST CONTINUE WALKING... SLOWLY... AND...

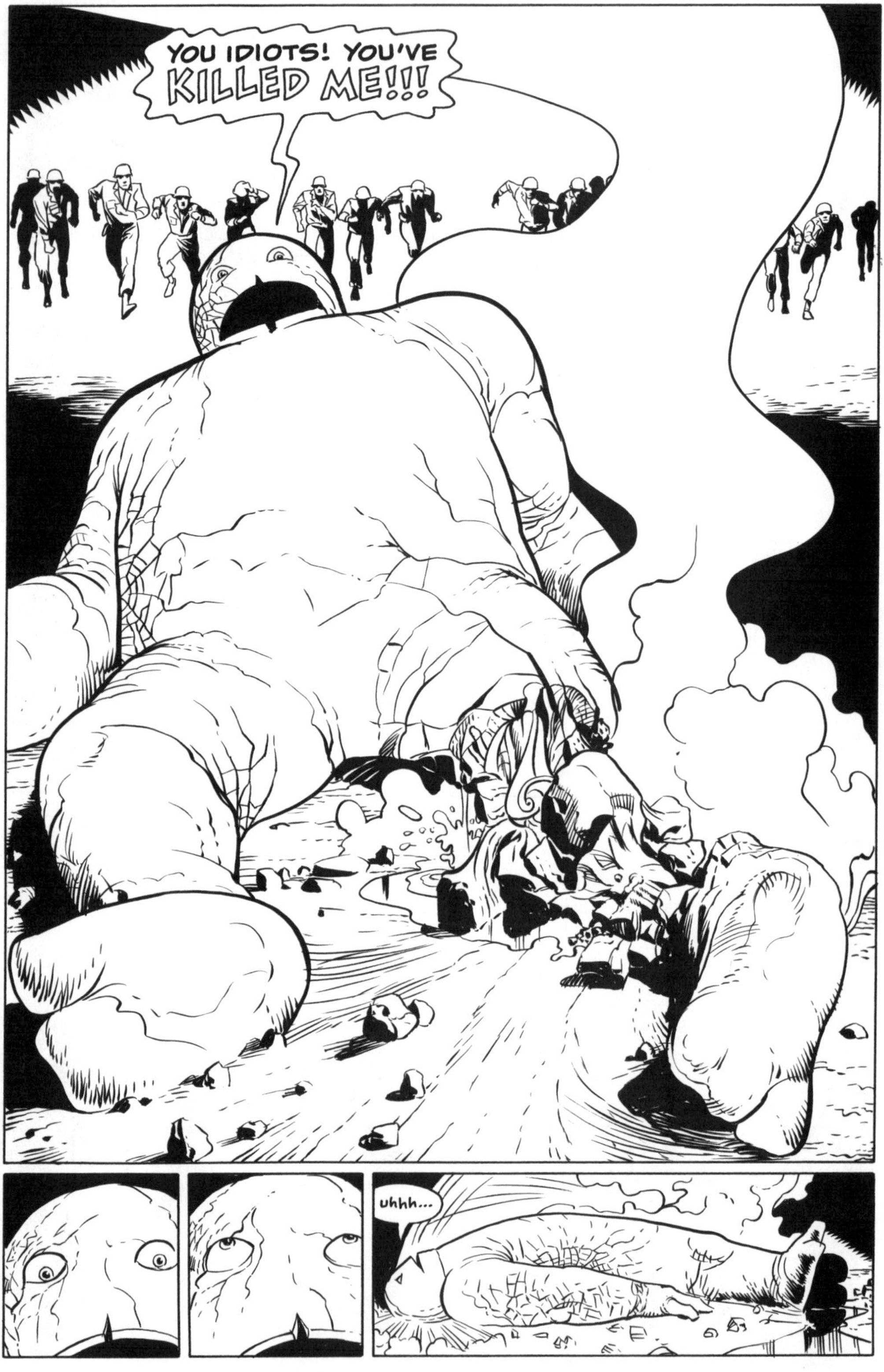
YOU IDIOTS! YOU'VE KILLED ME!!!
uhhh...

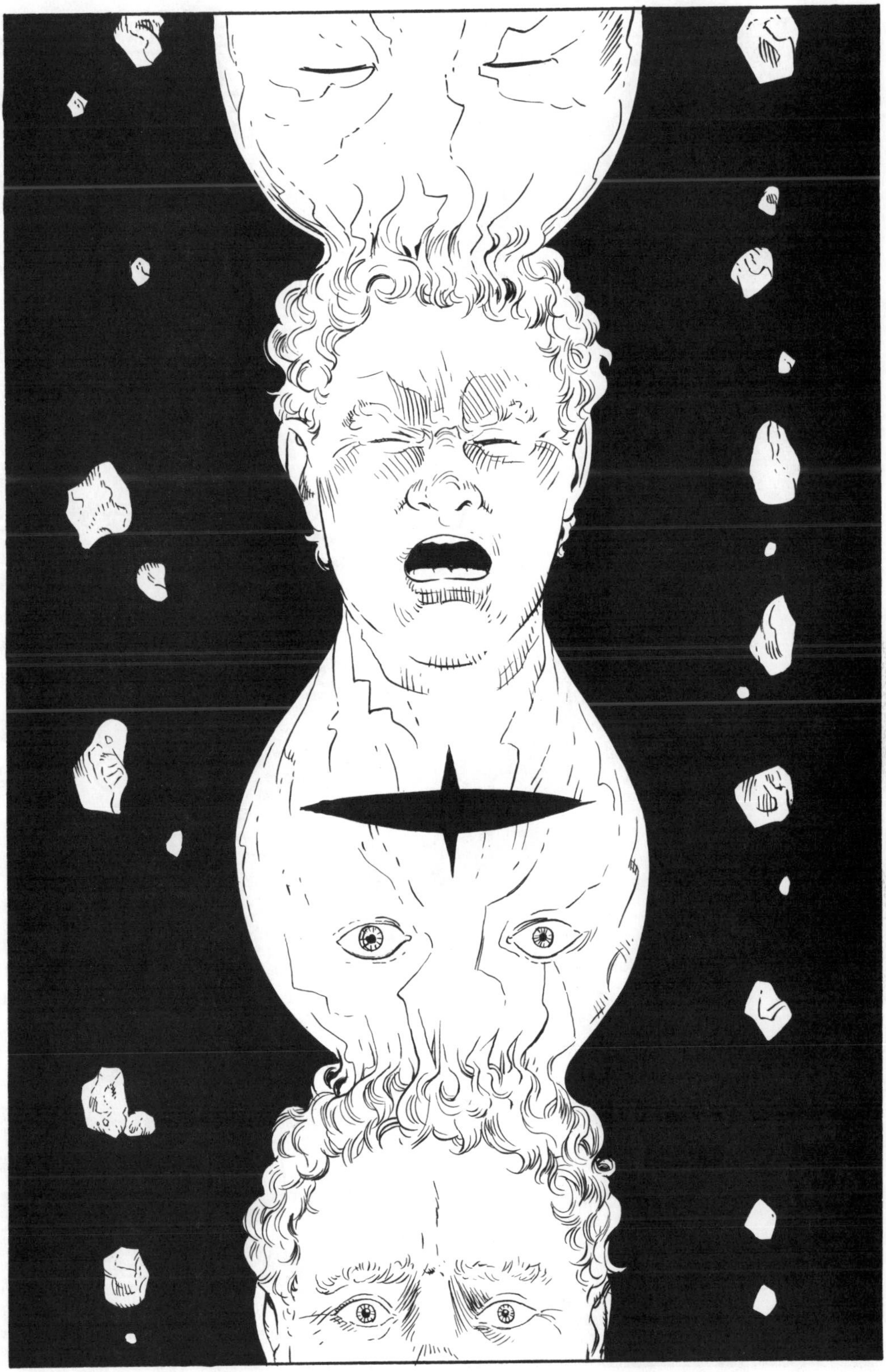

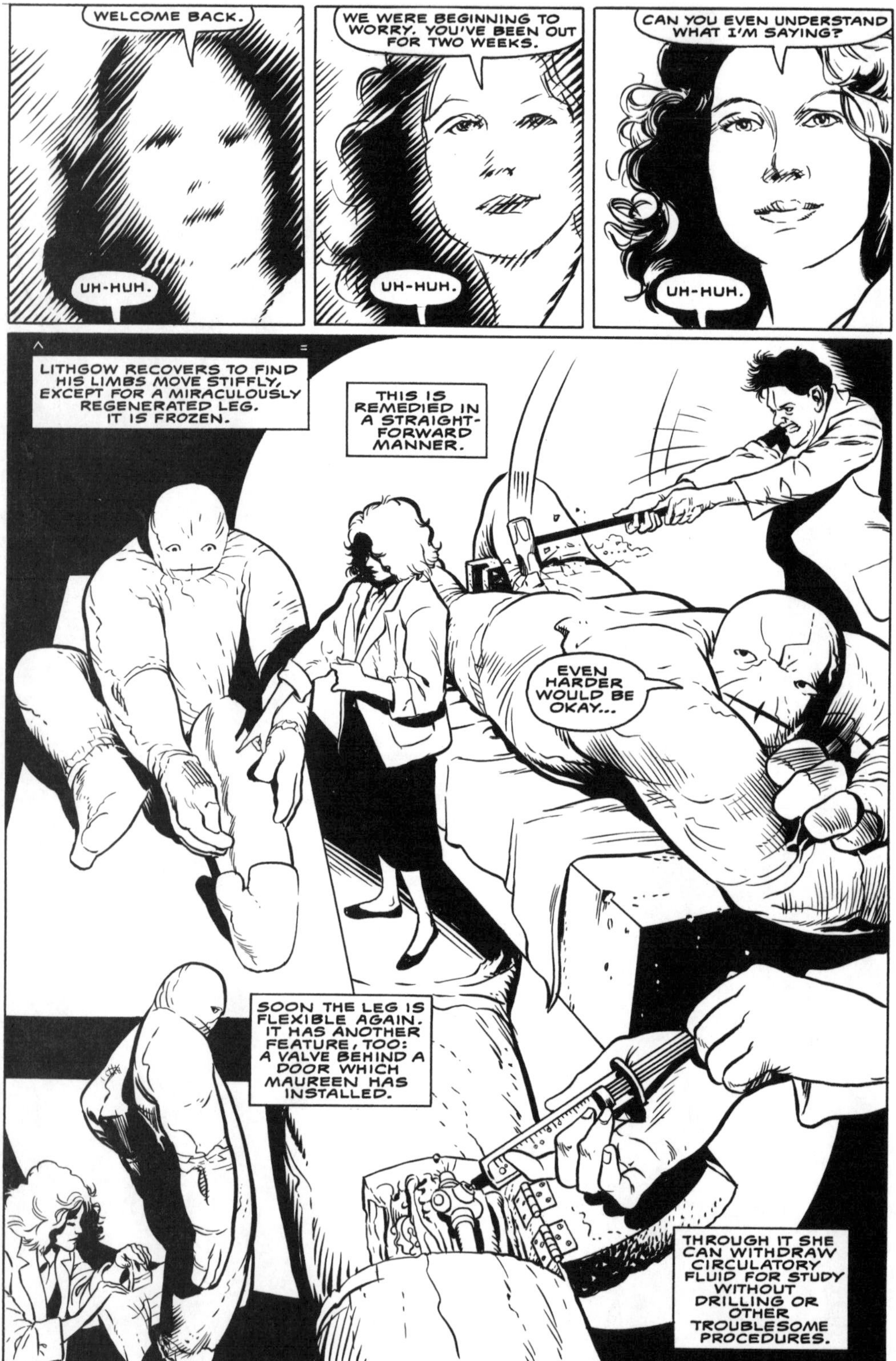
WELCOME BACK.
UH-HUH.
WE WERE BEGINNING TO WORRY. YOU'VE BEEN OUT FOR TWO WEEKS.
UH-HUH.
CAN YOU EVEN UNDERSTAND WHAT I'M SAYING?
UH-HUH.
LITHGOW RECOVERS TO FIND HIS LIMBS MOVE STIFFLY, EXCEPT FOR A MIRACULOUSLY REGENERATED LEG. IT IS FROZEN.
THIS IS REMEDIED IN A STRAIGHT-FORWARD MANNER.
EVEN HARDER WOULD BE OKAY...
SOON THE LEG IS FLEXIBLE AGAIN. IT HAS ANOTHER FEATURE, TOO: A VALVE BEHIND A DOOR WHICH MAUREEN HAS INSTALLED.
THROUGH IT SHE CAN WITHDRAW CIRCULATORY FLUID FOR STUDY WITHOUT DRILLING OR OTHER TROUBLESOME PROCEDURES.

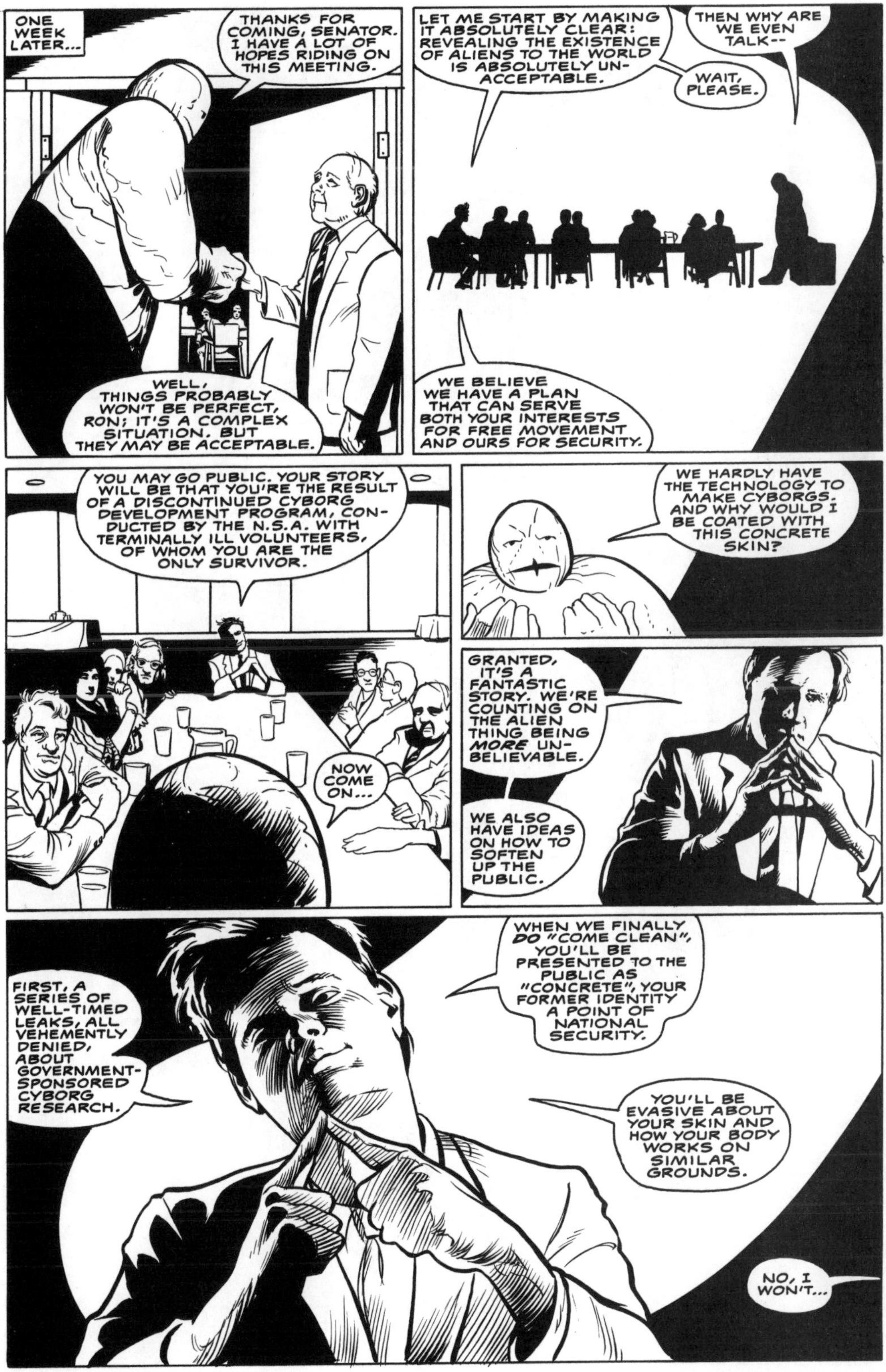
ONE WEEK LATER...
THANKS FOR COMING, SENATOR. I HAVE A LOT OF HOPES RIDING ON THIS MEETING.
WELL, THINGS PROBABLY WON'T BE PERFECT, RON; IT'S A COMPLEX SITUATION. BUT THEY MAY BE ACCEPTABLE.
LET ME START BY MAKING IT ABSOLUTELY CLEAR: REVEALING THE EXISTENCE OF ALIENS TO THE WORLD IS ABSOLUTELY UN-ACCEPTABLE.
THEN WHY ARE WE EVEN TALK--
WAIT, PLEASE.
WE BELIEVE WE HAVE A PLAN THAT CAN SERVE BOTH YOUR INTERESTS FOR FREE MOVEMENT AND OURS FOR SECURITY.
YOU MAY GO PUBLIC. YOUR STORY WILL BE THAT YOU'RE THE RESULT OF A DISCONTINUED CYBORG DEVELOPMENT PROGRAM, CON-DUCTED BY THE N.S.A. WITH TERMINALLY ILL VOLUNTEERS, OF WHOM YOU ARE THE ONLY SURVIVOR.
NOW COME ON...
WE HARDLY HAVE THE TECHNOLOGY TO MAKE CYBORGS. AND WHY WOULD I BE COATED WITH THIS CONCRETE SKIN?
GRANTED, IT'S A FANTASTIC STORY. WE'RE COUNTING ON THE ALIEN THING BEING *MORE* UN-BELIEVABLE.
WE ALSO HAVE IDEAS ON HOW TO SOFTEN UP THE PUBLIC.
FIRST, A SERIES OF WELL-TIMED LEAKS, ALL VEHEMENTLY DENIED, ABOUT GOVERNMENT-SPONSORED CYBORG RESEARCH.
WHEN WE FINALLY *DO* "COME CLEAN", YOU'LL BE PRESENTED TO THE PUBLIC AS "CONCRETE", YOUR FORMER IDENTITY A POINT OF NATIONAL SECURITY.
YOU'LL BE EVASIVE ABOUT YOUR SKIN AND HOW YOUR BODY WORKS ON SIMILAR GROUNDS.
NO, I WON'T...

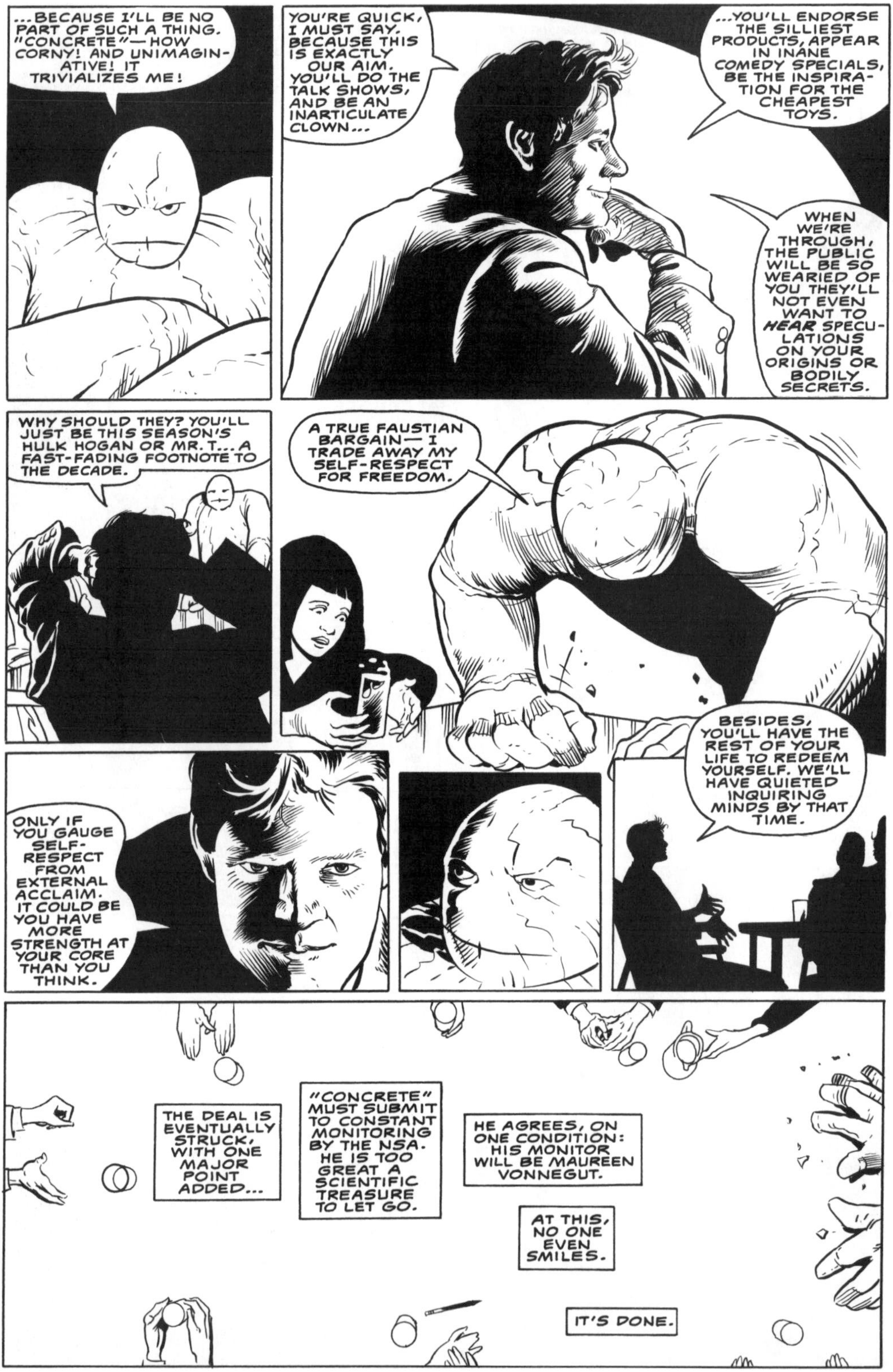
...BECAUSE I'LL BE NO PART OF SUCH A THING. "CONCRETE"—HOW CORNY! AND UNIMAGIN-ATIVE! IT TRIVIALIZES ME!
YOU'RE QUICK, I MUST SAY. BECAUSE THIS IS EXACTLY OUR AIM. YOU'LL DO THE TALK SHOWS, AND BE AN INARTICULATE CLOWN...
...YOU'LL ENDORSE THE SILLIEST PRODUCTS, APPEAR IN INANE COMEDY SPECIALS, BE THE INSPIRA-TION FOR THE CHEAPEST TOYS.
WHEN WE'RE THROUGH, THE PUBLIC WILL BE SO WEARIED OF YOU THEY'LL NOT EVEN WANT TO HEAR SPECU-LATIONS ON YOUR ORIGINS OR BODILY SECRETS.
WHY SHOULD THEY? YOU'LL JUST BE THIS SEASON'S HULK HOGAN OR MR. T... A FAST-FADING FOOTNOTE TO THE DECADE.
A TRUE FAUSTIAN BARGAIN— I TRADE AWAY MY SELF-RESPECT FOR FREEDOM.
ONLY IF YOU GAUGE SELF-RESPECT FROM EXTERNAL ACCLAIM. IT COULD BE YOU HAVE MORE STRENGTH AT YOUR CORE THAN YOU THINK.
BESIDES, YOU'LL HAVE THE REST OF YOUR LIFE TO REDEEM YOURSELF. WE'LL HAVE QUIETED INQUIRING MINDS BY THAT TIME.
THE DEAL IS EVENTUALLY STRUCK, WITH ONE MAJOR POINT ADDED...
"CONCRETE" MUST SUBMIT TO CONSTANT MONITORING BY THE NSA. HE IS TOO GREAT A SCIENTIFIC TREASURE TO LET GO.
HE AGREES, ON ONE CONDITION: HIS MONITOR WILL BE MAUREEN VONNEGUT.
AT THIS, NO ONE EVEN SMILES.
IT'S DONE.

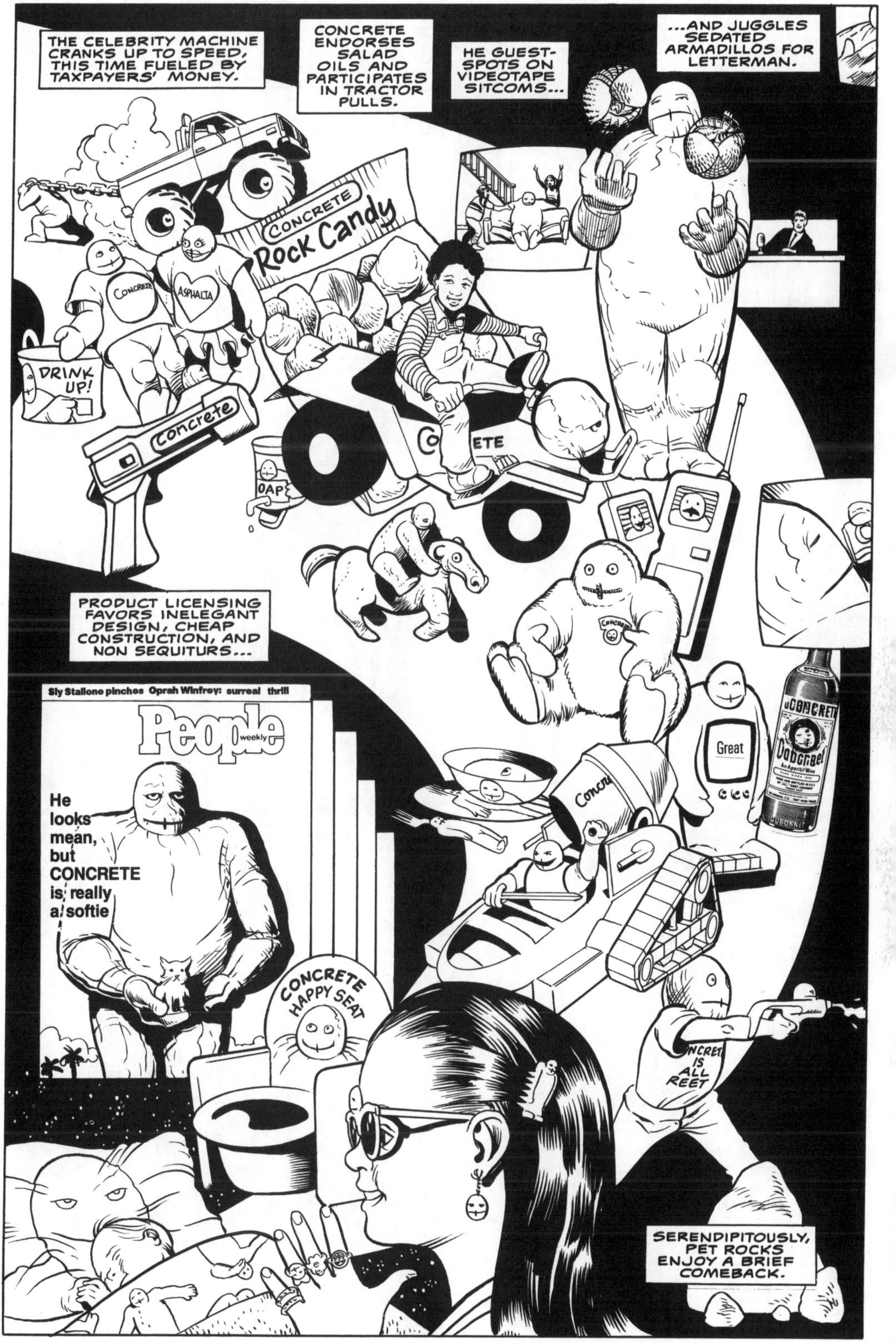
THE CELEBRITY MACHINE CRANKS UP TO SPEED, THIS TIME FUELED BY TAXPAYERS' MONEY.
CONCRETE ENDORSES SALAD OILS AND PARTICIPATES IN TRACTOR PULLS.
HE GUEST-SPOTS ON VIDEOTAPE SITCOMS...
...AND JUGGLES SEDATED ARMADILLOS FOR LETTERMAN.
CONCRETE Rock Candy
CONCRETE
ASPHALTA
DRINK UP!
Concrete
PRODUCT LICENSING FAVORS INELEGANT DESIGN, CHEAP CONSTRUCTION, AND NON SEQUITURS...
Sly Stallone pinches Oprah Winfrey: surreal thrill
People weekly
He looks mean, but CONCRETE is really a softie
Great
CONCRETE HAPPY SEAT
IS ALL REET
SERENDIPITOUSLY, PET ROCKS ENJOY A BRIEF COMEBACK.

MY NEXT GUEST IS EASILY RECOGNIZABLE—HE SHOULD BE: YOU PAID FOR HIS FACE LIFT! HE'S AUTHOR OF "CONCRETE'S ULTIMATE HI-FIBER DIET." PLEASE WELCOME...

CONCRETE'S ULTIMATE **HI-FIBER** DIET

...CONCRETE!

DOC AND THE BAND PLAY THE OLD SIMON AND GARFUNKEL TUNE, "I AM A ROCK."

CLAP CLAP CLAP CLAP CLAP

CLAP CLAP CLAP CLAP CLAP CLAP

THUD!

YOU MAKE A STRIKING ENTRANCE.

THANKS. I COULDN'T FIND A PARKING SPACE.

NOW, WE WERE TALKING EARLIER... YOU SAY YOU CAN'T TELL US ANYTHING ABOUT HOW THIS CYBORG BODY WORKS...

C'MON, NOW... BE BORING, LIKE WE AGREED.

RIGHT.

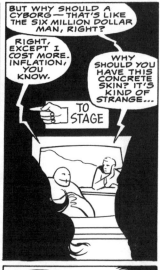

BUT WHY SHOULD A CYBORG—THAT'S LIKE THE SIX MILLION DOLLAR MAN, RIGHT?

RIGHT, EXCEPT I COST MORE. INFLATION, YOU KNOW.

WHY SHOULD YOU HAVE THIS CONCRETE SKIN? IT'S KIND OF STRANGE...

TO STAGE

WELL, LET ME PUT IT THIS WAY. TROWELING ON A LITTLE HERE AND THERE CAN HIDE A MULTITUDE OF SINS.

MORE THAN THAT I CANNOT SAY.

WHAT ABOUT YOUR FORMER LIFE—?

YOU WERE TERMINALLY ILL—?

WELL, ALL THAT'S CLASSIFIED, TOO. ALL I CAN TELL YOU IS THAT I WASN'T JIMMY HOFFA.

NOW LET ME GET THIS STRAIGHT...

YOU CAN'T TALK ABOUT YOUR BODY...

YOU CAN'T TALK ABOUT YOUR FORMER LIFE...

WHAT ARE YOU DOING ON A TALK SHOW?

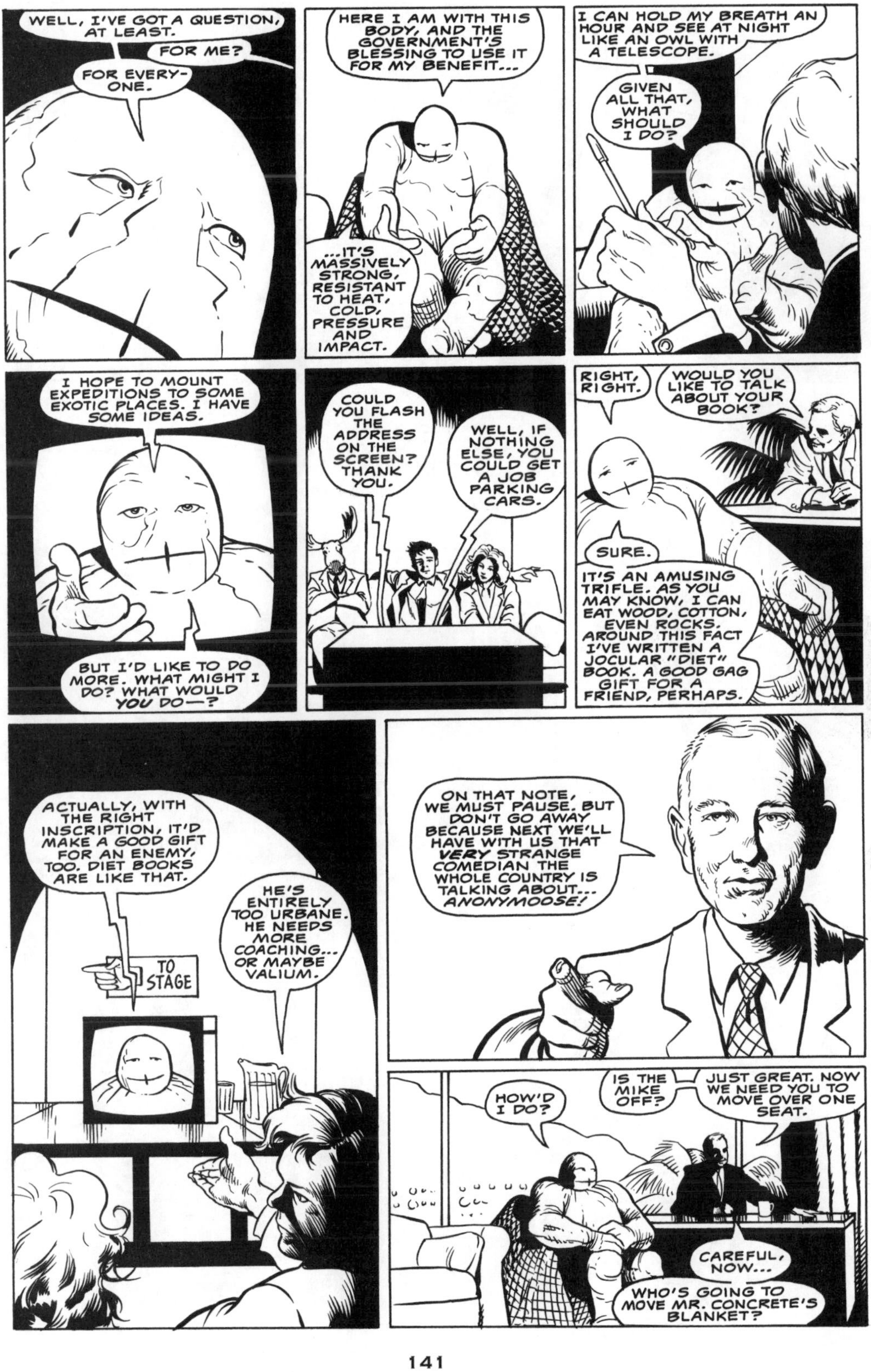

WELL, I'VE GOT A QUESTION, AT LEAST.
FOR ME?
FOR EVERY-ONE.
HERE I AM WITH THIS BODY, AND THE GOVERNMENT'S BLESSING TO USE IT FOR MY BENEFIT...
...IT'S MASSIVELY STRONG, RESISTANT TO HEAT, COLD, PRESSURE AND IMPACT.
I CAN HOLD MY BREATH AN HOUR AND SEE AT NIGHT LIKE AN OWL WITH A TELESCOPE.
GIVEN ALL THAT, WHAT SHOULD I DO?
I HOPE TO MOUNT EXPEDITIONS TO SOME EXOTIC PLACES. I HAVE SOME IDEAS.
BUT I'D LIKE TO DO MORE. WHAT MIGHT I DO? WHAT WOULD *YOU* DO—?
COULD YOU FLASH THE ADDRESS ON THE SCREEN? THANK YOU.
WELL, IF NOTHING ELSE, YOU COULD GET A JOB PARKING CARS.
RIGHT, RIGHT.
WOULD YOU LIKE TO TALK ABOUT YOUR BOOK?
SURE.
IT'S AN AMUSING TRIFLE. AS YOU MAY KNOW, I CAN EAT WOOD, COTTON, EVEN ROCKS. AROUND THIS FACT I'VE WRITTEN A JOCULAR "DIET" BOOK. A GOOD GAG GIFT FOR A FRIEND, PERHAPS.
ACTUALLY, WITH THE RIGHT INSCRIPTION, IT'D MAKE A GOOD GIFT FOR AN ENEMY, TOO. DIET BOOKS ARE LIKE THAT.
TO STAGE
HE'S ENTIRELY TOO URBANE. HE NEEDS MORE COACHING... OR MAYBE VALIUM.
ON THAT NOTE, WE MUST PAUSE. BUT DON'T GO AWAY BECAUSE NEXT WE'LL HAVE WITH US THAT *VERY* STRANGE COMEDIAN THE WHOLE COUNTRY IS TALKING ABOUT... *ANONYMOOSE!*
HOW'D I DO?
IS THE MIKE OFF?
JUST GREAT. NOW WE NEED YOU TO MOVE OVER ONE SEAT.
CAREFUL, NOW...
WHO'S GOING TO MOVE MR. CONCRETE'S BLANKET?

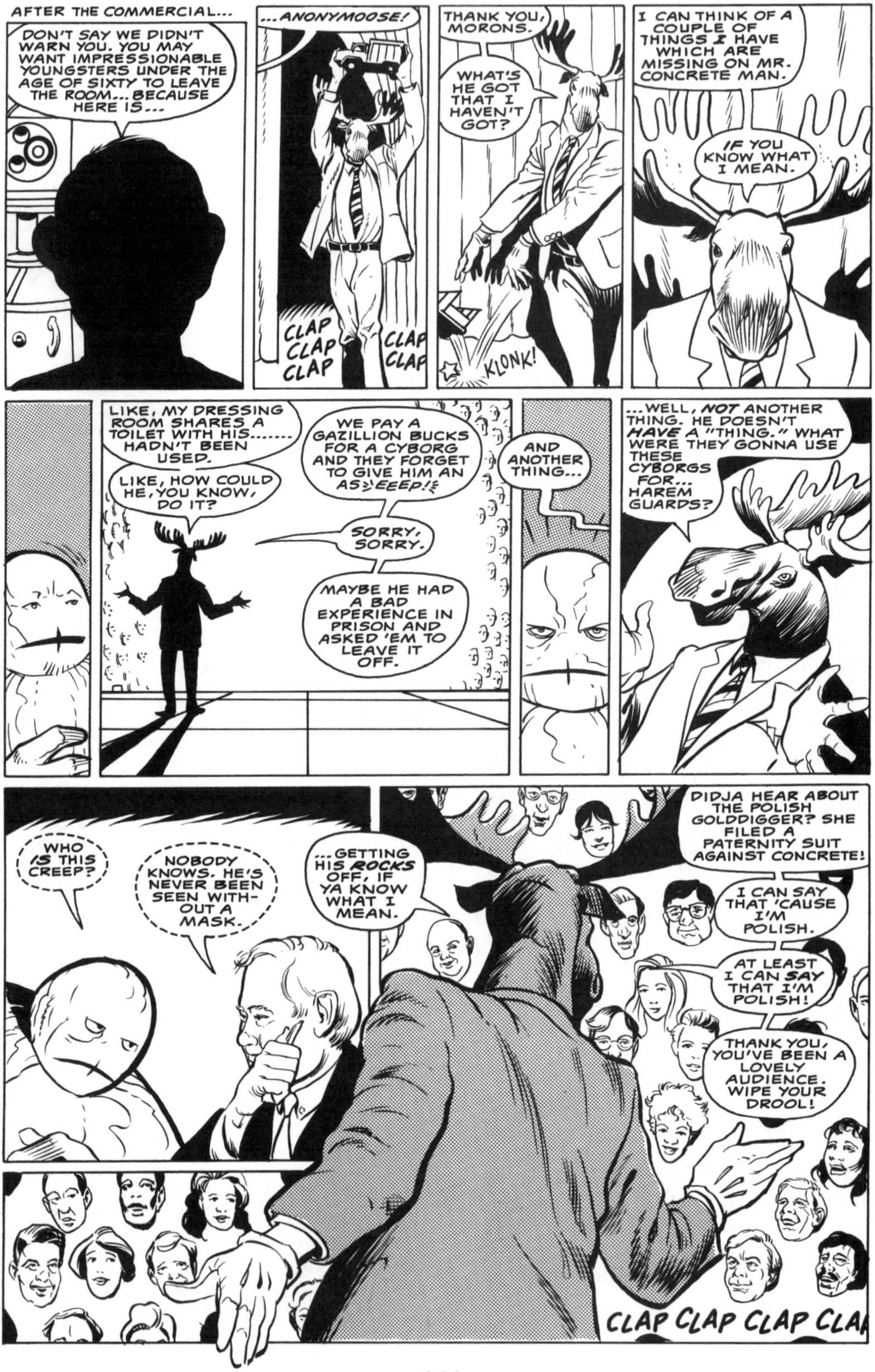
AFTER THE COMMERCIAL...
DON'T SAY WE DIDN'T WARN YOU. YOU MAY WANT IMPRESSIONABLE YOUNGSTERS UNDER THE AGE OF SIXTY TO LEAVE THE ROOM... BECAUSE HERE IS...
...ANONYMOOSE!
CLAP CLAP CLAP
CLAP CLAP
THANK YOU, MORONS.
WHAT'S HE GOT THAT I HAVEN'T GOT?
KLONK!
I CAN THINK OF A COUPLE OF THINGS I HAVE WHICH ARE MISSING ON MR. CONCRETE MAN.
IF YOU KNOW WHAT I MEAN.
LIKE, MY DRESSING ROOM SHARES A TOILET WITH HIS....... HADN'T BEEN USED.
LIKE, HOW COULD HE, YOU KNOW, DO IT?
WE PAY A GAZILLION BUCKS FOR A CYBORG AND THEY FORGET TO GIVE HIM AN AS EEEP!
SORRY, SORRY.
MAYBE HE HAD A BAD EXPERIENCE IN PRISON AND ASKED 'EM TO LEAVE IT OFF.
AND ANOTHER THING...
...WELL, NOT ANOTHER THING. HE DOESN'T HAVE A "THING." WHAT WERE THEY GONNA USE THESE CYBORGS FOR... HAREM GUARDS?
WHO IS THIS CREEP?
NOBODY KNOWS. HE'S NEVER BEEN SEEN WITHOUT A MASK.
...GETTING HIS ROCKS OFF, IF YA KNOW WHAT I MEAN.
DIDJA HEAR ABOUT THE POLISH GOLDDIGGER? SHE FILED A PATERNITY SUIT AGAINST CONCRETE!
I CAN SAY THAT 'CAUSE I'M POLISH.
AT LEAST I CAN SAY THAT I'M POLISH!
THANK YOU, YOU'VE BEEN A LOVELY AUDIENCE. WIPE YOUR DROOL!
CLAP CLAP CLAP CLA

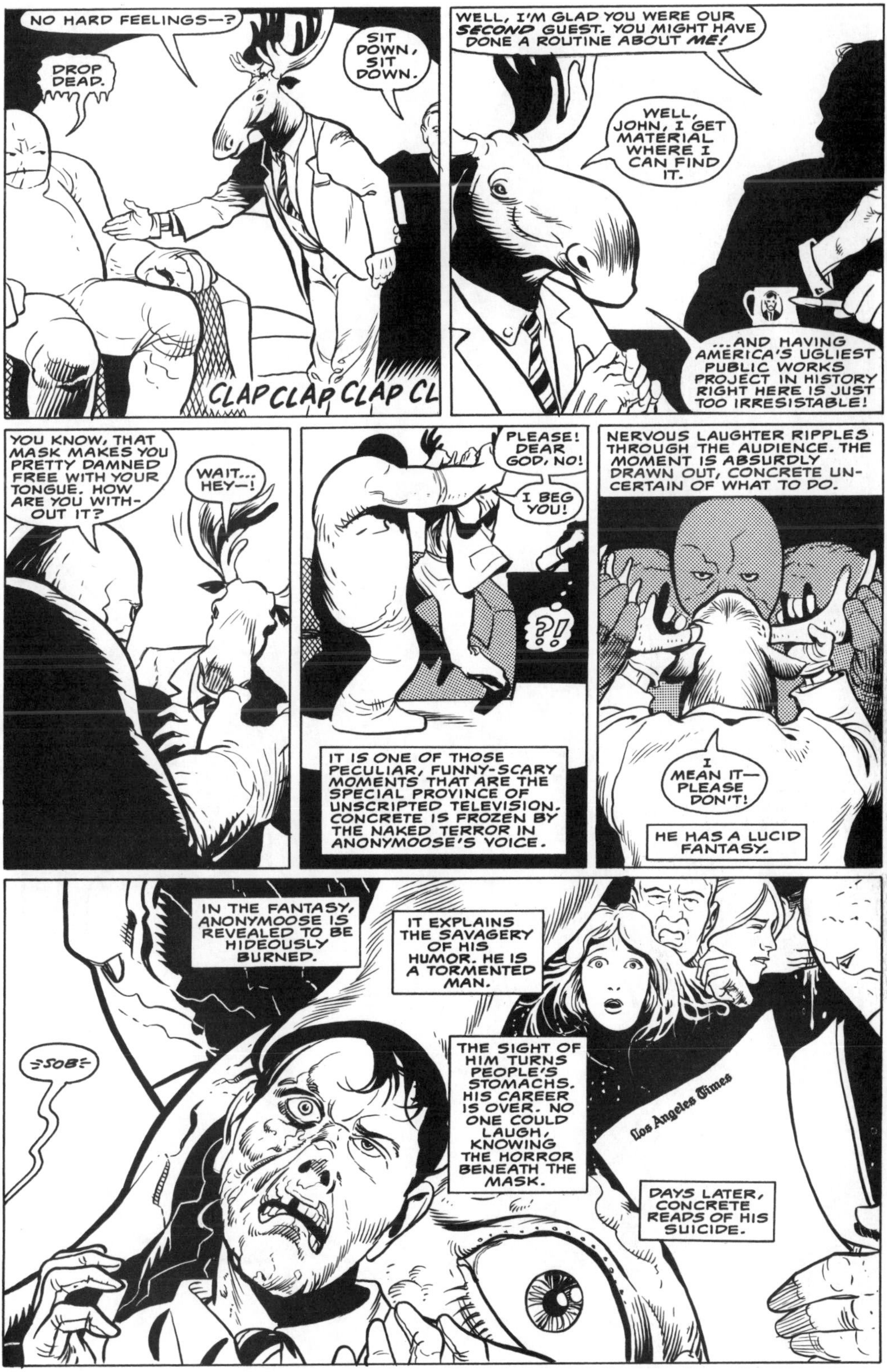
NO HARD FEELINGS—?
DROP DEAD.
SIT DOWN, SIT DOWN.
CLAP CLAP CLAP CL
WELL, I'M GLAD YOU WERE OUR SECOND GUEST. YOU MIGHT HAVE DONE A ROUTINE ABOUT ME!
WELL, JOHN, I GET MATERIAL WHERE I CAN FIND IT.
...AND HAVING AMERICA'S UGLIEST PUBLIC WORKS PROJECT IN HISTORY RIGHT HERE IS JUST TOO IRRESISTABLE!
YOU KNOW, THAT MASK MAKES YOU PRETTY DAMNED FREE WITH YOUR TONGUE. HOW ARE YOU WITHOUT IT?
WAIT... HEY—!
PLEASE! DEAR GOD, NO!
I BEG YOU!
?!
IT IS ONE OF THOSE PECULIAR, FUNNY-SCARY MOMENTS THAT ARE THE SPECIAL PROVINCE OF UNSCRIPTED TELEVISION. CONCRETE IS FROZEN BY THE NAKED TERROR IN ANONYMOOSE'S VOICE.
NERVOUS LAUGHTER RIPPLES THROUGH THE AUDIENCE. THE MOMENT IS ABSURDLY DRAWN OUT, CONCRETE UNCERTAIN OF WHAT TO DO.
I MEAN IT—PLEASE DON'T!
HE HAS A LUCID FANTASY.
IN THE FANTASY, ANONYMOOSE IS REVEALED TO BE HIDEOUSLY BURNED.
IT EXPLAINS THE SAVAGERY OF HIS HUMOR. HE IS A TORMENTED MAN.
SOB
THE SIGHT OF HIM TURNS PEOPLE'S STOMACHS. HIS CAREER IS OVER. NO ONE COULD LAUGH, KNOWING THE HORROR BENEATH THE MASK.
Los Angeles Times
DAYS LATER, CONCRETE READS OF HIS SUICIDE.

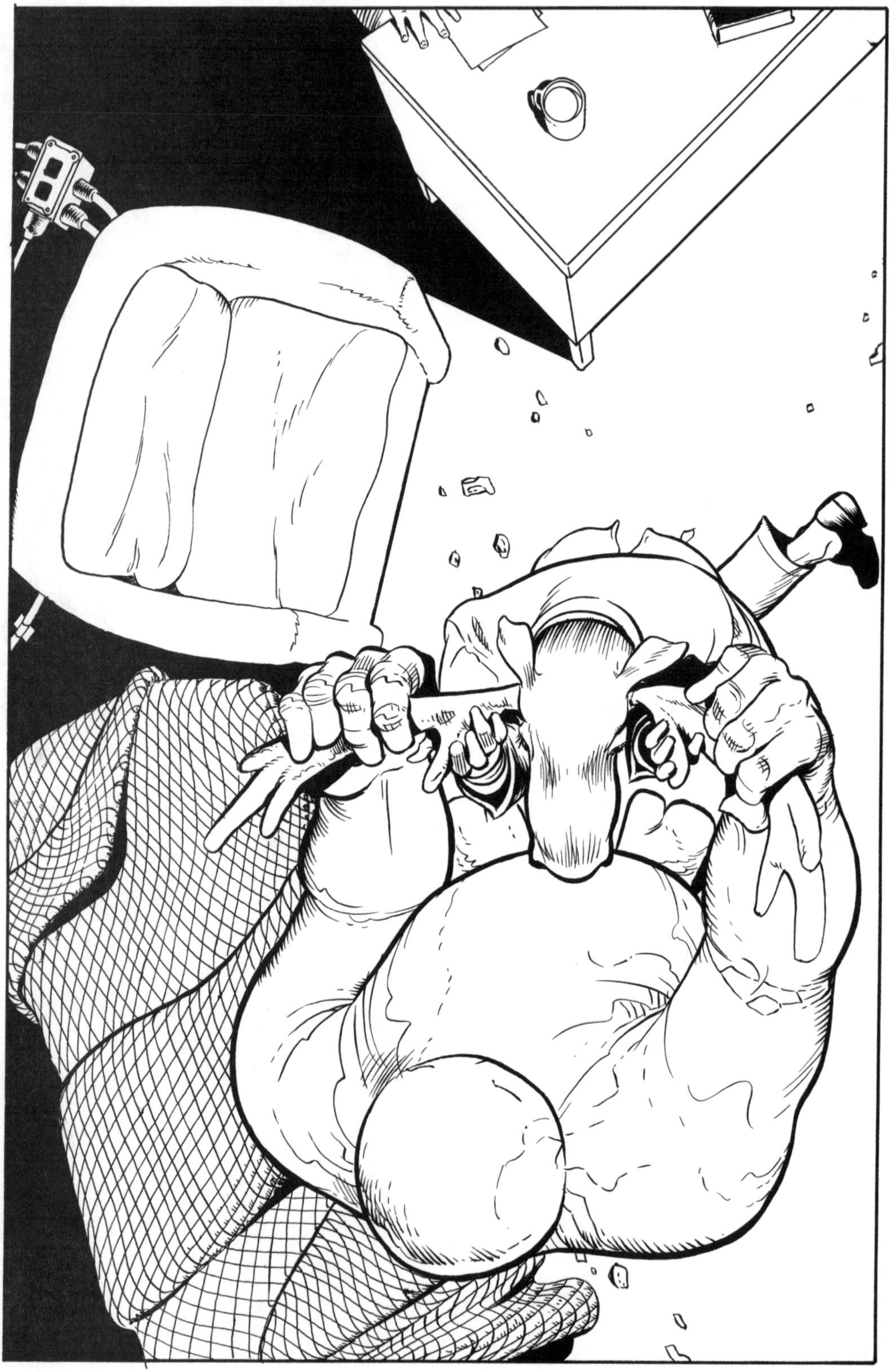

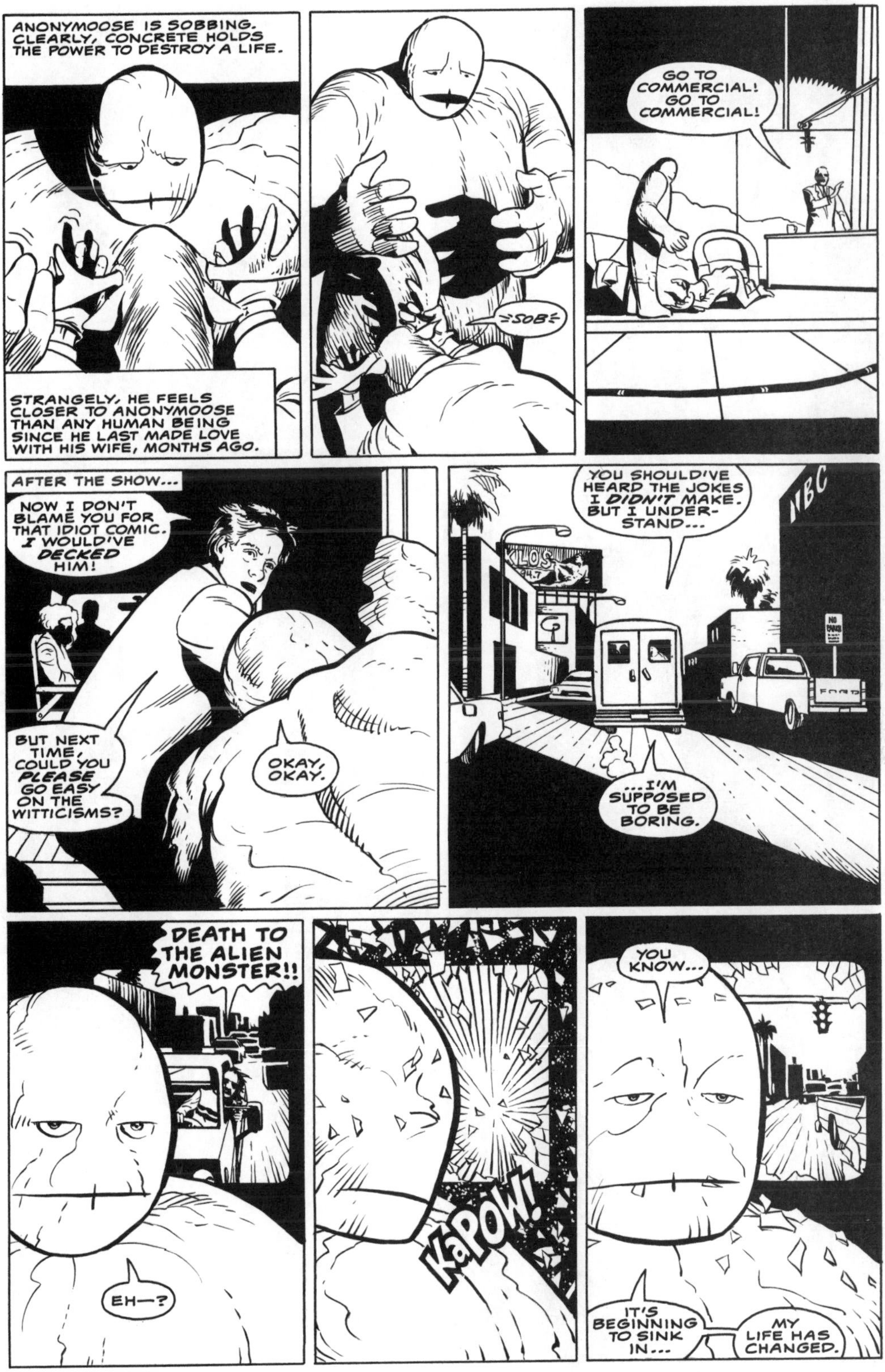
ANONYMOOSE IS SOBBING. CLEARLY, CONCRETE HOLDS THE POWER TO DESTROY A LIFE.
STRANGELY, HE FEELS CLOSER TO ANONYMOOSE THAN ANY HUMAN BEING SINCE HE LAST MADE LOVE WITH HIS WIFE, MONTHS AGO.
SOB
GO TO COMMERCIAL! GO TO COMMERCIAL!
AFTER THE SHOW...
NOW I DON'T BLAME YOU FOR THAT IDIOT COMIC. I WOULD'VE DECKED HIM!
BUT NEXT TIME, COULD YOU PLEASE GO EASY ON THE WITTICISMS?
OKAY, OKAY.
YOU SHOULD'VE HEARD THE JOKES I DIDN'T MAKE. BUT I UNDERSTAND...
NBC
...I'M SUPPOSED TO BE BORING.
DEATH TO THE ALIEN MONSTER!!
EH—?
KaPOW!
YOU KNOW...
IT'S BEGINNING TO SINK IN...
MY LIFE HAS CHANGED.

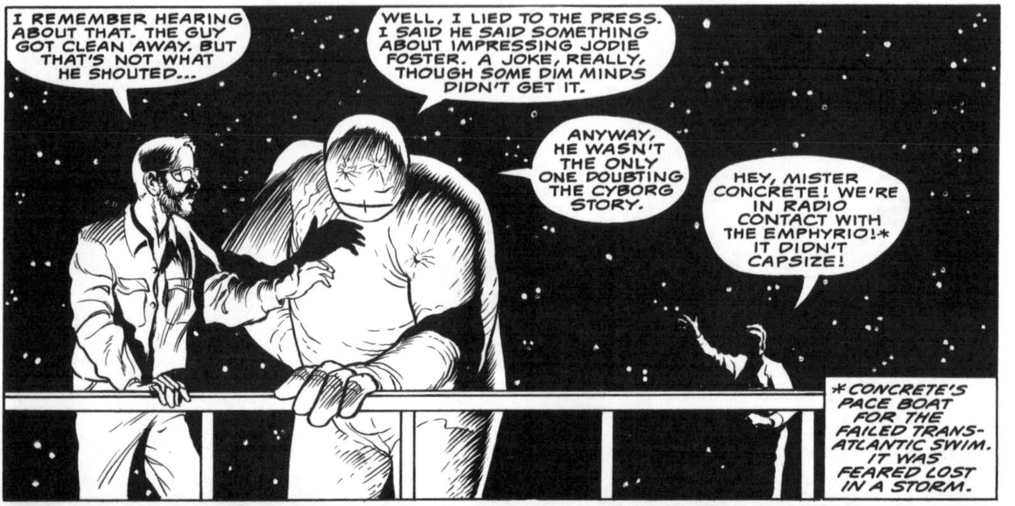
I REMEMBER HEARING ABOUT THAT. THE GUY GOT CLEAN AWAY. BUT THAT'S NOT WHAT HE SHOUTED...
WELL, I LIED TO THE PRESS. I SAID HE SAID SOMETHING ABOUT IMPRESSING JODIE FOSTER. A JOKE, REALLY, THOUGH SOME DIM MINDS DIDN'T GET IT.
ANYWAY, HE WASN'T THE ONLY ONE DOUBTING THE CYBORG STORY.
HEY, MISTER CONCRETE! WE'RE IN RADIO CONTACT WITH THE EMPHYRIO!* IT DIDN'T CAPSIZE!
*CONCRETE'S PACE BOAT FOR THE FAILED TRANS-ATLANTIC SWIM. IT WAS FEARED LOST IN A STORM.

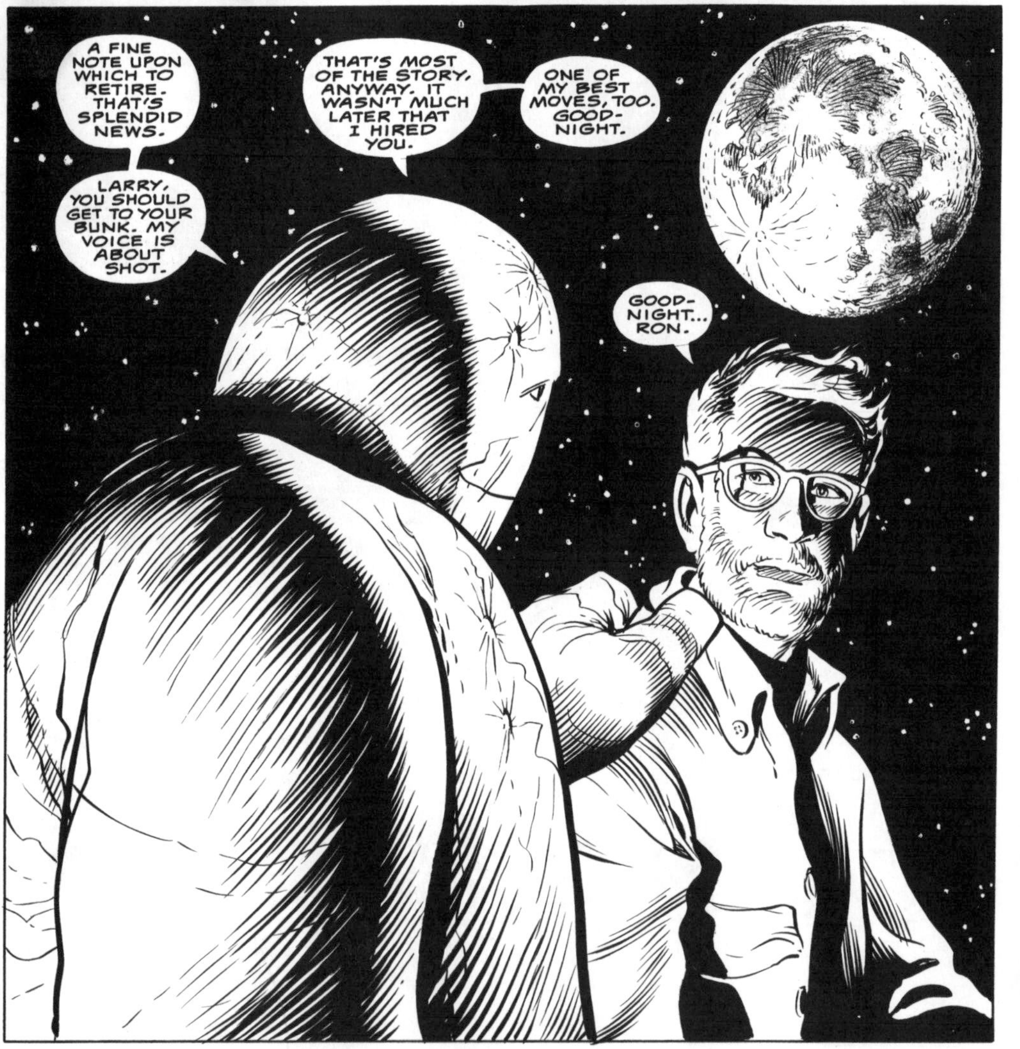
A FINE NOTE UPON WHICH TO RETIRE. THAT'S SPLENDID NEWS.
LARRY. YOU SHOULD GET TO YOUR BUNK. MY VOICE IS ABOUT SHOT.
THAT'S MOST OF THE STORY, ANYWAY. IT WASN'T MUCH LATER THAT I HIRED YOU.
ONE OF MY BEST MOVES, TOO. GOOD-NIGHT.
GOOD-NIGHT... RON.

Concrete

IF YOUR BROTHER ACTIVATED HIS EMERGENCY TRANSMISSION BEACON WHEN HE WENT DOWN, WHY CAN'T THEY TRIANGULATE HIS LOCATION, LARRY?

THE BATTERIES MUST HAVE BEEN WEAK. THEY LOST IT. WE'RE LUCKY TO KNOW THE GENERAL AREA OF THE CRASH, MAUREEN.

WHAT I WANT TO KNOW IS WHY HE WAS FLYING A BIPLANE IN MONTANA! I THOUGHT HE LIVED IN L.A.!

STORY & ART ©1987
PAUL CHADWICK

LETTERING:
BILL SPICER

Straight in the Eye

HE'S LIKE THAT. MR. ADVENTURE. ALL THOSE STUNTMEN ARE INTO THE MACHO THING.

WHEN HE FINISHES A PICTURE HE TAKES OFF IN HIS PLANE, FLYING PLACE TO PLACE, ASKING AROUND FOR RUNWAYS WITHIN A HUNDRED MILES.

THE PLANE CARRIES ONLY THAT MUCH FUEL. SLEEPS UNDER THE WING IN A SLEEPING BAG. HE LOVES IT.

OR LOVED IT.

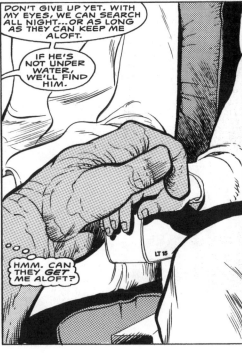

DON'T GIVE UP YET. WITH MY EYES, WE CAN SEARCH ALL NIGHT...OR AS LONG AS THEY CAN KEEP ME ALOFT.

IF HE'S NOT UNDER WATER, WE'LL FIND HIM.

LT 15

HMM. CAN THEY *GET* ME ALOFT?

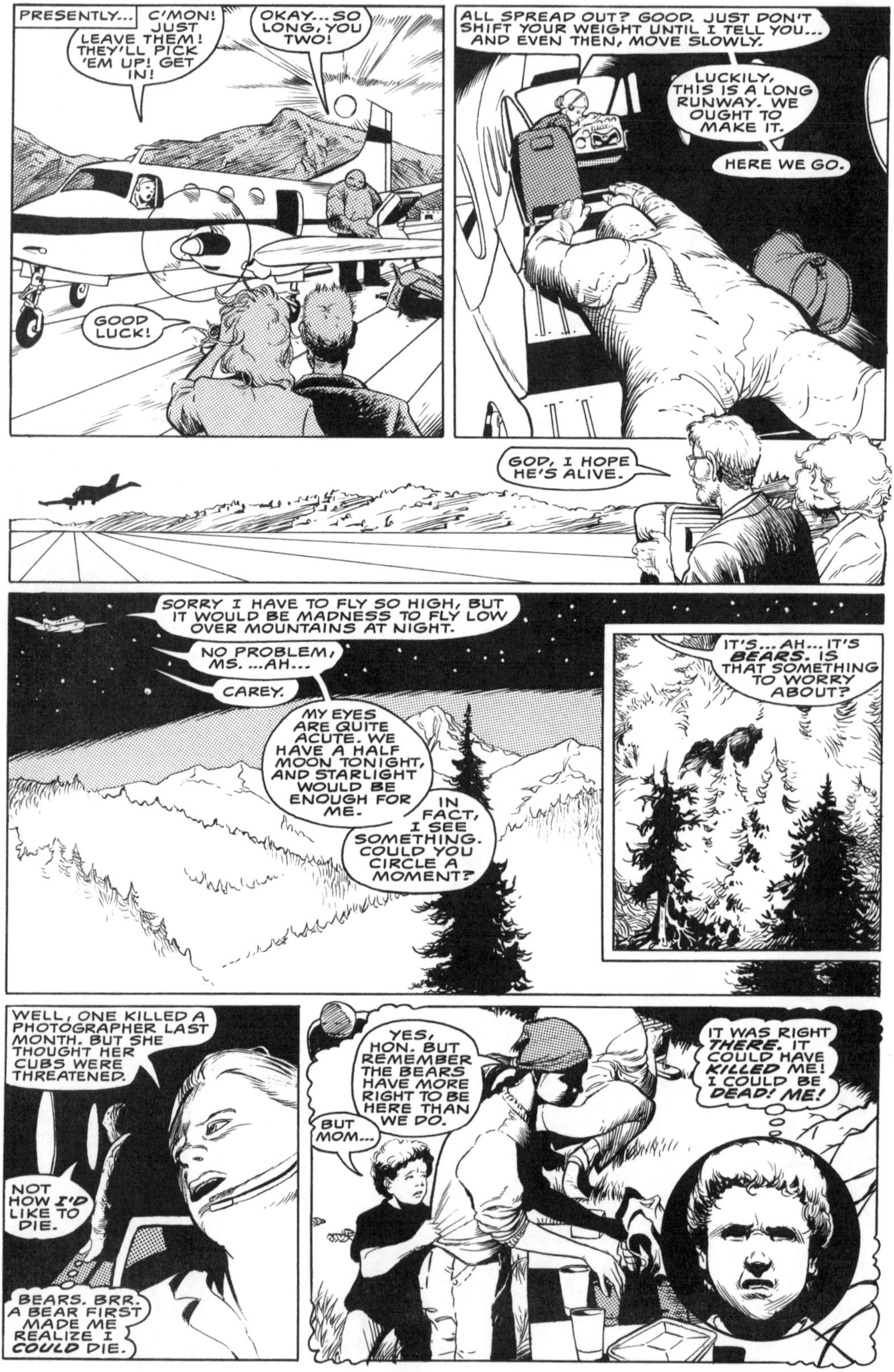
PRESENTLY...
C'MON! JUST LEAVE THEM! THEY'LL PICK 'EM UP! GET IN!
OKAY... SO LONG, YOU TWO!
GOOD LUCK!
ALL SPREAD OUT? GOOD. JUST DON'T SHIFT YOUR WEIGHT UNTIL I TELL YOU... AND EVEN THEN, MOVE SLOWLY.
LUCKILY, THIS IS A LONG RUNWAY. WE OUGHT TO MAKE IT.
HERE WE GO.
GOD, I HOPE HE'S ALIVE.
SORRY I HAVE TO FLY SO HIGH, BUT IT WOULD BE MADNESS TO FLY LOW OVER MOUNTAINS AT NIGHT.
NO PROBLEM, MS. ...AH...
CAREY.
MY EYES ARE QUITE ACUTE. WE HAVE A HALF MOON TONIGHT, AND STARLIGHT WOULD BE ENOUGH FOR ME.
IN FACT, I SEE SOMETHING. COULD YOU CIRCLE A MOMENT?
IT'S... AH... IT'S BEARS. IS THAT SOMETHING TO WORRY ABOUT?
WELL, ONE KILLED A PHOTOGRAPHER LAST MONTH. BUT SHE THOUGHT HER CUBS WERE THREATENED.
NOT HOW I'D LIKE TO DIE.
BEARS. BRR. A BEAR FIRST MADE ME REALIZE I COULD DIE.
BUT MOM...
YES, HON. BUT REMEMBER THE BEARS HAVE MORE RIGHT TO BE HERE THAN WE DO.
IT WAS RIGHT THERE. IT COULD HAVE KILLED ME! I COULD BE DEAD! ME!

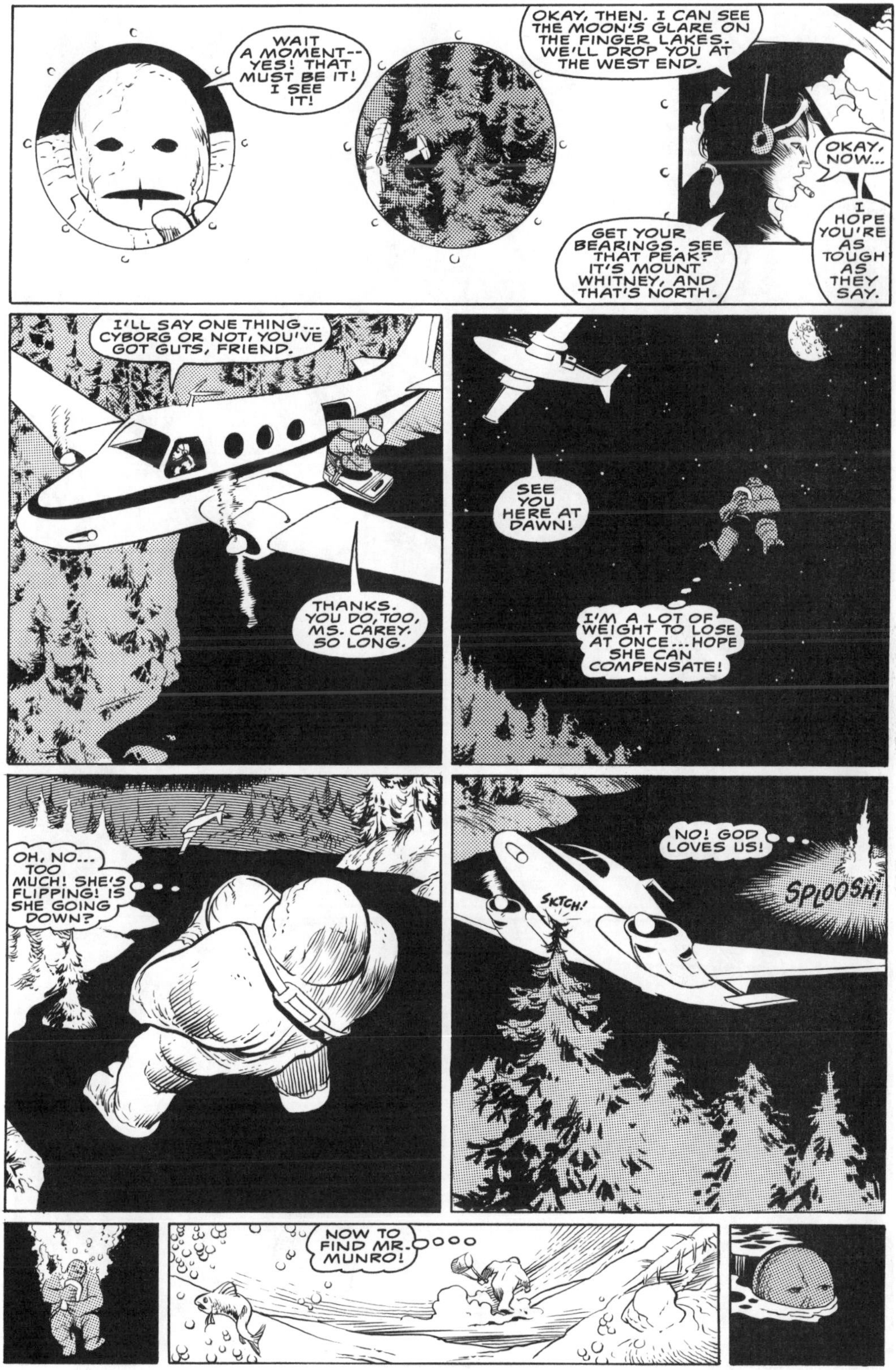
WAIT A MOMENT-- YES! THAT MUST BE IT! I SEE IT!
OKAY, THEN. I CAN SEE THE MOON'S GLARE ON THE FINGER LAKES. WE'LL DROP YOU AT THE WEST END.
OKAY, NOW...
GET YOUR BEARINGS. SEE THAT PEAK? IT'S MOUNT WHITNEY, AND THAT'S NORTH.
I HOPE YOU'RE AS TOUGH AS THEY SAY.
I'LL SAY ONE THING... CYBORG OR NOT, YOU'VE GOT GUTS, FRIEND.
THANKS. YOU DO, TOO, MS. CAREY. SO LONG.
SEE YOU HERE AT DAWN!
I'M A LOT OF WEIGHT TO LOSE AT ONCE... HOPE SHE CAN COMPENSATE!
OH, NO... TOO MUCH! SHE'S FLIPPING! IS SHE GOING DOWN?
NO! GOD LOVES US!
SKTCH!
SPLOOSH!
NOW TO FIND MR. MUNRO!

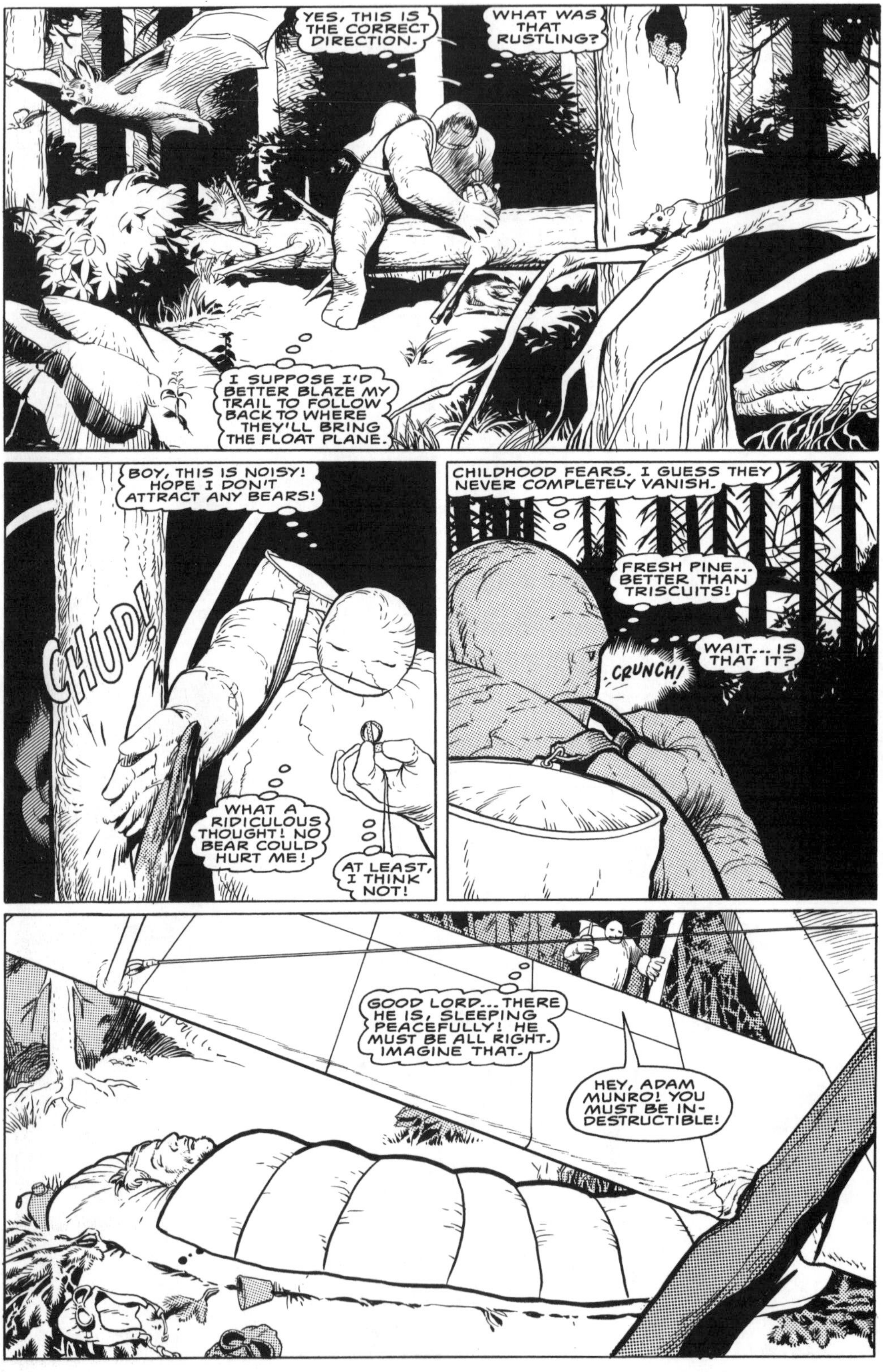

YES, THIS IS THE CORRECT DIRECTION.
WHAT WAS THAT RUSTLING?
I SUPPOSE I'D BETTER BLAZE MY TRAIL TO FOLLOW BACK TO WHERE THEY'LL BRING THE FLOAT PLANE.
BOY, THIS IS NOISY! HOPE I DON'T ATTRACT ANY BEARS!
CHUD!
WHAT A RIDICULOUS THOUGHT! NO BEAR COULD HURT ME!
AT LEAST, I THINK NOT!
CHILDHOOD FEARS. I GUESS THEY NEVER COMPLETELY VANISH.
FRESH PINE... BETTER THAN TRISCUITS!
CRUNCH!
WAIT... IS THAT IT?
GOOD LORD... THERE HE IS, SLEEPING PEACEFULLY! HE MUST BE ALL RIGHT. IMAGINE THAT.
HEY, ADAM MUNRO! YOU MUST BE IN-DESTRUCTIBLE!

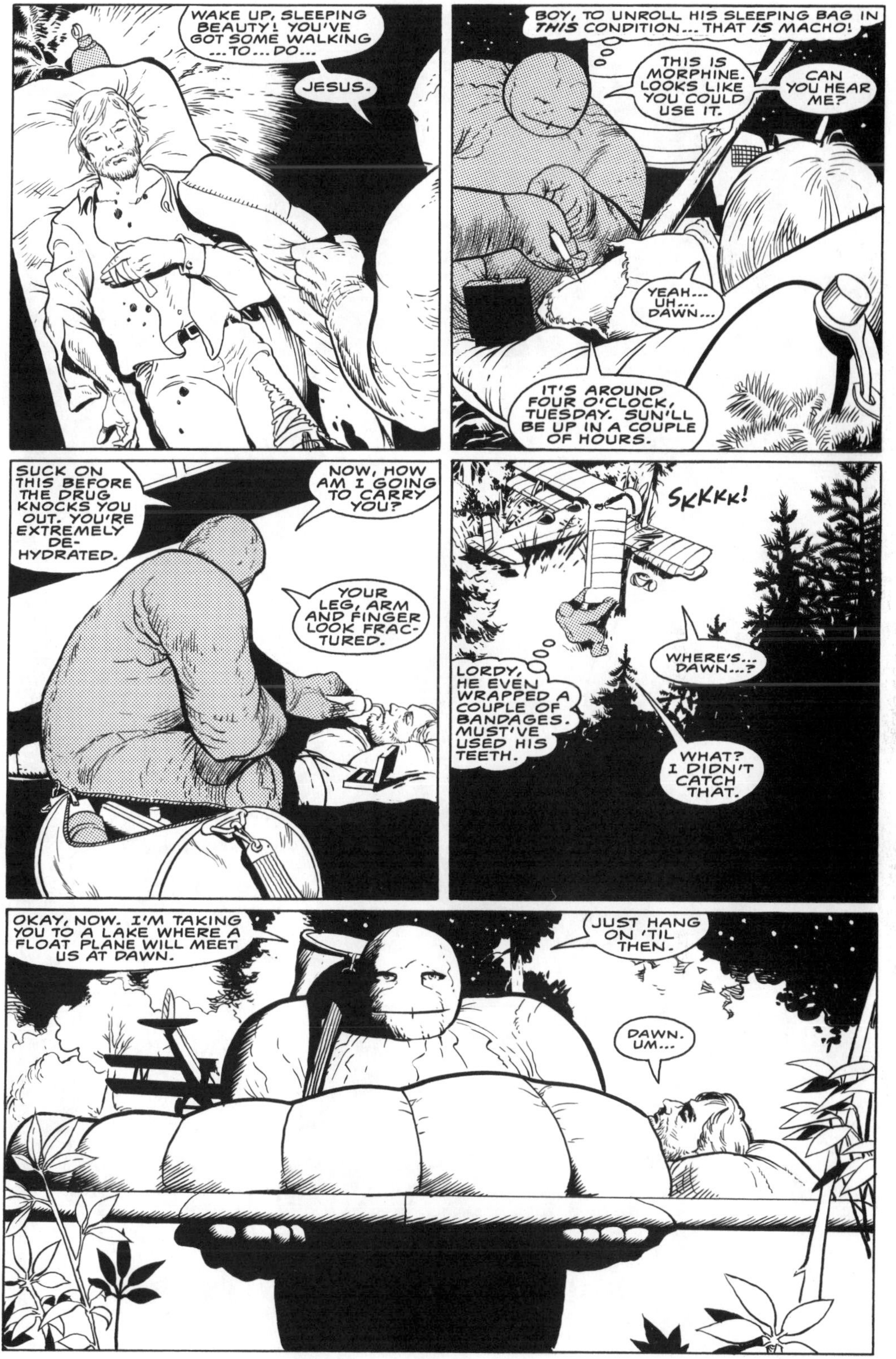

WAKE UP, SLEEPING BEAUTY! YOU'VE GOT SOME WALKING ...TO...DO...
JESUS.
BOY, TO UNROLL HIS SLEEPING BAG IN THIS CONDITION... THAT IS MACHO!
THIS IS MORPHINE. LOOKS LIKE YOU COULD USE IT.
CAN YOU HEAR ME?
YEAH... UH... DAWN...
IT'S AROUND FOUR O'CLOCK, TUESDAY. SUN'LL BE UP IN A COUPLE OF HOURS.
SUCK ON THIS BEFORE THE DRUG KNOCKS YOU OUT. YOU'RE EXTREMELY DE-HYDRATED.
NOW, HOW AM I GOING TO CARRY YOU?
YOUR LEG, ARM AND FINGER LOOK FRAC-TURED.
SKKKK!
LORDY, HE EVEN WRAPPED A COUPLE OF BANDAGES. MUST'VE USED HIS TEETH.
WHERE'S... DAWN...?
WHAT? I DIDN'T CATCH THAT.
OKAY, NOW. I'M TAKING YOU TO A LAKE WHERE A FLOAT PLANE WILL MEET US AT DAWN.
JUST HANG ON 'TIL THEN.
DAWN. UM...

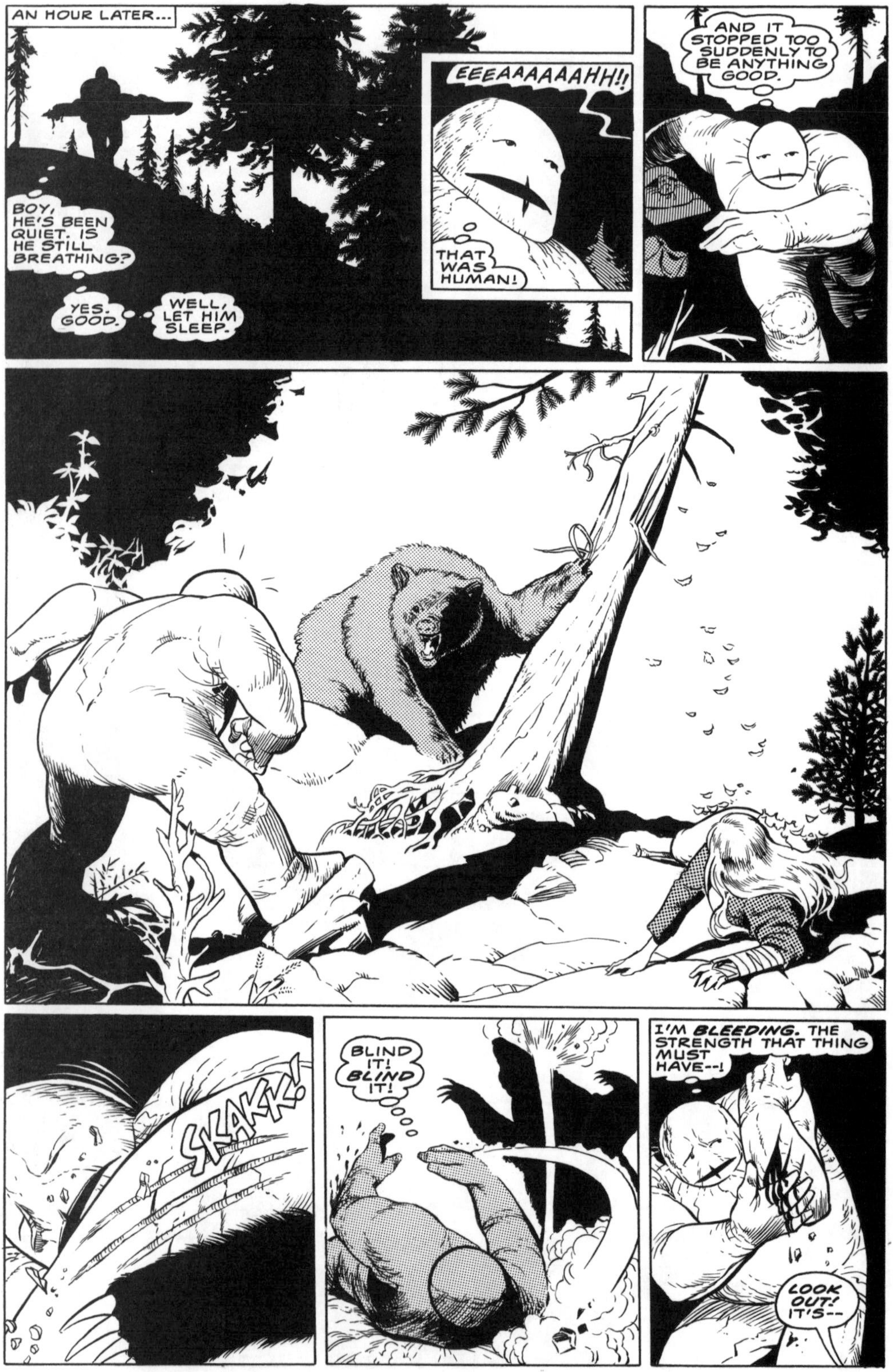
AN HOUR LATER...
BOY, HE'S BEEN QUIET. IS HE STILL BREATHING?
YES. GOOD.
WELL, LET HIM SLEEP.
EEEAAAAAAAHH!!
THAT WAS HUMAN!
AND IT STOPPED TOO SUDDENLY TO BE ANYTHING GOOD.
SKAKK!
BLIND IT! BLIND IT!
I'M BLEEDING. THE STRENGTH THAT THING MUST HAVE--!
LOOK OUT! IT'S--

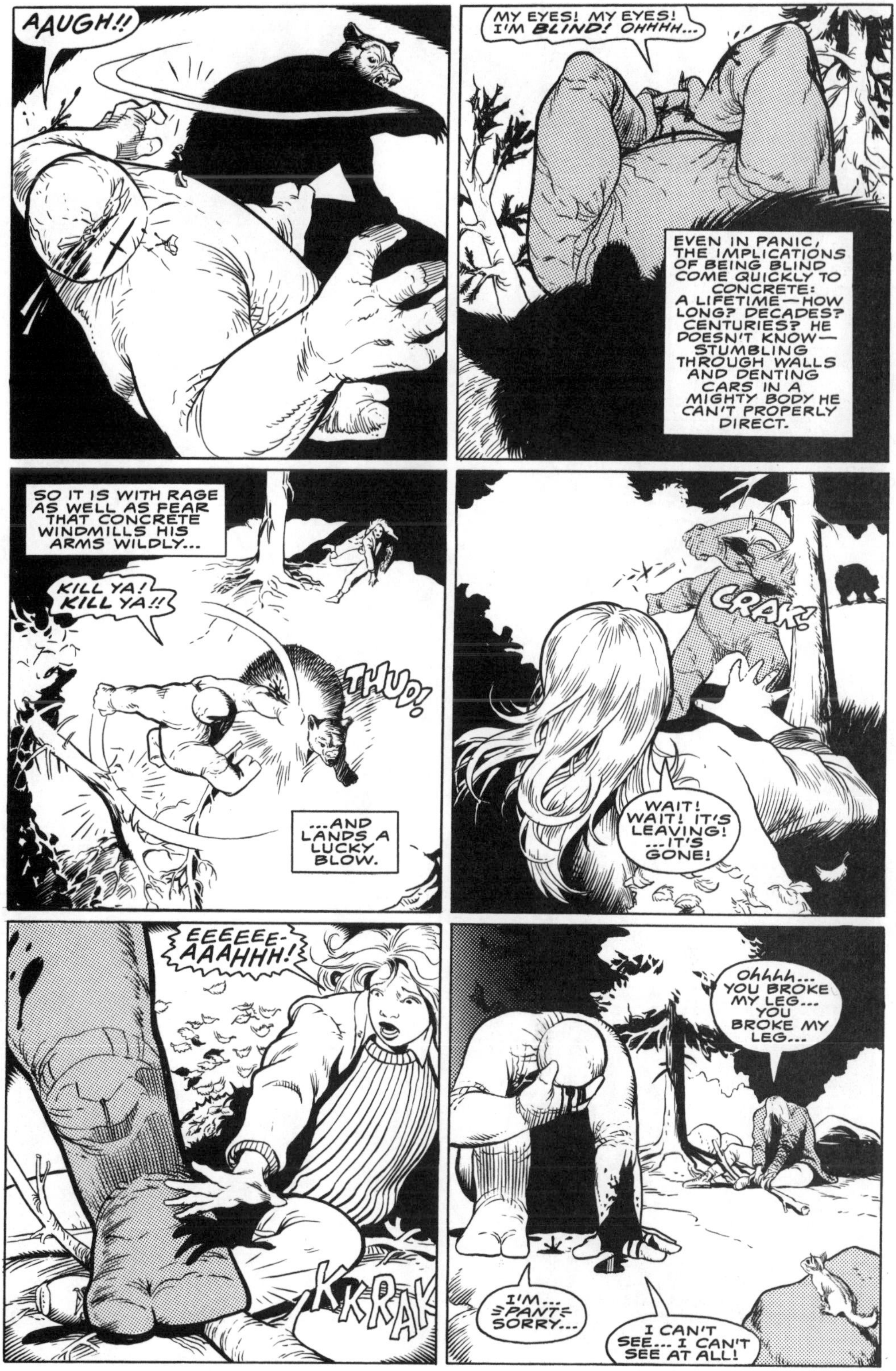
AAUGH!!
MY EYES! MY EYES! I'M BLIND! OHHHH...
EVEN IN PANIC, THE IMPLICATIONS OF BEING BLIND COME QUICKLY TO CONCRETE: A LIFETIME—HOW LONG? DECADES? CENTURIES? HE DOESN'T KNOW—STUMBLING THROUGH WALLS AND DENTING CARS IN A MIGHTY BODY HE CAN'T PROPERLY DIRECT.
SO IT IS WITH RAGE AS WELL AS FEAR THAT CONCRETE WINDMILLS HIS ARMS WILDLY...
KILL YA! KILL YA!!
THUD!
...AND LANDS A LUCKY BLOW.
CRAK!
WAIT! WAIT! IT'S LEAVING! ...IT'S GONE!
EEEEEE-AAAHHHH!
KKRAK
Ohhhh... YOU BROKE MY LEG... YOU BROKE MY LEG...
I'M... PANT SORRY...
I CAN'T SEE... I CAN'T SEE AT ALL!

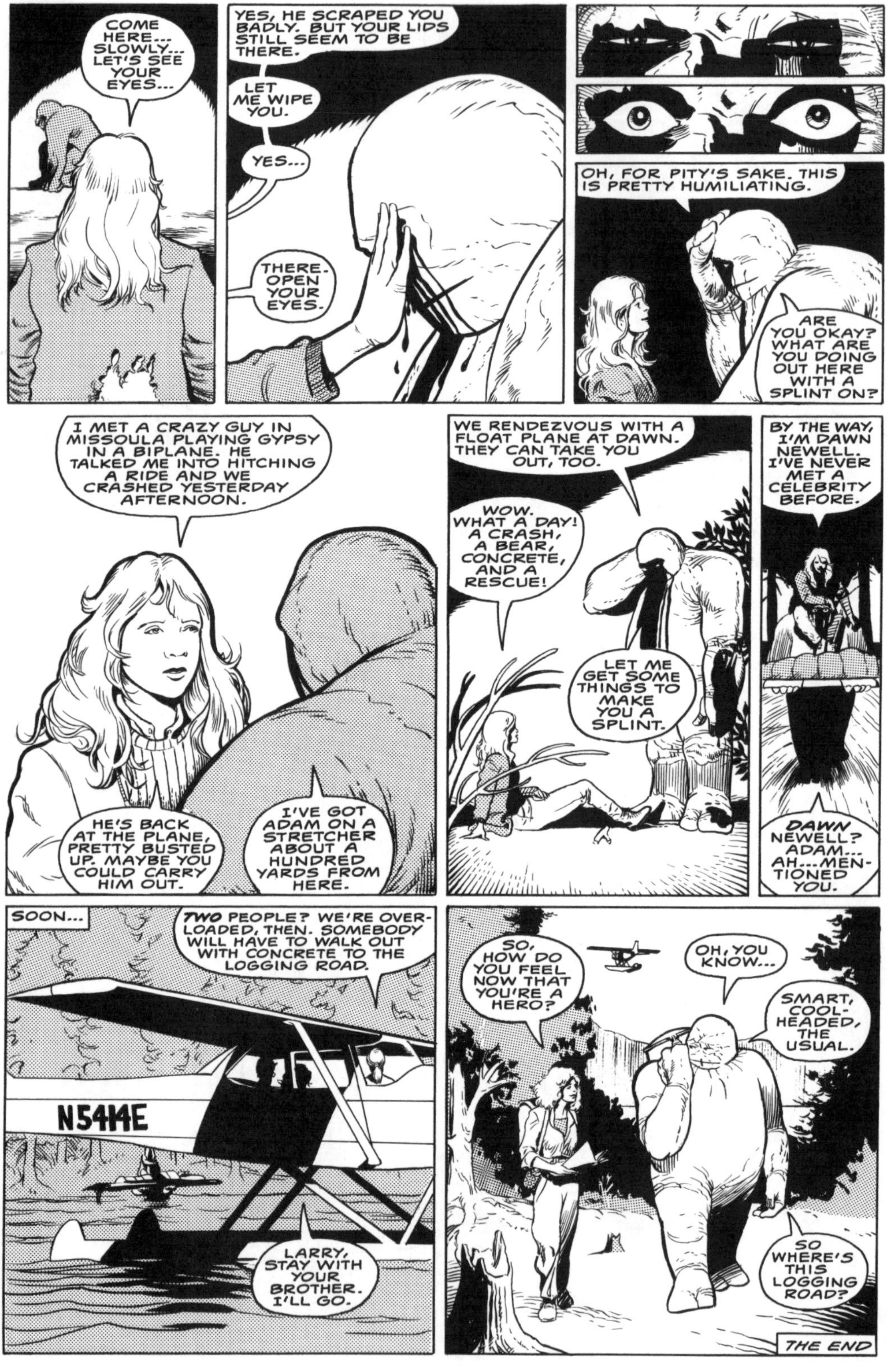
COME HERE... SLOWLY... LET'S SEE YOUR EYES...
YES, HE SCRAPED YOU BADLY. BUT YOUR LIDS STILL SEEM TO BE THERE.
LET ME WIPE YOU.
YES...
THERE. OPEN YOUR EYES.
OH, FOR PITY'S SAKE. THIS IS PRETTY HUMILIATING.
ARE YOU OKAY? WHAT ARE YOU DOING OUT HERE WITH A SPLINT ON?
I MET A CRAZY GUY IN MISSOULA PLAYING GYPSY IN A BIPLANE. HE TALKED ME INTO HITCHING A RIDE AND WE CRASHED YESTERDAY AFTERNOON.
HE'S BACK AT THE PLANE, PRETTY BUSTED UP. MAYBE YOU COULD CARRY HIM OUT.
I'VE GOT ADAM ON A STRETCHER ABOUT A HUNDRED YARDS FROM HERE.
WE RENDEZVOUS WITH A FLOAT PLANE AT DAWN. THEY CAN TAKE YOU OUT, TOO.
WOW. WHAT A DAY! A CRASH, A BEAR, CONCRETE, AND A RESCUE!
LET ME GET SOME THINGS TO MAKE YOU A SPLINT.
BY THE WAY, I'M DAWN NEWELL. I'VE NEVER MET A CELEBRITY BEFORE.
DAWN NEWELL? ADAM... AH... MENTIONED YOU.
SOON...
TWO PEOPLE? WE'RE OVERLOADED, THEN. SOMEBODY WILL HAVE TO WALK OUT WITH CONCRETE TO THE LOGGING ROAD.
N5414E
LARRY, STAY WITH YOUR BROTHER. I'LL GO.
SO, HOW DO YOU FEEL NOW THAT YOU'RE A HERO?
OH, YOU KNOW...
SMART, COOL-HEADED, THE USUAL.
SO WHERE'S THIS LOGGING ROAD?
THE END

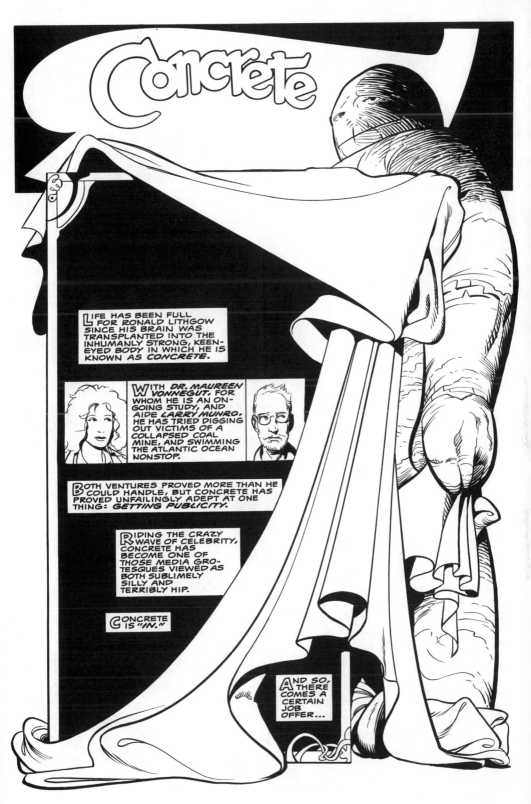

Concrete

LIFE HAS BEEN FULL FOR RONALD LITHGOW SINCE HIS BRAIN WAS TRANSPLANTED INTO THE INHUMANLY STRONG, KEEN-EYED BODY IN WHICH HE IS KNOWN AS *CONCRETE*.

WITH *DR. MAUREEN VONNEGUT*, FOR WHOM HE IS AN ON-GOING STUDY, AND AIDE *LARRY MUNRO*, HE HAS TRIED DIGGING OUT VICTIMS OF A COLLAPSED COAL MINE; AND SWIMMING THE ATLANTIC OCEAN NONSTOP.

BOTH VENTURES PROVED MORE THAN HE COULD HANDLE, BUT CONCRETE HAS PROVED UNFAILINGLY ADEPT AT ONE THING: *GETTING PUBLICITY*.

RIDING THE CRAZY WAVE OF CELEBRITY, CONCRETE HAS BECOME ONE OF THOSE MEDIA GRO-TESQUES VIEWED AS BOTH SUBLIMELY SILLY AND TERRIBLY HIP.

CONCRETE IS *"IN."*

AND SO, THERE COMES A CERTAIN JOB OFFER...

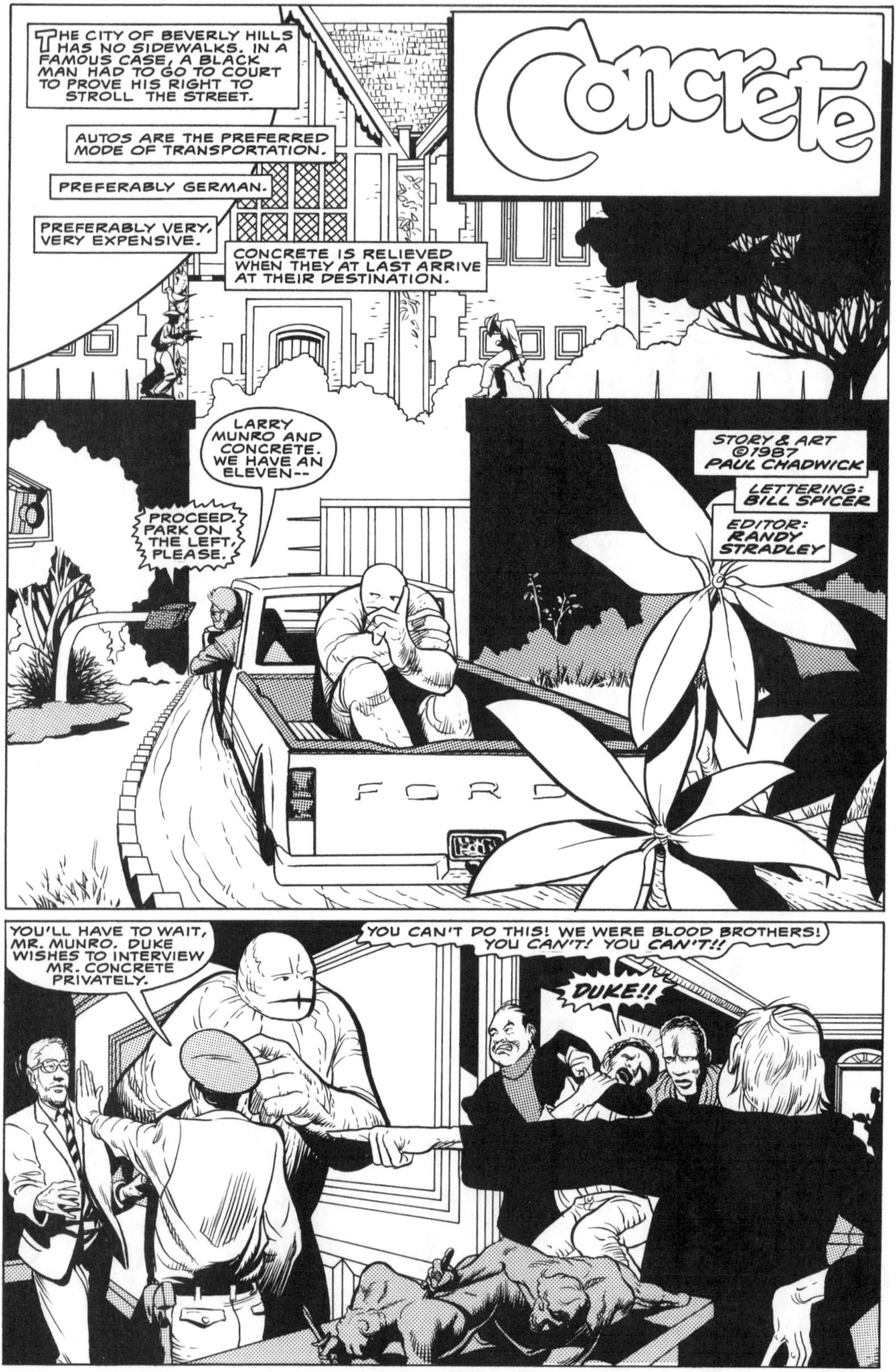
Concrete
THE CITY OF BEVERLY HILLS HAS NO SIDEWALKS. IN A FAMOUS CASE, A BLACK MAN HAD TO GO TO COURT TO PROVE HIS RIGHT TO STROLL THE STREET.
AUTOS ARE THE PREFERRED MODE OF TRANSPORTATION.
PREFERABLY GERMAN.
PREFERABLY VERY, VERY EXPENSIVE.
CONCRETE IS RELIEVED WHEN THEY AT LAST ARRIVE AT THEIR DESTINATION.
LARRY MUNRO AND CONCRETE. WE HAVE AN ELEVEN--
PROCEED. PARK ON THE LEFT, PLEASE.
STORY & ART ©1987 PAUL CHADWICK
LETTERING: BILL SPICER
EDITOR: RANDY STRADLEY
FORD
YOU'LL HAVE TO WAIT, MR. MUNRO. DUKE WISHES TO INTERVIEW MR. CONCRETE PRIVATELY.
YOU CAN'T DO THIS! WE WERE BLOOD BROTHERS! YOU CAN'T! YOU CAN'T!!
DUKE!!

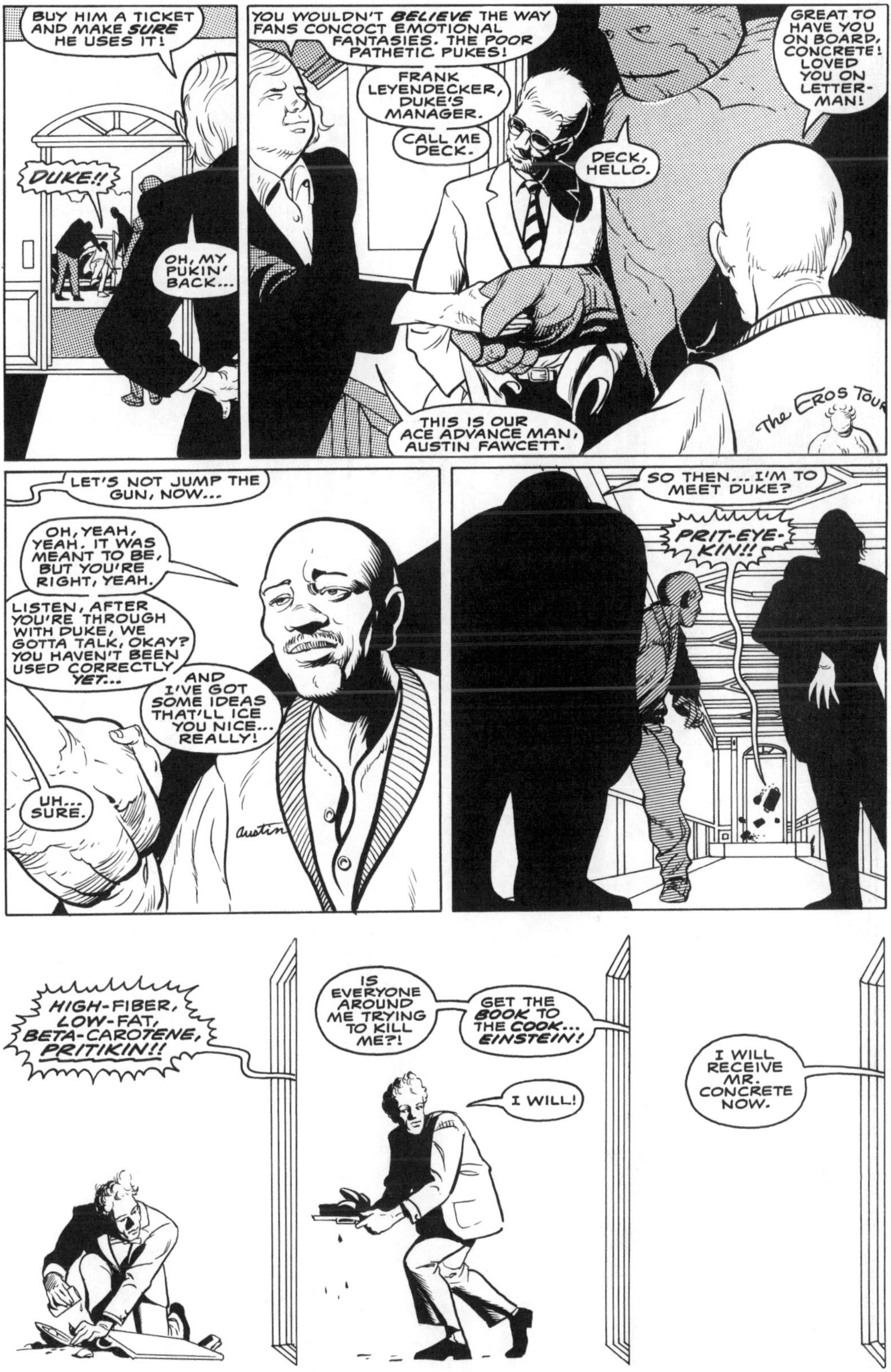
BUY HIM A TICKET AND MAKE SURE HE USES IT!
DUKE!!
OH, MY PUKIN' BACK...
YOU WOULDN'T BELIEVE THE WAY FANS CONCOCT EMOTIONAL FANTASIES. THE POOR PATHETIC PUKES!
FRANK LEYENDECKER, DUKE'S MANAGER.
CALL ME DECK.
DECK, HELLO.
GREAT TO HAVE YOU ON BOARD, CONCRETE! LOVED YOU ON LETTERMAN!
THIS IS OUR ACE ADVANCE MAN, AUSTIN FAWCETT.
The Eros Tour
LET'S NOT JUMP THE GUN, NOW...
OH, YEAH, YEAH. IT WAS MEANT TO BE, BUT YOU'RE RIGHT, YEAH.
LISTEN, AFTER YOU'RE THROUGH WITH DUKE, WE GOTTA TALK, OKAY? YOU HAVEN'T BEEN USED CORRECTLY YET...
AND I'VE GOT SOME IDEAS THAT'LL ICE YOU NICE... REALLY!
UH... SURE.
Austin
SO THEN... I'M TO MEET DUKE?
PRIT-EYE-KIN!!
HIGH-FIBER, LOW-FAT, BETA-CAROTENE, PRITIKIN!!
IS EVERYONE AROUND ME TRYING TO KILL ME?!
GET THE BOOK TO THE COOK... EINSTEIN!
I WILL!
I WILL RECEIVE MR. CONCRETE NOW.

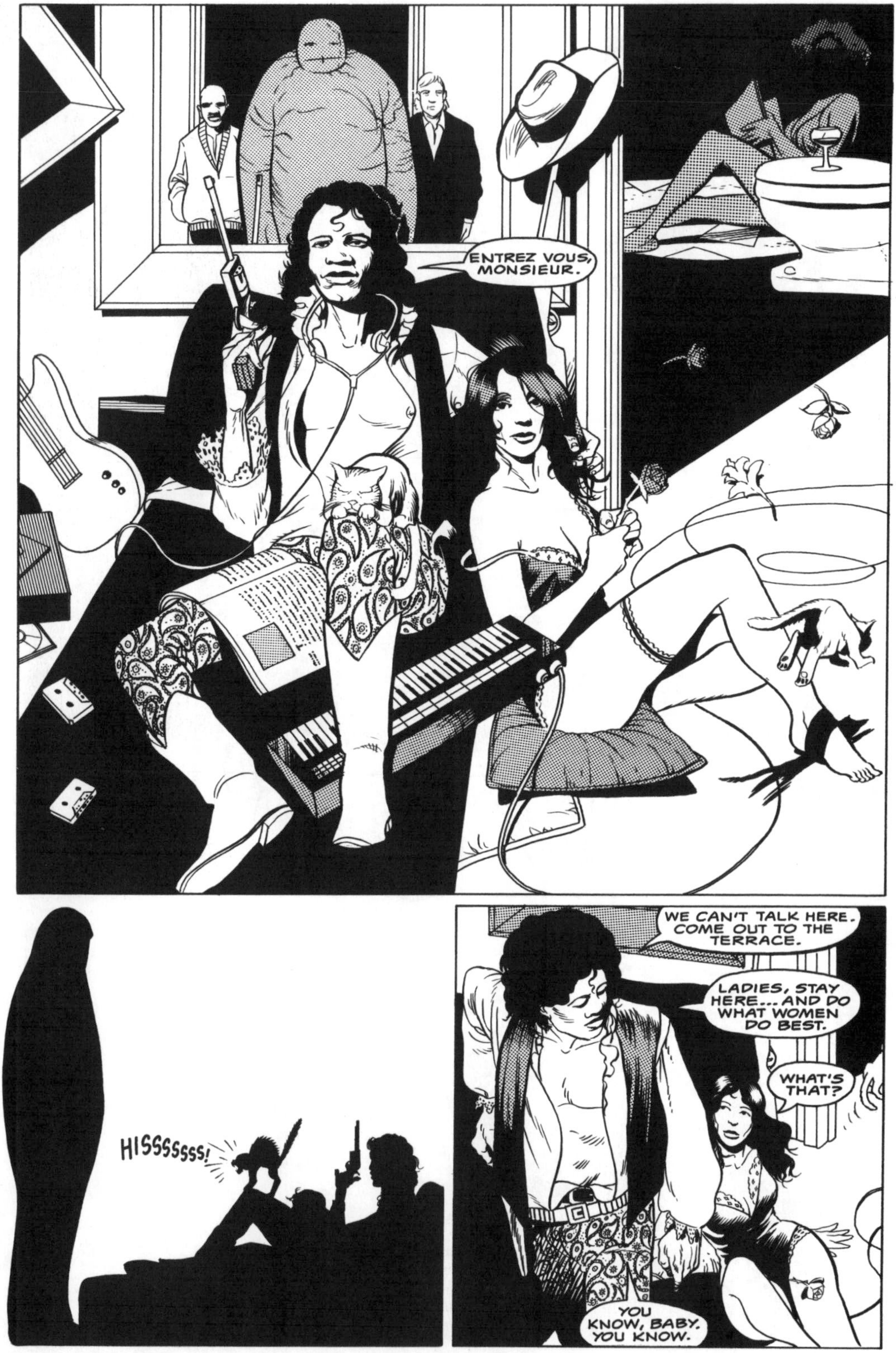
ENTREZ VOUS, MONSIEUR.
HISSSSSSSS!
WE CAN'T TALK HERE. COME OUT TO THE TERRACE.
LADIES, STAY HERE... AND DO WHAT WOMEN DO BEST.
WHAT'S THAT?
YOU KNOW, BABY. YOU KNOW.

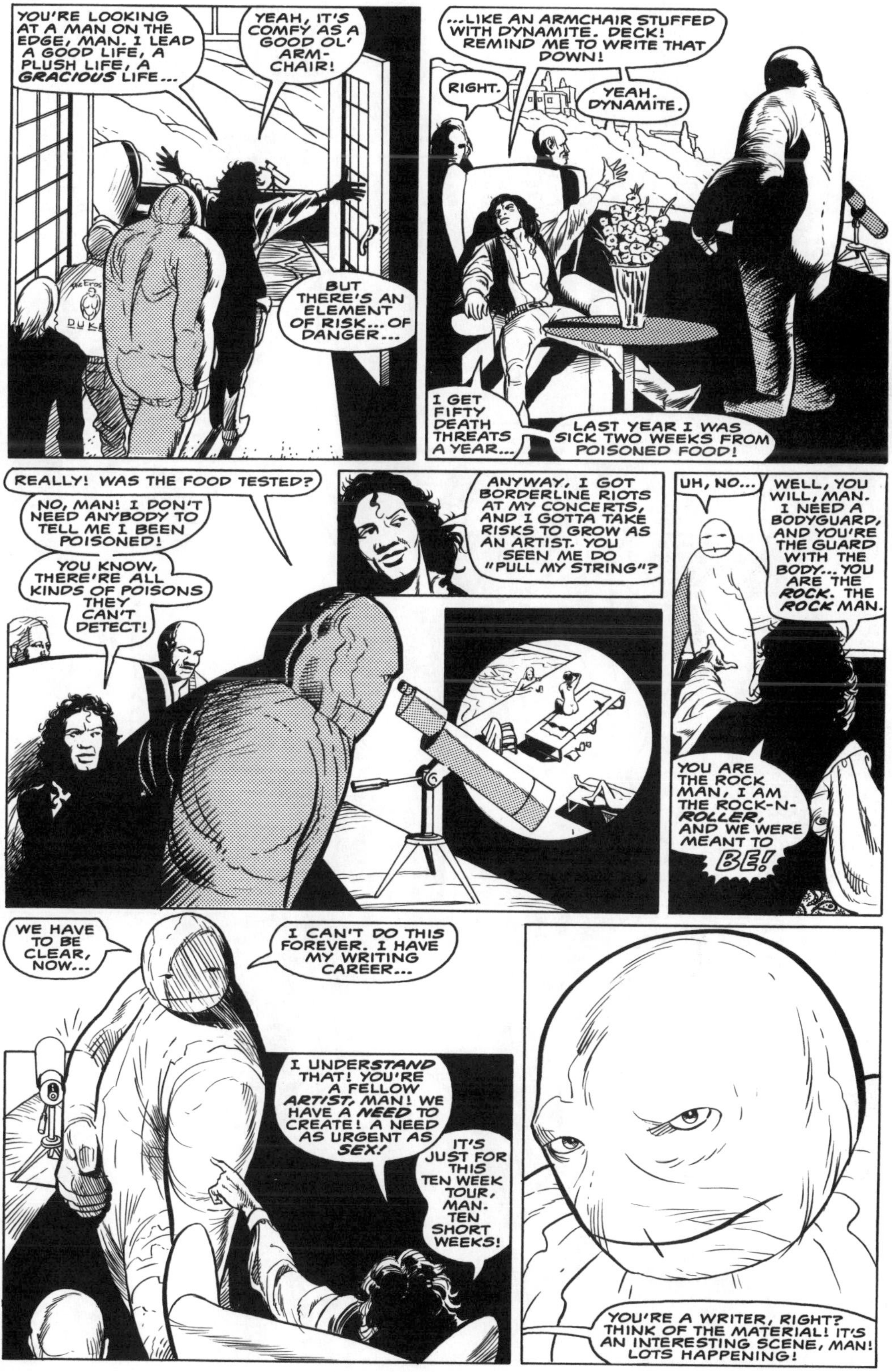
YOU'RE LOOKING AT A MAN ON THE EDGE, MAN. I LEAD A GOOD LIFE, A PLUSH LIFE, A GRACIOUS LIFE...
YEAH, IT'S COMFY AS A GOOD OL' ARM-CHAIR!
BUT THERE'S AN ELEMENT OF RISK... OF DANGER...
...LIKE AN ARMCHAIR STUFFED WITH DYNAMITE. DECK! REMIND ME TO WRITE THAT DOWN!
RIGHT.
YEAH. DYNAMITE.
I GET FIFTY DEATH THREATS A YEAR...
LAST YEAR I WAS SICK TWO WEEKS FROM POISONED FOOD!
REALLY! WAS THE FOOD TESTED?
NO, MAN! I DON'T NEED ANYBODY TO TELL ME I BEEN POISONED!
YOU KNOW, THERE'RE ALL KINDS OF POISONS THEY CAN'T DETECT!
ANYWAY, I GOT BORDERLINE RIOTS AT MY CONCERTS, AND I GOTTA TAKE RISKS TO GROW AS AN ARTIST. YOU SEEN ME DO "PULL MY STRING"?
UH, NO...
WELL, YOU WILL, MAN. I NEED A BODYGUARD, AND YOU'RE THE GUARD WITH THE BODY... YOU ARE THE ROCK. THE ROCK MAN.
YOU ARE THE ROCK MAN, I AM THE ROCK-N-ROLLER, AND WE WERE MEANT TO BE!
WE HAVE TO BE CLEAR, NOW...
I CAN'T DO THIS FOREVER. I HAVE MY WRITING CAREER...
I UNDERSTAND THAT! YOU'RE A FELLOW ARTIST, MAN! WE HAVE A NEED TO CREATE! A NEED AS URGENT AS SEX!
IT'S JUST FOR THIS TEN WEEK TOUR, MAN. TEN SHORT WEEKS!
YOU'RE A WRITER, RIGHT? THINK OF THE MATERIAL! IT'S AN INTERESTING SCENE, MAN! LOTS HAPPENING!

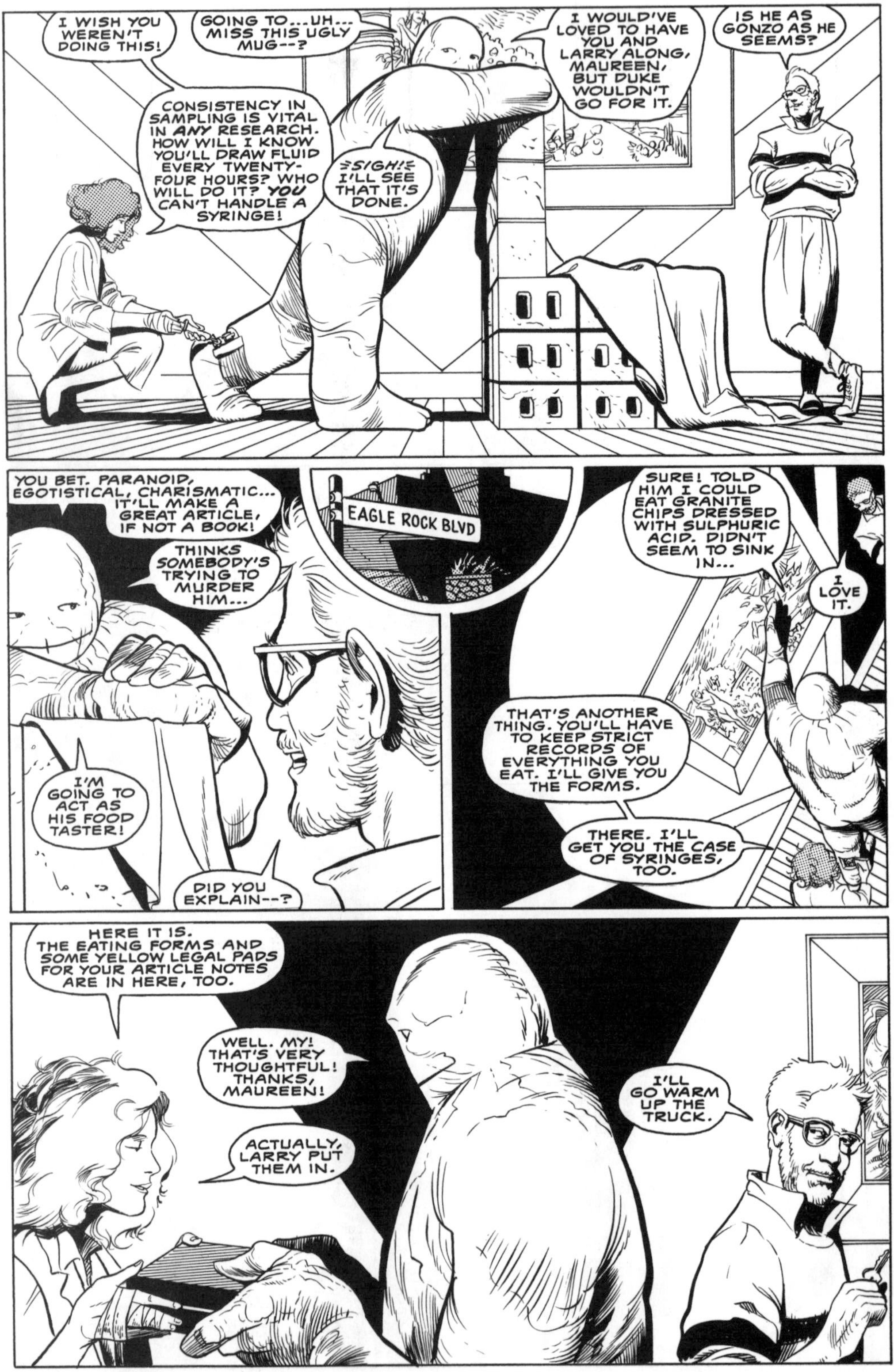
I WISH YOU WEREN'T DOING THIS!
GOING TO...UH... MISS THIS UGLY MUG--?
I WOULD'VE LOVED TO HAVE YOU AND LARRY ALONG, MAUREEN, BUT DUKE WOULDN'T GO FOR IT.
IS HE AS GONZO AS HE SEEMS?
CONSISTENCY IN SAMPLING IS VITAL IN ANY RESEARCH. HOW WILL I KNOW YOU'LL DRAW FLUID EVERY TWENTY-FOUR HOURS? WHO WILL DO IT? YOU CAN'T HANDLE A SYRINGE!
SIGH! I'LL SEE THAT IT'S DONE.
YOU BET. PARANOID, EGOTISTICAL, CHARISMATIC... IT'LL MAKE A GREAT ARTICLE, IF NOT A BOOK!
THINKS SOMEBODY'S TRYING TO MURDER HIM...
I'M GOING TO ACT AS HIS FOOD TASTER!
DID YOU EXPLAIN--?
EAGLE ROCK BLVD
SURE! TOLD HIM I COULD EAT GRANITE CHIPS DRESSED WITH SULPHURIC ACID. DIDN'T SEEM TO SINK IN...
I LOVE IT.
THAT'S ANOTHER THING. YOU'LL HAVE TO KEEP STRICT RECORDS OF EVERYTHING YOU EAT. I'LL GIVE YOU THE FORMS.
THERE. I'LL GET YOU THE CASE OF SYRINGES, TOO.
HERE IT IS. THE EATING FORMS AND SOME YELLOW LEGAL PADS FOR YOUR ARTICLE NOTES ARE IN HERE, TOO.
WELL. MY! THAT'S VERY THOUGHTFUL! THANKS, MAUREEN!
ACTUALLY, LARRY PUT THEM IN.
I'LL GO WARM UP THE TRUCK.

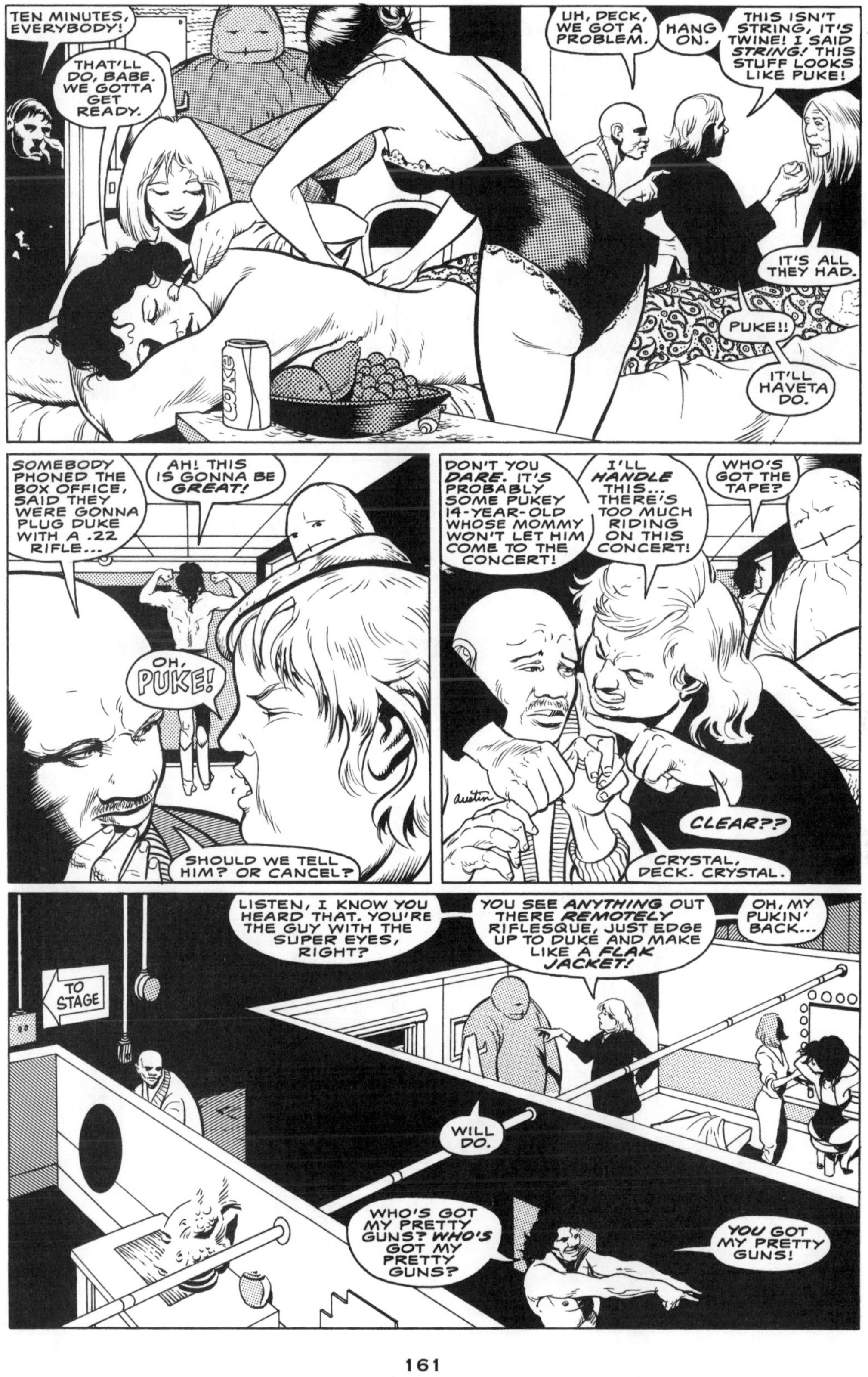

TEN MINUTES, EVERYBODY!
THAT'LL DO, BABE. WE GOTTA GET READY.
UH, DECK, WE GOT A PROBLEM.
HANG ON.
THIS ISN'T STRING, IT'S TWINE! I SAID STRING! THIS STUFF LOOKS LIKE PUKE!
IT'S ALL THEY HAD.
PUKE!!
IT'LL HAVETA DO.
SOMEBODY PHONED THE BOX OFFICE, SAID THEY WERE GONNA PLUG DUKE WITH A .22 RIFLE...
AH! THIS IS GONNA BE GREAT!
OH, PUKE!
SHOULD WE TELL HIM? OR CANCEL?
DON'T YOU DARE. IT'S PROBABLY SOME PUKEY 14-YEAR-OLD WHOSE MOMMY WON'T LET HIM COME TO THE CONCERT!
I'LL HANDLE THIS... THERE'S TOO MUCH RIDING ON THIS CONCERT!
WHO'S GOT THE TAPE?
CLEAR??
CRYSTAL, DECK. CRYSTAL.
TO STAGE
LISTEN, I KNOW YOU HEARD THAT. YOU'RE THE GUY WITH THE SUPER EYES, RIGHT?
YOU SEE ANYTHING OUT THERE REMOTELY RIFLESQUE, JUST EDGE UP TO DUKE AND MAKE LIKE A FLAK JACKET!
OH, MY PUKIN' BACK...
WILL DO.
WHO'S GOT MY PRETTY GUNS? WHO'S GOT MY PRETTY GUNS?
YOU GOT MY PRETTY GUNS!

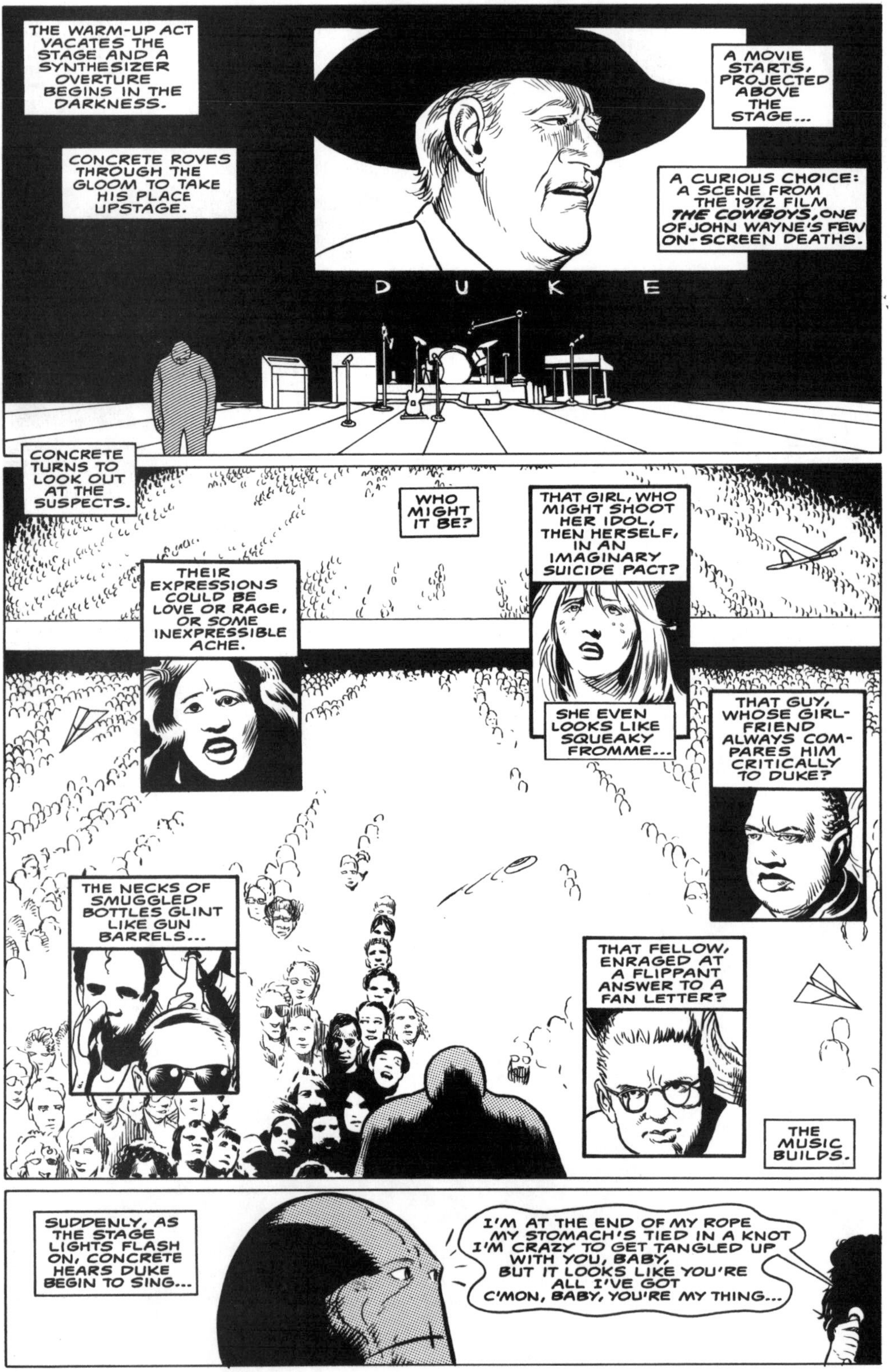
THE WARM-UP ACT VACATES THE STAGE AND A SYNTHESIZER OVERTURE BEGINS IN THE DARKNESS.
A MOVIE STARTS, PROJECTED ABOVE THE STAGE...
CONCRETE ROVES THROUGH THE GLOOM TO TAKE HIS PLACE UPSTAGE.
A CURIOUS CHOICE: A SCENE FROM THE 1972 FILM *THE COWBOYS*, ONE OF JOHN WAYNE'S FEW ON-SCREEN DEATHS.
D U K E
CONCRETE TURNS TO LOOK OUT AT THE SUSPECTS.
WHO MIGHT IT BE?
THAT GIRL, WHO MIGHT SHOOT HER IDOL, THEN HERSELF, IN AN IMAGINARY SUICIDE PACT?
THEIR EXPRESSIONS COULD BE LOVE OR RAGE, OR SOME INEXPRESSIBLE ACHE.
SHE EVEN LOOKS LIKE SQUEAKY FROMME...
THAT GUY, WHOSE GIRL-FRIEND ALWAYS COM-PARES HIM CRITICALLY TO DUKE?
THE NECKS OF SMUGGLED BOTTLES GLINT LIKE GUN BARRELS...
THAT FELLOW, ENRAGED AT A FLIPPANT ANSWER TO A FAN LETTER?
THE MUSIC BUILDS.
SUDDENLY, AS THE STAGE LIGHTS FLASH ON, CONCRETE HEARS DUKE BEGIN TO SING...
I'M AT THE END OF MY ROPE MY STOMACH'S TIED IN A KNOT I'M CRAZY TO GET TANGLED UP WITH YOU, BABY, BUT IT LOOKS LIKE YOU'RE ALL I'VE GOT C'MON, BABY, YOU'RE MY THING...

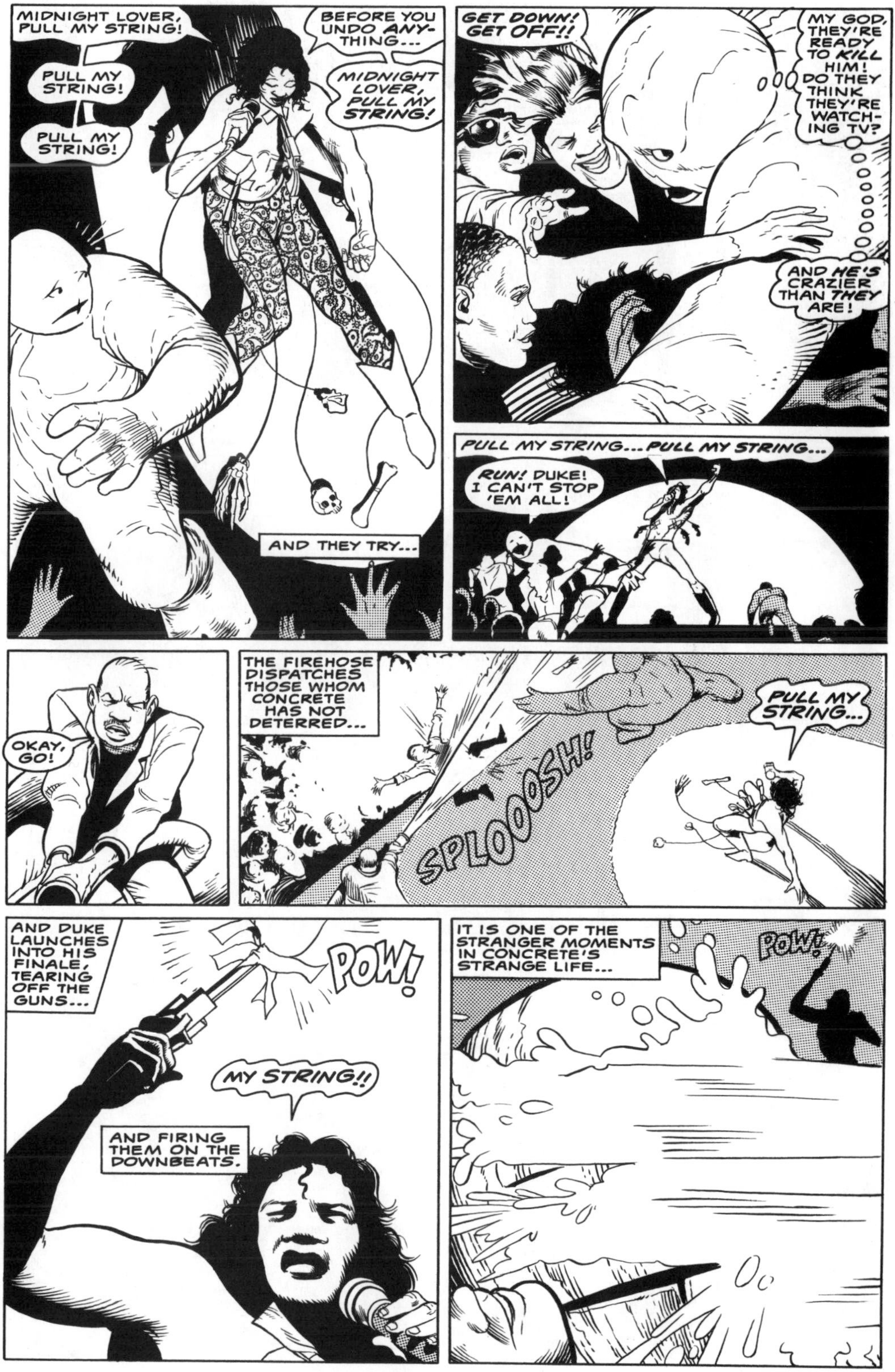
MIDNIGHT LOVER, PULL MY STRING!
BEFORE YOU UNDO ANY-THING...
PULL MY STRING!
MIDNIGHT LOVER, PULL MY STRING!
PULL MY STRING!
AND THEY TRY...
GET DOWN! GET OFF!!
MY GOD, THEY'RE READY TO KILL HIM! DO THEY THINK THEY'RE WATCHING TV?
AND HE'S CRAZIER THAN THEY ARE!
PULL MY STRING... PULL MY STRING...
RUN! DUKE! I CAN'T STOP 'EM ALL!
OKAY, GO!
THE FIREHOSE DISPATCHES THOSE WHOM CONCRETE HAS NOT DETERRED...
PULL MY STRING...
SPLOOOSH!
AND DUKE LAUNCHES INTO HIS FINALE, TEARING OFF THE GUNS...
POW!
MY STRING!!
AND FIRING THEM ON THE DOWNBEATS.
IT IS ONE OF THE STRANGER MOMENTS IN CONCRETE'S STRANGE LIFE...
POW!

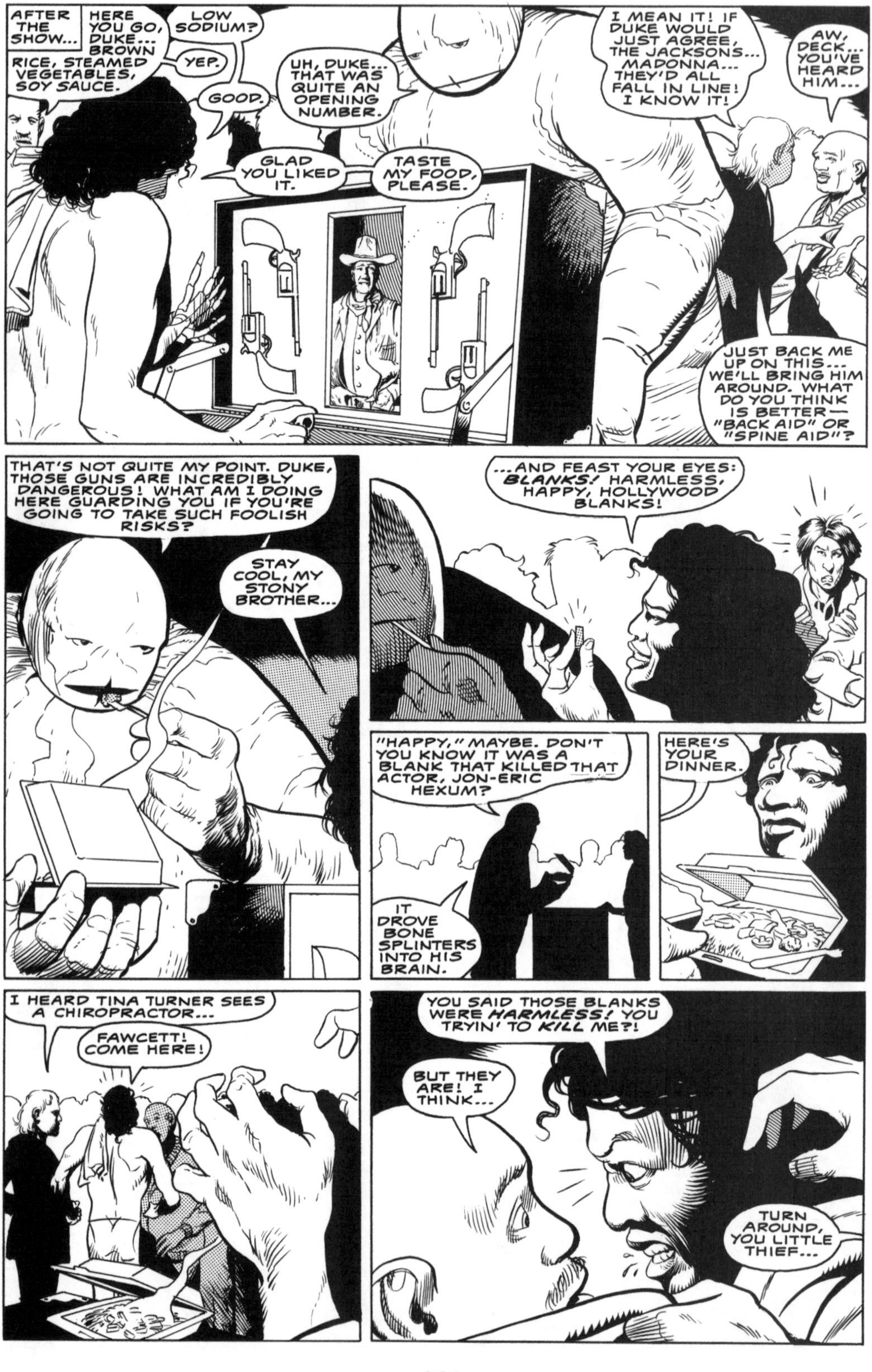
AFTER THE SHOW...
HERE YOU GO, DUKE... BROWN RICE, STEAMED VEGETABLES, SOY SAUCE.
LOW SODIUM?
YEP.
GOOD.
UH, DUKE... THAT WAS QUITE AN OPENING NUMBER.
GLAD YOU LIKED IT.
TASTE MY FOOD, PLEASE.
I MEAN IT! IF DUKE WOULD JUST AGREE, THE JACKSONS... MADONNA... THEY'D ALL FALL IN LINE! I KNOW IT!
AW, DECK... YOU'VE HEARD HIM...
JUST BACK ME UP ON THIS... WE'LL BRING HIM AROUND. WHAT DO YOU THINK IS BETTER— "BACK AID" OR "SPINE AID"?
THAT'S NOT QUITE MY POINT. DUKE, THOSE GUNS ARE INCREDIBLY DANGEROUS! WHAT AM I DOING HERE GUARDING YOU IF YOU'RE GOING TO TAKE SUCH FOOLISH RISKS?
STAY COOL, MY STONY BROTHER...
...AND FEAST YOUR EYES: *BLANKS!* HARMLESS, HAPPY, HOLLYWOOD BLANKS!
"HAPPY," MAYBE. DON'T YOU KNOW IT WAS A BLANK THAT KILLED THAT ACTOR, JON-ERIC HEXUM?
IT DROVE BONE SPLINTERS INTO HIS BRAIN.
HERE'S YOUR DINNER.
I HEARD TINA TURNER SEES A CHIROPRACTOR...
FAWCETT! COME HERE!
YOU SAID THOSE BLANKS WERE *HARMLESS!* YOU TRYIN' TO *KILL* ME?!
BUT THEY ARE! I THINK...
TURN AROUND, YOU LITTLE THIEF...

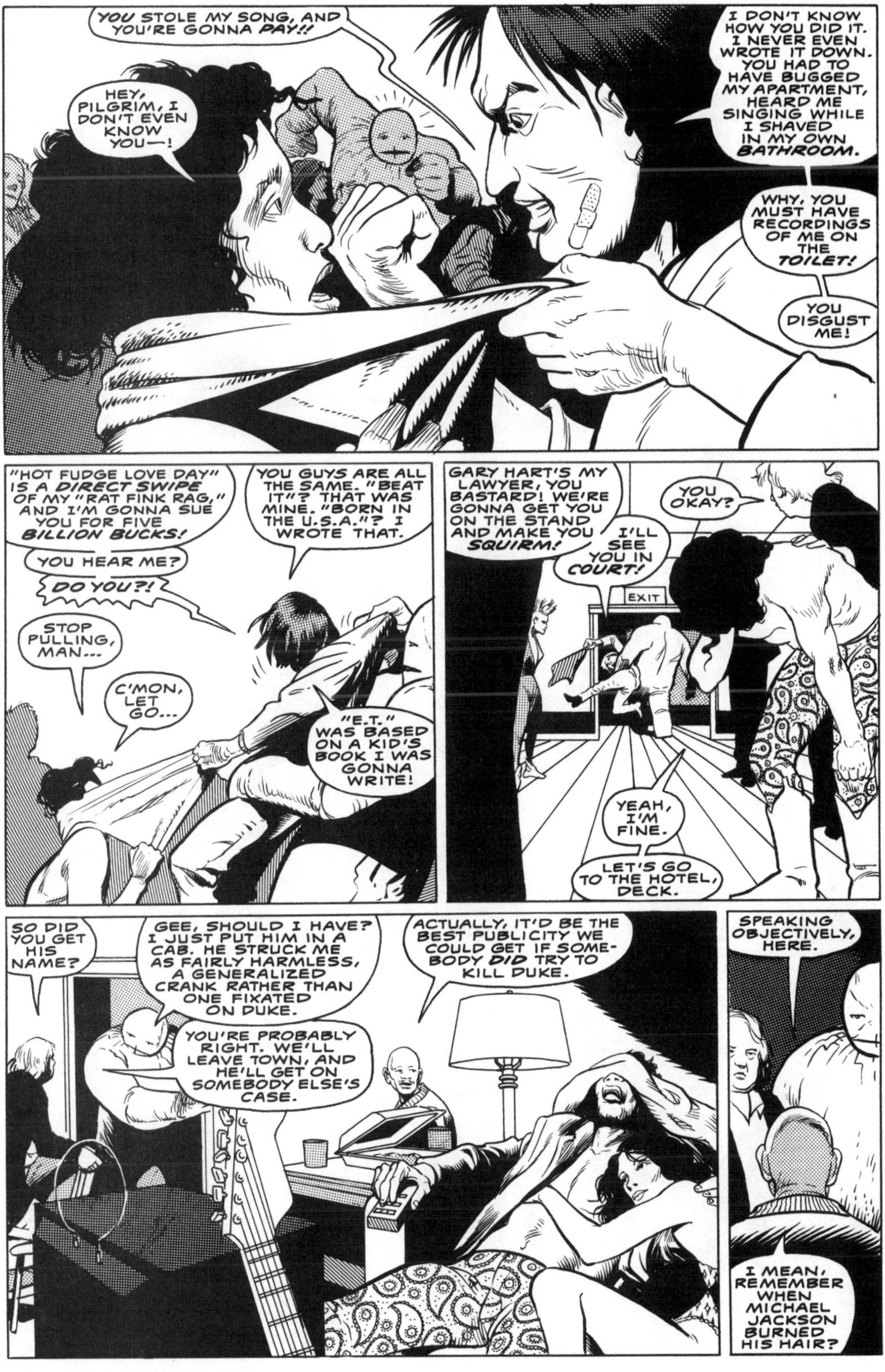
YOU STOLE MY SONG, AND YOU'RE GONNA PAY!!
HEY, PILGRIM, I DON'T EVEN KNOW YOU—!
I DON'T KNOW HOW YOU DID IT. I NEVER EVEN WROTE IT DOWN. YOU HAD TO HAVE BUGGED MY APARTMENT, HEARD ME SINGING WHILE I SHAVED IN MY OWN BATHROOM.
WHY, YOU MUST HAVE RECORDINGS OF ME ON THE TOILET!
YOU DISGUST ME!
"HOT FUDGE LOVE DAY" IS A DIRECT SWIPE OF MY "RAT FINK RAG," AND I'M GONNA SUE YOU FOR FIVE BILLION BUCKS!
YOU HEAR ME?
DO YOU?!
YOU GUYS ARE ALL THE SAME. "BEAT IT"? THAT WAS MINE. "BORN IN THE U.S.A."? I WROTE THAT.
STOP PULLING, MAN...
C'MON, LET GO...
"E.T." WAS BASED ON A KID'S BOOK I WAS GONNA WRITE!
GARY HART'S MY LAWYER, YOU BASTARD! WE'RE GONNA GET YOU ON THE STAND AND MAKE YOU SQUIRM!
I'LL SEE YOU IN COURT!
YOU OKAY?
EXIT
YEAH, I'M FINE.
LET'S GO TO THE HOTEL, DECK.
SO DID YOU GET HIS NAME?
GEE, SHOULD I HAVE? I JUST PUT HIM IN A CAB. HE STRUCK ME AS FAIRLY HARMLESS, A GENERALIZED CRANK RATHER THAN ONE FIXATED ON DUKE.
YOU'RE PROBABLY RIGHT. WE'LL LEAVE TOWN, AND HE'LL GET ON SOMEBODY ELSE'S CASE.
ACTUALLY, IT'D BE THE BEST PUBLICITY WE COULD GET IF SOMEBODY DID TRY TO KILL DUKE.
SPEAKING OBJECTIVELY, HERE.
I MEAN, REMEMBER WHEN MICHAEL JACKSON BURNED HIS HAIR?

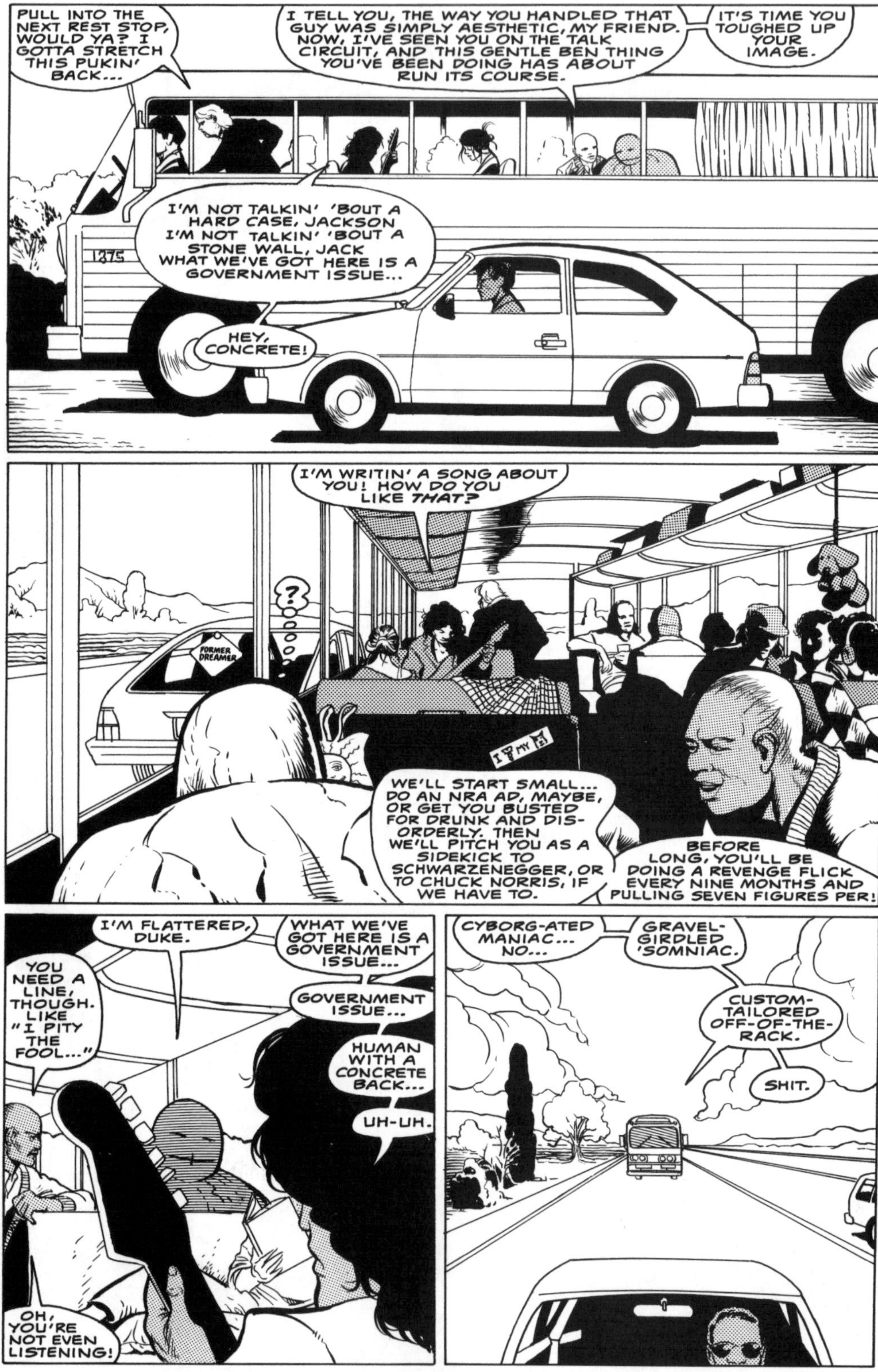
PULL INTO THE NEXT REST STOP, WOULD YA? I GOTTA STRETCH THIS PUKIN' BACK...
I TELL YOU, THE WAY YOU HANDLED THAT GUY WAS SIMPLY AESTHETIC, MY FRIEND. NOW, I'VE SEEN YOU ON THE TALK CIRCUIT, AND THIS GENTLE BEN THING YOU'VE BEEN DOING HAS ABOUT RUN ITS COURSE.
IT'S TIME YOU TOUGHED UP YOUR IMAGE.
I'M NOT TALKIN' 'BOUT A HARD CASE, JACKSON I'M NOT TALKIN' 'BOUT A STONE WALL, JACK WHAT WE'VE GOT HERE IS A GOVERNMENT ISSUE...
1375
HEY, CONCRETE!
I'M WRITIN' A SONG ABOUT YOU! HOW DO YOU LIKE THAT?
?
FORMER DREAMER
WE'LL START SMALL... DO AN NRA AD, MAYBE, OR GET YOU BUSTED FOR DRUNK AND DIS-ORDERLY. THEN WE'LL PITCH YOU AS A SIDEKICK TO SCHWARZENEGGER, OR TO CHUCK NORRIS, IF WE HAVE TO.
BEFORE LONG, YOU'LL BE DOING A REVENGE FLICK EVERY NINE MONTHS AND PULLING SEVEN FIGURES PER!
I'M FLATTERED, DUKE.
YOU NEED A LINE, THOUGH. LIKE "I PITY THE FOOL..."
WHAT WE'VE GOT HERE IS A GOVERNMENT ISSUE...
GOVERNMENT ISSUE...
HUMAN WITH A CONCRETE BACK...
UH-UH.
OH, YOU'RE NOT EVEN LISTENING!
CYBORG-ATED MANIAC... NO...
GRAVEL-GIRDLED 'SOMNIAC.
CUSTOM-TAILORED OFF-OF-THE-RACK.
SHIT.

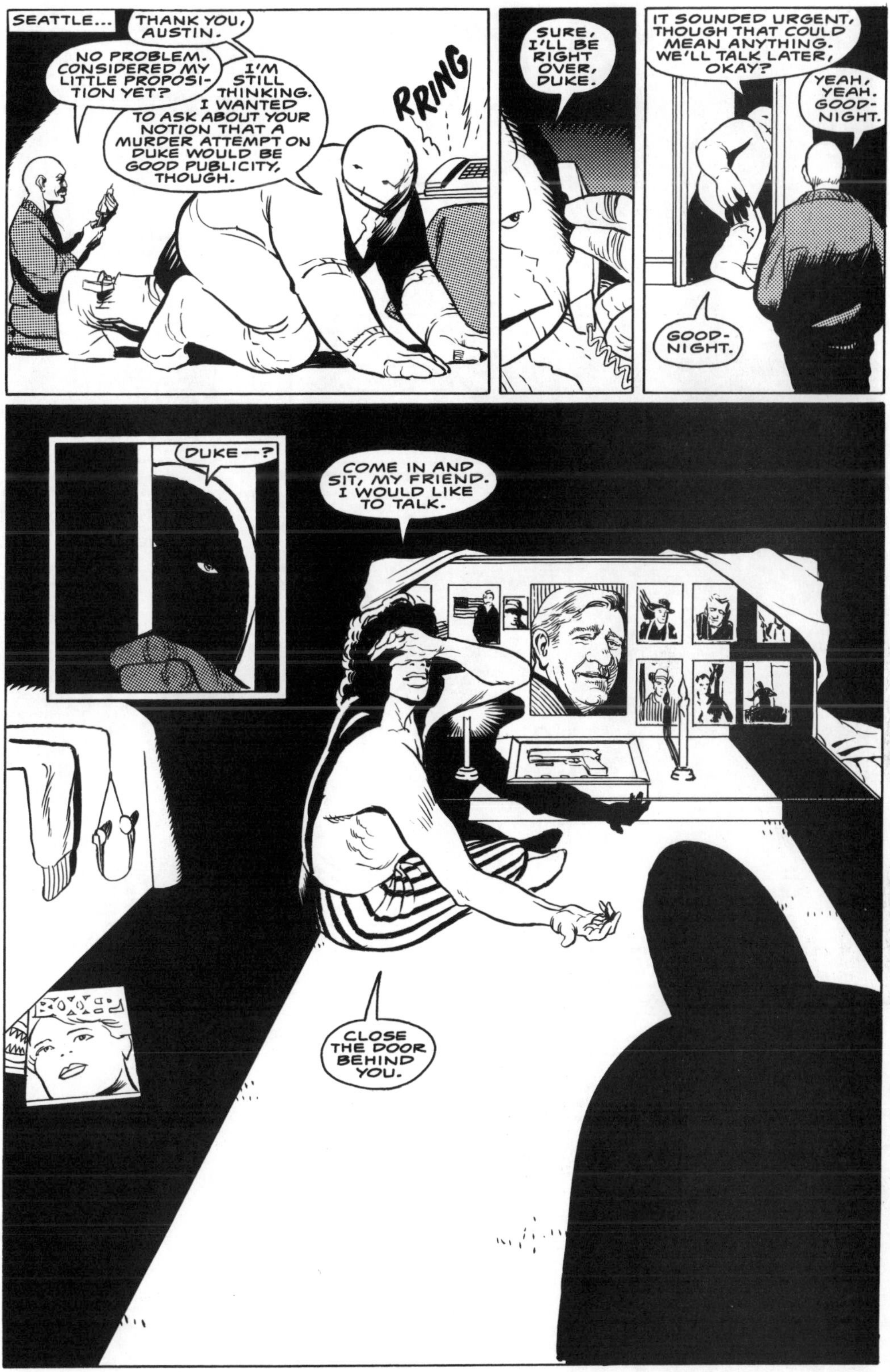
SEATTLE...
THANK YOU, AUSTIN.
NO PROBLEM. CONSIDERED MY LITTLE PROPOSITION YET?
I'M STILL THINKING. I WANTED TO ASK ABOUT YOUR NOTION THAT A MURDER ATTEMPT ON DUKE WOULD BE GOOD PUBLICITY, THOUGH.
RRING
SURE, I'LL BE RIGHT OVER, DUKE.
IT SOUNDED URGENT, THOUGH THAT COULD MEAN ANYTHING. WE'LL TALK LATER, OKAY?
YEAH, YEAH. GOOD-NIGHT.
GOOD-NIGHT.
DUKE—?
COME IN AND SIT, MY FRIEND. I WOULD LIKE TO TALK.
CLOSE THE DOOR BEHIND YOU.

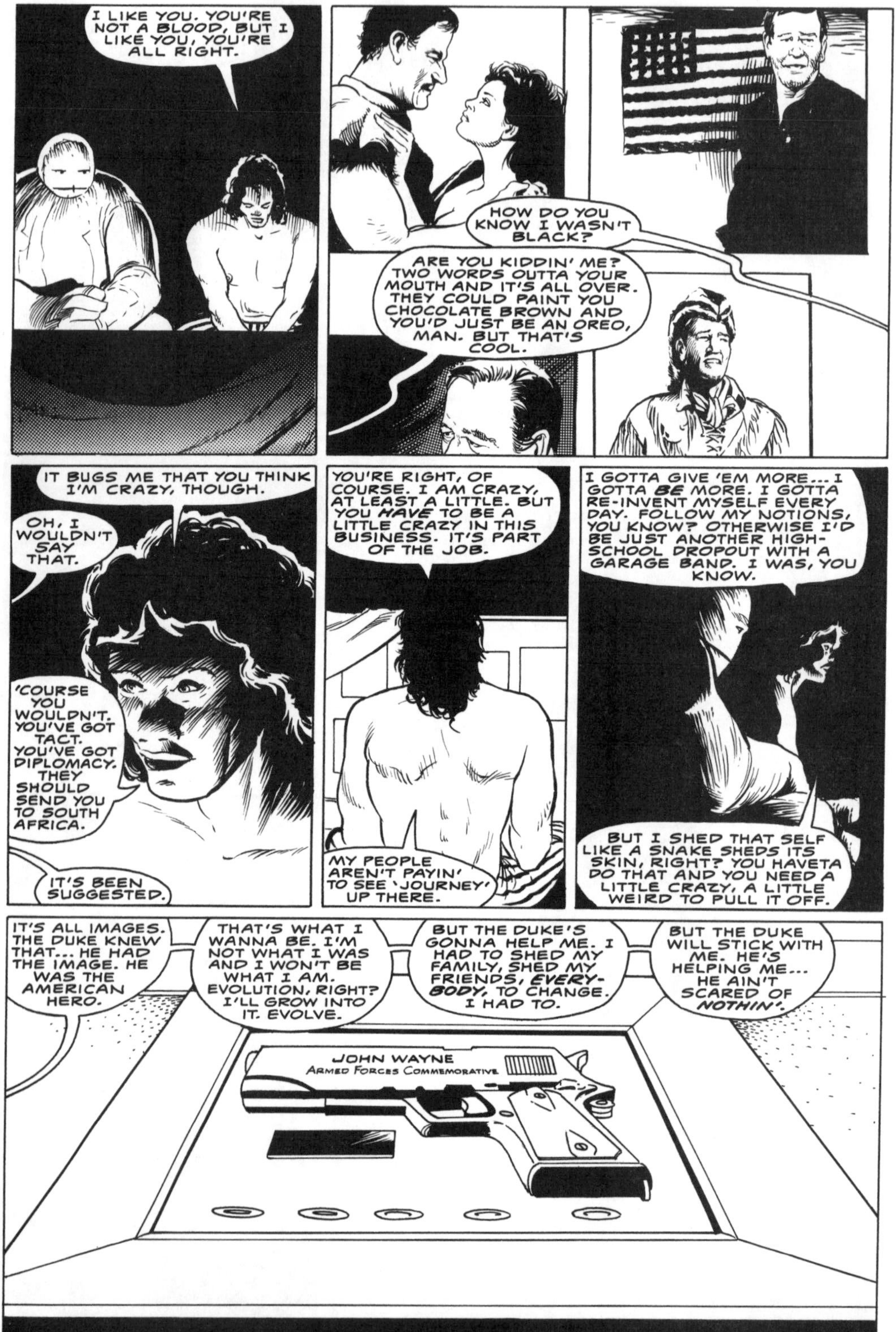
I LIKE YOU. YOU'RE NOT A BLOOD, BUT I LIKE YOU, YOU'RE ALL RIGHT.
HOW DO YOU KNOW I WASN'T BLACK?
ARE YOU KIDDIN' ME? TWO WORDS OUTTA YOUR MOUTH AND IT'S ALL OVER. THEY COULD PAINT YOU CHOCOLATE BROWN AND YOU'D JUST BE AN OREO, MAN. BUT THAT'S COOL.
IT BUGS ME THAT YOU THINK I'M CRAZY, THOUGH.
OH, I WOULDN'T SAY THAT.
'COURSE YOU WOULDN'T. YOU'VE GOT TACT. YOU'VE GOT DIPLOMACY. THEY SHOULD SEND YOU TO SOUTH AFRICA.
IT'S BEEN SUGGESTED.
YOU'RE RIGHT, OF COURSE. I AM CRAZY, AT LEAST A LITTLE. BUT YOU *HAVE* TO BE A LITTLE CRAZY IN THIS BUSINESS. IT'S PART OF THE JOB.
MY PEOPLE AREN'T PAYIN' TO SEE 'JOURNEY' UP THERE.
I GOTTA GIVE 'EM MORE... I GOTTA *BE* MORE. I GOTTA RE-INVENT MYSELF EVERY DAY. FOLLOW MY NOTIONS, YOU KNOW? OTHERWISE I'D BE JUST ANOTHER HIGH-SCHOOL DROPOUT WITH A GARAGE BAND. I WAS, YOU KNOW.
BUT I SHED THAT SELF LIKE A SNAKE SHEDS ITS SKIN, RIGHT? YOU HAVETA DO THAT AND YOU NEED A LITTLE CRAZY, A LITTLE WEIRD TO PULL IT OFF.
IT'S ALL IMAGES. THE DUKE KNEW THAT... HE HAD THE IMAGE. HE WAS THE AMERICAN HERO.
THAT'S WHAT I WANNA BE. I'M NOT WHAT I WAS AND I WON'T BE WHAT I AM. EVOLUTION, RIGHT? I'LL GROW INTO IT. EVOLVE.
BUT THE DUKE'S GONNA HELP ME. I HAD TO SHED MY FAMILY, SHED MY FRIENDS, *EVERY-BODY*, TO CHANGE. I HAD TO.
BUT THE DUKE WILL STICK WITH ME. HE'S HELPING ME... HE AIN'T SCARED OF *NOTHIN'*.
JOHN WAYNE
ARMED FORCES COMMEMORATIVE

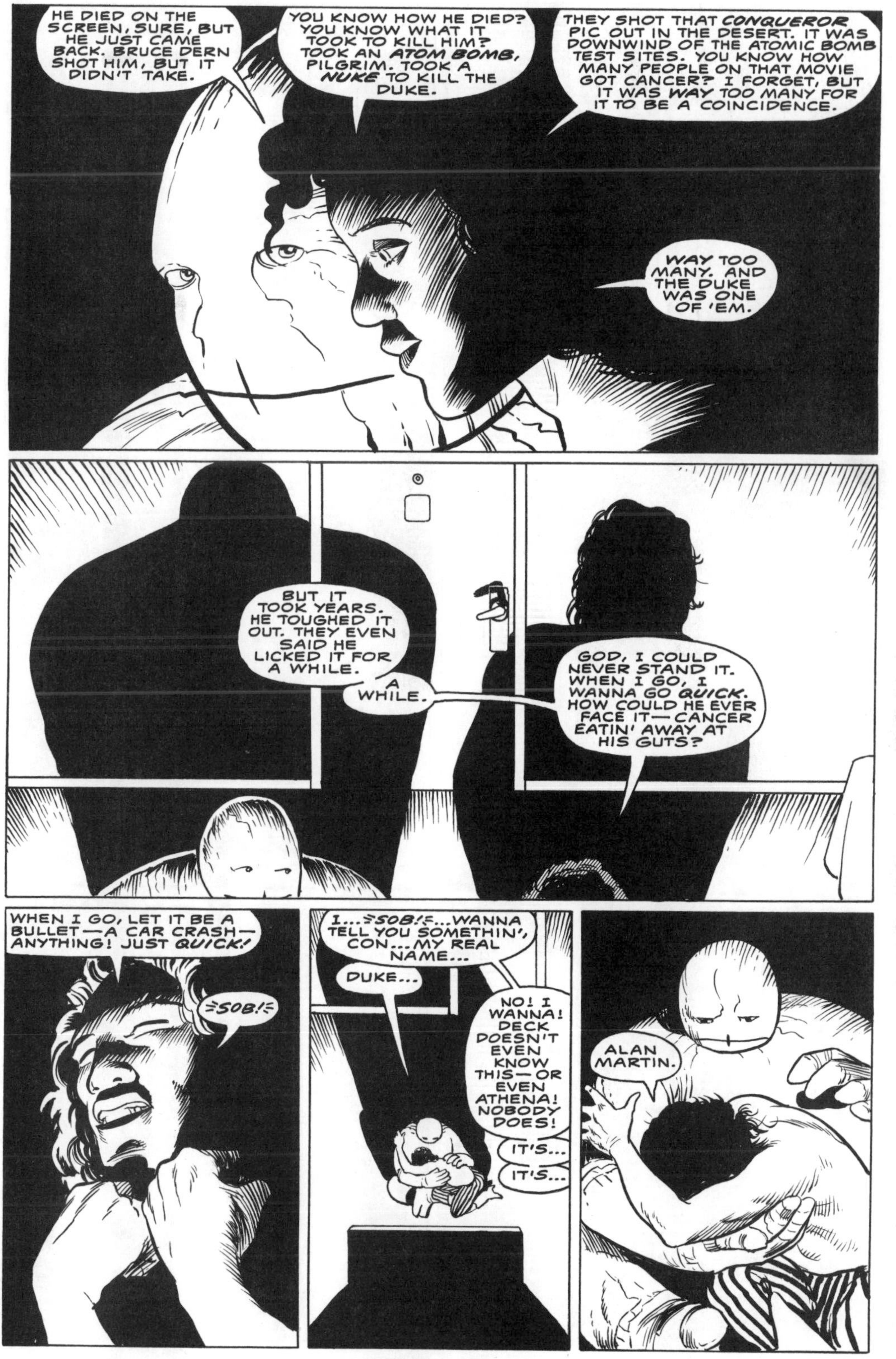
HE DIED ON THE SCREEN, SURE, BUT HE JUST CAME BACK. BRUCE DERN SHOT HIM, BUT IT DIDN'T TAKE.
YOU KNOW HOW HE DIED? YOU KNOW WHAT IT TOOK TO KILL HIM? TOOK AN ATOM BOMB, PILGRIM. TOOK A NUKE TO KILL THE DUKE.
THEY SHOT THAT CONQUEROR PIC OUT IN THE DESERT. IT WAS DOWNWIND OF THE ATOMIC BOMB TEST SITES. YOU KNOW HOW MANY PEOPLE ON THAT MOVIE GOT CANCER? I FORGET, BUT IT WAS WAY TOO MANY FOR IT TO BE A COINCIDENCE.
WAY TOO MANY. AND THE DUKE WAS ONE OF 'EM.
BUT IT TOOK YEARS. HE TOUGHED IT OUT. THEY EVEN SAID HE LICKED IT FOR A WHILE.
A WHILE.
GOD, I COULD NEVER STAND IT. WHEN I GO, I WANNA GO QUICK. HOW COULD HE EVER FACE IT—CANCER EATIN' AWAY AT HIS GUTS?
WHEN I GO, LET IT BE A BULLET—A CAR CRASH—ANYTHING! JUST QUICK!
SOB!
I... SOB!... WANNA TELL YOU SOMETHIN', CON... MY REAL NAME...
DUKE...
NO! I WANNA! DECK DOESN'T EVEN KNOW THIS—OR EVEN ATHENA! NOBODY DOES!
IT'S...
IT'S...
ALAN MARTIN.

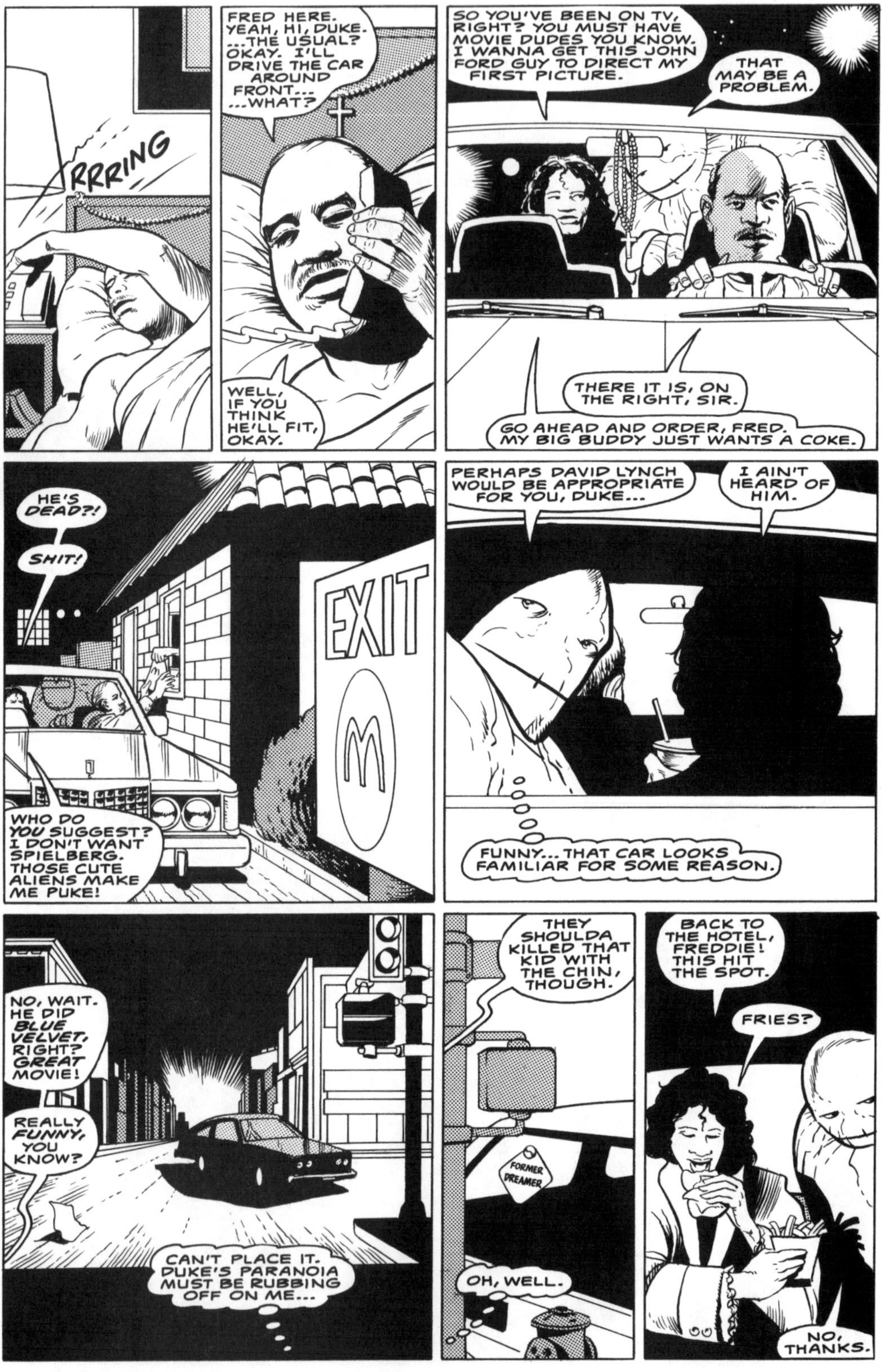
RRRING
FRED HERE. YEAH, HI, DUKE. ...THE USUAL? OKAY. I'LL DRIVE THE CAR AROUND FRONT... ...WHAT?
WELL, IF YOU THINK HE'LL FIT, OKAY.
SO YOU'VE BEEN ON TV, RIGHT? YOU MUST HAVE MOVIE DUDES YOU KNOW. I WANNA GET THIS JOHN FORD GUY TO DIRECT MY FIRST PICTURE.
THAT MAY BE A PROBLEM.
THERE IT IS, ON THE RIGHT, SIR.
GO AHEAD AND ORDER, FRED. MY BIG BUDDY JUST WANTS A COKE.
HE'S DEAD?!
SHIT!
EXIT
WHO DO YOU SUGGEST? I DON'T WANT SPIELBERG. THOSE CUTE ALIENS MAKE ME PUKE!
PERHAPS DAVID LYNCH WOULD BE APPROPRIATE FOR YOU, DUKE...
I AIN'T HEARD OF HIM.
FUNNY... THAT CAR LOOKS FAMILIAR FOR SOME REASON.
NO, WAIT. HE DID BLUE VELVET, RIGHT? GREAT MOVIE!
REALLY FUNNY, YOU KNOW?
CAN'T PLACE IT. DUKE'S PARANOIA MUST BE RUBBING OFF ON ME...
THEY SHOULDA KILLED THAT KID WITH THE CHIN, THOUGH.
FORMER DREAMER
OH, WELL.
BACK TO THE HOTEL, FREDDIE! THIS HIT THE SPOT.
FRIES?
NO, THANKS.

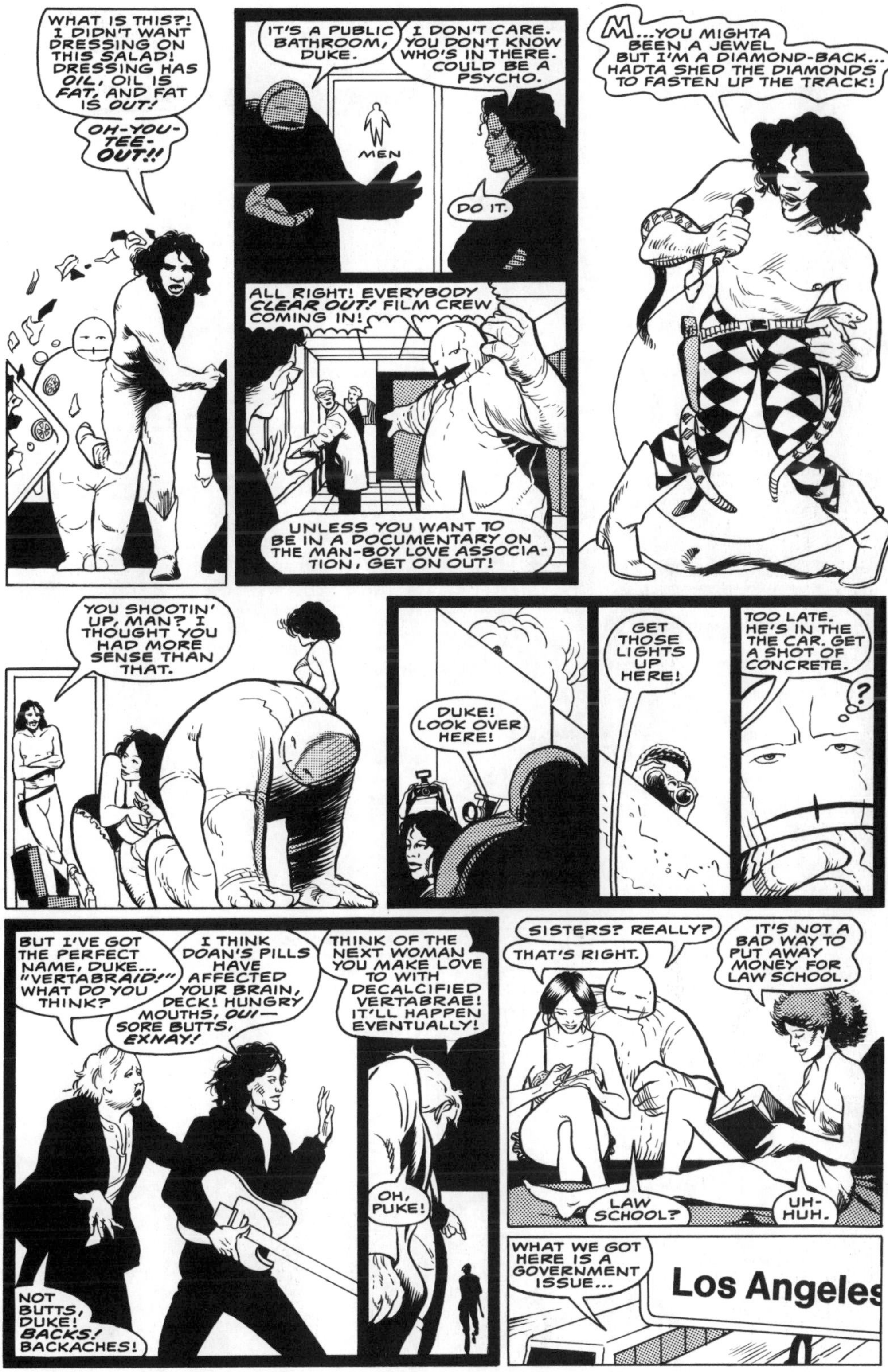
WHAT IS THIS?! I DIDN'T WANT DRESSING ON THIS SALAD! DRESSING HAS OIL, OIL IS FAT, AND FAT IS OUT!
OH-YOU-TEE-OUT!!
IT'S A PUBLIC BATHROOM, DUKE.
I DON'T CARE. YOU DON'T KNOW WHO'S IN THERE. COULD BE A PSYCHO.
MEN
DO IT.
ALL RIGHT! EVERYBODY CLEAR OUT! FILM CREW COMING IN!
UNLESS YOU WANT TO BE IN A DOCUMENTARY ON THE MAN-BOY LOVE ASSOCIATION, GET ON OUT!
M...YOU MIGHTA BEEN A JEWEL BUT I'M A DIAMOND-BACK... HADTA SHED THE DIAMONDS TO FASTEN UP THE TRACK!
YOU SHOOTIN' UP, MAN? I THOUGHT YOU HAD MORE SENSE THAN THAT.
DUKE! LOOK OVER HERE!
GET THOSE LIGHTS UP HERE!
TOO LATE. HE'S IN THE THE CAR. GET A SHOT OF CONCRETE.
?
BUT I'VE GOT THE PERFECT NAME, DUKE... "VERTABRAID!" WHAT DO YOU THINK?
I THINK DOAN'S PILLS HAVE AFFECTED YOUR BRAIN, DECK! HUNGRY MOUTHS, OUI— SORE BUTTS, EXNAY!
NOT BUTTS, DUKE! BACKS! BACKACHES!
THINK OF THE NEXT WOMAN YOU MAKE LOVE TO WITH DECALCIFIED VERTABRAE! IT'LL HAPPEN EVENTUALLY!
OH, PUKE!
SISTERS? REALLY?
THAT'S RIGHT.
IT'S NOT A BAD WAY TO PUT AWAY MONEY FOR LAW SCHOOL.
LAW SCHOOL?
UH-HUH.
WHAT WE GOT HERE IS A GOVERNMENT ISSUE...
Los Angeles

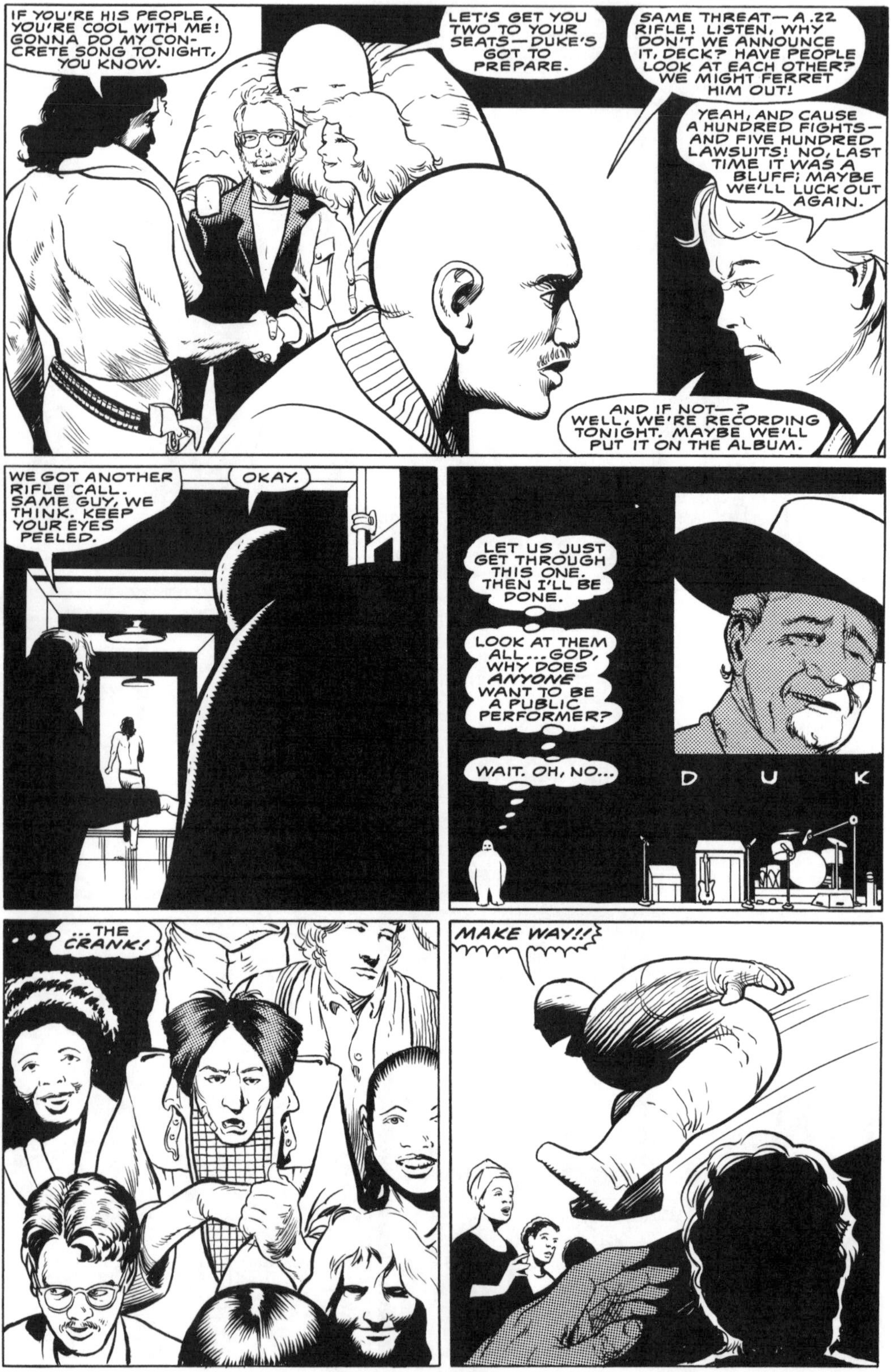
IF YOU'RE HIS PEOPLE, YOU'RE COOL WITH ME! GONNA DO MY CONCRETE SONG TONIGHT, YOU KNOW.
LET'S GET YOU TWO TO YOUR SEATS—DUKE'S GOT TO PREPARE.
SAME THREAT—A .22 RIFLE! LISTEN, WHY DON'T WE ANNOUNCE IT, DECK? HAVE PEOPLE LOOK AT EACH OTHER? WE MIGHT FERRET HIM OUT!
YEAH, AND CAUSE A HUNDRED FIGHTS—AND FIVE HUNDRED LAWSUITS! NO, LAST TIME IT WAS A BLUFF; MAYBE WE'LL LUCK OUT AGAIN.
AND IF NOT—? WELL, WE'RE RECORDING TONIGHT. MAYBE WE'LL PUT IT ON THE ALBUM.
WE GOT ANOTHER RIFLE CALL. SAME GUY, WE THINK. KEEP YOUR EYES PEELED.
OKAY.
LET US JUST GET THROUGH THIS ONE. THEN I'LL BE DONE.
LOOK AT THEM ALL... GOD, WHY DOES *ANYONE* WANT TO BE A PUBLIC PERFORMER?
WAIT. OH, NO...
D U K
...THE *CRANK!*
MAKE WAY!!

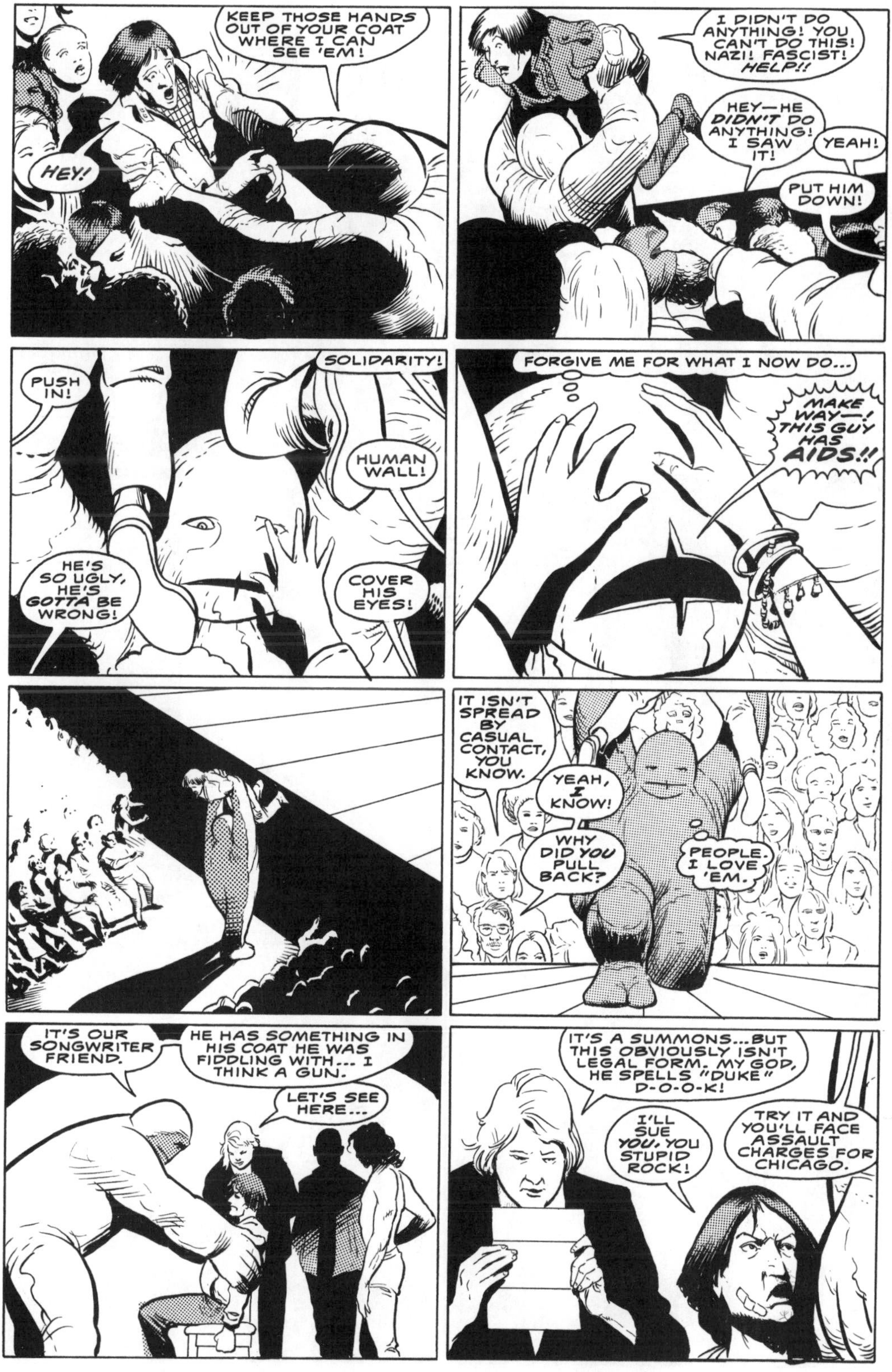
KEEP THOSE HANDS OUT OF YOUR COAT WHERE I CAN SEE 'EM!
HEY!
I DIDN'T DO ANYTHING! YOU CAN'T DO THIS! NAZI! FASCIST! HELP!!
HEY—HE DIDN'T DO ANYTHING! I SAW IT!
YEAH!
PUT HIM DOWN!
PUSH IN!
SOLIDARITY!
HUMAN WALL!
HE'S SO UGLY, HE'S GOTTA BE WRONG!
COVER HIS EYES!
FORGIVE ME FOR WHAT I NOW DO...
MAKE WAY—! THIS GUY HAS AIDS!!
IT ISN'T SPREAD BY CASUAL CONTACT, YOU KNOW.
YEAH, I KNOW!
WHY DID YOU PULL BACK?
PEOPLE. I LOVE 'EM.
IT'S OUR SONGWRITER FRIEND.
HE HAS SOMETHING IN HIS COAT HE WAS FIDDLING WITH... I THINK A GUN.
LET'S SEE HERE...
IT'S A SUMMONS...BUT THIS OBVIOUSLY ISN'T LEGAL FORM. MY GOD, HE SPELLS "DUKE" D-O-O-K!
I'LL SUE YOU, YOU STUPID ROCK!
TRY IT AND YOU'LL FACE ASSAULT CHARGES FOR CHICAGO.

C'MON AND GET OUT THERE! THE FILM CLIP'S OVER!

REMEMBER, YOU'RE A PERFORMER TONIGHT.

TIME TO DO IT!!

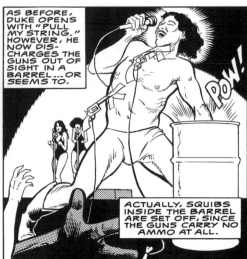

AS BEFORE, DUKE OPENS WITH "PULL MY STRING." HOWEVER, HE NOW DISCHARGES THE GUNS OUT OF SIGHT IN A BARREL...OR SEEMS TO.

POW!

ACTUALLY, SQUIBS INSIDE THE BARREL ARE SET OFF, SINCE THE GUNS CARRY NO AMMO AT ALL.

AS A FINALE, THE BARREL IS OVERTURNED, DISGORGING WATER, GUNS, AND—WITH LIMITED CONCEPTUAL SIGNIFICANCE—FISH.

THE CONCERT CONTINUES WITH DUKE'S UNIQUE BLEND OF MUSIC, SPECTACLE AND CONCEPTUAL PLAY.

UNTIL AT LAST IT IS TIME FOR CONCRETE'S MOMENT OF HONOR.

HOM

I AIN'T TALKIN' 'BOUT A HARD CASE, JACKSON...

I'M NOT TALKIN' 'BOUT A STONE WALL, JACK...

WHAT WE'VE GOT HERE IS A GOVERNMENT ISSUE...

HOMEBOY

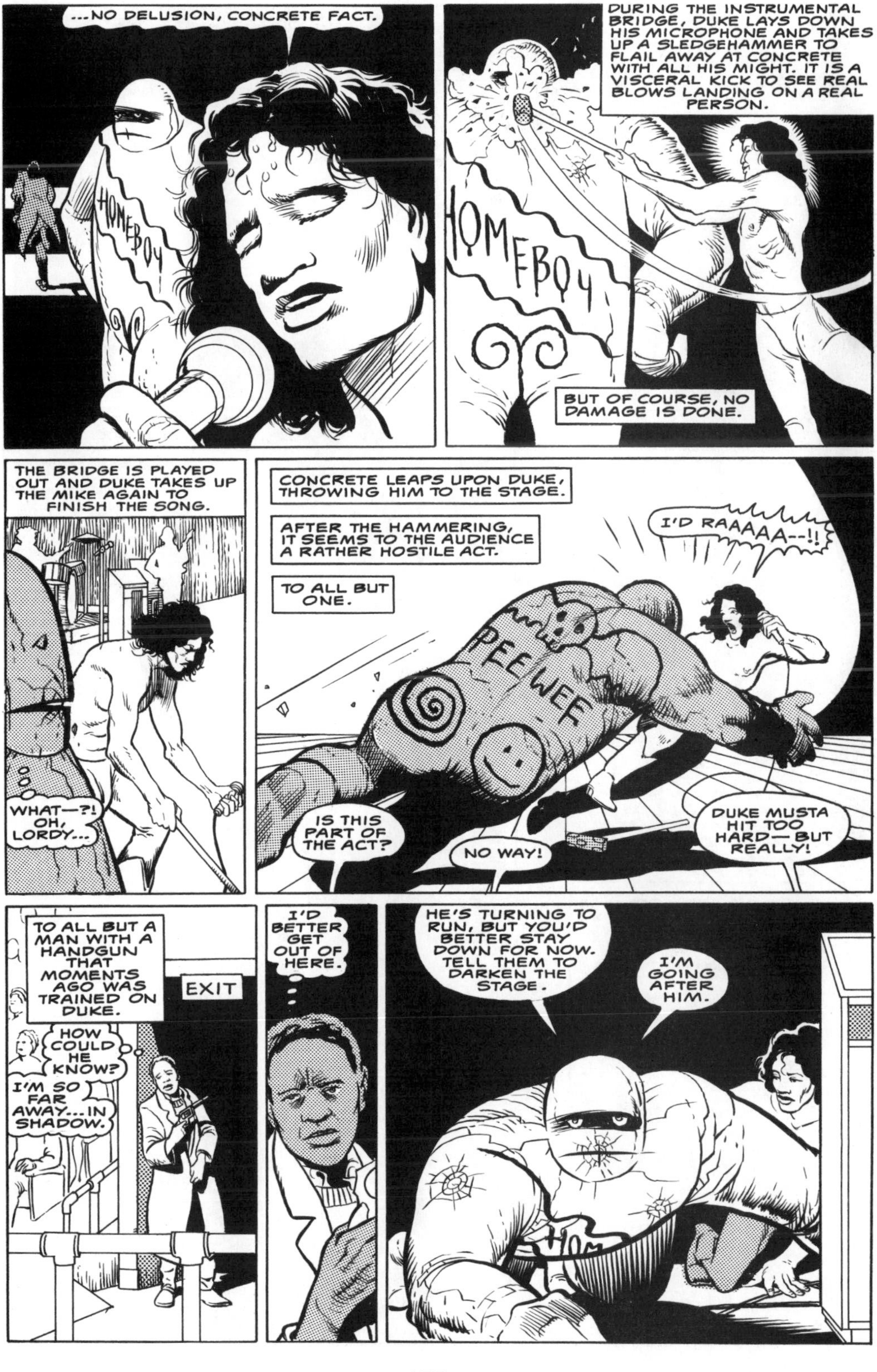
...NO DELUSION, CONCRETE FACT.
HOMEBOY
DURING THE INSTRUMENTAL BRIDGE, DUKE LAYS DOWN HIS MICROPHONE AND TAKES UP A SLEDGEHAMMER TO FLAIL AWAY AT CONCRETE WITH ALL HIS MIGHT. IT IS A VISCERAL KICK TO SEE REAL BLOWS LANDING ON A REAL PERSON.
HOMEBOY
BUT OF COURSE, NO DAMAGE IS DONE.
THE BRIDGE IS PLAYED OUT AND DUKE TAKES UP THE MIKE AGAIN TO FINISH THE SONG.
WHAT—?! OH, LORDY...
CONCRETE LEAPS UPON DUKE, THROWING HIM TO THE STAGE.
AFTER THE HAMMERING, IT SEEMS TO THE AUDIENCE A RATHER HOSTILE ACT.
TO ALL BUT ONE.
I'D RAAAAAA--!!
PEEWEE
IS THIS PART OF THE ACT?
NO WAY!
DUKE MUSTA HIT TOO HARD— BUT REALLY!
TO ALL BUT A MAN WITH A HANDGUN THAT MOMENTS AGO WAS TRAINED ON DUKE.
EXIT
HOW COULD HE KNOW?
I'M SO FAR AWAY...IN SHADOW.
I'D BETTER GET OUT OF HERE.
HE'S TURNING TO RUN, BUT YOU'D BETTER STAY DOWN FOR NOW. TELL THEM TO DARKEN THE STAGE.
I'M GOING AFTER HIM.
HOM

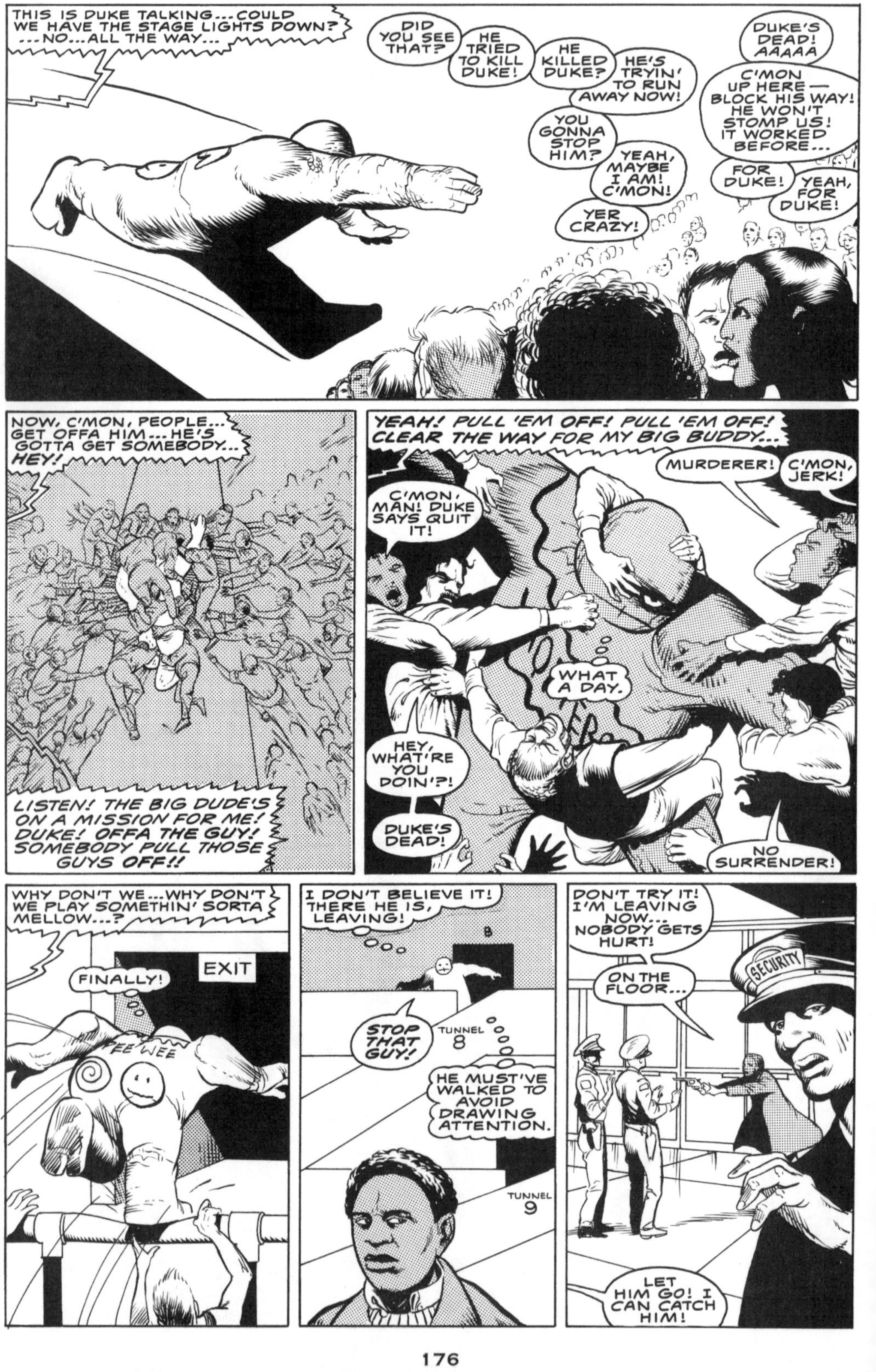

THIS IS DUKE TALKING... COULD WE HAVE THE STAGE LIGHTS DOWN? ...NO... ALL THE WAY...
DID YOU SEE THAT?
HE TRIED TO KILL DUKE!
HE KILLED DUKE?
HE'S TRYIN' TO RUN AWAY NOW!
YOU GONNA STOP HIM?
YEAH, MAYBE I AM! C'MON!
YER CRAZY!
DUKE'S DEAD! AAAAA
C'MON UP HERE— BLOCK HIS WAY! HE WON'T STOMP US! IT WORKED BEFORE...
FOR DUKE!
YEAH, FOR DUKE!
NOW, C'MON, PEOPLE... GET OFFA HIM... HE'S GOTTA GET SOMEBODY... HEY!
LISTEN! THE BIG DUDE'S ON A MISSION FOR ME! DUKE! OFFA THE GUY! SOMEBODY PULL THOSE GUYS OFF!!
YEAH! PULL 'EM OFF! PULL 'EM OFF! CLEAR THE WAY FOR MY BIG BUDDY...
MURDERER!
C'MON, JERK!
C'MON, MAN! DUKE SAYS QUIT IT!
WHAT A DAY.
HEY, WHAT'RE YOU DOIN'?!
DUKE'S DEAD!
NO SURRENDER!
WHY DON'T WE... WHY DON'T WE PLAY SOMETHIN' SORTA MELLOW...?
EXIT
FINALLY!
PEE WEE
I DON'T BELIEVE IT! THERE HE IS, LEAVING!
STOP THAT GUY!
TUNNEL 8
HE MUST'VE WALKED TO AVOID DRAWING ATTENTION.
TUNNEL 9
DON'T TRY IT! I'M LEAVING NOW... NOBODY GETS HURT!
ON THE FLOOR...
SECURITY
LET HIM GO! I CAN CATCH HIM!

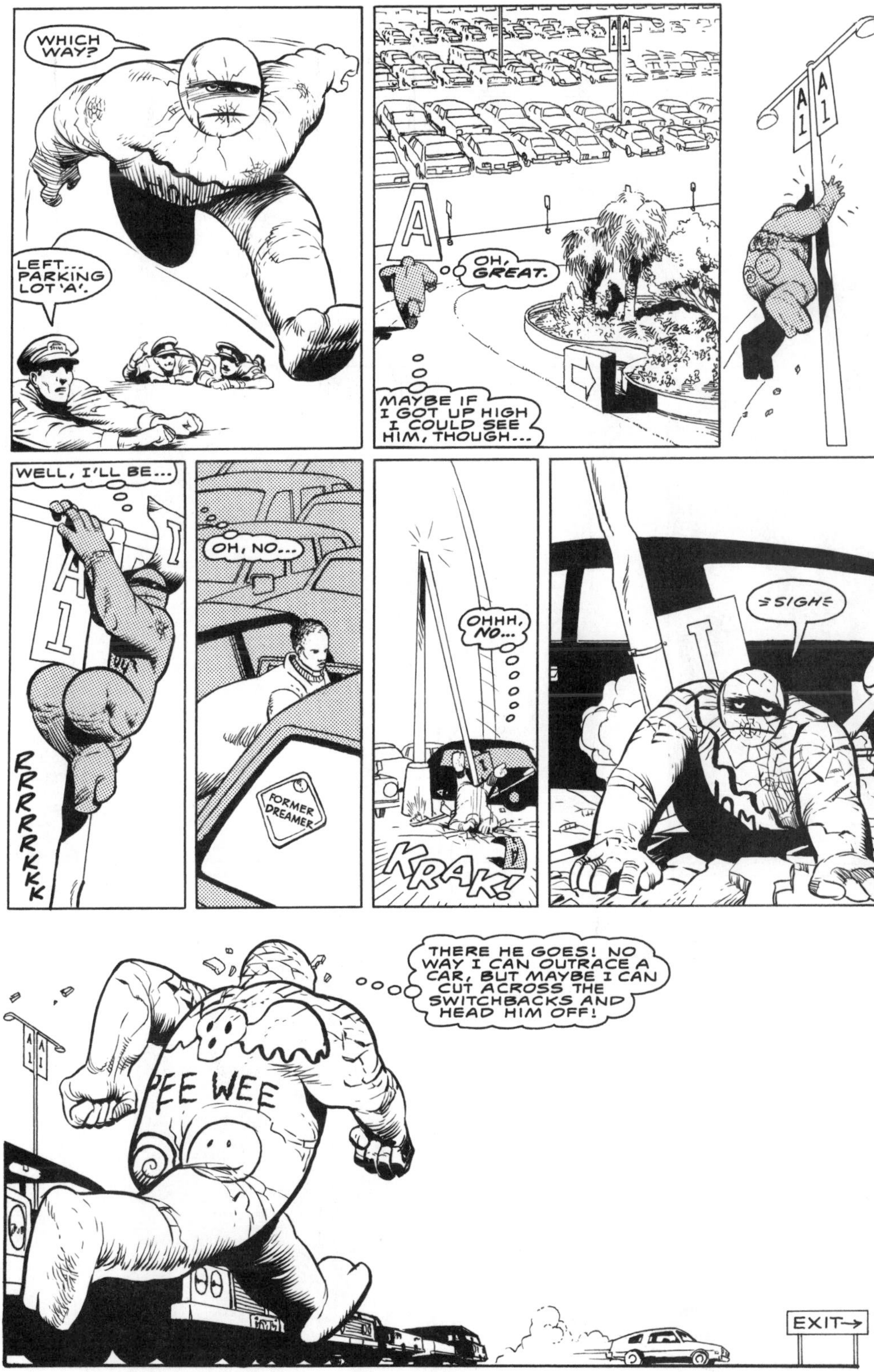
WHICH WAY?
LEFT... PARKING LOT 'A'.
A1
OH, GREAT.
MAYBE IF I GOT UP HIGH I COULD SEE HIM, THOUGH...
WELL, I'LL BE...
RRRRRKKK
OH, NO...
FORMER DREAMER
OHHH, NO...
KRAK!
SIGH
THERE HE GOES! NO WAY I CAN OUTRACE A CAR, BUT MAYBE I CAN CUT ACROSS THE SWITCHBACKS AND HEAD HIM OFF!
PEE WEE
EXIT→

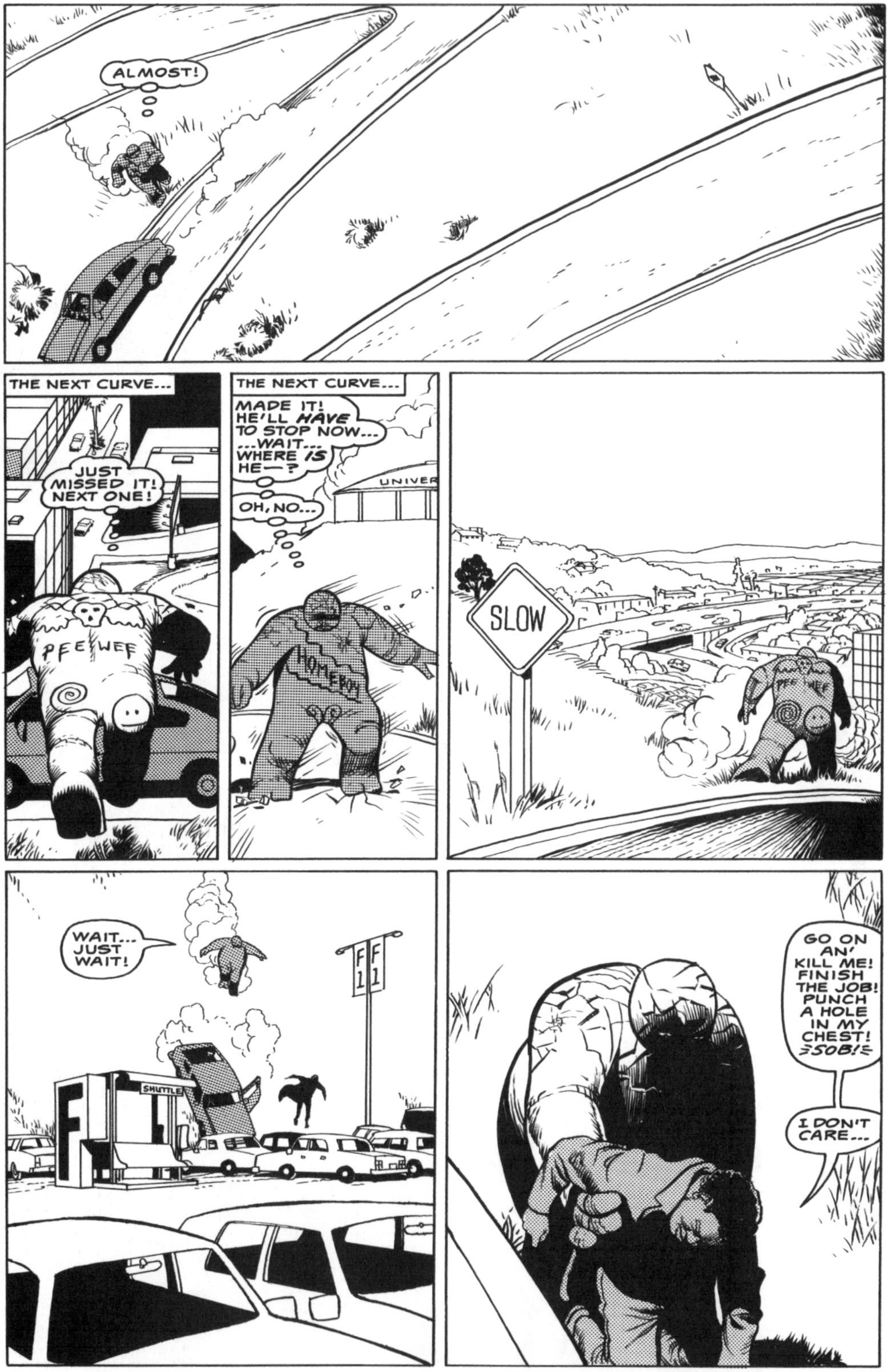
ALMOST!
THE NEXT CURVE...
JUST MISSED IT! NEXT ONE!
PEE WEE
THE NEXT CURVE...
MADE IT! HE'LL HAVE TO STOP NOW... ...WAIT... WHERE IS HE—?
OH, NO...
UNIVER
HOMEROY
SLOW
PEE WEE
WAIT... JUST WAIT!
F 1
F 1
F
SHUTTLE
GO ON AN' KILL ME! FINISH THE JOB! PUNCH A HOLE IN MY CHEST! SOB!
I DON'T CARE...

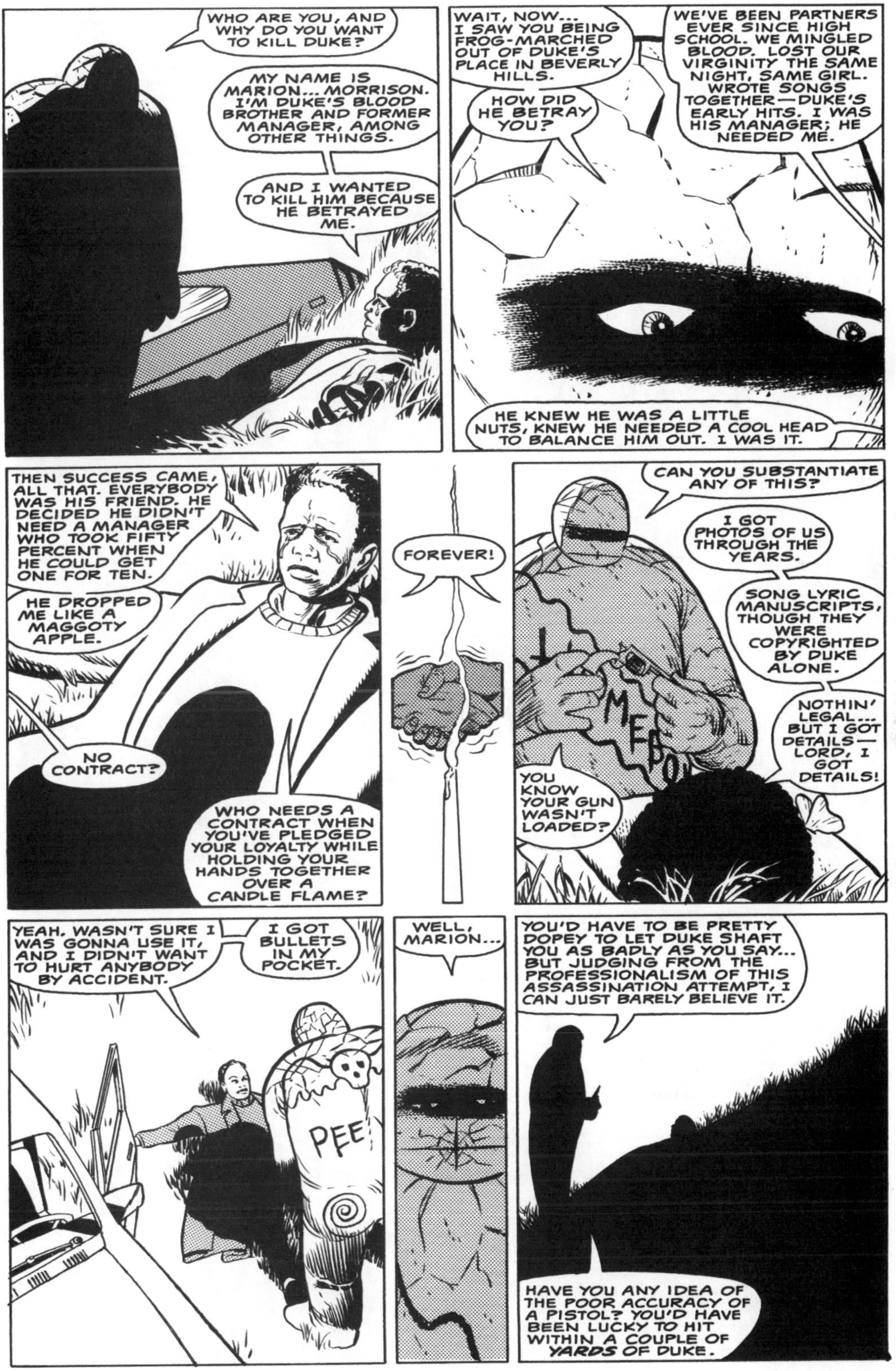
WHO ARE YOU, AND WHY DO YOU WANT TO KILL DUKE?
MY NAME IS MARION... MORRISON. I'M DUKE'S BLOOD BROTHER AND FORMER MANAGER, AMONG OTHER THINGS.
AND I WANTED TO KILL HIM BECAUSE HE BETRAYED ME.
WAIT, NOW... I SAW YOU BEING FROG-MARCHED OUT OF DUKE'S PLACE IN BEVERLY HILLS.
HOW DID HE BETRAY YOU?
WE'VE BEEN PARTNERS EVER SINCE HIGH SCHOOL. WE MINGLED BLOOD. LOST OUR VIRGINITY THE SAME NIGHT, SAME GIRL. WROTE SONGS TOGETHER—DUKE'S EARLY HITS. I WAS HIS MANAGER; HE NEEDED ME.
HE KNEW HE WAS A LITTLE NUTS, KNEW HE NEEDED A COOL HEAD TO BALANCE HIM OUT. I WAS IT.
THEN SUCCESS CAME, ALL THAT. EVERYBODY WAS HIS FRIEND. HE DECIDED HE DIDN'T NEED A MANAGER WHO TOOK FIFTY PERCENT WHEN HE COULD GET ONE FOR TEN.
HE DROPPED ME LIKE A MAGGOTY APPLE.
NO CONTRACT?
WHO NEEDS A CONTRACT WHEN YOU'VE PLEDGED YOUR LOYALTY WHILE HOLDING YOUR HANDS TOGETHER OVER A CANDLE FLAME?
FOREVER!
CAN YOU SUBSTANTIATE ANY OF THIS?
I GOT PHOTOS OF US THROUGH THE YEARS.
SONG LYRIC MANUSCRIPTS, THOUGH THEY WERE COPYRIGHTED BY DUKE ALONE.
NOTHIN' LEGAL... BUT I GOT DETAILS—LORD, I GOT DETAILS!
YOU KNOW YOUR GUN WASN'T LOADED?
YEAH. WASN'T SURE I WAS GONNA USE IT, AND I DIDN'T WANT TO HURT ANYBODY BY ACCIDENT.
I GOT BULLETS IN MY POCKET.
PEE
WELL, MARION...
YOU'D HAVE TO BE PRETTY DOPEY TO LET DUKE SHAFT YOU AS BADLY AS YOU SAY... BUT JUDGING FROM THE PROFESSIONALISM OF THIS ASSASSINATION ATTEMPT, I CAN JUST BARELY BELIEVE IT.
HAVE YOU ANY IDEA OF THE POOR ACCURACY OF A PISTOL? YOU'D HAVE BEEN LUCKY TO HIT WITHIN A COUPLE OF *YARDS* OF DUKE.

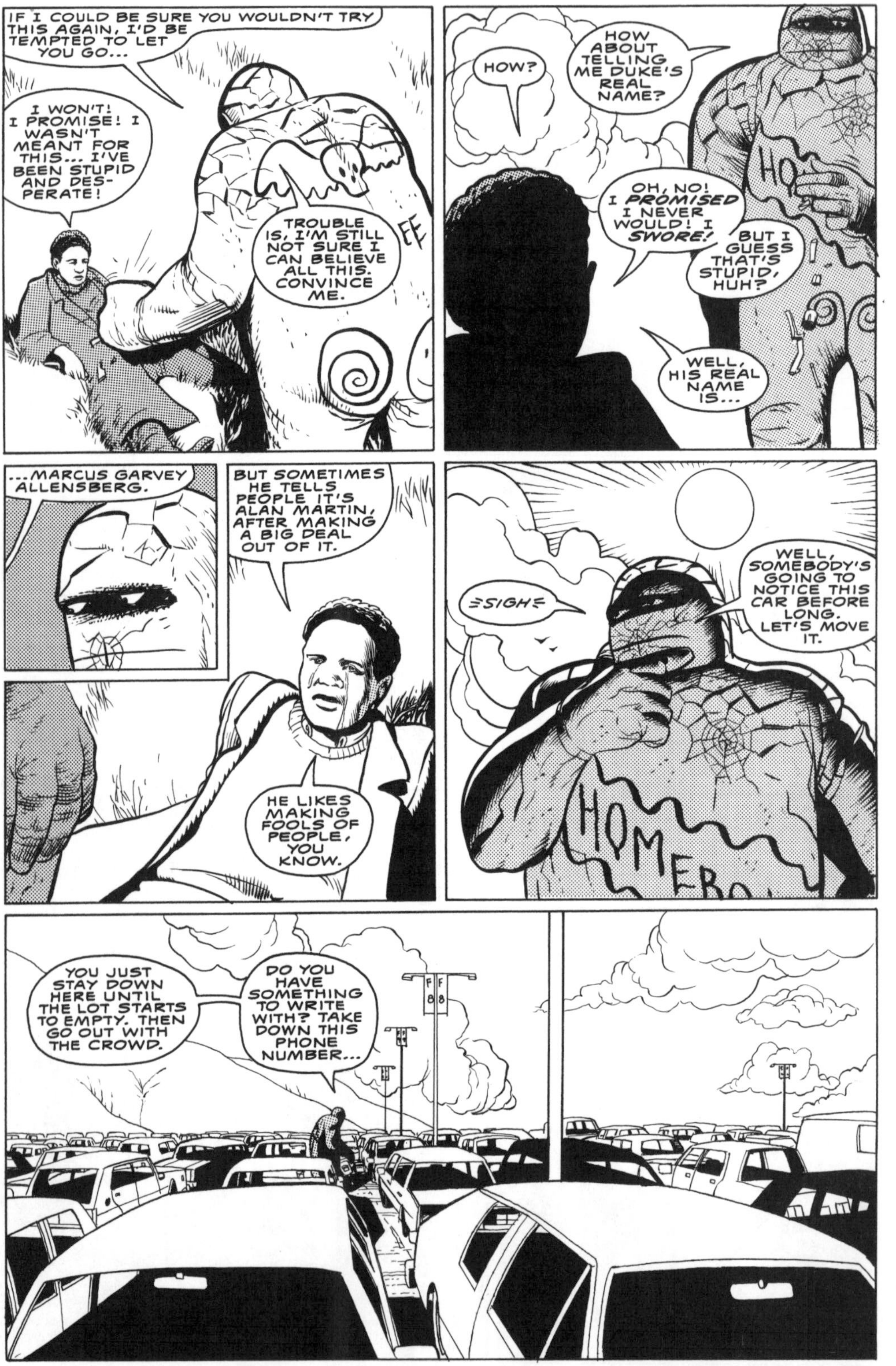
IF I COULD BE SURE YOU WOULDN'T TRY THIS AGAIN, I'D BE TEMPTED TO LET YOU GO...
I WON'T! I PROMISE! I WASN'T MEANT FOR THIS... I'VE BEEN STUPID AND DES-PERATE!
TROUBLE IS, I'M STILL NOT SURE I CAN BELIEVE ALL THIS. CONVINCE ME.
HOW?
HOW ABOUT TELLING ME DUKE'S REAL NAME?
OH, NO! I PROMISED I NEVER WOULD! I SWORE!
BUT I GUESS THAT'S STUPID, HUH?
WELL, HIS REAL NAME IS...
...MARCUS GARVEY ALLENSBERG.
BUT SOMETIMES HE TELLS PEOPLE IT'S ALAN MARTIN, AFTER MAKING A BIG DEAL OUT OF IT.
HE LIKES MAKING FOOLS OF PEOPLE, YOU KNOW.
=SIGH=
WELL, SOMEBODY'S GOING TO NOTICE THIS CAR BEFORE LONG. LET'S MOVE IT.
YOU JUST STAY DOWN HERE UNTIL THE LOT STARTS TO EMPTY. THEN GO OUT WITH THE CROWD.
DO YOU HAVE SOMETHING TO WRITE WITH? TAKE DOWN THIS PHONE NUMBER...

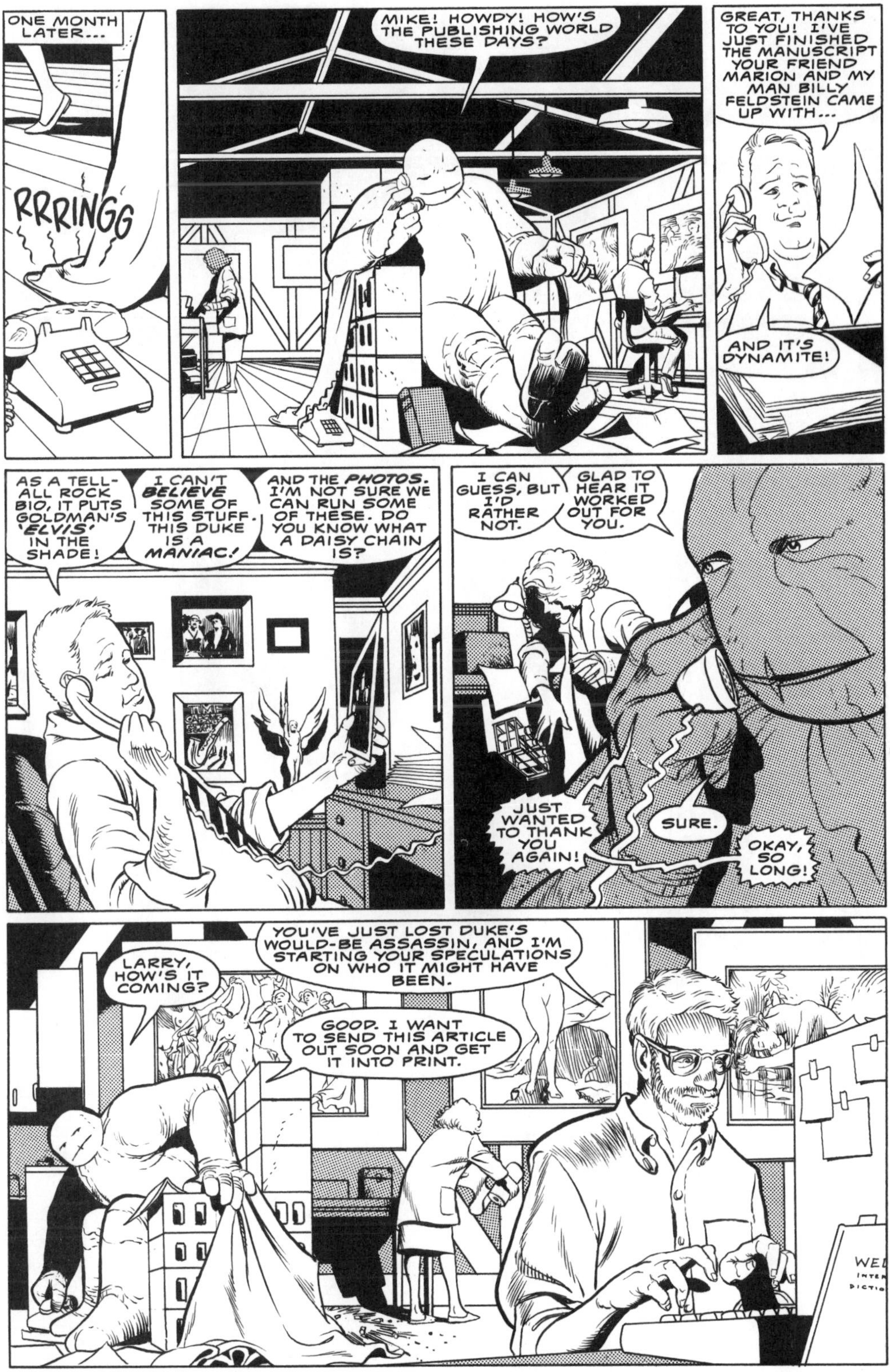
ONE MONTH LATER...
RRRINGG
MIKE! HOWDY! HOW'S THE PUBLISHING WORLD THESE DAYS?
GREAT, THANKS TO YOU! I'VE JUST FINISHED THE MANUSCRIPT YOUR FRIEND MARION AND MY MAN BILLY FELDSTEIN CAME UP WITH...
AND IT'S DYNAMITE!
AS A TELL-ALL ROCK BIO, IT PUTS GOLDMAN'S 'ELVIS' IN THE SHADE!
I CAN'T BELIEVE SOME OF THIS STUFF. THIS DUKE IS A MANIAC!
AND THE PHOTOS. I'M NOT SURE WE CAN RUN SOME OF THESE. DO YOU KNOW WHAT A DAISY CHAIN IS?
I CAN GUESS, BUT I'D RATHER NOT.
GLAD TO HEAR IT WORKED OUT FOR YOU.
JUST WANTED TO THANK YOU AGAIN!
SURE.
OKAY, SO LONG!
LARRY, HOW'S IT COMING?
YOU'VE JUST LOST DUKE'S WOULD-BE ASSASSIN, AND I'M STARTING YOUR SPECULATIONS ON WHO IT MIGHT HAVE BEEN.
GOOD. I WANT TO SEND THIS ARTICLE OUT SOON AND GET IT INTO PRINT.

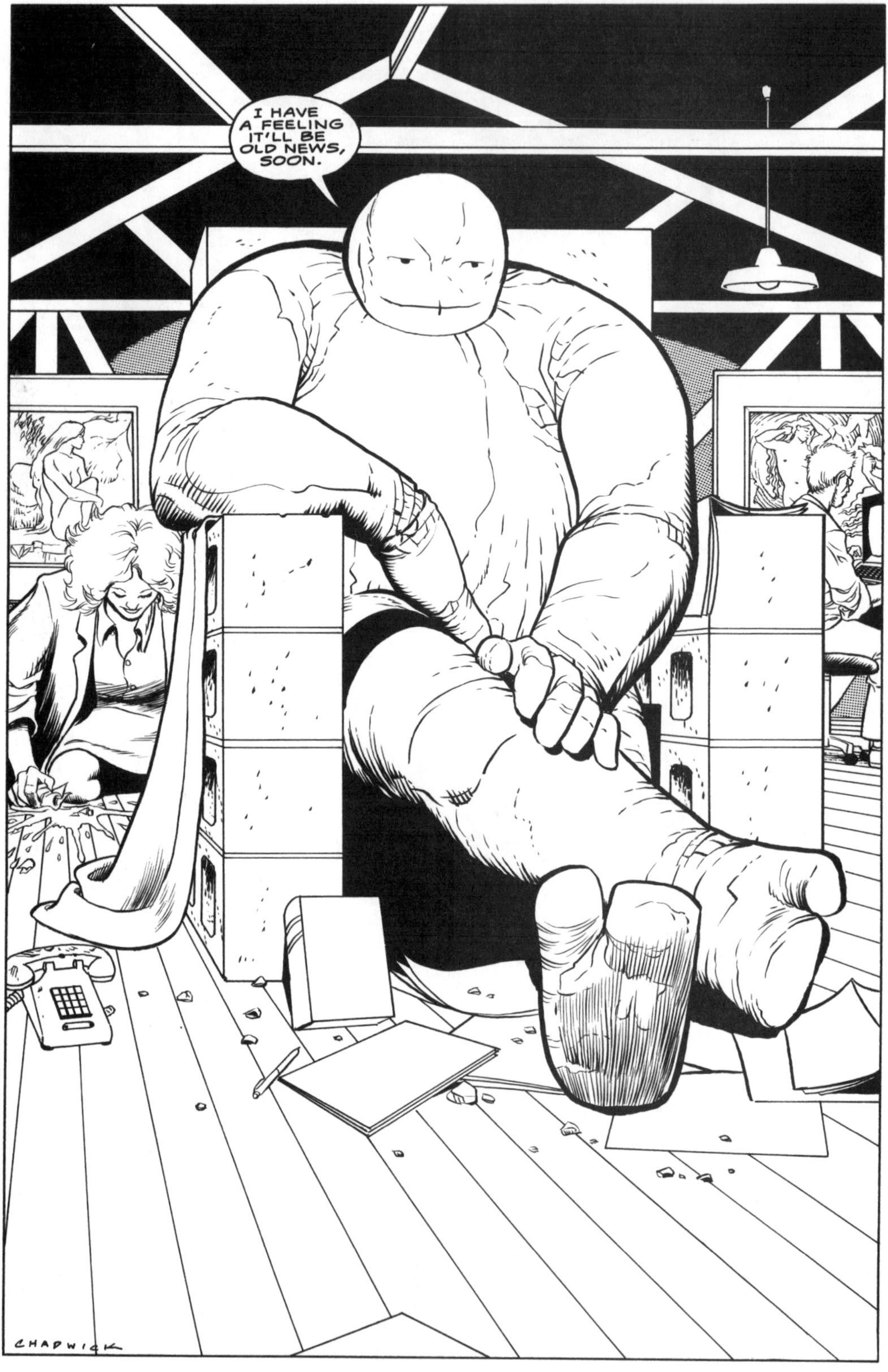
I HAVE A FEELING IT'LL BE OLD NEWS, SOON.
CHADWICK

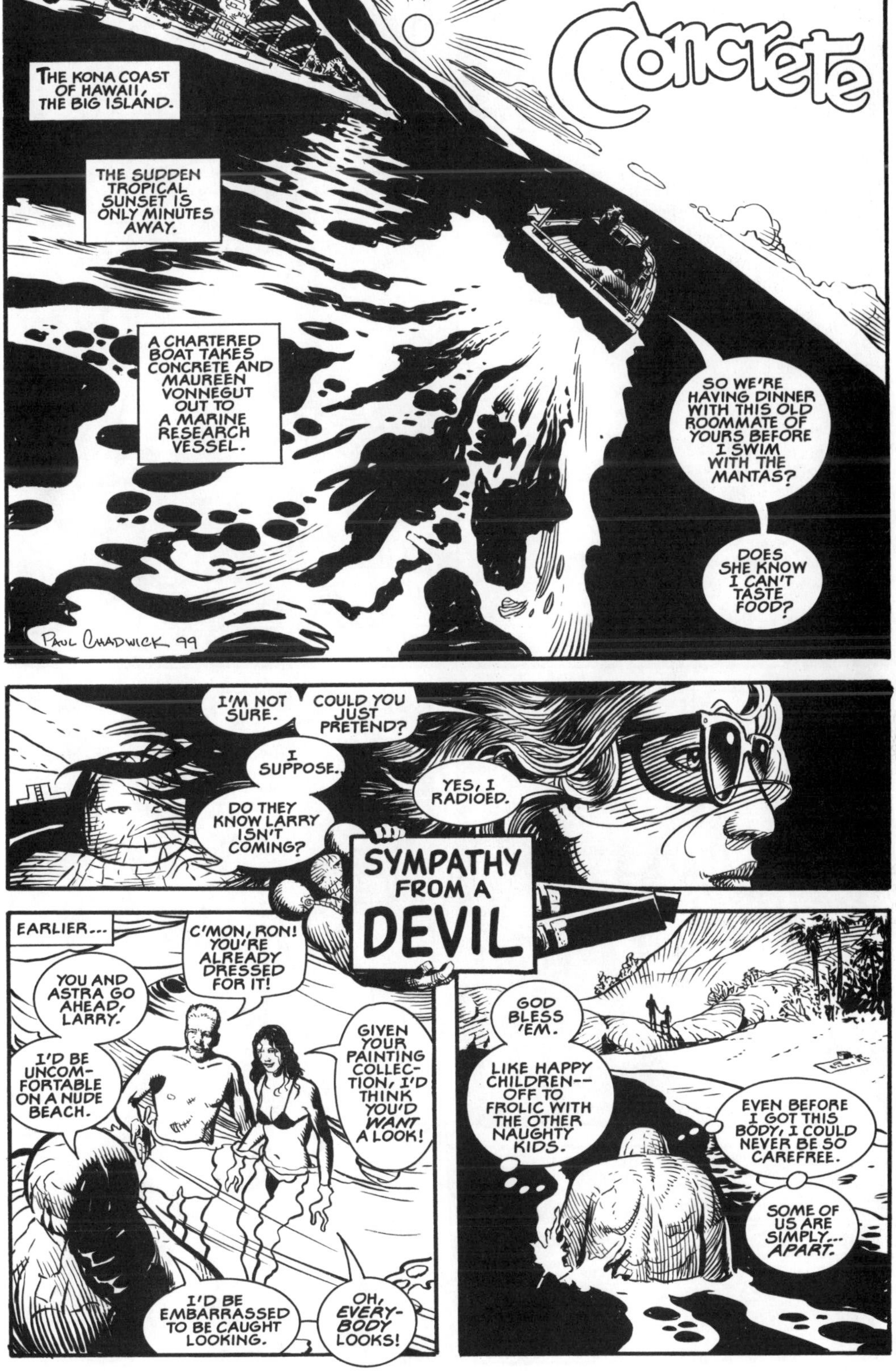
Concrete
THE KONA COAST OF HAWAII, THE BIG ISLAND.
THE SUDDEN TROPICAL SUNSET IS ONLY MINUTES AWAY.
A CHARTERED BOAT TAKES CONCRETE AND MAUREEN VONNEGUT OUT TO A MARINE RESEARCH VESSEL.
SO WE'RE HAVING DINNER WITH THIS OLD ROOMMATE OF YOURS BEFORE I SWIM WITH THE MANTAS?
DOES SHE KNOW I CAN'T TASTE FOOD?
PAUL CHADWICK 99
I'M NOT SURE.
COULD YOU JUST PRETEND?
I SUPPOSE..
DO THEY KNOW LARRY ISN'T COMING?
YES, I RADIOED.
SYMPATHY FROM A DEVIL
EARLIER...
YOU AND ASTRA GO AHEAD, LARRY.
C'MON, RON! YOU'RE ALREADY DRESSED FOR IT!
I'D BE UNCOMFORTABLE ON A NUDE BEACH.
GIVEN YOUR PAINTING COLLECTION, I'D THINK YOU'D WANT A LOOK!
I'D BE EMBARRASSED TO BE CAUGHT LOOKING.
OH, EVERYBODY LOOKS!
GOD BLESS 'EM.
LIKE HAPPY CHILDREN-- OFF TO FROLIC WITH THE OTHER NAUGHTY KIDS.
EVEN BEFORE I GOT THIS BODY, I COULD NEVER BE SO CAREFREE.
SOME OF US ARE SIMPLY... APART.

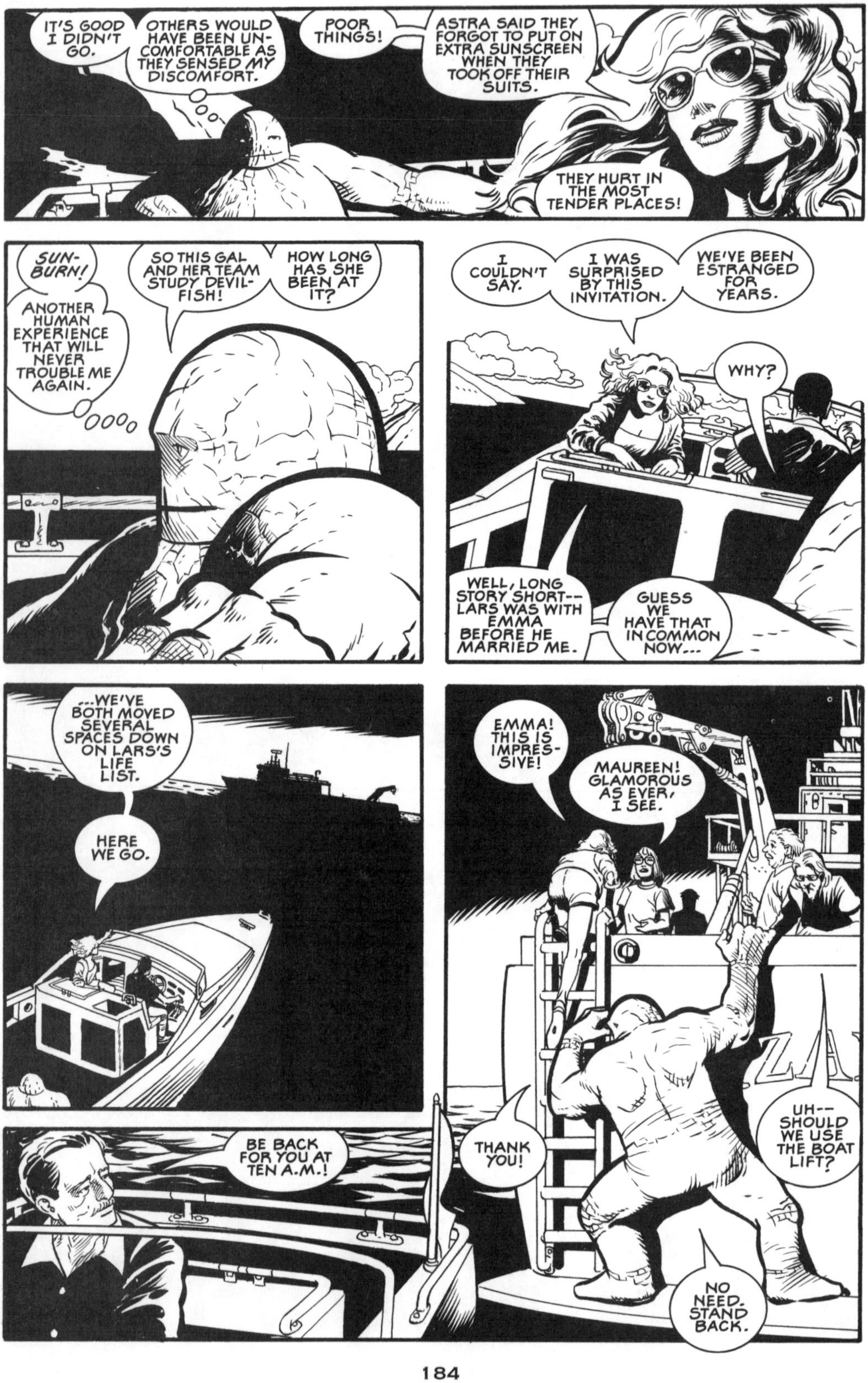
IT'S GOOD I DIDN'T GO.
OTHERS WOULD HAVE BEEN UN-COMFORTABLE AS THEY SENSED MY DISCOMFORT.
POOR THINGS!
ASTRA SAID THEY FORGOT TO PUT ON EXTRA SUNSCREEN WHEN THEY TOOK OFF THEIR SUITS.
THEY HURT IN THE MOST TENDER PLACES!
SUN-BURN!
ANOTHER HUMAN EXPERIENCE THAT WILL NEVER TROUBLE ME AGAIN.
SO THIS GAL AND HER TEAM STUDY DEVIL-FISH!
HOW LONG HAS SHE BEEN AT IT?
I COULDN'T SAY.
I WAS SURPRISED BY THIS INVITATION.
WE'VE BEEN ESTRANGED FOR YEARS.
WHY?
WELL, LONG STORY SHORT-- LARS WAS WITH EMMA BEFORE HE MARRIED ME.
GUESS WE HAVE THAT IN COMMON NOW...
...WE'VE BOTH MOVED SEVERAL SPACES DOWN ON LARS'S LIFE LIST.
HERE WE GO.
EMMA! THIS IS IMPRES-SIVE!
MAUREEN! GLAMOROUS AS EVER, I SEE.
BE BACK FOR YOU AT TEN A.M.!
THANK YOU!
UH-- SHOULD WE USE THE BOAT LIFT?
NO NEED. STAND BACK.

REALLY--GET *WAY* BACK.

ONE...

TWO...

ELIZ

SEAT

KTOOM!

ELIZ

THE DENTS IN THE DECK ARE HARDLY VISIBLE.

SEAT

...SO I GOT INVOLVED WITH THE PROJECT RESPONSIBLE FOR CONCRETE HERE.

A SEMI-LIE.

WHAT DID LARS THINK OF HIS WIFE DOING THIS HUSH-HUSH WORK?

WE'D DIVORCED BY THEN, EMMA.

AHH.

CONCRETE, I'M SO PLEASED YOU AGREED TO THIS.

I REALIZE PHOTOGRAPHING MANTA RAYS HARDLY COMPARES TO YOUR FAMOUS ADVENTURES.

BUT IT'S QUITE A BIG DEAL TO US SMALL-TIMERS.

IS YOUR FOOD ALL RIGHT?

OH, YES. SPLENDID.

I NOTICE YOU'VE EATEN THE SALT SHAKER.

DO YOU NEED MORE?

OH! NO!

I--AH-- THOUGHT I WAS REACH- ING FOR A ROLL.

UM--YOU KNOW I CAN ALMOST EAT ANY- THING.

IN FACT, I NEED ROCKS FOR MY COAT- ING.

YOU'RE COMPLAINING WE DIDN'T SERVE *ROCKS!?*

NO, NO! FOOD'S GREAT!

PRICKLY!

I'M SURE SOMEONE AS *WEALTHY* AS YOU IS USED TO FANCIER FOOD.

MIKE, GET MORE SALT, WILL YOU?

REALLY, IT'S FINE.

I'M NOT WEALTHY!

I WANT SOME SALT!

ROCKS! JESUS!

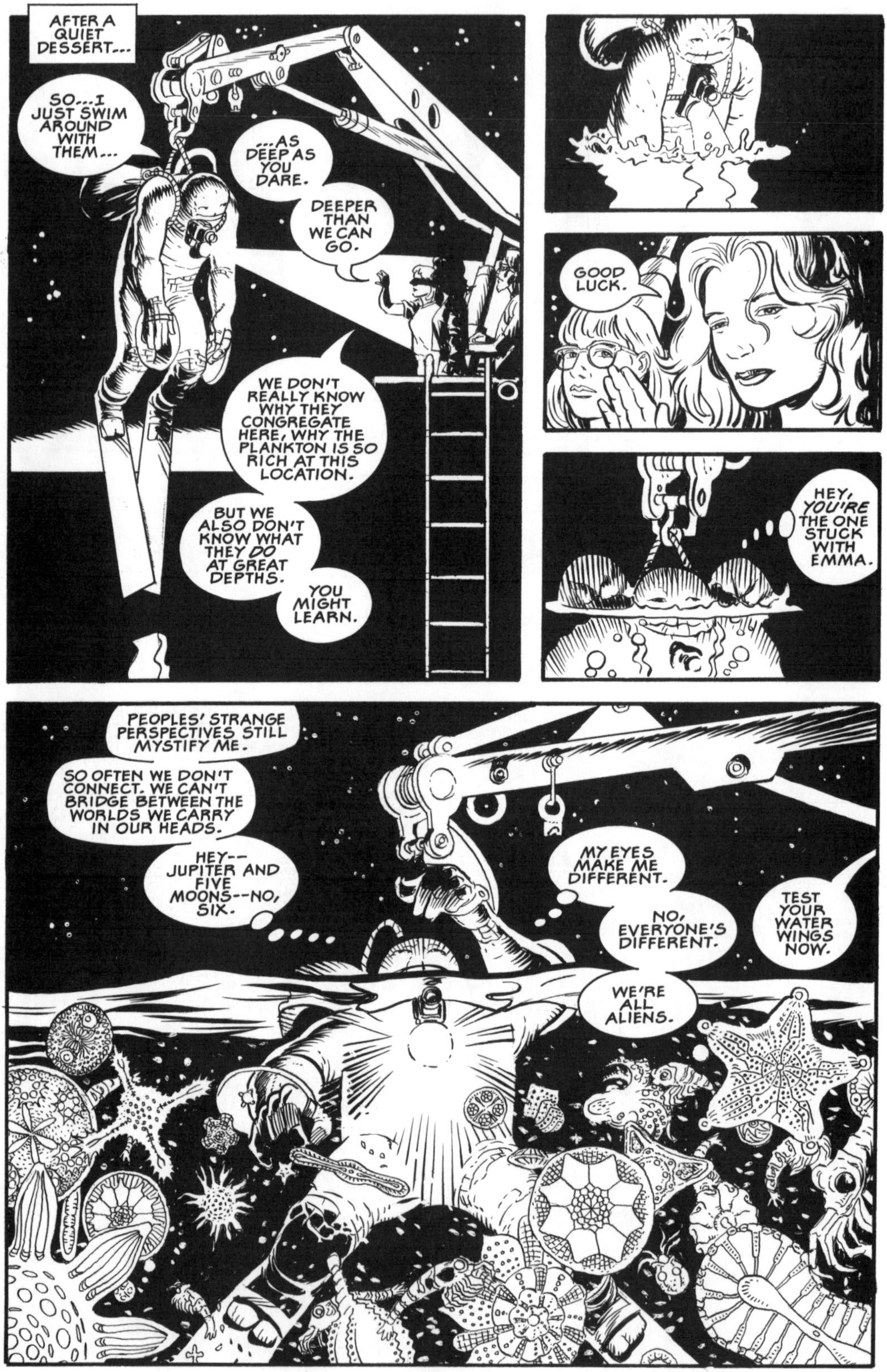
AFTER A QUIET DESSERT...
SO...I JUST SWIM AROUND WITH THEM...
...AS DEEP AS YOU DARE.
DEEPER THAN WE CAN GO.
WE DON'T REALLY KNOW WHY THEY CONGREGATE HERE, WHY THE PLANKTON IS SO RICH AT THIS LOCATION.
BUT WE ALSO DON'T KNOW WHAT THEY *DO* AT GREAT DEPTHS.
YOU MIGHT LEARN.
GOOD LUCK.
HEY, *YOU'RE* THE ONE STUCK WITH EMMA.
PEOPLES' STRANGE PERSPECTIVES STILL MYSTIFY ME.
SO OFTEN WE DON'T CONNECT. WE CAN'T BRIDGE BETWEEN THE WORLDS WE CARRY IN OUR HEADS.
HEY-- JUPITER AND FIVE MOONS--NO, SIX.
MY EYES MAKE ME DIFFERENT.
NO, EVERYONE'S DIFFERENT.
WE'RE ALL ALIENS.
TEST YOUR WATER WINGS NOW.

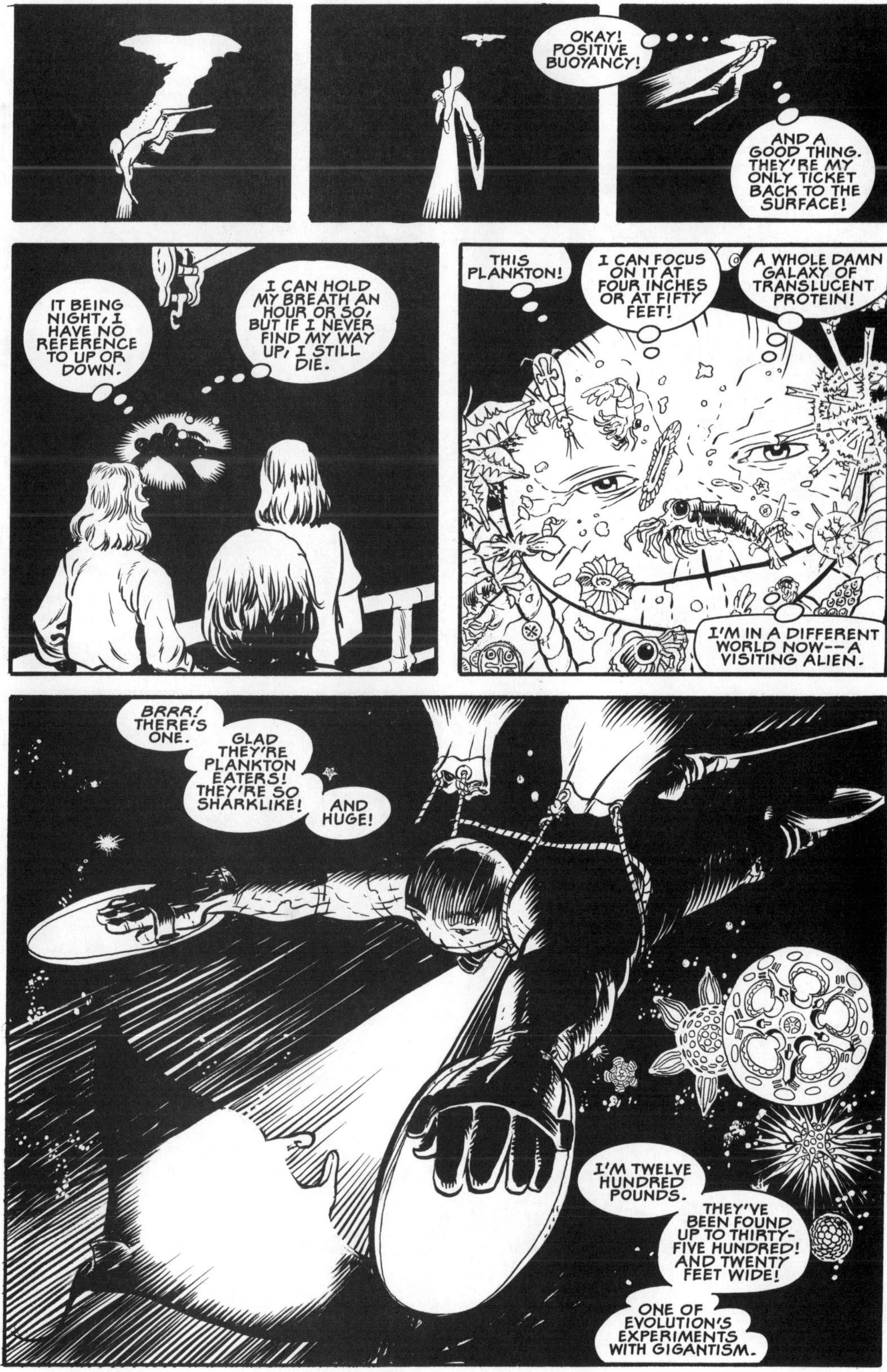
OKAY! POSITIVE BUOYANCY!
AND A GOOD THING. THEY'RE MY ONLY TICKET BACK TO THE SURFACE!
IT BEING NIGHT, I HAVE NO REFERENCE TO UP OR DOWN.
I CAN HOLD MY BREATH AN HOUR OR SO, BUT IF I NEVER FIND MY WAY UP, I STILL DIE.
THIS PLANKTON!
I CAN FOCUS ON IT AT FOUR INCHES OR AT FIFTY FEET!
A WHOLE DAMN GALAXY OF TRANSLUCENT PROTEIN!
I'M IN A DIFFERENT WORLD NOW-- A VISITING ALIEN.
BRRR! THERE'S ONE.
GLAD THEY'RE PLANKTON EATERS! THEY'RE SO SHARKLIKE!
AND HUGE!
I'M TWELVE HUNDRED POUNDS.
THEY'VE BEEN FOUND UP TO THIRTY-FIVE HUNDRED! AND TWENTY FEET WIDE!
ONE OF EVOLUTION'S EXPERIMENTS WITH GIGANTISM.

EMMA CHIDED ME FOR CALLING THEM DEVILFISH.

BUT THOSE-- "CEPHALIC FINS" SURE LOOK LIKE HORNS.

WHAT GRACE! THE OPPOSITE OF ME!

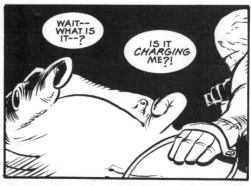

WAIT-- WHAT IS IT--?

IS IT CHARGING ME?!

NO.

CURIOUS, I GUESS.

I'VE NEVER BEEN SO DEEP, EXCEPT WHEN I GOT MUD DURING THE TRANS- ATLANTIC SWIM.

BUT THAT WAS MIDDAY, WITH A TROPICAL SUN.

BLUE WAS UP.

I'M GETTING NERVOUS. WHAT-- WHAT'S THAT EMERGING?!

SHARK!!

IT'S HUGE!!

GET AWAY!!

CONCRETE FLAILS WILDLY.

HIS ROCKY SKIN ABRADES HIS ROPE.

A WATER WING BREAKS FREE....

188

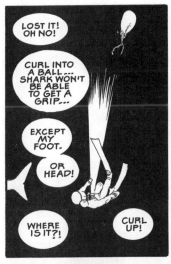

LOST IT! OH NO!

CURL INTO A BALL... SHARK WON'T BE ABLE TO GET A GRIP...

EXCEPT MY FOOT.

OR HEAD!

WHERE IS IT?!

CURL UP!

ONLY ONE FLOAT LEFT.

THAT MEANS I'M SINKING, SLOWLY.

SHARK GONE?

SINKING. I WILL DROWN.

NO.

I CAN SWIM UP.

IF I HOLD IT OUT, I CAN SEE WHICH WAY IT'S PULLING.

THEN I CAN SWIM UP THAT WAY.

SHARK GONE?

EXCEPT WHILE I'M SWIMMING, IT'S PULLED BACK.

OKAY, I'LL SWIM AND STOP, OVER AND OVER.

NO--- TELL ME I DIDN'T!

IDIOT!

I OPENED MY HAND!

THAT'S IT.

I HAVE NO MORE ORIENTATION THAN THESE DIATOMS AND SHRIMP.

LIKE THEM, I DRIFT, THEN I DIE.

FIFTY MINUTES AFTER DESCENT...

THAT'S IT!

EVERYBODY SUIT UP! ALL LIGHTS ON!

BUT I DON'T SEE WHAT WE COULD DO...

HE'S SO HEAVY...

WE'RE NOT LETTING YOUR PIECES-OF-SHIT EQUIPMENT KILL HIM WITHOUT A FIGHT!

GET LINE! ALL YOU HAVE!

LIGHTS ON!

HEY-- ATTACH A LIGHT TO YOUR ANCHOR LINE!

IT'S TOO DEEP TO ANCHOR HERE!

THAT'S NOT THE POINT. HE MIGHT SEE IT, FOLLOW IT UP.

OR PULL HIMSELF UP.

DOWN THEY COME FROM A BLAZING UPPER REALM OF LIGHT, HALOED WITH BACKLIT HAIR AND AIR BUBBLES...

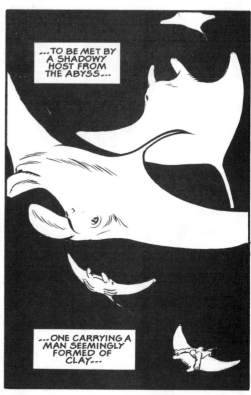

...TO BE MET BY A SHADOWY HOST FROM THE ABYSS...

...ONE CARRYING A MAN SEEMINGLY FORMED OF CLAY...

...JUST IN TIME.

GASSP!

THING IS, I THINK IT WAS TAKING ME UP EVEN BEFORE THE LIGHTS WERE ON.

IN THE DARK, I FELT WEIRDLY CLOSE TO IT, ALIEN AS IT WAS.

THOUGH NOT AS ALIEN AS THAT FREAK SHARK.

IT WAS A MEGAMOUTH, FROM WHAT YOU SAY.

A PLANKTON EATER, NOT DISCOVERED UNTIL THE SEVENTIES.

WELL, FUNNY THAT *I'M* THE GUY TO GET THIS LESSON.

BUT I WON'T BE IN SUCH A RUSH TO ASSUME THAT WHICH IS *STRANGE* IS AN *ENEMY*...

...BECAUSE IT CAN TURN OUT TO BE JUST THE OPPOSITE.

SHALL WE LOOK AT THE VIDEO, EMMA?

THE END

190

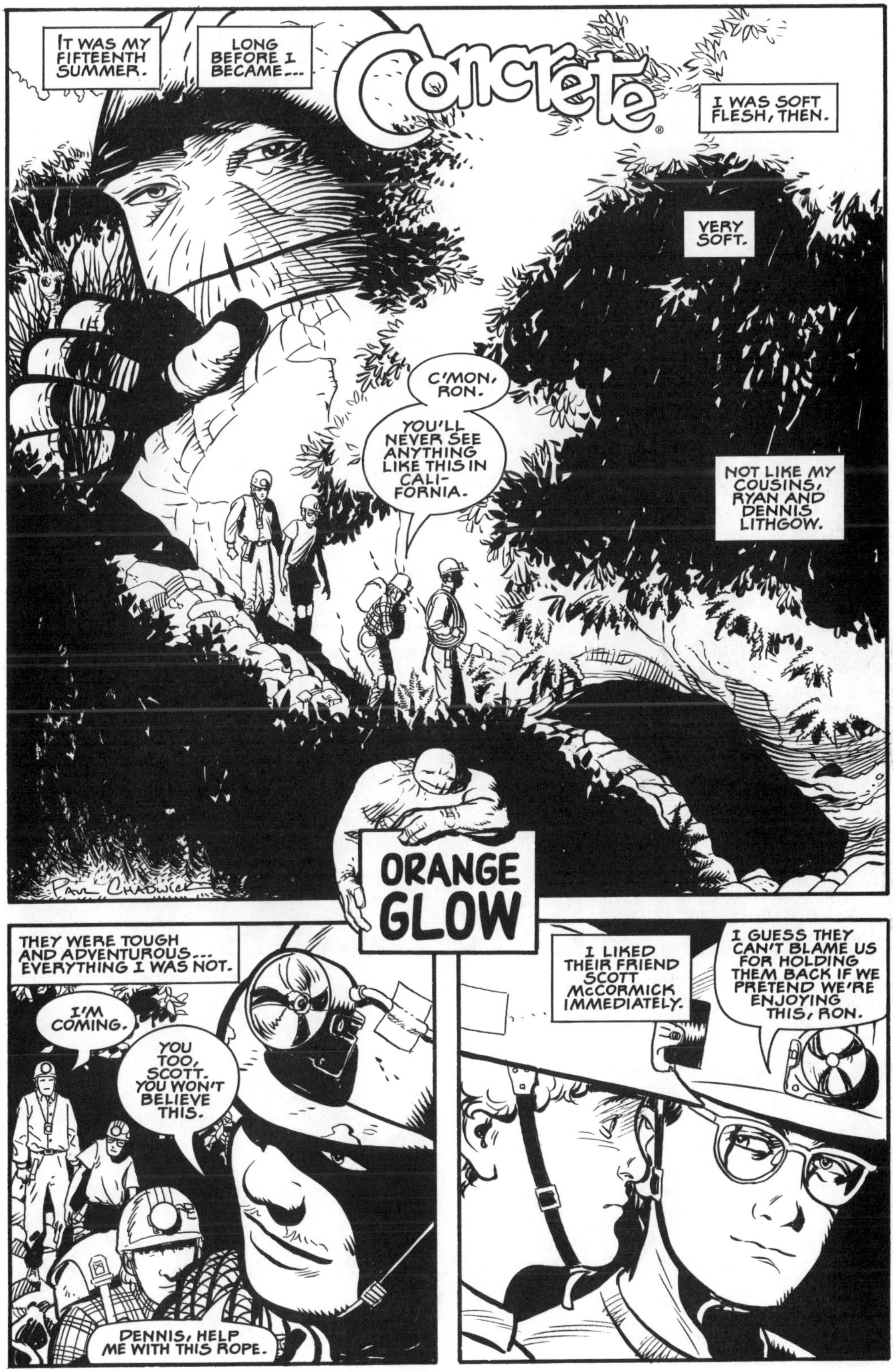
IT WAS MY FIFTEENTH SUMMER.
LONG BEFORE I BECAME...
Concrete®
I WAS SOFT FLESH, THEN.
VERY SOFT.
C'MON, RON.
YOU'LL NEVER SEE ANYTHING LIKE THIS IN CALI-FORNIA.
NOT LIKE MY COUSINS, RYAN AND DENNIS LITHGOW.
PAUL CHADWICK
ORANGE GLOW
THEY WERE TOUGH AND ADVENTUROUS... EVERYTHING I WAS NOT.
I'M COMING.
YOU TOO, SCOTT. YOU WON'T BELIEVE THIS.
DENNIS, HELP ME WITH THIS ROPE.
I LIKED THEIR FRIEND SCOTT McCORMICK IMMEDIATELY.
I GUESS THEY CAN'T BLAME US FOR HOLDING THEM BACK IF WE PRETEND WE'RE ENJOYING THIS, RON.

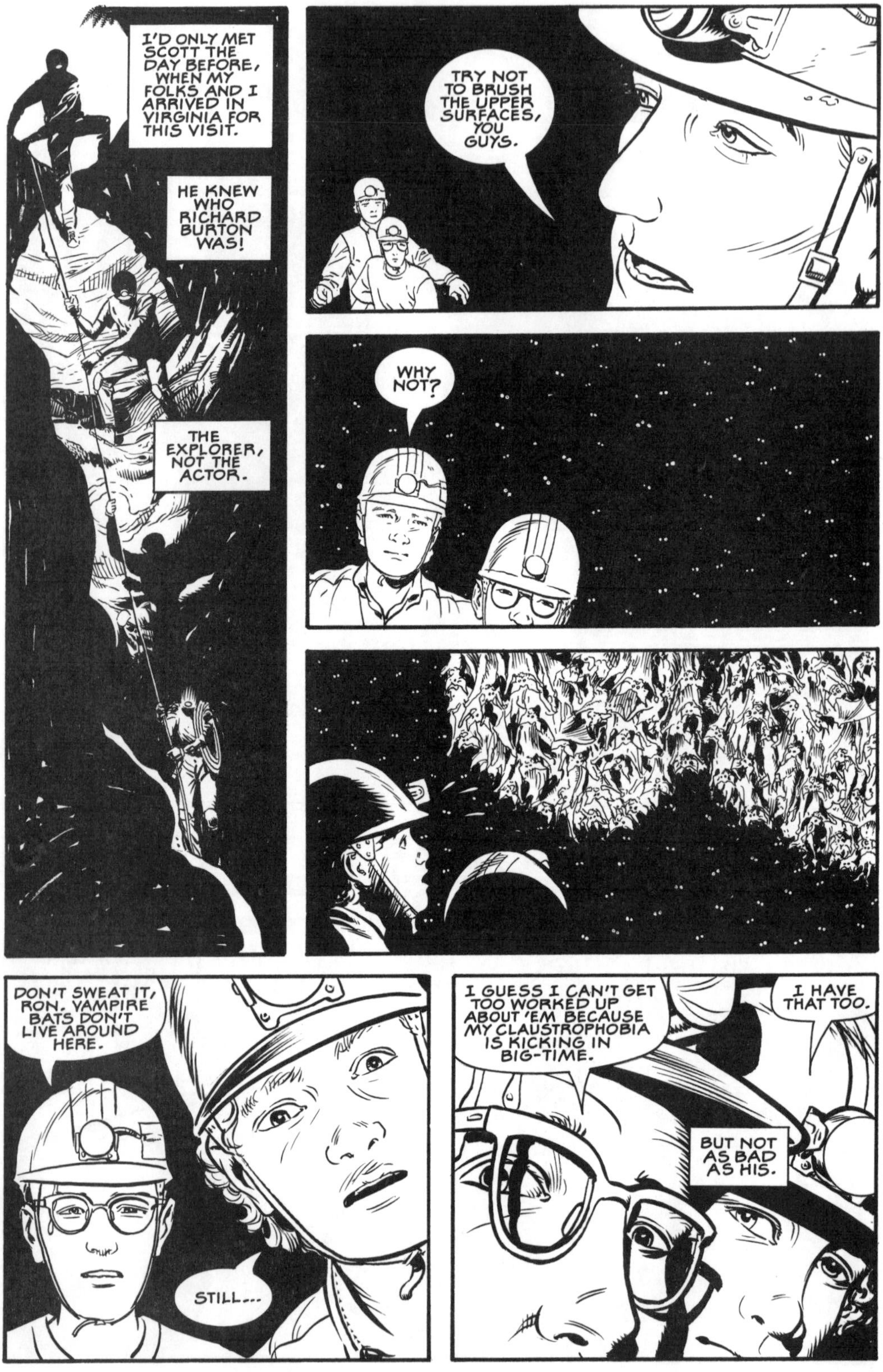
I'D ONLY MET SCOTT THE DAY BEFORE, WHEN MY FOLKS AND I ARRIVED IN VIRGINIA FOR THIS VISIT.
HE KNEW WHO RICHARD BURTON WAS!
THE EXPLORER, NOT THE ACTOR.
TRY NOT TO BRUSH THE UPPER SURFACES, YOU GUYS.
WHY NOT?
DON'T SWEAT IT, RON. VAMPIRE BATS DON'T LIVE AROUND HERE.
STILL...
I GUESS I CAN'T GET TOO WORKED UP ABOUT 'EM BECAUSE MY CLAUSTROPHOBIA IS KICKING IN BIG-TIME.
I HAVE THAT TOO.
BUT NOT AS BAD AS HIS.

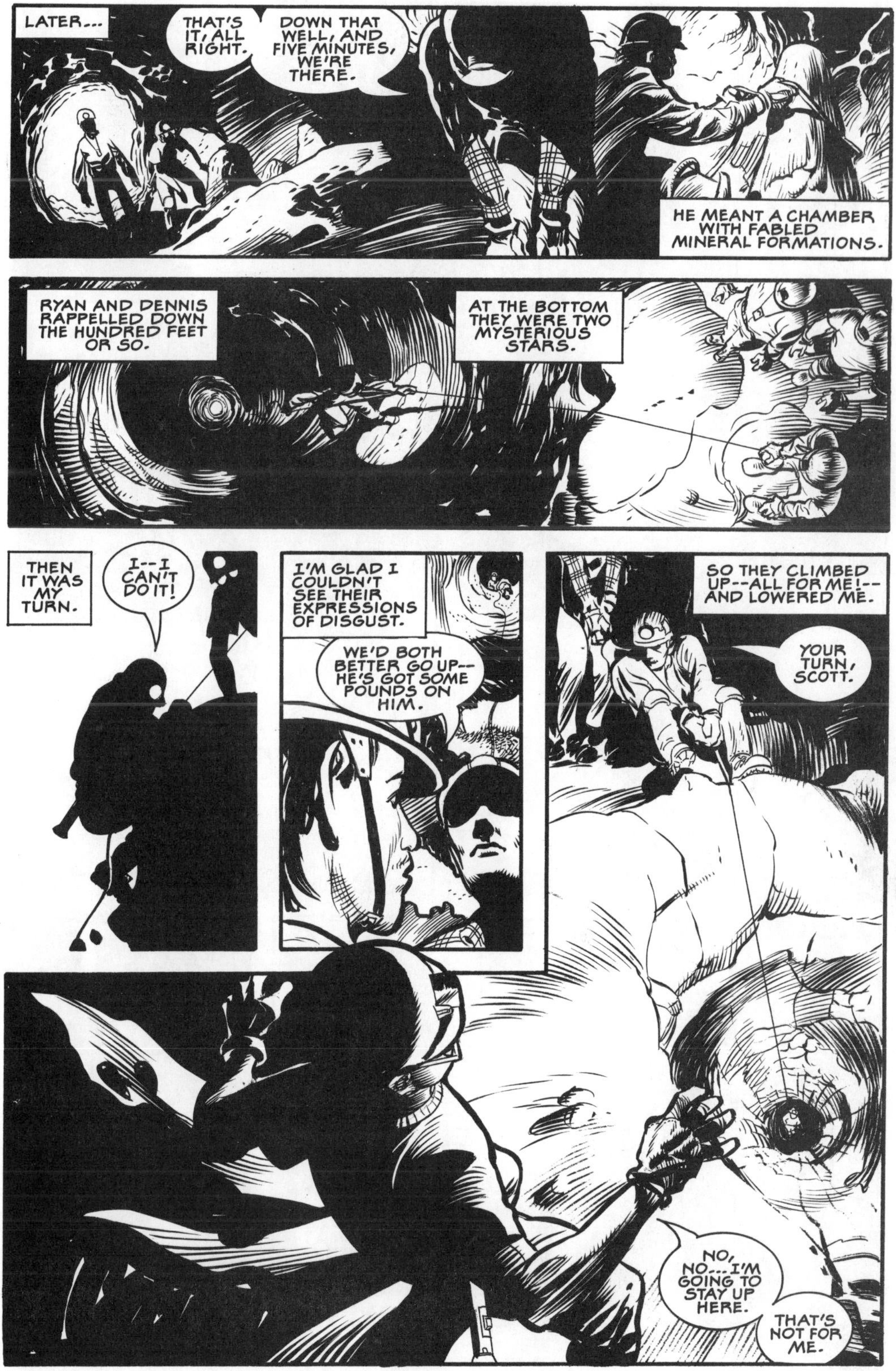
LATER...
THAT'S IT, ALL RIGHT.
DOWN THAT WELL, AND FIVE MINUTES, WE'RE THERE.
HE MEANT A CHAMBER WITH FABLED MINERAL FORMATIONS.
RYAN AND DENNIS RAPPELLED DOWN THE HUNDRED FEET OR SO.
AT THE BOTTOM THEY WERE TWO MYSTERIOUS STARS.
THEN IT WAS MY TURN.
I--I CAN'T DO IT!
I'M GLAD I COULDN'T SEE THEIR EXPRESSIONS OF DISGUST.
WE'D BOTH BETTER GO UP-- HE'S GOT SOME POUNDS ON HIM.
SO THEY CLIMBED UP--ALL FOR ME!-- AND LOWERED ME.
YOUR TURN, SCOTT.
NO, NO... I'M GOING TO STAY UP HERE.
THAT'S NOT FOR ME.

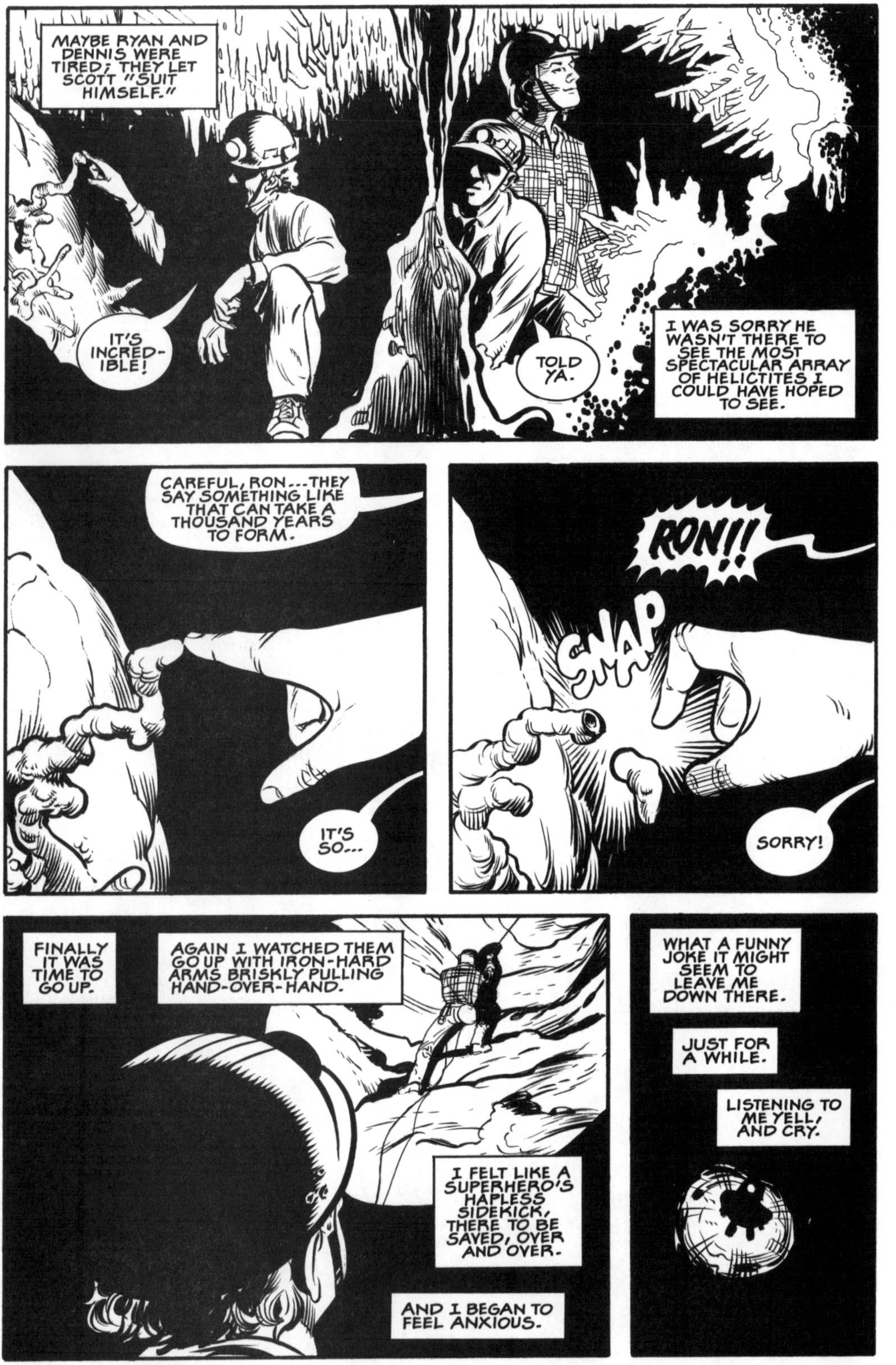
MAYBE RYAN AND DENNIS WERE TIRED; THEY LET SCOTT "SUIT HIMSELF."
IT'S INCRED-IBLE!
TOLD YA.
I WAS SORRY HE WASN'T THERE TO SEE THE MOST SPECTACULAR ARRAY OF HELICTITES I COULD HAVE HOPED TO SEE.
CAREFUL, RON...THEY SAY SOMETHING LIKE THAT CAN TAKE A THOUSAND YEARS TO FORM.
IT'S SO...
RON!!
SNAP
SORRY!
FINALLY IT WAS TIME TO GO UP.
AGAIN I WATCHED THEM GO UP WITH IRON-HARD ARMS BRISKLY PULLING HAND-OVER-HAND.
I FELT LIKE A SUPERHERO'S HAPLESS SIDEKICK, THERE TO BE SAVED, OVER AND OVER.
AND I BEGAN TO FEEL ANXIOUS.
WHAT A FUNNY JOKE IT MIGHT SEEM TO LEAVE ME DOWN THERE.
JUST FOR A WHILE.
LISTENING TO ME YELL, AND CRY.

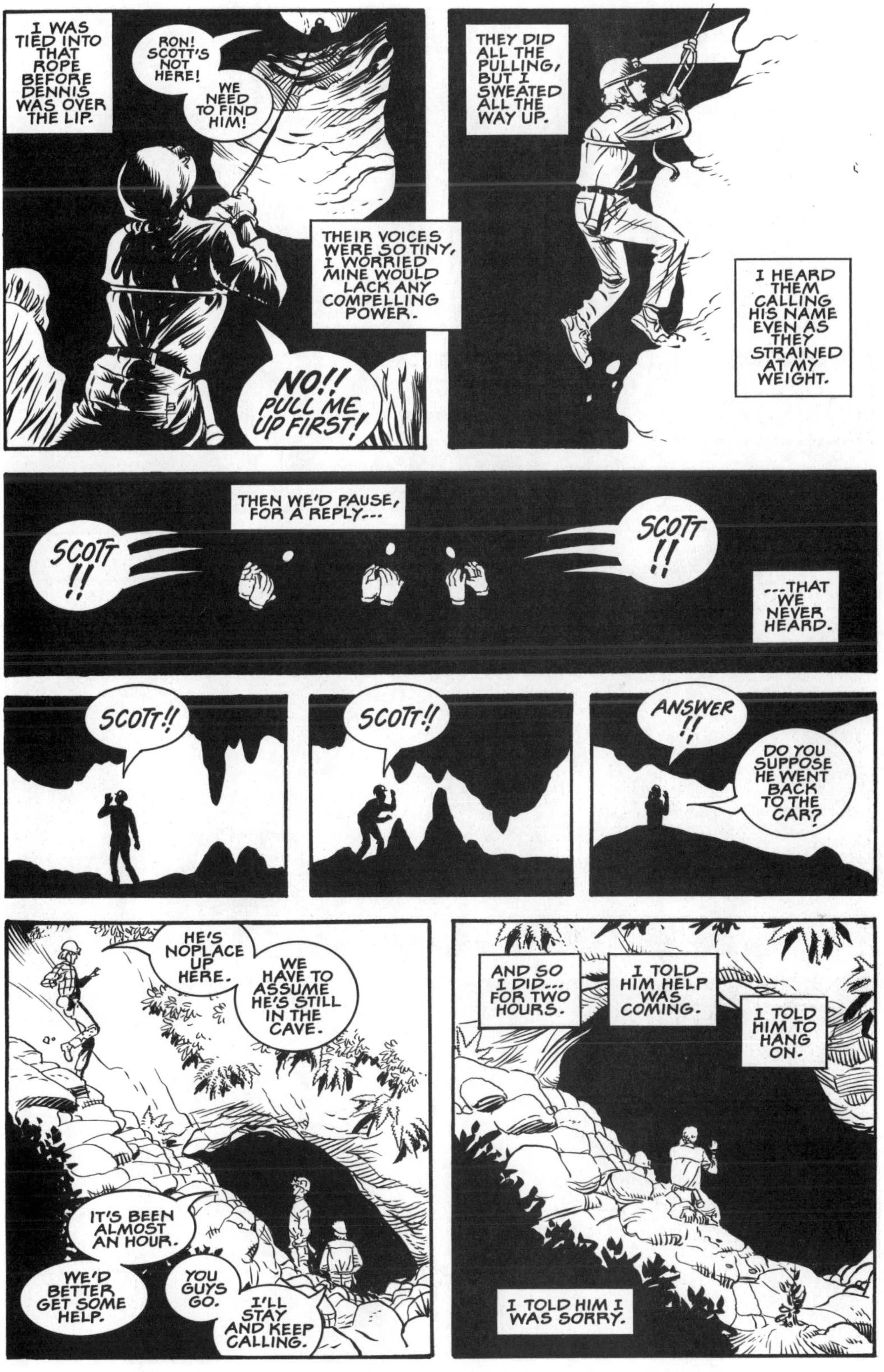

I WAS TIED INTO THAT ROPE BEFORE DENNIS WAS OVER THE LIP.
RON! SCOTT'S NOT HERE!
WE NEED TO FIND HIM!
THEIR VOICES WERE SO TINY, I WORRIED MINE WOULD LACK ANY COMPELLING POWER.
NO!! PULL ME UP FIRST!
THEY DID ALL THE PULLING, BUT I SWEATED ALL THE WAY UP.
I HEARD THEM CALLING HIS NAME EVEN AS THEY STRAINED AT MY WEIGHT.
THEN WE'D PAUSE, FOR A REPLY---
SCOTT !!
SCOTT !!
---THAT WE NEVER HEARD.
SCOTT!!
SCOTT!!
ANSWER !!
DO YOU SUPPOSE HE WENT BACK TO THE CAR?
HE'S NOPLACE UP HERE.
WE HAVE TO ASSUME HE'S STILL IN THE CAVE.
IT'S BEEN ALMOST AN HOUR.
WE'D BETTER GET SOME HELP.
YOU GUYS GO.
I'LL STAY AND KEEP CALLING.
AND SO I DID... FOR TWO HOURS.
I TOLD HIM HELP WAS COMING.
I TOLD HIM TO HANG ON.
I TOLD HIM I WAS SORRY.

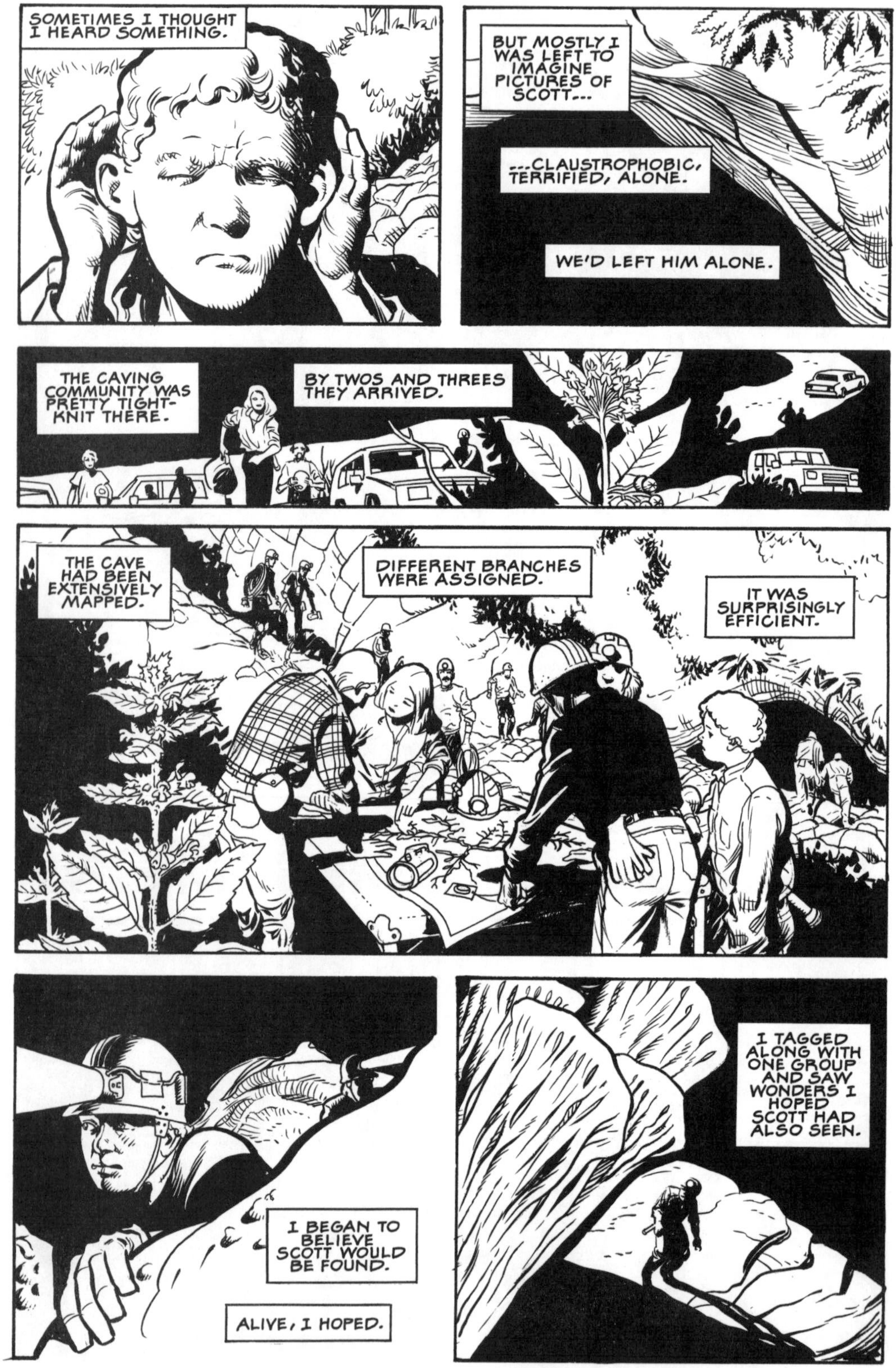
SOMETIMES I THOUGHT I HEARD SOMETHING.
BUT MOSTLY I WAS LEFT TO IMAGINE PICTURES OF SCOTT...
...CLAUSTROPHOBIC, TERRIFIED, ALONE.
WE'D LEFT HIM ALONE.
THE CAVING COMMUNITY WAS PRETTY TIGHT-KNIT THERE.
BY TWOS AND THREES THEY ARRIVED.
THE CAVE HAD BEEN EXTENSIVELY MAPPED.
DIFFERENT BRANCHES WERE ASSIGNED.
IT WAS SURPRISINGLY EFFICIENT.
I BEGAN TO BELIEVE SCOTT WOULD BE FOUND.
ALIVE, I HOPED.
I TAGGED ALONG WITH ONE GROUP AND SAW WONDERS I HOPED SCOTT HAD ALSO SEEN.

I HAD A FANTASY THAT I FOUND SCOTT.

I'D BE A HERO.

IT'D CEMENT OUR FRIENDSHIP.

SCOTT?

MAYBE WE'D WRITE BOOKS TOGETHER.

BUT AS THE HOURS WORE ON, DOUBT BEGAN TO RISE IN OUR MINDS.

THIS MAKES NO SENSE!

HE'S A VIRGIN CAVER!

I THINK HE'S HIDING IN SOMEBUDDY'S HOUSE RIGHT NOW, SCARED OF ALL THIS FUSS HE'S CAUSED.

BUT THEN HIS HELMET WAS FOUND, DEEP WITHIN A PASSAGE RYAN, DENNIS AND I NEVER CAME NEAR.

THAT GAVE NEW ENERGY TO EVERYBODY.

BUT DAYS OF SEARCHING AFTER THAT TURNED UP NOTHING MORE.

I HEARD THEY GAVE THE HELMET TO HIS PARENTS.

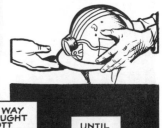

AND ALL THE WAY HOME, I THOUGHT ABOUT SCOTT LYING IN THE DARK, WATCHING THE GLOW FROM HIS FLASHLIGHT.

UNTIL IT WENT OUT.

FINALLY IT WAS TIME TO LEAVE VIRGINIA.

OUR PARTING FROM MY AUNT AND UNCLE AND COUSINS WAS SUBDUED.

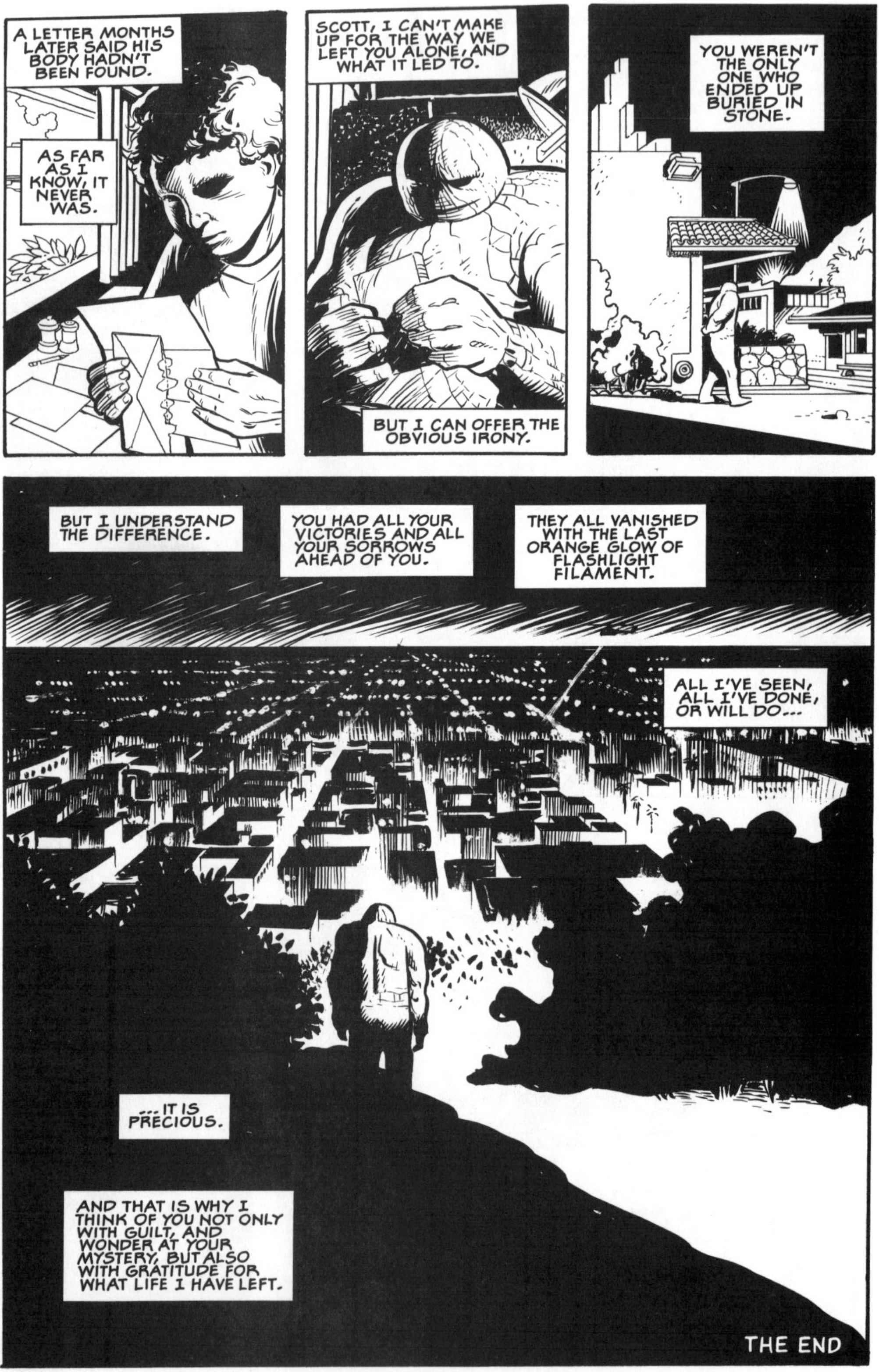
A LETTER MONTHS LATER SAID HIS BODY HADN'T BEEN FOUND.
AS FAR AS I KNOW, IT NEVER WAS.
SCOTT, I CAN'T MAKE UP FOR THE WAY WE LEFT YOU ALONE, AND WHAT IT LED TO.
BUT I CAN OFFER THE OBVIOUS IRONY.
YOU WEREN'T THE ONLY ONE WHO ENDED UP BURIED IN STONE.
BUT I UNDERSTAND THE DIFFERENCE.
YOU HAD ALL YOUR VICTORIES AND ALL YOUR SORROWS AHEAD OF YOU.
THEY ALL VANISHED WITH THE LAST ORANGE GLOW OF FLASHLIGHT FILAMENT.
ALL I'VE SEEN, ALL I'VE DONE, OR WILL DO...
...IT IS PRECIOUS.
AND THAT IS WHY I THINK OF YOU NOT ONLY WITH GUILT, AND WONDER AT YOUR MYSTERY, BUT ALSO WITH GRATITUDE FOR WHAT LIFE I HAVE LEFT.
THE END

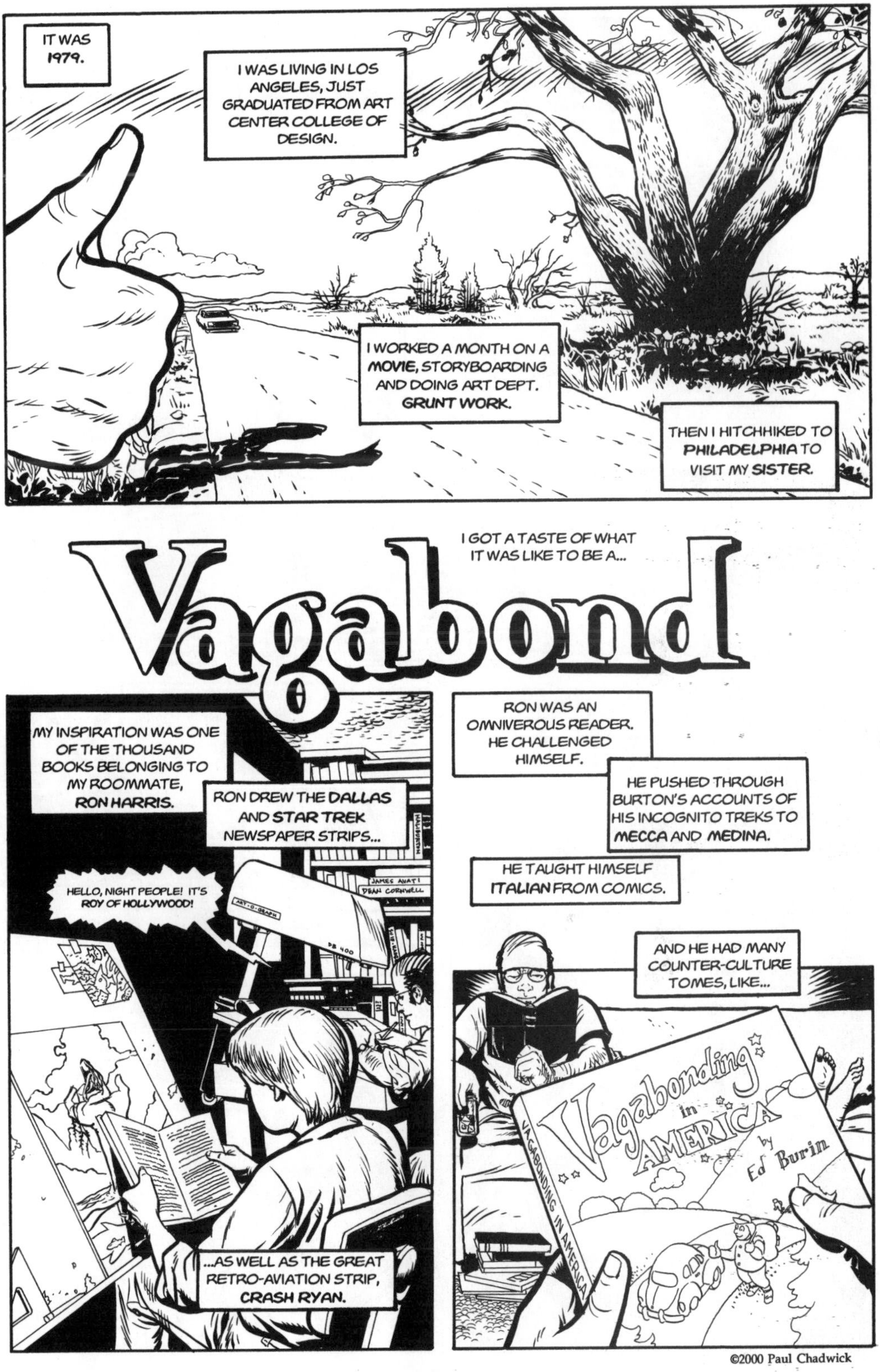
IT WAS 1979.
I WAS LIVING IN LOS ANGELES, JUST GRADUATED FROM ART CENTER COLLEGE OF DESIGN.
I WORKED A MONTH ON A MOVIE, STORYBOARDING AND DOING ART DEPT. GRUNT WORK.
THEN I HITCHHIKED TO PHILADELPHIA TO VISIT MY SISTER.
I GOT A TASTE OF WHAT IT WAS LIKE TO BE A...
Vagabond
MY INSPIRATION WAS ONE OF THE THOUSAND BOOKS BELONGING TO MY ROOMMATE, RON HARRIS.
RON DREW THE DALLAS AND STAR TREK NEWSPAPER STRIPS...
HELLO, NIGHT PEOPLE! IT'S ROY OF HOLLYWOOD!
JAMES AVATI
DEAN CORNWELL
ART-O-GRAPH
DB 400
...AS WELL AS THE GREAT RETRO-AVIATION STRIP, CRASH RYAN.
RON WAS AN OMNIVEROUS READER. HE CHALLENGED HIMSELF.
HE PUSHED THROUGH BURTON'S ACCOUNTS OF HIS INCOGNITO TREKS TO MECCA AND MEDINA.
HE TAUGHT HIMSELF ITALIAN FROM COMICS.
AND HE HAD MANY COUNTER-CULTURE TOMES, LIKE...
Vagabonding in AMERICA by Ed Burin
VAGABONDING IN AMERICA

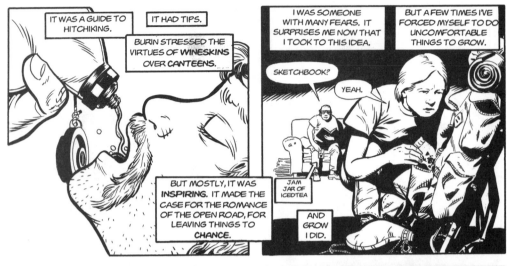

IT WAS A GUIDE TO HITCHIKING.

IT HAD TIPS.

BURIN STRESSED THE VIRTUES OF **WINESKINS** OVER **CANTEENS.**

BUT MOSTLY, IT WAS **INSPIRING.** IT MADE THE CASE FOR THE ROMANCE OF THE OPEN ROAD, FOR LEAVING THINGS TO **CHANCE.**

I WAS SOMEONE WITH MANY FEARS. IT SURPRISES ME NOW THAT I TOOK TO THIS IDEA.

BUT A FEW TIMES I'VE FORCED MYSELF TO DO UNCOMFORTABLE THINGS TO GROW.

SKETCHBOOK?

YEAH.

JAM JAR OF ICEDTEA

AND GROW I DID.

RON LEFT ME OFF AT THE ONRAMP TO FREEWAY 10.

IT WENT RIGHT OUT OF CALIFORNIA AND ENDED IN NEW MEXICO.

RON'S COOL BUT ENDLESSLY TROUBLESOME STUDEBAKER

I WORE A MOLDED PLASTIC **PITH HELMET.**

IT WAS GOOFY, BUT I THOUGHT IT MIGHT HELP GET RIDES.

MY ONLY WEAPON WAS A ONE-EDGED RAZOR BLADE.

IT WAS A TALISMAN.

AN ART CENTER INSTRUCTOR, THE CHARISMATIC **BARRON STOREY,** USED THOSE BLADES FOR EVERYTHING.

COOL!

SQUEEGEE AWAY THE EXCESS MEDIUM...

MY FIRST RIDE.

H-HI! WHERE'RE YA HEADED?

EAST!!

YOU GONNA GET IN OR NOT?!?

I GUESS...

ONE THING I EXCELLED AT DURING COLLEGE WAS CHARCOAL DRAWING.

SO I OFFERED DRIVERS PORTRAITS.

TROUBLE IS, THIS GUY **INSISTED** ON A 3/4 VIEW.

LIKE THIS!!

UH -- YOU SURE?

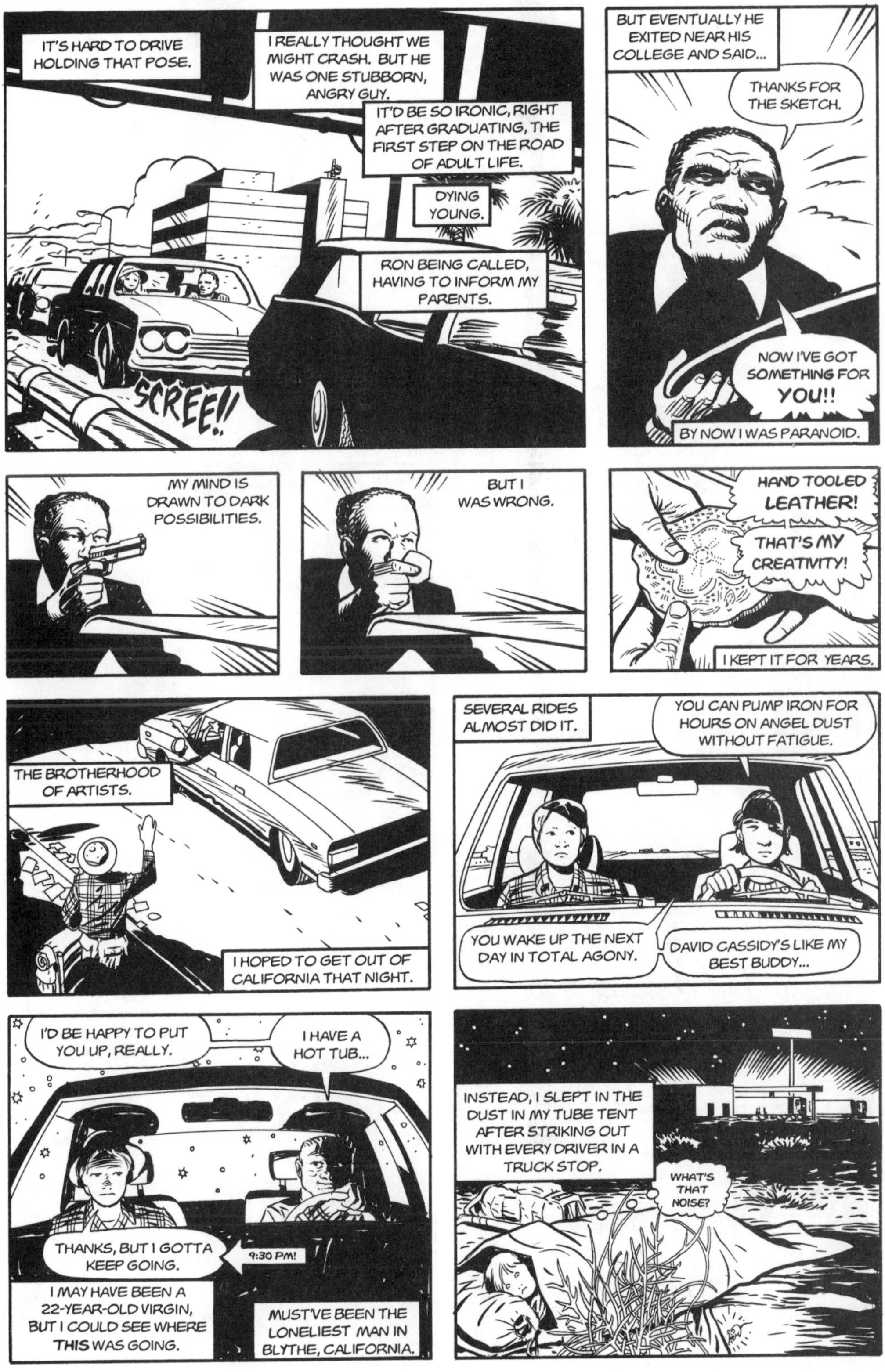
IT'S HARD TO DRIVE HOLDING THAT POSE.
I REALLY THOUGHT WE MIGHT CRASH. BUT HE WAS ONE STUBBORN, ANGRY GUY.
IT'D BE SO IRONIC, RIGHT AFTER GRADUATING, THE FIRST STEP ON THE ROAD OF ADULT LIFE.
DYING YOUNG.
RON BEING CALLED, HAVING TO INFORM MY PARENTS.
SCREE!!
BUT EVENTUALLY HE EXITED NEAR HIS COLLEGE AND SAID...
THANKS FOR THE SKETCH.
NOW I'VE GOT SOMETHING FOR YOU!!
BY NOW I WAS PARANOID.
MY MIND IS DRAWN TO DARK POSSIBILITIES.
BUT I WAS WRONG.
HAND TOOLED LEATHER!
THAT'S MY CREATIVITY!
I KEPT IT FOR YEARS.
THE BROTHERHOOD OF ARTISTS.
I HOPED TO GET OUT OF CALIFORNIA THAT NIGHT.
SEVERAL RIDES ALMOST DID IT.
YOU CAN PUMP IRON FOR HOURS ON ANGEL DUST WITHOUT FATIGUE.
YOU WAKE UP THE NEXT DAY IN TOTAL AGONY.
DAVID CASSIDY'S LIKE MY BEST BUDDY...
I'D BE HAPPY TO PUT YOU UP, REALLY.
I HAVE A HOT TUB...
THANKS, BUT I GOTTA KEEP GOING.
9:30 PM!
I MAY HAVE BEEN A 22-YEAR-OLD VIRGIN, BUT I COULD SEE WHERE THIS WAS GOING.
MUST'VE BEEN THE LONELIEST MAN IN BLYTHE, CALIFORNIA.
INSTEAD, I SLEPT IN THE DUST IN MY TUBE TENT AFTER STRIKING OUT WITH EVERY DRIVER IN A TRUCK STOP.
WHAT'S THAT NOISE?

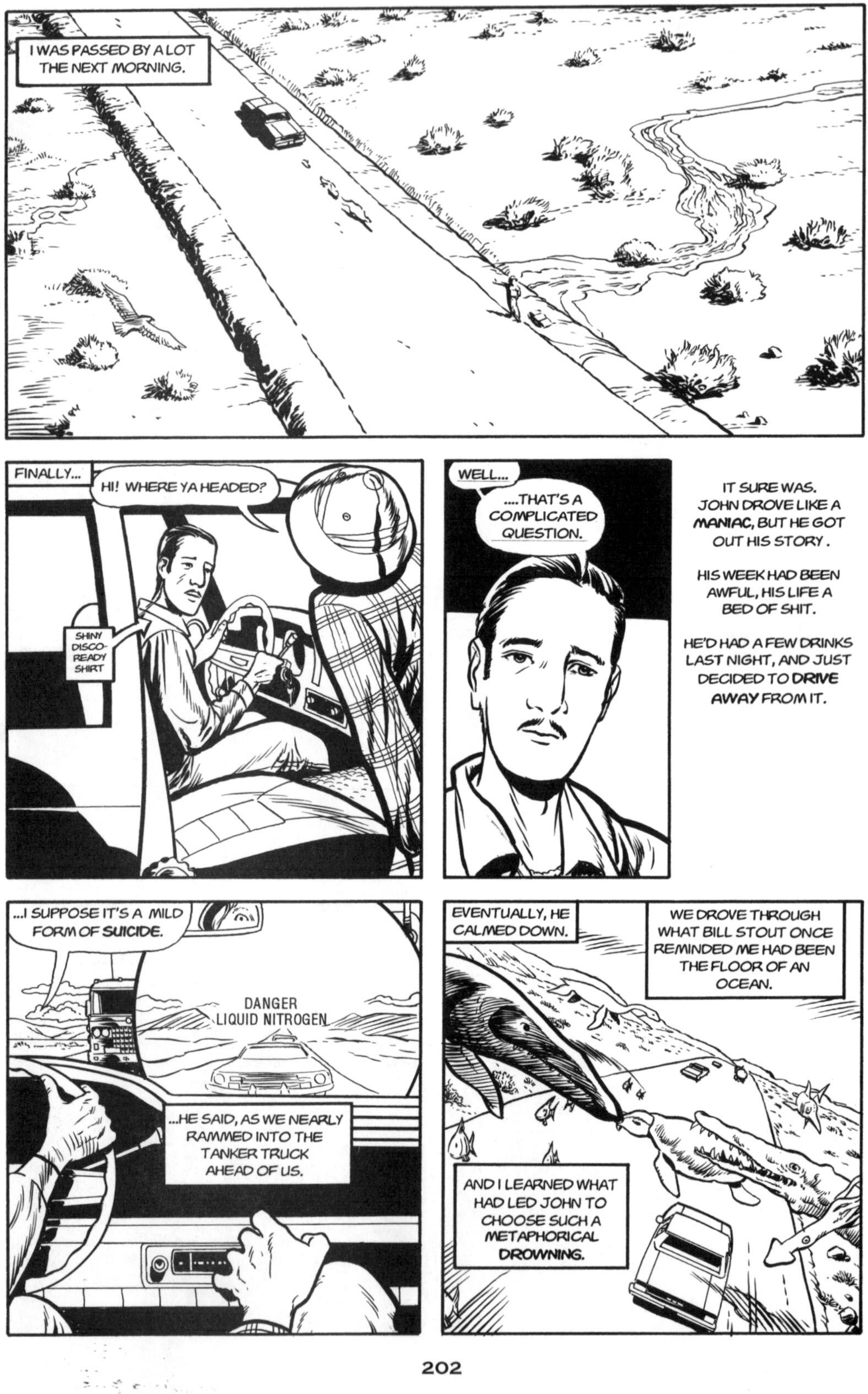
I WAS PASSED BY A LOT THE NEXT MORNING.
FINALLY...
HI! WHERE YA HEADED?
SHINY DISCO-READY SHIRT
WELL...
....THAT'S A COMPLICATED QUESTION.
IT SURE WAS. JOHN DROVE LIKE A **MANIAC**, BUT HE GOT OUT HIS STORY.
HIS WEEK HAD BEEN AWFUL, HIS LIFE A BED OF SHIT.
HE'D HAD A FEW DRINKS LAST NIGHT, AND JUST DECIDED TO **DRIVE AWAY** FROM IT.
...I SUPPOSE IT'S A MILD FORM OF **SUICIDE**.
DANGER
LIQUID NITROGEN
...HE SAID, AS WE NEARLY RAMMED INTO THE TANKER TRUCK AHEAD OF US.
EVENTUALLY, HE CALMED DOWN.
WE DROVE THROUGH WHAT BILL STOUT ONCE REMINDED ME HAD BEEN THE FLOOR OF AN OCEAN.
AND I LEARNED WHAT HAD LED JOHN TO CHOOSE SUCH A METAPHORICAL **DROWNING**.

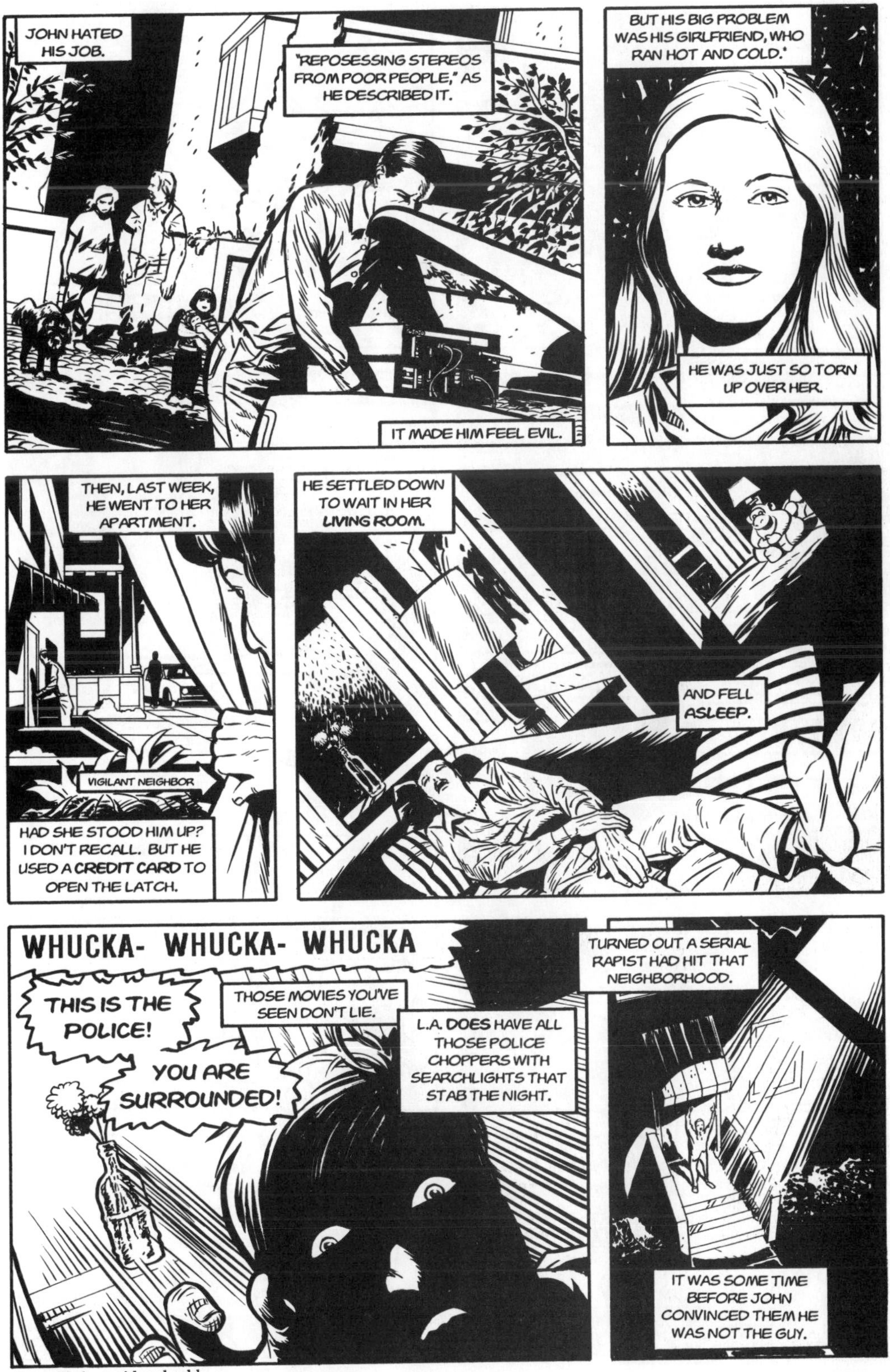
JOHN HATED HIS JOB.
"REPOSESSING STEREOS FROM POOR PEOPLE," AS HE DESCRIBED IT.
IT MADE HIM FEEL EVIL.
BUT HIS BIG PROBLEM WAS HIS GIRLFRIEND, WHO RAN HOT AND COLD.*
HE WAS JUST SO TORN UP OVER HER.
THEN, LAST WEEK, HE WENT TO HER APARTMENT.
VIGILANT NEIGHBOR
HAD SHE STOOD HIM UP? I DON'T RECALL. BUT HE USED A CREDIT CARD TO OPEN THE LATCH.
HE SETTLED DOWN TO WAIT IN HER LIVING ROOM.
AND FELL ASLEEP.
WHUCKA- WHUCKA- WHUCKA
THIS IS THE POLICE!
YOU ARE SURROUNDED!
THOSE MOVIES YOU'VE SEEN DON'T LIE.
L.A. DOES HAVE ALL THOSE POLICE CHOPPERS WITH SEARCHLIGHTS THAT STAB THE NIGHT.
TURNED OUT A SERIAL RAPIST HAD HIT THAT NEIGHBORHOOD.
IT WAS SOME TIME BEFORE JOHN CONVINCED THEM HE WAS NOT THE GUY.

*More likely, tepid and cold

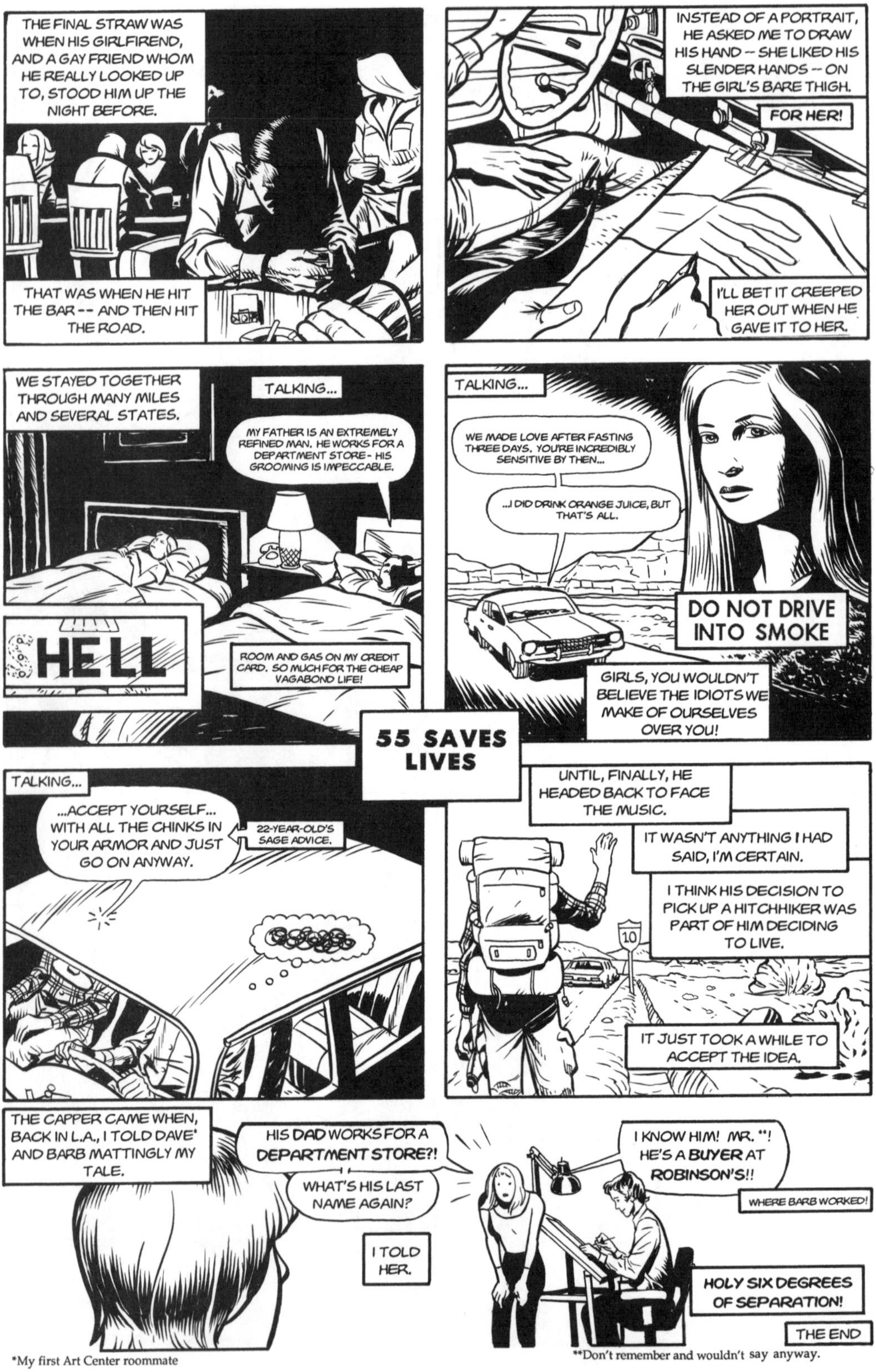
THE FINAL STRAW WAS WHEN HIS GIRLFIREND, AND A GAY FRIEND WHOM HE REALLY LOOKED UP TO, STOOD HIM UP THE NIGHT BEFORE.
THAT WAS WHEN HE HIT THE BAR -- AND THEN HIT THE ROAD.
INSTEAD OF A PORTRAIT, HE ASKED ME TO DRAW HIS HAND -- SHE LIKED HIS SLENDER HANDS -- ON THE GIRL'S BARE THIGH.
FOR HER!
I'LL BET IT CREEPED HER OUT WHEN HE GAVE IT TO HER.
WE STAYED TOGETHER THROUGH MANY MILES AND SEVERAL STATES.
TALKING...
MY FATHER IS AN EXTREMELY REFINED MAN. HE WORKS FOR A DEPARTMENT STORE- HIS GROOMING IS IMPECCABLE.
HELL
ROOM AND GAS ON MY CREDIT CARD. SO MUCH FOR THE CHEAP VAGABOND LIFE!
TALKING...
WE MADE LOVE AFTER FASTING THREE DAYS. YOU'RE INCREDIBLY SENSITIVE BY THEN...
...I DID DRINK ORANGE JUICE, BUT THAT'S ALL.
DO NOT DRIVE INTO SMOKE
GIRLS, YOU WOULDN'T BELIEVE THE IDIOTS WE MAKE OF OURSELVES OVER YOU!
55 SAVES LIVES
TALKING...
...ACCEPT YOURSELF... WITH ALL THE CHINKS IN YOUR ARMOR AND JUST GO ON ANYWAY.
22-YEAR-OLD'S SAGE ADVICE.
UNTIL, FINALLY, HE HEADED BACK TO FACE THE MUSIC.
IT WASN'T ANYTHING I HAD SAID, I'M CERTAIN.
I THINK HIS DECISION TO PICK UP A HITCHHIKER WAS PART OF HIM DECIDING TO LIVE.
IT JUST TOOK A WHILE TO ACCEPT THE IDEA.
THE CAPPER CAME WHEN, BACK IN L.A., I TOLD DAVE* AND BARB MATTINGLY MY TALE.
HIS DAD WORKS FOR A DEPARTMENT STORE?!
WHAT'S HIS LAST NAME AGAIN?
I TOLD HER.
I KNOW HIM! MR. **! HE'S A BUYER AT ROBINSON'S!!
WHERE BARB WORKED!
HOLY SIX DEGREES OF SEPARATION!
THE END

*My first Art Center roommate

**Don't remember and wouldn't say anyway.

Concrete®

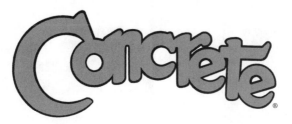

GALLERY

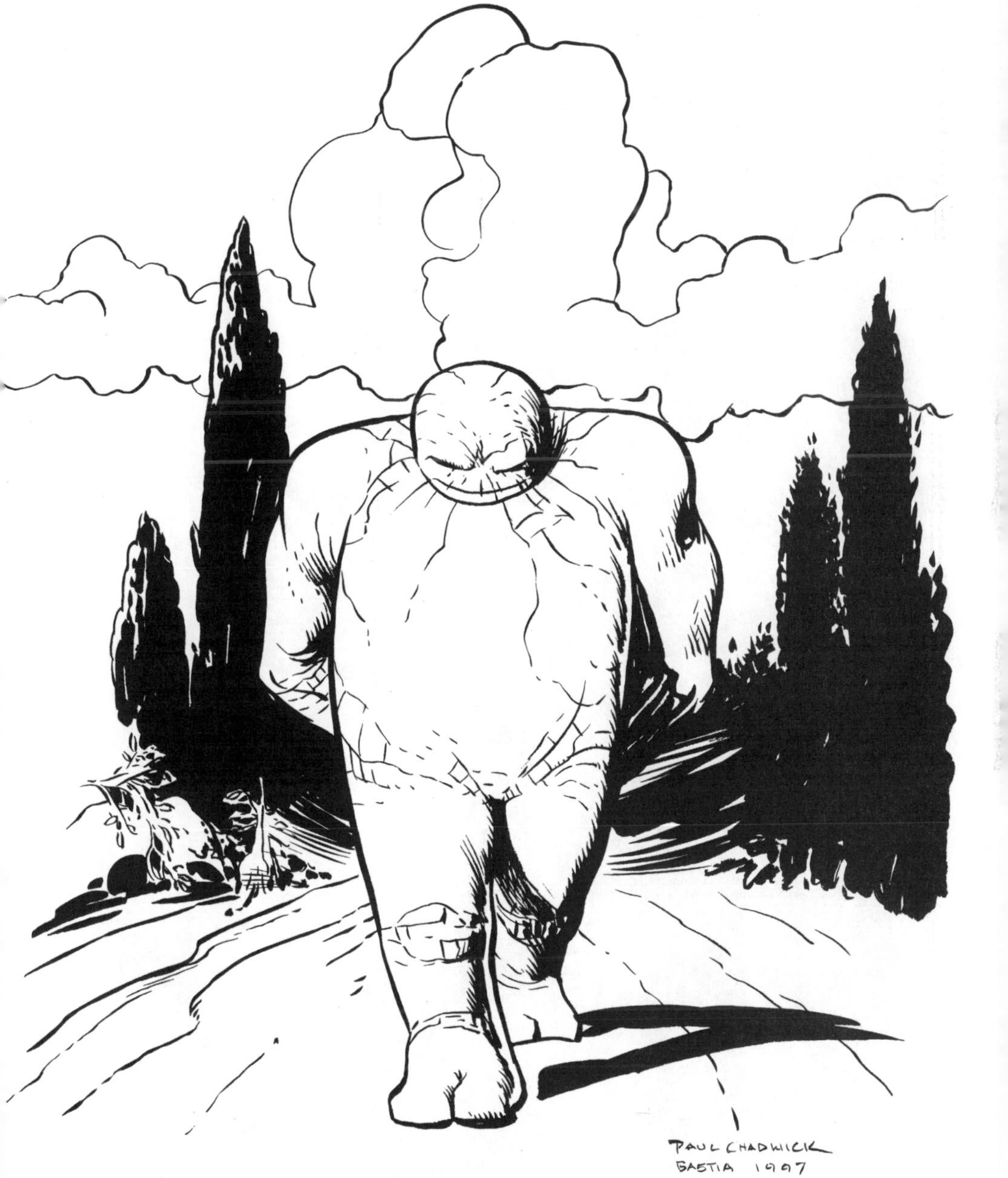
PAUL CHADWICK
BASTIA 1997

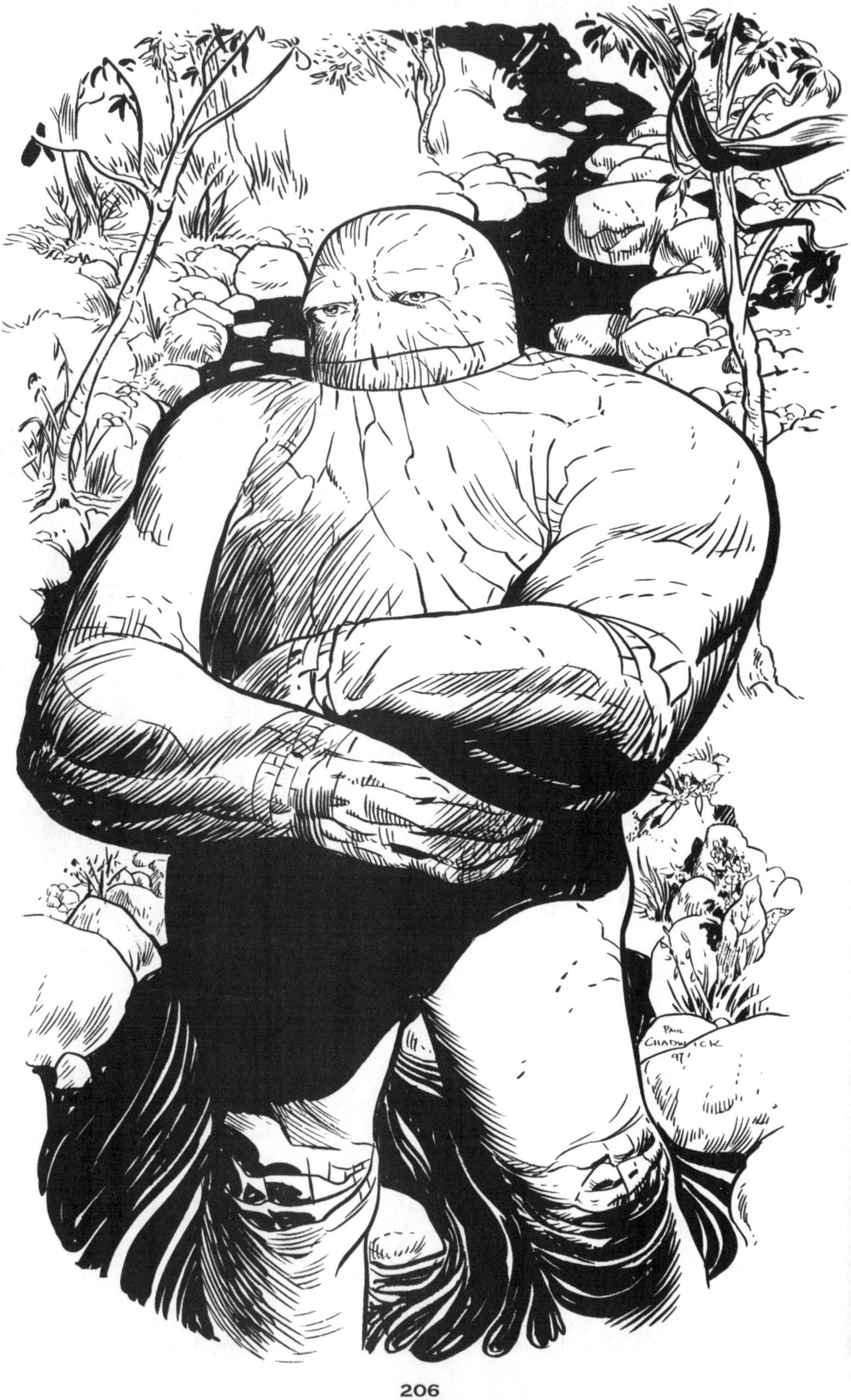
PAUL
CHADWICK
97

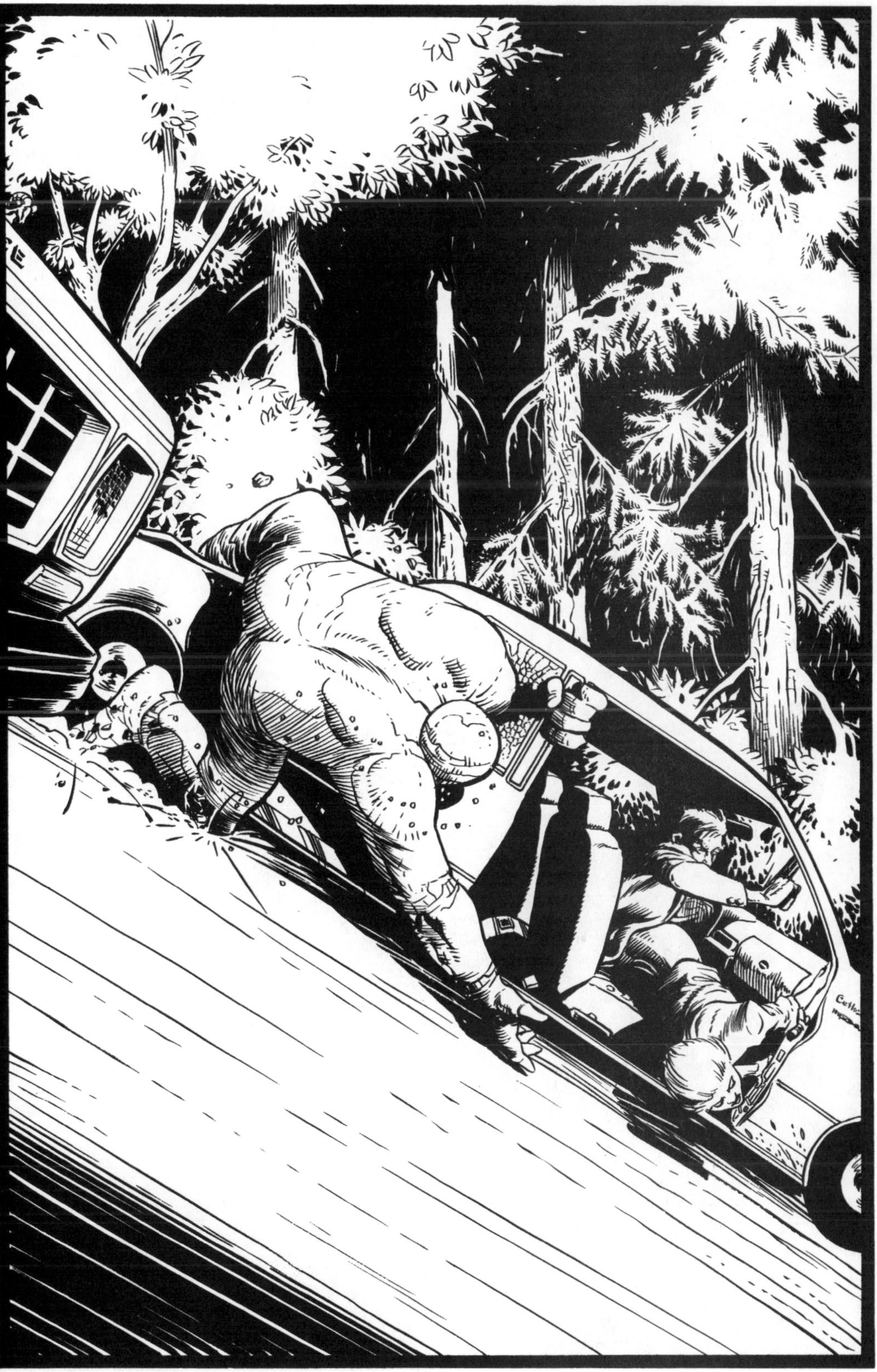

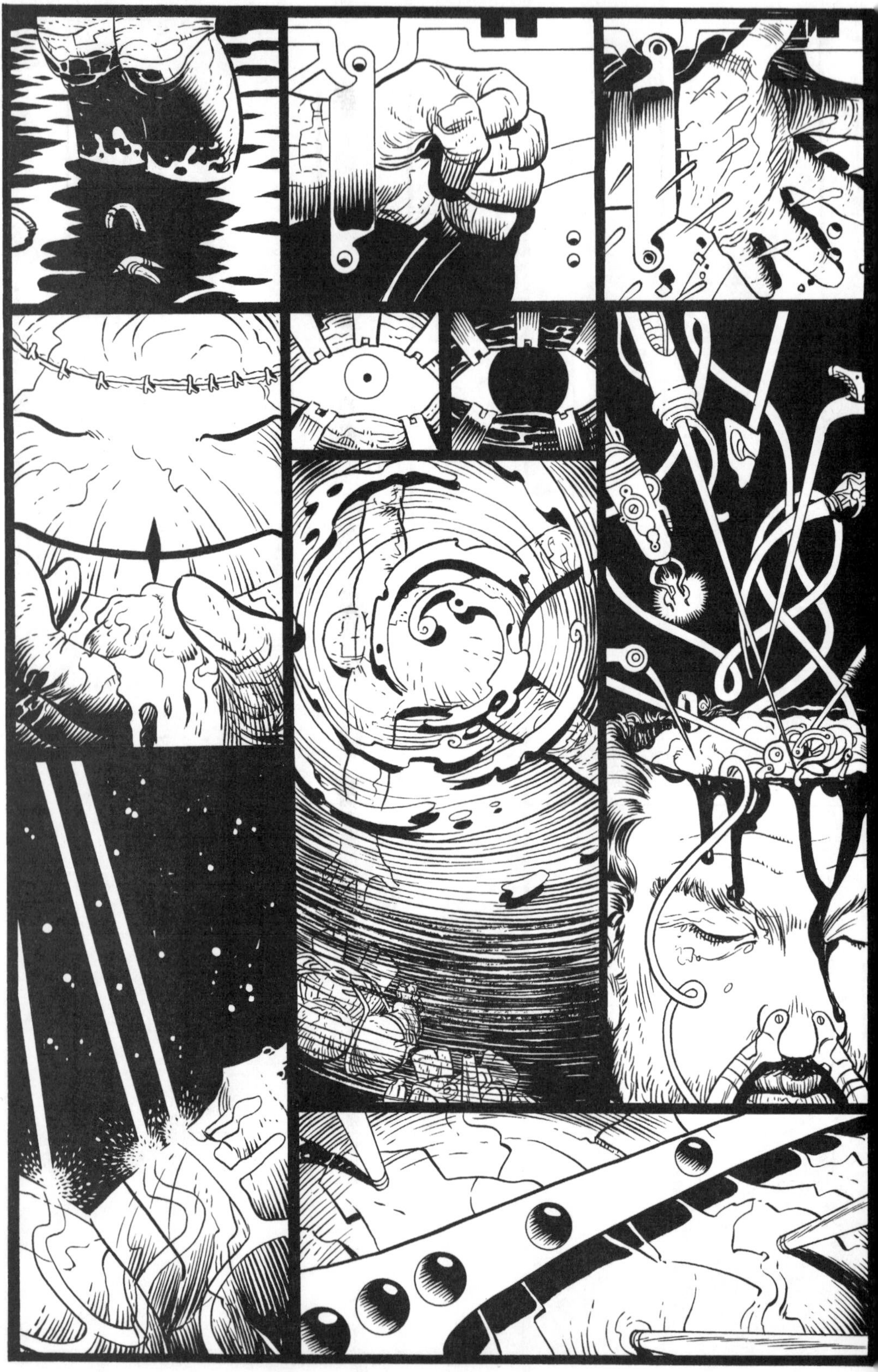